contemporary operations management

PRENTICE-HALL, INC., ENGLEWOOD CLIFFS, NEW JERSEY 07632

THOMAS M. COOK
The University of Tulsa

ROBERT A. RUSSELL
The University of Tulsa

contemporary operations management

text and cases

Library of Congress Cataloging in Publication Data

COOK, THOMAS M   (date)
  Contemporary operations management.

  Includes bibliographies and index.
  1. Management—Mathematical models. 2. Operation
research. 3. Production management—Mathematical
models. I. Russell, Robert A., (date)   joint author.
II. Title.
HD30.25.C66   658.4′034   79-17130
ISBN 0-13-170407-9

Editorial/production supervision by Alice Erdman
Interior design by Linda J. Conway and Alice Erdman
Cover design by Linda J. Conway
Manufacturing buyer: Harry P. Baisley

Printed in the United States of America

10 9 8 7 6 5 4 3 2 1

PRENTICE-HALL INTERNATIONAL, INC., *London*
PRENTICE-HALL OF AUSTRALIA PTY. LIMITED, *Sydney*
PRENTICE-HALL OF CANADA, LTD., *Toronto*
PRENTICE-HALL OF INDIA PRIVATE LIMITED, *New Delhi*
PRENTICE-HALL OF JAPAN, INC., *Tokyo*
PRENTICE-HALL OF SOUTHEAST ASIA PTE. LTD., *Singapore*
WHITEHALL BOOKS LIMITED, *Wellington, New Zealand*

contents

v

preface

This book is intended for use in a semester or quarter course that introduces the student to the field of operations/production management. The book is aimed at the business or engineering student who will most likely pursue a career in an organization requiring some managerial ability and decision-making skill. The level of the text is designed to be appropriate for an introductory course at the graduate or undergraduate level.

The approach in this text is somewhat traditional, in that it is organized along the functional lines of designing, operating, scheduling, and controlling productive systems. These primary functions guide the development of concepts, tools, and applications throughout the text. The text does, however, differ from older production texts in that emphasis is placed on nonfactory operations as well as factory operations. Concepts, examples, and case studies are presented throughout the text that deal with not only factories but also hospitals, government agencies, service organizations, and educational institutions. Many of the concepts and tools presented in the text are relevant to both private- and public-sector problems, but whenever differences do exist, they are pointed out.

One of the objectives in the text was to select those topics that are considered to be in the mainstream of the POM area. The text is designed as an introduction and not as an encyclopedia of the POM field. It has been designed with AACSB guidelines in mind and should satisfy text requirements for introductory courses in production/operations management or applied quantitative methods.

The mathematical level of the book is purposely kept low in order to make the material readable for both the student and the layman. A course in college algebra or finite mathematics is sufficient mathematical preparation. In Chapter 2 on linear programming, the simplex method and more mathematical material have been placed in an appendix at the end of the chapter and may be skipped without loss of continuity. Although the mathematical level of the book is relatively low, the book is decision-oriented and devotes significant time to the explanation of quantitative methods that are of particular use to operations managers; the limitations of these methods are discussed, as well as their utility.

A special effort is made in this text to bridge the gap between the theory and the practice of operations management. Numerous references to successful applications are made throughout the chapters of the text. Particularly relevant applications from the literature are briefly described as small cases or scenarios. A Harvard-type case is presented at the end of each chapter and may be used as an assignment or a basis of discussion. These cases should stimulate student interest and help the student develop a more realistic view of POM problems. Case discussions and solutions are provided in the instructor's manual.

The format of the chapters has been designed to facilitate the learning of both descriptive and analytical material. Key concepts and words are italicized in the text (these are defined in the glossary at the end of the book), and each chapter contains a summary and set of review questions. In addition, several solved problems are presented at the end of each chapter to further illustrate the application of various methods and concepts. An ample number of unresolved problems and review questions are included with each chapter, along with answers to selected problems at the end of the book.

The book is divided into five parts. The first section is an introduction to the POM area. The second contains a description of three quantitative tools—linear programming, simulation, and queuing theory—that are especially helpful to the operations manager in his decision-making role. The third section is concerned with the design of the productive system. Topics such as plant location, facility layout, process design, and job design are discussed in this section. The fourth and fifth parts address the problems inherent in operating and controlling an ongoing productive system. Important topics in these sections are forecasting, aggregate planning, inventory control systems, materials requirements planning, scheduling, and quality assurance.

Although it is not strongly emphasized throughout the book, a unifying thread that underlies the text is the systems approach to operations management. It is felt that taking the view of the organization as a whole and integrating important decisions are vital for the successful management of future organizations. It is true that implementations of true systems approaches are infrequent today, but many firms are making progress, and this trend will probably characterize the development of operations management throughout the rest of this century.

Several people have been extremely helpful to us at various stages of this project. We would like to thank the reviewers, whose comments and suggestions led to an improved manuscript: Prof. F. J. Brewerton, Middle Tennessee State University, Prof. David M. Dougherty, University of Texas at El Paso, Prof. Douglas A. Eluers, University of North Carolina at Chapel Hill, Prof. William N. Ledbetter, Auburn University, Prof. Jugoslav S. Milutinovich, Temple University, Prof. Richard G. Newman, Indiana University Northwest.

We would like to thank the staff at Prentice-Hall for its assistance, particularly Business Management Editor Barbara Piercecchi and Production Editor Alice Erdman. We would like to thank our typist, Margaret Carpenter, who did her usual outstanding job preparing the manuscript.

Finally, we would like to thank our families for their understanding and encouragement during the course of this project.

Thomas M. Cook
Robert A. Russell

contemporary operations management

part ONE

introduction

early in the fifteenth century, the Venetian shipbuilders seem to have used a type of assembly-line process in the outfitting of ships, and instituted standardization in key parts of ships.

The real roots of what we call operations management did not begin to develop until the Industrial Revolution. This period is characterized by the emergence of the factory system (with its advantages and disadvantages) and greatly increased productivity. In 1764, James Watt improved the steam engine to the extent that it could be used as a source of power in industry. Shortly thereafter, in 1776, Scottish economist Adam Smith wrote his book, *The Wealth of Nations*, in which he advocated division of labor. In his observations regarding the manufacture of straight pins, he noted three economic advantages of such division: (1) development of dexterity upon repetitive performance of a single task, (2) time savings owing to less changeover effort, and (3) likely development of machines that simplify work and increase worker productivity. Smith's book laid the foundation for modern work simplification methods, but it also helped create some monotonous jobs that are very limited in scope.

In 1832, an English mathematician and genius, Charles Babbage, wrote his milestone treatise, *On Economy of Machines and Manufactures*. In his book, Babbage recommended scientific methods in analyzing business problems. He agreed with Smith concerning the division of labor, but he further proposed skill differential in wages—that not all workers be paid the same amount; but rather be paid on the basis of the skill required to do the job.

Around the turn of the century, Frederick Taylor formally advocated a scientific approach to the problems of manufacturing. He formalized some of the ideas Babbage had espoused and focused mainly on work standards and wage incentives. He demonstrated that scientifically conceived work standards and wage incentives could improve productivity. Taylor wanted to replace old work methods with the development of a science for each element of work. His ideas, which came to be known as scientific management theory, were not popular with everyone, especially in the case of labor unions. However, Taylor's ideas made a revolutionary impact, and he was to be known as the father of scientific management. His efforts were largely responsible for developing industrial engineering as a profession. Modern fields most affected by Taylor's early efforts include methods engineering and work measurement, human engineering, and personnel.

Henry Gantt, a contemporary of Taylor's refined the content of early scientific management by bringing into consideration the human aspect of management's attitude toward labor. He espoused the importance of the personnel department to the scientific approach to management. Perhaps his greatest contribution, however, was his scheduling system for loading jobs on machines. Basically a recording procedure, Gantt's system was devised to minimize job completion delays; it permitted machine loadings to be planned months in advance. Other contemporaries of Taylor were Frank and Lillian Gilbreth, who pioneered time and motion study and industrial psychology.

In 1913, Henry Ford introduced the first moving assembly line for automobiles. The innovation allowed cars to be produced about eight times faster than before, and high levels of output fueled consumerism in the U.S. economy. In 1915, F.W. Harris published a simple lot-size formula that constituted the basis for inventory control for several decades and still finds wide use today.

During the twenties and thirties, most of the contributions to operations management were quantitative in nature. A.K. Erlang developed formulas to predict waiting times for callers using automatic telephone exchanges. His work founded modern waiting-line analysis, or queuing theory (see Chapter 4). Statistical quality control methods were introduced by Walter Shewhart in 1931, and L.H.C. Tippett developed statistical sampling to determine standard work times in 1934. Aside from these developments in statistics during the thirties, the well-known Hawthorne experiments were carried out to determine the effects of environmental changes on the work output of employees at a Western Electric plant. Their surprising results were that workers responded more to mere changes in their environment rather than to the nature of those changes. For example, increasing the lighting or temperature raised output, but so did returning all environmental conditions to their original state. These results tended to refute the scientific management theories and led to schools of thought founded more on human behavioral theories, such as human relations.

During World War II, the British organized a team of talented people, called "Blackett's Circus," ranging from mathematicians and physicists to physiologists and army officers, to study the military and logistics problems facing Great Britain during the war. This interdisciplinary scientific approach to operations-type problems was successful in British military efforts and soon spread to the U.S. military. Such a scientific team approach, using mathematical models and techniques, became known as *operations research* (also called *management science*), and its applications soon spread to business.

Operations research/management science is a sister discipline that provides many of the quantitative tools for use in operations management and other functional areas of business. In 1947, George Dantzig helped develop linear programming (see Chapter 2), and, along with the development of high-speed computers, this brought about a modeling and systems type of approach to business problems. At the beginning of the fifties, a new era had begun in much the same way that scientific management had emerged at the beginning of the century. Rapid progress was made in the fifties with computer hardware, data processing, and mathematical solution techniques. Operations research/management science and industrial engineering were rapidly becoming a profession, but production/operations management had not yet "come into its own." Most of the research focused upon well-defined operational problems for which an analytical solution could be found.

In the late fifties and early sixties, some books and articles began to appear that dealt specifically with production management as opposed to industrial engineering or mathematical programming. Earlier courses in production management dealt with such topics as plant layout, process design, time and motion studies, aggregate planning, inventory, and quality control. Meanwhile, the practice of production management was becoming recognized as a profession in itself, and much progress was being made in the use of the computer to solve production problems. Commercial computer programming packages became available from major computer manufacturers for areas like scheduling, inventory control, plant location, and forecasting. The founding of the American Production and Inventory Control Society (APICS) in 1957 did much to advance the practice of production and inventory management, as well as the status of production management as a profession.

The late sixties and the seventies, the current era, have been characterized by the systems approach and an attitude toward solving real management problems more than narrow mathematical problems. The discipline is now usually called operations management rather than production management, as it applies also to the management of operations outside the factory. Many of the planning, scheduling, and controlling methods are now applied to service and nonmanufacturing organizations, Operations management is now recognized as a profession in itself, and a student pursuing such a career is often known as a student of POM (production/operations management).

The modern *systems approach* requires the organization to consider its decisions in relation to the whole of the organization and its environment. Implementing the true systems approach is somewhat difficult, since it requires management to consider higher-order and lower-order implications of any decision. The current practice of operations management does not always employ a true systems approach, although some efforts such as materials requirements planning systems (see Chapter 11) come very close. The current era is characterized by very rapid data processing and the increasing trend to the use of machines for power and computation. Further progress in incorporating human or behavioral considerations and a more thorough or pervasive use of the systems approach should characterize future advancements in the field of operations management.

THE NATURE OF OPERATIONS MANAGEMENT

The brief history in the preceding section outlines how man has greatly increased his ability to produce goods and services. A productive system is the mechanism by which goods and services are created. Operations management, quite simply is the management of productive systems.

We must stress the fact that operations management goes well beyond the manufacturing operations of assembly and fabrication. Productive systems also include the operation of banks; city, state, and federal government agencies; hospitals; public utilities; school systems; insurance companies; retail department stores; and so on. We shall see that many of the basic principles of operations management can be applied to both manufacturing and service organizations.

The management of both service and manufacturing organizations can be unified by viewing a productive system as one that transforms inputs into outputs. Figure 1-1 illustrates a basic diagram of a productive system.

We may define operations management more formally as the management of a productive system that transforms inputs into outputs. The responsibility of the operations manager can be seen in Figure 1-1 as the area between inputs and outputs. The operations manager, whether his official title is production manager, or vice-

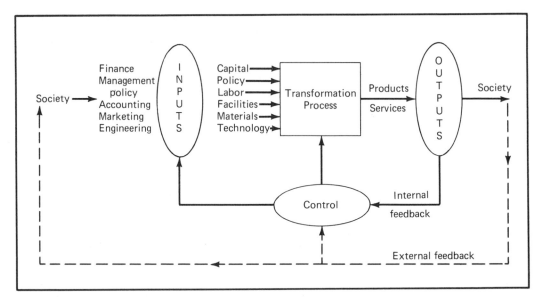

FIGURE 1-1   Diagram of Productive System

president of operations, or whatever, must follow the policies set by top management and work cooperatively with other organizational functions such as finance, marketing, and engineering. He has some control over the inputs, such as labor, use of capital, facilities, and available technology. His primary concern is the management of the transformation process to create quality products or services efficiently. Listed in Table 1-1 are some systems that typify the transformation process for both products and services.

You might have learned in your first management course that management functions in general involve planning, organizing, staffing, direction, and control. These same functions apply to the operations manager. There are also several important functions that apply specifically to the management of the transformation process of any productive system. These four basic functions are designing, scheduling, operation, and controlling.

Designing

Designing the transformation process involves basic issues such as equipment selection, type of process, and work-flow patterns. Transformation processes are usually either continuous, intermittent, or "one-shot" projects. Continuous processes are generally highly specialized to produce one type of product or service. Associated equipment is usually of a special-purpose type with little flexibility. Intermittent processes are more general and utilize a variety of multipurpose equipment. Classical examples of continuous, intermittent, and project processes are automobile assembly lines, job shops, and building construction respectively. The choice of the best type of process is dictated by economical considerations and volume of output desired.

Table 1-1 Systems Transformation Processes

TYPE OF SYSTEM	MAIN INPUTS	COMPONENTS	FUNCTION	MAIN OUTPUT
Automobile plant	Steel, parts	Assembly line, equipment, workers	Assembly of autos	Automobiles
Hospital	Patients	Doctors, nurses, equipment, supplies	Health care	Healthy people
Insurance claims office	Claims, phone calls	Claims agents	Rejecting, accepting, settling claims	Settled claims
University	Students	Professors, books, facilities	Imparting knowledge and information	Educated students
Computer center	Jobs to be processed	Programmers, CPU, peripheral equipment	Processing of computer jobs	Processed jobs

Other design factors include the layout of the facility and pattern of work flow to achieve a smooth flow of output.

Scheduling

After a process is designed, it must be scheduled to produce the desired product or service at the right time. Scheduling can be broken down into long-range and short-range planning. In long-range scheduling, forecasts of future demand are obtained and aggregate plans are devised to estimate needed amounts of manpower, capacity, and materials. Long-range scheduling involves the tentative scheduling of future activities to meet future demand. It requires the planning of manpower and materials to have them available at the right time and the right place to transform the inputs to the desired outputs. Much attention is given to this type of scheduling in Chapter 11 on materials requirements planning (MRP). Another type of scheduling involves the management of projects over time and utilizes the PERT/CPM method to pinpoint bottleneck activities and avoid delays. Short-range scheduling gets down to the micro level of weekly or daily operations. It involves sequencing activities such as jobs through machines, vehicles through routes, and patients through a hospital. In Chapter 12 we will examine systematic methods for scheduling.

Operating

Operating the transformation process is closely related to scheduling. But whereas scheduling refers to a type of planning prior to execution, operating often refers to the actual implementation of the transformation procedures. Effective operation requires the ability to react to last-minute changes and unexpected delays in planned schedules. The operating phase also involves longer-range decision activities not pertaining to scheduling, such as purchasing, implementing market strategies, and process redesign.

Control

The control function is graphically depicted in Figure 1-1. It involves the monitoring of the transformation process to ensure a quality end product or service. The control mechanism usually consists of some means of measuring the product or service before its completion; people and automated machines are both used. Often, computers are used to monitor inventory levels and can signal an out-of-stock or backorder situation. Machines also exist to measure chemical processes such as the octane rating of various gasolines. Another type of feedback can occur externally to the firm, from society. However, the purpose of quality control (see Chapter 13) is to help ensure an acceptable product or service before it reaches the customer.

We have taken a brief look at the basic functions of managing a production system. We have mentioned some of the primary responsibilities of the operations manager, but certainly not all of them. Table 1-2 further delineates the major responsibilities associated with managing a productive system.

Table 1-2   Major Responsibilities of the Operations Manager

DESIGN	SCHEDULING
1. Product design	1. Aggregate planning
2. Job and process design	2. Scheduling manpower levels
3. Capital equipment selection	3. Project management
4. Setting labor standards	4. Timing inventory replenishments
5. Developing labor skills	5. Routing and sequencing
6. Plant location and layout	6. Job-shop scheduling
OPERATING	CONTROL
1. Purchasing	1. Quality control
2. Forecasting requirements	2. Inventory control policies
3. Process redesign	3. Monitoring of production processes
4. Operation of transformation process	4. Cost control
5. Maintenance	5. Resource allocation

A SYSTEMS APPROACH

Operations managers must all be involved with the basic functions of designing, scheduling, operating, and controlling. The managerial approach that is used in performing these four functions can and does vary widely. An underlying philosophy of this text (and most others) is that a systems approach is the most effective approach to operations management decision problems.

The word *system* is much used in our society. We hear of computer systems, solar systems, and political systems. In the broad definition of general systems theory, a system is a whole comprising interrelated parts intended to accomplish a specific objective. Thus, a computer system is made up of hardware components such as the central processor unit, card reader, disk drives, and tape drives, and software components such as the operating system software and compiler programs. These components interact to accomplish the objective of processing computer jobs.

Organizations, too, conform to our definition of a system. The operations manager, for example, is concerned with human/machine systems comprising components such as machinery, departments, divisions, and individual people. The main thrust of the systems approach is to broadly define problems that when solved yield benefits that are in line with the highest order and overall goals of the organization.

Failure to use the systems approach can sometimes yield good results for a component of the system, but not for the system as a whole. For example, suppose the inventory division of an organization is experiencing higher-than-average inventory levels and costs. Reducing inventory levels may reduce costs in the inventory division but may reduce sales for marketing and cause unemployment on the production line; this may not be consistent with the goals of the organization as a whole. This is called suboptimization rather than optimization of the organization goals.

Traditional approaches to operations management viewed the organizational boundaries of the firm as being relatively fixed. The basic idea was for each department of the organization to do its job as well as possible, but apart from other departments. This approach can lead to optimization of departmental goals but suboptimization of the goals of the organization as a whole.

In order to optimize the goals of the organization, the systems approach requires the inclusion of all factors relevant to the problem. In the example above, we would require input from not only inventory but also marketing and personnel. The modern systems approach cuts across departmental and divisional lines. It recognizes the interdependence of the various functions of an organization. Decisions made by operations managers have an effect on the engineering, marketing, and finance functions of the organization. Likewise, decisions made in these departments can have significant impact on the productive function.

The systems approach calls for an integration of the goals, policies, and decisions of the separate functions of the organization. This blend of viewpoints will result in an integrated decision that leads to the best overall good of the firm as perceived by management. Figure 1-2 depicts the synthesis of input and output between the various organizational departments and integrated decisions.

The systems approach, although the most effective, is not always the easiest approach to implement. It requires cooperation between departments and an examination of perhaps more alternatives than does a traditional approach. It may also require the resolution of conflict between departments whose objectives are not in complete agreement. Such decisions often require common sense and the subjective judgment of management. There is never a guarantee that the resulting decisions will always be perfect; in the business world, decisions are too complex and contingencies too pre-

12

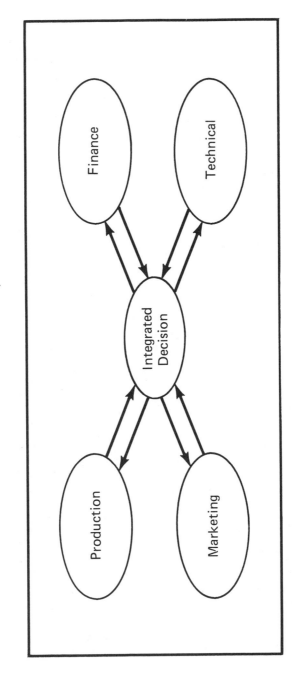

FIGURE 1-2 Integrated Decisions through the Systems Approach

valent. However, the use of the systems approach will lead to a systematic way to reach the goals of the organization and balance between departments.

Just as a systems approach help us to have a balanced perspective concerning an organization's components, it also helps us to view the organization as a component, or subsystem, of the environment in which it exists. Figure 1-3 depicts the productive system as a subsystem of the organization and its environment.

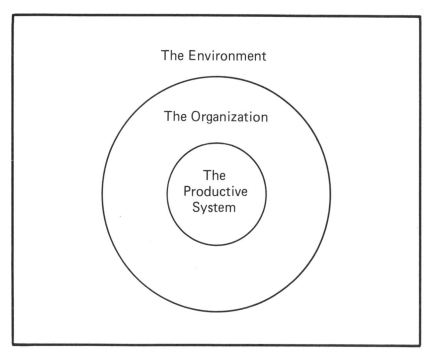

FIGURE 1-3   The Productive System as a Subsystem

Systems methodology is very broad and applicable to other endeavors in addition to operations management. It is particularly valuable in decision structuring or decision-making endeavors such as business and economic policy of quantitative decision making.

DECISION MAKING

All decision problems can be classified as either (1) strategic, (2) tactical, or (3) operational.

Strategic problems involve the establishment of organizational goals and objectives. These kinds of problems generally affect the organization as a whole and entail decisions that have long-term impact on the organization. Strategic decision making is usually the role of top management, but operations management is often involved in the design phases. For example, decisions regarding product mix, plant locations, and the degree of automation are all strategic decisions.

Tactical decisions generally involve not the organization as a whole but rather some component or subsystem. Tactical decisions deal with means of implementing strategic decisions. Operations managers must make hundreds of tactical decisions in their managerial careers. Examples of tactical decisions are allocation of resources such as raw materials and capital, yearly manpower levels, selection of equipment, and process redesign or improvement.

Operational decisions are concerned most with efficiency of performance and deal with an even more limited subsystem of the organization, such as an inventory department or machine shop. Thousands of operational decisions must be made yearly by the operations manager and perhaps foremen or first-line management. Operational decisions involve a wide range of activities, from scheduling of day-to-day activities to pricing and production levels. The main concern of operational decisions is the performance of specific jobs in a timely and cost-efficient manner.

Given the systems approach as the general structure for decision making, we can distinguish between decision alternatives as affecting system effectiveness or system efficiency. Starr defines strategic decisions as affecting the organization as a whole and thus affecting system effectiveness.[1] Tactical and operational decisions affect only various subsystems and hence system efficiency. Obviously, system effectiveness is more important than system efficiency. Decisions to improve system efficiency should not be made at the expense of system effectiveness. However, given a high level of system effectiveness, it is desirable to achieve system efficiency as well.

There are several ways for the operations manager to arrive at decisions for strategic, tactical, or operational problems. He can use his subjective judgment, mathematical decision models, or heuristic decision methods. The appropriate choice of methods depends upon the nature of the decision problem. One of the main purposes of this text is to familiarize you with effective approaches to various decision-making problems.

An important factor in any decision problem pertains to the amount of risk or uncertainty underlying the problem. Figure 1-4 illustrates the range of risk in decision making. Deterministic problems are those in which all information regarding the

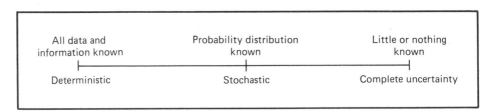

FIGURE 1-4 **Continuum of Uncertainty in Decision Problems**

[1]M.K. Starr, *Production Management: Systems and Synthesis* (Englewood Cliffs, N.J.: Prentice-Hall, 1972).

problem is known with certainty. Stochastic problems involve more risk, as only a probability distribution is known. In decision problems under uncertainty, little or nothing is known about the decision environment. To illustrate these three types of problems, let's consider a simplified decision problem for an inventory manager who has to place an order at the beginning of each month to replenish stock. In a deterministic problem, he would know next month's demand with certainty, so he could order exactly that amount. In a stochastic problem, he would not know next month's demand, but he would know the probability distribution of demand; for instance, the demand may be normally distributed with a mean of 250 units. Last, under uncertainty, he would have little or no idea what the next month's demand would be or how much to order. Most decision problems are neither completely deterministic or completely uncertain.

For decision problems that are completely deterministic, objective decision methods have been most helpful in achieving an effective solution. Tactical and operational as well as some strategic problems have been solved successfully by objective means such as mathematical models and heuristics. Earlier efforts with objective methods tended to focus on simple, well-defined problems in which efficiency was the prime consideration. More recently, however, attention has begun to focus on more general operations management problems and system effectiveness. Nevertheless, as decision problems become more complex and less clearly defined, and as multiple objectives are considered, then the decision maker's own personal judgment becomes more involved in the final decision.

Models

Models can be very useful in making objective decisions about decision problems in general. Model development and solution have been a key development in the discipline of operations research/management science. Many of these models and problem-solving techniques are applicable to operations management problems.

A *model* is a representation or an abstraction of an object or a particular real-world phenomenon. A good model accurately displays the key properties of the entity it represents. Models are used in many disciplines besides operations management; economics and engineering are two other areas that make extensive use of them. The purpose in using a model is to gain specific information about and general insight into the phenomenon it represents. By using models, it is possible to investigate certain cause-and-effect relationships and the interaction between key variables.

In operations management, the primary models of interest are mathematical models. We can use equations and algebraic relationships to express certain managerial goals and physical constraints. Consider, for example, a production scheduling problem in which many possible products can be selected and scheduled for production. The human mind could probably find an acceptable production schedule, but a good model solved by an optimization technique can usually achieve a 10–15 percent better solution. Models also offer the capability of exploring various alternatives.

Given an accurate model of a productive system, we can solve it many different times in order to determine the effects of changing various inputs. This type of *sensitivity analysis* is extremely useful and allows management to ask "what-if" questions. For instance, if management was uncertain about the availability of a certain raw material, it could input several different raw-material levels to this model and obtain production schedules and estimated profits in each case.

Models can thus be especially helpful in the decision-making process, but management must realize their limitations and the fact that a solution is usually a good starting point but not necessarily the final answer.

Heuristics

Models can be an effective tool for decision making, but in some cases a model cannot be constructed, or its solution is too cumbersome and impractical. Many decision problems in operations management are complex and involve many interacting variables and relationships; this is particularly true in the area of scheduling. Heuristics have been devised as a simple means to determine effective objective solutions to problems. A *heuristic* is a method or rule of thumb that determines good but not necessarily optimal solutions to a problem. Heuristics are widespread in operations management, and we shall consider several throughout this book.

As an example, consider a cargo-loading problem in which the load placed on a truck is to have maximum value. There are 99 cartons of various volumes and values, but not all the cartons will fit in the truck simultaneously. Which cartons should be loaded? Let's consider two heuristic decision rules:

Heuristic 1:   Load cartons in decreasing order of value.
Heuristic 2:   Load cartons in decreasing order of value per volume.

The first heuristic simply loads those cartons having highest value first. The second heuristic is usually more effective, as it considers not only the value but the volume of the cartons.

Neither heuristic would guarantee an optimal solution. But an important analogy can be made here. Management is usually practical-minded and is interested in getting an effective solution quickly and then proceeding to the next important problem. Sometimes an additional 5 percent improvement offered by an exact model or optimization procedure is not worth the additional time and effort.

Most decision problems encountered by operations managers are still resolved by human judgment. As mathematical techniques and heuristics improve and become more widespread, we can expect progressive operations managers to turn more to these approaches; however, there are still situations in which the human mind is superior to quantitative techniques. Managers must deal with not only people and behavioral considerations, but multiple and sometimes conflicting goals of the organization. These kinds of decisions seem to be predominant in managerial activities. Research is in progress on multiple-criteria decision making. Perhaps with further advancements in this area, management will have some objective quantitative methods that will prove useful in a much wider range of real-world decision problems.

Management Information Systems (MIS)

Recent progress in operations management can be partially attributed to the systems approach and the use of scientific decision methods. But a factor that has perhaps been utilized even more by practicing operations managers is a *management information system*. No matter what decision method is used, accurate and timely information is critical to effective managerial decision making; each of the phases of designing, scheduling, operating, and controlling requires the collection, processing, and presentation of data. Computer-assisted planning and control extend the abilities of management to perform these important functions.

A management information system (MIS) is a means of collecting, storing, and processing data so that they are useful for decision making. The system consists of the personnel and the computer hardware and software necessary to process the data, and it serves the purpose of converting raw data to timely, usable information for management. The MIS manipulates the data or statistically summarizes them so that a more accurate scientific decision process can be used. Even though information systems do not generate decisions, they do automate many routine tasks and provide quantitative data for evaluation.

Management information systems can support all three levels of managerial planning. However, operations problems are characterized by frequent repetition of planning, making this area more attractive for computer support than strategic planning, which occurs less frequently.

There are many important examples of information systems used in operations management. They are perhaps most widely used in the management of inventory. In many firms, it is important to have immediate access to the inventory status of various items. With a computer-based information system, it is possible to continuously monitor inventory transactions. We shall see in Chapter 11 that information systems are an indispensable part of MRP for management of inventories subject to dependent demand.

Forecasting and other planning activities are aided by the accurate and sometimes voluminous historical data that can be stored and manipulated with a computer-based information system. This same type of data can be easily converted to a form that is acceptable to computerized planning models. The control function of the operations manager is also aided by a computer-based information system, since such a system makes it possible to monitor system performance continuously rather than periodically.

Other operations management applications of MIS (such as scheduling) can be cited, but the use of MIS is so widespread that it is found in nearly all aspects of medium- to large-sized manufacturing and service industries. It is accurate to say that MIS is revolutionizing the speed and reliability of information that is required by management for decision making.

Thus far in this chapter, we have tried to convey what operations management is all about and its key characteristics. At this point, it seems best to show you some real-world scenarios of successful operations management applications. Many possible examples exist in manufacturing and service industries, and in the private and public sectors. We have chosen the following three applications because they are representative of modern scientific approaches and because they report their results.

Scheduling Policies for Surgical Patients[2]

Rising medical costs, limited facility space, and increasing pressure for surgical-suite utilization caused the Deaconess Hospital in St. Louis, Missouri, to review its policies for scheduling patients through its surgical suite (capacity five patients) and recovery room (capacity twelve patients). The hospital had been using a random-input policy for scheduling patients for surgery. A team of researchers suggested a computer simulation approach to scientifically study different queueing decision rules for scheduling patients. It was not allowable to experiment with different schedules using actual patients, and the simulation approach permitted the testing of different policies on the computer without affecting hospital functions.

Not all patients require a recovery room after surgery, so data had to be collected regarding the statistical distribution of types of surgery, their times, and the patient's duration of stay (if any) in the recovery room. The GPSS simulation language was used to write a simulator that could analyze five different scheduling rules for the 27 patients that needed to be scheduled each day. The scheduling had to allow for certain priorities, such as the fact that a patient needing the recovery room must always have a bed available for him.

Each of the five patient scheduling rules was used by the simulator on a previous 103-day schedule involving 2,781 patients. It was found that significant improvement could be obtained by using any of the four new scheduling rules. In particular, one scheduling rule, which was based on scheduling those patients requiring the longest surgery first, offered the following improvements: higher operating- and recovery-room utilization rates, increased patient load in the recovery room during a shorter day, and more timely completion of the surgical and recovery schedule. Additionally, the average length of workday in the recovery room was reduced 21 percent, allowing the reduction of manpower requirements of one registered nurse and one operating-room technician. The $17,000-a-year cost savings more than outweighed the cost of the simulator and scheduling.

These improvements were found using very simple scheduling rules; the Deanconess Hospital planned to adopt the one scheduling rule while continuing to investigate other scientific scheduling approaches.

---

[2]N.K. Kwak, P.J. Kuzdrall, and H. Schmitz, "The GPSS Simulation of Scheduling Policies for Surgical Patients," *Management Science*, 22 (May 1976), 982–89.

will provide some motivation and also further bridge the gap between theory and practice.

Following this introductory chapter, Part Two of the book presents quantitative methods of particular importance to operations managers in the analysis of productive systems. Chapter 2 looks at linear programming modeling and applications to operations management. Linear programming is valuable not only for its usefulness in resource allocation, production scheduling, and distribution, but also for its introduction to modeling. Chapter 3 explores computer simulation, a tool extremely valuable for analyzing stochastic decision problems. Simulation is probably the most widely used quantitative method for studying and predicting the behavior of complex productive systems. Chapter 4 is concerned with the analysis of waiting lines and their characteristics. The study of waiting lines is useful in capacity planning and process design as well as the scheduling of productive systems.

In Part Three of the text, we focus on the design of productive systems. Chapters 5, 6, and 7 all pertain to various design phases of operations management. In Chapter 5, we study the factors in the design of the transformation process for converting inputs to desired outputs. Key topics include product and process design and facilities layout. Chapter 6 is devoted to job design and studies the human element of the man–machine system. The emphasis in Chapter 6 is on behavioral considerations, work measurement, and time studies. Chapter 7 is concerned with strategic decisions as to where to locate facilities such as plants or warehouses.

The operation and planning aspects of productive systems are covered in Part Four. One of the important functions of the operations manager is the forecasting and anticipation of future demand levels and capacity needs. Chapter 8 discusses several forecasting alternatives and their strengths and weaknesses. Chapter 9, on aggregate planning, is concerned with using forecasts to develop intermediate-range plans for meeting demand levels. Strategies and methods for the absorption of fluctuating demand levels are presented.

In Part Five of the text we look at the scheduling and control functions of operations management. Chapter 10 deals with classical approaches to the management of inventory. Inventory models are presented that help not only to control inventory costs but also to schedule purchases and production. Whereas Chapter 10 deals with independent demand items, Chapter 11 examines materials requirements planning (MRP) for dependent demand items. This is particularly important in the management of inventories for parts and subassemblies in manufacturing operations. MRP also provides capability in capacity planning and scheduling of operations. Chapter 12 studies the scheduling problem in operations management. Initially, the chapter looks at project scheduling and the PERT method for effective project management; then the scheduling of production and services is studied and various heuristics for complex job-shop scheduling problems are presented. Finally, Chapter 13 is devoted to the control function. The major theme of the chapter is the development of a quality assurance system and statistical tests that ensure the quality of the final product or service.

REVIEW QUESTIONS

1. In your opinion, what has been the single most important event in the advancement of operations management?
2. What are some of the characteristics of the modern approach to operations management?
3. Paraphrase the definition of operations management in your own words.
4. Characterize the inputs, components, and outputs of the transformation process of systems such as (a) a bank, (b) book publishing, (c) a football team, (d) a job shop.
5. What are the four basic functions of the operations manager?
6. Briefly explain the nature of the systems approach.
7. Differentiate between decision making under deterministic conditions, stochastic conditions, and uncertainty.
8. What is the primary benefit of using models in the analysis of a problem?
9. What is a heuristic? Give an example of one.
10. What is an MIS? How have these systems improved the practice of operations management?
11. List any application you have seen that you would consider operations management in action.
12. Distinguish between system effectiveness and system efficiency.
13. Characterize strategic, tactical, and operational decision problems.

REFERENCES

BUFFA, E.S., *Operations Management: The Management of Productive Systems*. New York: John Wiley, 1976.

CHASE, R.B., and H.J. AQUILANO, *Production and Operations Management*. Homewood, Ill.: Richard D. Irwin, 1977.

DRAKE, A.W., R.L. KEENEY, and P.M. MORSE, eds., *Analysis of Public Systems*. Cambridge, Mass.: M.I.T. Press, 1972.

EASTON, A., *Complex Managerial Decisions Involving Multiple Objectives*. New York: John Wiley, 1973.

GEORGE, CLAUDE S., *The History of Management Thought*. Englewood Cliffs, N.J.: Prentice-Hall, 1968.

JOHNSON, R.A., F.E. KAST, and J.E. ROSENZWEIG, *The Theory and Management of Systems*. New York: McGraw-Hill, 1967.

OLSEN, R.A., *Manufacturing Management: A Quantitative Approach.* Scranton, Pa.: International Textbook, 1968.

STARR, M.K., *Production Management: Systems and Synthesis.* Englewood Cliffs, N.J.: Prentice-Hall, 1972.

VOLLMAN, T.E., *Operations Management: A Systems Model-Building Approach.* Reading, Mass.: Addison-Wesley, 1973.

part TWO

quantitative methods for operations management

chapter 2

LINEAR
PROGRAMMING

In this chapter we begin our study of quantitative methods of particular importance to operations managers. First we shall study linear programming, its methodology, and its applications to operations management. In Chapter 3 we will examine the extremely useful tool of computer simulation, and in Chapter 4 we will study queuing theory and its usefulness in analyzing waiting lines.

Of all the quantitative tools available to the operations manager, *linear programming* is one of the most widely used. It is primarily concerned with the determination of the best allocation of scarce resources. Thus, it can be used to allocate limited resources such as capital or raw materials among competing alternatives in order to maximize the objectives of a particular enterprise. Linear programming is not limited to allocation problems however; it has many applications in scheduling and distribution functions. These applications are extensive not only in production and non-manufacturing industries, but also in government agencies and companies in the public sector.

Linear programming is just one technique in the more general area of mathematical programming. Mathematical programming is concerned with the development of modeling and solution procedures for the purpose of maximizing the extent to which the goals and objectives of the decision maker are realized. Special linearity conditions must hold before a general mathematical programming problem is actually an LP problem; we shall examine these conditions later in the chapter.

Despite the implication of its name, LP has little to do with computer programming. In LP, the word *programming* is related to planning. Specifically, it refers to modeling a problem and subsequently solving it by mathematical techniques. As we shall see, LP is very similar to setting up and solving a system of linear equations.

Even though LP is quite different from computer programming, computer development has played an integral part in the successful application of LP. Real-world LP problems often involve hundreds of variables and equations. These problems would be impossible to solve without a high-speed computer.

Linear programming has numerous applications to the production and operations functions. In a survey sent to the directors of production/operations at roughly half of *Fortune*'s top 500 companies, we found that 95 percent of those responding used LP to some extent in managing their operations. Undoubtedly, smaller companies use LP less. In some cases, it is not needed; in other cases, managers may not understand LP or realize its potential.

AREAS OF APPLICATION

Linear programming has applications in a wide range of disciplines, from economic theory to the social sciences. Industrial, agricultural, and military applications are the most extensive. In this section, we focus on a small portion of applications that are relevant to operations management. Linear programming is usually not the only means used in solving the following problems, but is an effective tool to use in the decision-making process.

Production Applications

Blending. In blending problems, the objective is to determine the combination of raw ingredients that will result in a satisfactory end product and minimize costs. Examples of blending problems are the blending of petroleum products, mixing of cattle feed, mixing of meats to make sausage, and mixing of paint.

Production Scheduling. This problem involves the determination of a production schedule that meets demand subject to fluctuations. The objective is to meet demand and yet maintain reasonable inventory levels and employment levels, while minimizing the overall costs of production and inventory.

Manpower Planning. LP can be used to make decisions for departmental staffing requirements for a given period of time. It has also been used to evaluate long-range hiring, promotion, and retirement schemes, as well as proposed compensation schemes[1] and the assignment of salesmen to territories.

Physical Distribution. Distributing products from plants to warehouses or customer demand points has been one of the more fruitful areas of application of LP. The objective is to meet demand while minimizing transportation costs. Models have also been developed to minimize the combined cost of production and distribution.

Aggregate Planning. Aggregate planning or scheduling involves the determination of minimum-cost production levels for several months into the future. Changing demand rates require decisions aimed at minimizing the costs of varying production rates, varying work-force levels, inventory, overtime, and subcontracting.

Process Control. The operation of various processes that generate scrap can be aided by LP models that help to minimize waste. Examples are the cutting of stock paper, fabric materials, and steel parts to fill various orders.

---

[1]Richard C. Grinold, "Input Policies for a Longitudinal Manpower Flow Model," *Management Science*, Vol. 22 (1976), 570–75.

Government and Nonmanufacturing Applications

Agriculture.   Among the agricultural applications of linear programming have been land allocation and animal diet problems.[2] LP can be used to determine the allocation of land areas to crops in order to minimize costs or maximize profits and meet certain crop requirements. It can be applied to diet problems, both animal and human, in order to meet nutritional requirements at minimal cost.

Environmental Protection.   Linear programming has been used to analyze alternatives for handling liquid waste material in order to satisfy antipollution requirements. LP has also been used as a tool in the analysis of paper recycling,[3] air cleaner design,[4] and analysis of alternative energy policies.[5]

Urban Development.   More recently, LP has been used to analyze public expenditure planning,[6] school busing, and drug control. Political redistricting and financial analysis of new community development processes have also been tackled with LP.[7]

Facilities Location.   Location analysis by linear programming includes the location of public parks and recreation areas within communities,[8] of hospitals, ambulance depots,[9] nuclear power plants,[10] telephone exchanges, and warehouses for centralized distribution.

NATURE OF LINEAR MODELS

We have presented a smattering of LP applications. Let us now focus on the nature of a linear model, what it is, and how to formulate it. Linearity is a very simple relationship between variables. To be precise, any linear expression is of the form:

$$a_1x_1 + a_2x_2 + \ldots + a_nx_n$$

---

[2]D.F. Lyons and V.A. Dodd, "The Mix-Feed Problem," *Operational Research* (Amsterdam: North-Holland Publishing, 1975); V.E. Smith, "A Diet Model with Protein Quality Variable," *Management Science*, February 1974, pp. 971–80.

[3]C.R. Glassey and V.K. Gupta, "A Linear Programming Analysis of Paper Recycling," *Management Science*, December 1974, pp. 392–408.

[4]S. Advani, "A Linear Programming Approach to Air Cleaner Design," *Operations Research*, March–April 1974, pp. 295–97.

[5]W. Marcuse, L. Bodin, E. Cherniavsky, and Yasuko Sanborn, "A Dynamic Time Dependent Model for the Analysis of Alternative Energy Policies," *Operational Research* (Amsterdam: North-Holland Publishing, 1975).

[6]M. Feldstein and Harold Luft, "Distributional Constraints in Public Expenditure Planning," *Management Science*, August 1973, pp. 1414–22.

[7]R.L. Heroux and W.A. Wallace, "Linear Programming and Financial Analysis of the New Community Development Process," *Management Science*, April 1973, pp. 857–72.

[8]C. Revelle, D. Marks, and J. Liebman, "An Analysis of Private and Public Sector Location Models," *Management Science*, Vol. 16 (1970), 692–707.

[9]E. Savas, "Simulation and Cost-Effectiveness of New York's Emergency Ambulance Service," *Management Science*, Vol. 15 (1969), B608–27.

[10]R. Dutton, G. Hinman, and C.B. Millham, "The Optimal Location of Nuclear Power Facilities in the Pacific Northwest," *Operations Research*, May–June 1974, pp. 478–87.

where the a_i represent coefficients and the x_i represent variables. A linear model is constructed from linear expressions. A linear expression called the *objective function* represents the goal or objective to be achieved; for example, the objective function may represent profit maximization or cost minimization. The remainder of any LP model is made up of *constraints*; these constraints are linear expressions that mathematically state the limited resource availability, various conditions, policies, or technical specifications.

The canonical form of an LP model is as follows:

2.1   Maximize (or Minimize) $c_1x_1 + c_2x_2 + \ldots + c_nx_n$

subject to the restrictions: $a_{11}x_1 + a_{12}x_2 + \cdots + a_{1n}x_n \leq b_1$

$$a_{21}x_1 + a_{22}x_2 + \cdots + a_{2n}x_n \leq b_2$$

2.2

$$\vdots$$

$$a_{m1}x_1 + a_{m2}x_2 + \cdots + a_{mn}x_n \leq b_m$$

2.3   and $x_1 \geq 0, x_2 \geq 0, \ldots, x_n \geq 0$

Any problem whose mathematical formulation fits this general model is an LP problem. The expression 2.1 is the objective function, inequalities 2.2 are the constraints, and the inequalities 2.3 are called nonnegativity conditions; they prevent the variables from assuming negative values. We should note that the constraints need not be stated with just less-than-or-equal-to ($\leq$) signs, but may also be stated with equalities ($=$), or greater-than-or-equal-to ($\geq$) signs.

The x_j variables in the general model above are decision variables; that is, they are variables whose values are determined when the LP model is solved. Their values provide the answers that are being sought in the LP analysis. In order to determine the values of the decision variables, the LP model needs data. The objective function coefficients c_j, the constraint coefficients a_{ij}, and the right-hand-side coefficients b_i are parameters of the model. The particular values of the parameters determine the final solution to the decision variables.

Not all mathematical models fit the general form of expressions 2.1–2.3. Any mathematical model not of this form is called a nonlinear model. Operations management applications also exist for nonlinear models, but, owing to their limited use and relatively complex nature, they are considered in advanced courses. In order for linear programming to be applicable to any mathematical model, the following conditions must hold.

Assumptions of Linear Programming

1. The objective function and constraints must be linear. This implies that the variables' values are additive. Thus, 2 units of profit contribution from decision variable x_1 and 3 units of profit contribution from decision variable x_3 must add

together to contribute 5 units to profit. Linearity also implies proportionality. If variable x_2 requires 2 hours of labor, then 2 units of x_2 require 4 hours. The last implication of linearity is that the decision variables are divisible. Fractional values such as $3\frac{3}{4}$ or 4.78 must be acceptable in the final solution. If whole-number solutions are required, we must resort to a mathematical programming technique called integer programming.

2. The parameters of the model must be known or accurately estimated. Numerical values must be provided for each parameter.

FORMULATING LP MODELS

In formulating any mathematical model, the decision maker is attempting to represent the essence of some problem in terms of relationships between symbols; in linear models, these relationships are all linear. Model building is more an art than a science; thus, formulating accurate models depends greatly upon the decision maker's own ingenuity and experience. Formulation is the most critical aspect of an LP analysis, for once the model is *correctly* formulated, it can be solved readily on a computer. The following guidelines serve as an aid in the formulation process:

1. Understand the problem.
2. Identify the decision variables (i.e., those variables whose values, if found, would solve the problem).
3. Choose a numerical measure of effectiveness for the objective function.
4. Represent this measure of effectiveness as a linear expression involving the decision variables.
5. Identify and represent all constraints as linear expressions involving the decision variables.
6. Collect data or make appropriate estimations for all parameters of the model.

We illustrate these guidelines in the following LP formulations.

Product-Mix Example

The Electrovox Company is a relatively new firm that manufactures CB radios. It currently manufactures a deluxe hi-gain unit and a standard model; Electrovox has the facilities to produce either the deluxe or the standard model, or a combination of both. Since production resources are limited, it is critical that the firm produce the appropriate number of deluxe and standard models. The deluxe unit sells for $150 and contributes $50 to profit; the standard unit sells for $100 and contributes $20 to profit. There are only three production resources that limit the production quantities, and the production requirements of the two CB radios are summarized in Table 2-1.

Additionally, there are 40 hi-gain transistors, 240 assembly hours, and 81 inspection hours available on a daily basis. We shall assume that the firm can sell all the

Table 2-1

PRODUCT	HI-GAIN TRANSISTORS	ASSEMBLY HOURS	INSPECTION HOURS
Hi-gain	1	4	1
Standard	0	1.2	.5

components it can produce and that plant equipment and labor skills are interchangeable between hi-gain and standard units.

Defining the Decision Variables and Objective Function. Assuming that we understand the problem, the next step is to define the decision variables. What is the Electrovox Company trying to decide? Specifically, how many hi-gain and how many standard CB radios it should produce? To answer the basic question, let x_1 equal the number of standard units to be produced daily, and let x_2 equal the number of hi-gain radios to be produced each day. Since x_1 and x_2 contribute \$20 and \$50, respectively, to profit, we may state the objective function as:

$$\text{Maximize } 20x_1 + 50x_2$$

Constructing the Constraints. The production process is limited only by the daily limitation of hi-gain transistors, assembly man-hours, and inspection man-hours. Thus we will have three constraints, one for each of the scarce resources.

The limited supply of hi-gain transistors will affect only the production of hi-gain CBs. Thus, the first constraint limits the production of hi-gain CBs to 40 per day and is stated as $x_2 \leq 40$.

Both CBs require assembly time; thus, the assembly-time constraint must ensure that the combined assembly time of both units must not exceed 240 hours. This may be expressed as $1.2x_1 + 4x_2 \leq 240$. Similarly, the inspection-time constraint is stated as $.50x_1 + 1x_2 \leq 81$. Since it is impossible to produce a negative number of CB radios, we impose the nonnegativity conditions $x_1, x_2 \geq 0$. The final LP formulation is thus:

$$\text{Maximize } 20x_1 + 50x_2$$
$$\text{subject to:} \quad x_2 \leq 40$$
$$1.2x_1 + 4x_2 \leq 240$$
$$.50x_1 + 1x_2 \leq 81$$
$$x_1, x_2 \geq 0$$

R&D Budget Allocation Example

The Viscus Oil Company must decide how to allocate its budget for energy research and development. The government grants certain tax breaks if the company invests funds in research concerned with energy conservation. However, the government stipulates that at least 60 percent of the funds must be funneled into research for automobile efficiency. Viscus has a $1 million budget for energy research and development this year; the research proposal data are shown in Table 2-2.

Table 2-2

PROJECT	MANAGEMENT POLICY ON UPPER LIMIT OF EXPENDITURES ($)	FORECASTED RETURN ON INVESTMENT (%)
Methanol fuel research	400,000	4.0
Electrically operated cars	200,000	0.1
Emission reduction	400,000	3.0
Solar cells	300,000	2.0
Windmills	200,000	1.0

Assuming that Viscus wants to maximize return on its investment and yet receive the government tax break, let us formulate the problem as an LP model.

The decision variables should reflect the question management is asking; that is, How much should we invest in each research alternative? Therefore, let x_1 = Amount invested in methanol fuel research, x_2 = Amount invested in electrically operated cars, x_3 = Amount applied toward emission reduction, x_4 = Amount allocated to solar cells, and x_5 = Amount invested in windmills.

The objective function should measure return on investment and is stated as:

$$\text{Maximize } 4.0x_1 + .1x_2 + 3.0x_3 + 2.0x_4 + 1.0x_5$$

One constraint is the budget limit itself. Thus, the total spent must not exceed $1 million, or:

$$x_1 + x_2 + x_3 + x_4 + x_5 \leq 1{,}000{,}000$$

Furthermore, at least $600,000 must be spent on research for automobile efficiency:

$$x_1 + x_2 + x_3 \geq 600{,}000$$

Finally, management has limited the expenditures on any single project:

$$x_1 \leq 400{,}000$$
$$x_2 \leq 200{,}000$$
$$x_3 \leq 400{,}000$$
$$x_4 \leq 300{,}000$$
$$x_5 \leq 200{,}000$$

Since it is impossible to allocate negative dollars in this case, the nonnegativity conditions also apply:

$$x_1, x_2, x_3, x_4, x_5 \geq 0$$

The Graphical Method of Solution

Thus far we have examined the applications of linear programming and the formulation of linear models. The next consideration is how to solve these linear models in order to obtain specific values for the decision variables. In this section we shall look at the graphical method of solution; it is particularly useful in yielding insight into the nature of LP problems. The graphical method is not useful, however, for obtaining the solution to real-world LP problems; the method cannot handle more than three variables, since we cannot graph in more than three dimensions. In actual applications, LP problems are solved by the *simplex method* on a computer. The simplex method is discussed in the appendix at the end of this chapter.

The graphical method of solution simply involves plotting each of a problem's constraints to form a region of possible solutions. We then examine this region to select the best alternative. Let's return to the Electrovox product-mix example and solve it by the graphical method. Recall that the objective is to produce the appropriate number of hi-gain and standard CBs in order to maximize profit. The model we formulated is:

Maximize $20x_1 + 50x_2$	profit
subject to: $\quad\quad\quad x_2 \leq\ 40$	transistor availability
$1.2x_1 + 4x_2 \leq 240$	assembly time
$.5x_1 + 1x_2 \leq\ 81$	inspection time
$x_1, x_2 \geq 0$	

The first step in the graphical method is to plot the constraints on a graph. Since the Electrovox constraints are inequalities rather than equations, their graphs are regions rather than lines. However, the easiest way to graph an inequality is first to graph it as an equality, then simply shade in the appropriate area.

The first constraint, $x_2 \leq 40$, can be located on the graph by first locating its x_1 and x_2 intercepts on the x_1 and x_2 axes respectively. Treating the constraint as an equation ($x_2 = 40$), we find that the x_2 intercept is 40 and the x_1 intercept does not exist. Thus, the graph of $x_2 = 40$ is parallel to the x_1 axis. The inequality $x_2 \leq 40$ is graphed from $x_2 = 40$ by simply observing on which side of the line the origin (0, 0) is located. Substituting $x_1 = 0$ and $x_2 = 0$ into the inequality $x_2 \leq 40$, we find that $0 < 40$, and the origin is thus included in the inequality. The graph of $x_2 \leq 40$ is the region established by the line $x_2 = 40$ and the shaded area in Figure 2-1. Notice that the nonnegativity conditions restrict the shaded area in Figure 2-1 to the first quadrant.

In the second constraint, we determine the x_1 intercept by letting $x_2 = 0$ and

Any point on the line $20x_1 + 50x_2 = 2,000$ within the feasible region will yield a profit of \$2,000. Letting $P = \$3,000$, we obtain a different isoprofit line in Figure 2-3. Moving the isoprofit lines toward the northeast increases the profit. Moving the isoprofit lines as far as possible (and remaining in the feasible region) intersects the point C. Thus, the point C is the optimum solution to the Electrovox problem.

How does the point C yield the optimum? This is answered by determining the x_1 and x_2 coordinate values associated with the point C. Since C occurs at the intersection of the two lines $1.2x_1 + 4x_2 = 240$ and $.5x_1 + 1x_2 = 81$, we can solve these two linear equations simultaneously to obtain x_1 and x_2.

$$
\begin{array}{rl}
1.2x_1 + 4x_2 = & 240 \\
-2.0x_1 - 4x_2 = & -324 \\
\hline
-.8x_1 \quad\quad = & -84 \\
x_1 = & 105
\end{array}
$$

Substituting 105 for x_1 in the first equation, we obtain $x_2 = [240 - 1.2(105)]/4 = 28.5$. Thus, the optimal product mix is to produce 105 standard and 28.5 hi-gain units each day. The profit associated with the optimal solution is $20(105) + 50(28.5) = \$3,525$ per day.

Notice that the optimal LP solution calls for the production of 28.5 hi-gain units per day. We can interpret this as the production of 28 whole units and half of another unit that is to be finished the next day. This solution reflects the divisibility assumption of LP. If we want integer solutions, then we must round off or resort to integer programming. However, rounding off LP solutions does not necessarily yield optimal or even feasible solutions.

A LINEAR DISTRIBUTION MODEL

The graphical method illustrates the solution of the general LP model. Some LP models are designed for solving special classes of problems. In particular, LP has probably been most widely applied in the distribution aspect of operations management. These applications have generated specially structured LP models that, although solvable by general methods, are usually solved by techniques that exploit the special properties of the models; the end result is a much more efficient solution procedure.

To illustrate the use of LP in distribution-type problems, let us consider the distribution problem faced by the East of the Rockies Region of Shell Oil Co.[11] Since approximately 20 percent of Shell's revenues go to pay for transportation costs, efficient distribution is critical. Figure 2-4 illustrates the Shell distribution problem. Shell's problem is relatively complex; basically, it is to distribute three products among four refineries and a large number of transshipment points and terminals. To further complicate the model, Shell has a choice among three different modes of transportation (pipelines, barges, and tankers).

---

[11]T.K. Zierer, W.A. Mitchell, and T.R. White, "Practical Applications of Linear Programming to Shell's Distribution Problems," *Interfaces*, Vol. 6, No. 4 (August 1976), 13–26.

FIGURE 2-4 Shell's East of the Rockies Distribution Problem

SOURCE: T.K. Zierer, W.A. Mitchell, and T.R. White, "Practical Applications of Linear Programming to Shell's Distribution Problems," *Interfaces*, Vol. 6, No. 4 (August 1976), 13–26.

The resulting LP model has 1,050 decision variables and 575 total constraints. The model operates in the IBM 370 series using IBM's MPSX as the LP programming code. A well-designed report generator offers more than ten optional reports, depending upon the system goals and different users. Even though the LP model is fairly large, its computer solution on an IBM 370/168 costs only $20 to $30 in daytime and $15 to $20 at night. Thus, the LP model is a cost-effective means of improving Shell's distribution efforts, as its benefits outweigh its costs.

We now focus on a much simpler distribution model that is probably the most widely used specially structured LP model. It is called the Hitchcock Koopmans transportation model, and it is concerned with determining the least-cost means of distributing from origins to destinations.

To illustrate the transportation problem, let's consider the distribution problem of the Electrovox Company. Electrovox is very progressive and has already used LP to determine its optimal product mix. The company is now faced with the problem of how to distribute its electrical components from plants to regional warehouses. Electrovox has plants located in Washington, D. C.; Denver; and Los Angeles. Regional warehouses are located in New York, Chicago, Dallas, and San Francisco (see Figure 2-5). This month, the company has available 50 units in Washington, 80 units in

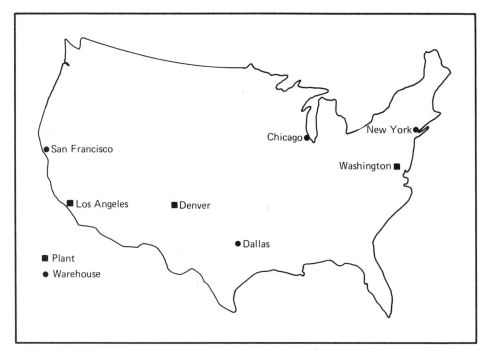

FIGURE 2-5   Location of Plants and Warehouses for Electrovox

SOURCE: *Introduction to Management Science* by Thomas M. Cook and Robert A. Russell (Englewood Cliffs, N.J.: Prentice-Hall, Inc., 1977). Reprinted with permission.

Denver, and 120 units in Los Angeles. In order to meet predicted demand, Electrovox must ship 90 units to New York, 70 to Chicago, 40 to Dallas, and 50 to San Francisco. Relevant per-unit transportation costs for each component, as well as demand-and-supply data, are given in Table 2-3. Electrovox wants to determine the shipping pattern that meets all demand at minimum transportation cost.

Table 2-3   Data for Electrovox Distribution Problems

FROM / TO	NEW YORK	CHICAGO	DALLAS	SAN FRANCISCO	SUPPLY
(WAREHOUSE)					
Plant:					
Washington, D.C.	$ .80	$ .90	$1.10	$1.60	50
Denver	1.20	.70	.50	.80	80
Los Angeles	1.40	1.00	.60	.70	120
Demand	90	70	40	50	250

The Electrovox distribution problem is actually an LP problem. To formulate it, let x_{ij} denote the amount to be shipped from plant i to warehouse j, where $i = 1, 2, 3$, and $j = 1, 2, 3, 4$. In this notation, x_{23} represents the number of units to be shipped from Denver to Dallas. Notice that the first subscript refers to the row (plant) in Table 2-3 and the second subscript refers to the column (warehouse). The problem may be formulated as:

$$\text{Minimize } .8x_{11} + .9x_{12} + 1.1x_{13} + 1.6x_{14} + 1.2x_{21} + .7x_{22} + .5x_{23} + .8x_{24}$$
$$+ 1.4x_{31} + 1.0x_{32} + .6x_{33} + .7x_{34}$$

$$\text{subject to: } x_{11} + x_{12} + x_{13} + x_{14} = 50$$
$$x_{21} + x_{22} + x_{23} + x_{24} = 80$$
$$x_{31} + x_{32} + x_{33} + x_{34} = 120$$
$$x_{11} + x_{21} + x_{31} = 90$$
$$x_{12} + x_{22} + x_{32} = 70$$
$$x_{13} + x_{23} + x_{33} = 40$$
$$x_{14} + x_{24} + x_{34} = 50$$
$$x_{ij} \geq 0; i = 1, 2, 3; j = 1, 2, 3, 4$$

The foregoing model may be solved directly by the general simplex method, as explained in the appendix to this chapter. However, streamlined simplex procedures are available that offer special computational benefits. Charnes and Cooper developed the stepping-stone method, which was one of the first specialized simplex procedures for transportation problems. Later, Dantzig developed the *modified distribution* (or MODI) *method*, which remains the best approach for solving transportation problems. Computational researchers have further refined the MODI method so that really significant computational savings can be achieved. For instance, transportation problems that have 1,000 plants and 1,000 warehouses (that is, 1 million decision variables) have been solved in 17 seconds or so on a CDC 6600 computer. Problems of this size are not even solvable without using special-purpose algorithms.

We can generalize the 3-by-4 transportation model above to m origins by n destinations. Special-purpose algorithms such as the MODI method can be used to optimize transportation problems. These optimization procedures are quite efficient, readily available, and would normally be used to solve transportation-type problems in actual practice. However, in this chapter we solve them by using a more intuitive approach, called a *heuristic*. A heuristic is a rule of thumb that may be used to obtain a good but not necessarily optimal solution to a problem. Heuristics do not guarantee an optimal solution, but good heuristics are usually within 10 percent of optimality. The advantage of heuristics is that they are usually much faster than optimization procedures and can sometimes be solved by hand without using a computer. Also, heuristics are often used for complex problems when no optimization method exists.

The VAM Heuristic for Solving Transportation Problems

Vogel's Approximation Method (VAM) is an effective heuristic for finding near-optimal solutions to transportation problems. It is an interesting heuristic that can be applied to problems other than transportation problems. To explain the VAM heuristic, we shall need a transportation tableau. This type of table is helpful in solving transportation-type problems. Table 2-4 illustrates a transportation tableau for the Electrovox problem. Usually, the sources are listed as rows in the tableau, and the destinations are columns. The available supply for each source is listed in the far-right column, and the required demands at each destination are summarized in the bottom row. The per-unit transportation cost for shipping from source to destination is found in the upper left-hand corner of the square in the row associated with the source and the column associated with the destination. For example, the per-unit transportation

Table 2-4   Transportation Tableau for Electrovox

TO / FROM	NEW YORK	CHICAGO	DALLAS	SAN FRANCISCO	SUPPLY
Washington, D.C.	.8	.9	1.1	1.6	50
Denver	1.2	.7	.5	.8	80
Los Angeles	1.4	1.0	.6	.7	120
Demand	90	70	40	50	250

cost from the L.A. source to the Chicago destination is $1.00. The twelve squares (or cells) formed by the three sources and four destinations correspond to direct routes over which shipments can be made. In any feasible solution, the sum of the shipments across any row must not exceed the supply available, and the sum of the shipments down any column must satisfy the demand required.

The basic idea in VAM is to avoid shipments that have a high cost. VAM looks at the opportunity cost of not assigning to the minimum-cost cell in a row or column of the transportation tableau. This is conservatively estimated to be the difference in costs between the lowest- and next-lowest-cost cells in that particular row or column. It then assigns to the minimum-cost cell in the row or column having the highest potential opportunity loss. If we view the opportunity cost as a possible penalty, the idea is to avoid a high penalty. This assignment, then, avoids incurring the highest opportunity loss. The details of VAM are presented as follows:

1. For each row, calculate the potential opportunity loss as the difference between the minimum-cost cell and the next-lowest-cost cell in that row.
2. For each column, calculate the potential opportunity loss as the difference between the minimum-cost cell and the next-lowest-cost cell in that column.
3. Find the highest potential opportunity loss from among all rows and columns, and find the minimum-cost cell associated with that row or column. If a tie exists in opportunity losses among rows and columns, then break the tie arbitrarily.
4. Allocate the maximum possible amount of supply to the minimum-cost cell in step 3. This will delete a row or column. Reduce the supplies and demands appropriately.
5. If a row has been deleted, recalculate the column opportunity losses. If a column has been deleted, recalculate the row opportunity losses.
6. If all allocations have been made, stop. Otherwise, begin another iteration by returning to step 3.

We illustrate the VAM procedure by applying it to the Electrovox distribution problem. The VAM heuristic begins by calculating the potential opportunity losses of not assigning to the lowest-cost cell in each row and column. The beginning calculations are shown in Table 2-5. The highest opportunity loss is 4, which is associated with column 1. This means that if we do not ship in the least-cost cell having cost $.80 per unit, we will have to ship in a cell having a cost of at least $.40 per unit more. In fact, the additional cost will be either $.40 or $.60 per unit. Thus, we allocate all the supply possible, which is 50 units, to cell 1,1, having the minimum cost of $.80. The supply for row 1 is exhausted, so we cross out the remaining cells in row 1 as a reminder that these costs are no longer usable in calculating opportunity losses.

In Table 2-6, we recalculate the column opportunity losses and illustrate the next iteration. The highest opportunity loss is now .3 and is associated with column 2. Thus, we allocate all that we can to the lowest-cost cell 2,2; this allocation is 70 units, which is all the demand that is required in column 2. We adjust the supplies and demands, delete column 2 by crossing out its remaining cells, and update the row opportunity losses in Table 2-7. This time, the largest opportunity loss is .3, which is associated with row 2. Allocating the available ten units deletes row 2 and leaves only

Table 2-5 Initial VAM Calculations for Electrovox

COLUMN OPPORTUNITY COSTS

ROW OPPORTUNITY COST	From \ To	New York (.4)	Chicago (.2)	Dallas (.1)	San Francisco (.1)	Supply
.1	Washington, D.C.	.8 50	.9	1.1	1.6	~~50~~
.2	Denver	1.2	.7	.5	.8	80
.1	Los Angeles	1.4	1.0	.6	.7	120
	Demand	~~90~~ 40	70	40	50	250

Table 2-6 Second Iteration for VAM

COLUMN OPPORTUNITY COSTS

ROW OPPORTUNITY COSTS	From \ To	New York (~~.4~~ .2)	Chicago (~~.2~~ .3)	Dallas (.1)	San Francisco (.1)	Supply
~~.1~~	Washington, D.C.	.8 50	.9	1.1	1.8	~~50~~
.2	Denver	1.2	.7 70	.5	.8	~~80~~ 10
.1	Los Angeles	1.4	1.0	.6	.7	120
	Demand	~~90~~ 40	~~70~~	40	50	250

Table 2-7 Third Iteration for VAM

COLUMN OPPORTUNITY COSTS

ROW OPPORTUNITY COSTS	From \ To	New York (~~.4~~ .2)	Chicago (~~.2~~ ~~.3~~)	Dallas (.1)	San Francisco (.1)	Supply
~~.1~~	Washington, D.C.	.8	.9	1.1	1.6	~~50~~
.3 ~~.2~~	Denver	1.2	.7 70	.5 10	.8	~~80~~ ~~10~~
.1	Los Angeles	1.4	1.0	.6	.7	120
	Demand	~~90~~ 40	~~70~~	~~40~~ 30	50	250

row 3 with available supply. Three more iterations are required to reach the final VAM solution. The final tableau is shown in Table 2-8.

The cost of the VAM solution is found by multiplying each shipment by its per-unit transportation cost. The distribution cost of the VAM solution is .8(50) + .7(70) + .5(10) + 1.4(40) + .6(30) + .7(50) = $203. The final distribution pattern is shown in Figure 2-6.

Table 2-8   Final Solution for VAM

COLUMN OPPORTUNITY COSTS: .4 .2 0 | .2 .3 | .1 0 | .1 0

ROW OPPORTUNITY COSTS:
- Washington, D.C.: .1
- Denver: .3 .2
- Los Angeles: .7 .1

From \ To	New York	Chicago	Dallas	San Francisco	Supply
Washington, D.C.	.8 50	.9	1.1	1.6	~~50~~
Denver	1.2	.7 70	.5 10	.8	~~80~~ ~~10~~
Los Angeles	1.4 40	1.0	.6 30	.7 50	~~120~~ ~~90~~ 40
Demand	~~90~~ ~~40~~	~~70~~	~~40~~ ~~30~~	~~50~~	250

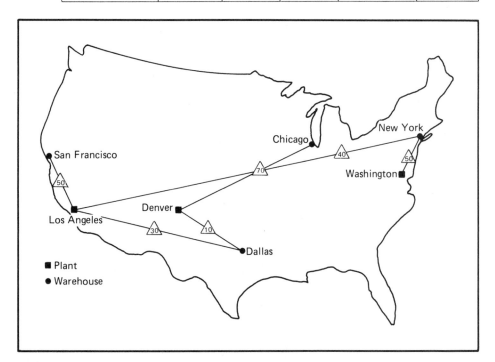

FIGURE 2-6   Final Distribution Pattern for VAM Solution

In this example, the total supply and demand are equal. In situations where supply exceeds demand, some supply will be left unshipped at some plant(s). Likewise, if demand exceeds supply, some demand will have to go unsatisfied; in either case, VAM can be used to determine a low-cost distribution pattern.

NETWORK MODELS IN OPERATIONS MANAGEMENT

Transportation models fall into a broader class of problems called network models. A *network* is a collection of nodes or points connected by links. Figure 2-7 depicts a network representation of the final VAM solution to the Electrovox problem.

Networks enjoy many applications in operations management because of the many situations they can accurately represent. Many problems can be represented as a collection of nodes connected by links. Most operations management applications of networks are in distribution and scheduling. However, networks analysis is used in

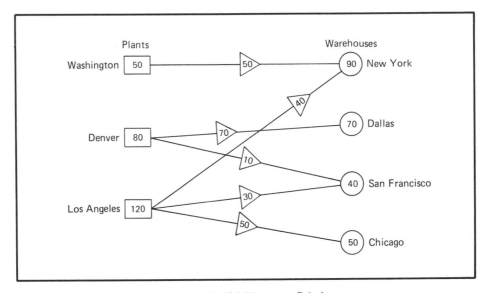

FIGURE 2-7   Network Representation of VAM Electrovox Solution

such areas as communications networks, transportation systems, water systems analysis, information theory, cybernetics, and project planning and control. In addition to their widespread applicability, network models constitute one of the few categories of mathematical models that is amenable to really large-scale analysis. Network models involving thousands—in some cases millions—of variables are solvable using some of the large computers.

We will run across network-type models further on in the text. Transportation models have further application in production scheduling, warehouse location, and aggregate planning. We will also consider PERT, a network approach to scheduling and controlling projects.

SUMMARY

Linear programming is an important operations management tool that has many applications, ranging from production scheduling to political redistricting. In spite of its power, we should be aware of the assumptions and limitations of LP, for it is not an appropriate tool for the majority of operations management problems.

In order for linear programming to be applicable to a particular decision problem, all relationships should be linear, with data obtainable and known with certainty. In other words, it must be possible to completely specify the conditions of the problem. Unfortunately, many operations management problems are not clear-cut and involve many factors that cannot be quantified in a linear model. The manager needs to know that LP can be an effective tool for a restricted class of problems; it can provide valuable input to the decision process, but is not an end in itself.

The graphical method is useful for illustrating the simplex method and how to solve LP problems. The simplex method and a computer are required for solving real-world LP problems.

The transportation model is a special LP model that is quite useful in analyzing distribution problems; it is a versatile model that has other applications, such as scheduling and aggregate planning. Its special structure facilitates the use of special-purpose algorithms in order to solve transportation problems more efficiently.

In the supplement to this chapter, we study the details of the simplex method and look at sensitivity analysis, which is very helpful in further analyzing the problem after an optimal solution has been obtained. The postoptimality phase of linear programming can be the most important to the manager. Sensitivity analysis can help answer various "what-if"–type questions. It can also be used to provide a range of alternative solutions, which is more helpful than a single solution, especially in today's dynamic and constantly changing business environment.

SOLVED PROBLEMS

Problem Statement

The Superstar Rent-A-Car Co. is interested in cutting gasoline costs for its fleet of cars. It has decided to use a blend of premium and regular gasoline to achieve the minimal required octane rating of 91 for the cars. Premium gas has an octane rating of 95; regular has a rating of 88. Premium gas costs $.80 per gallon, and regular is $.70. The company's storage tanks can hold 6,000 gallons this month, and the distributor can supply only 3,000 gallons of premium. How many gallons of premium and regular should Superstar Co. purchase in order to minimize costs (assuming it wants to fill its tank)?

Solution

First, we need to formulate the problem and then solve it graphically. The decision variables should answer the purchasing question. Therefore, let x_1 = No. of gallons of premium to purchase, and x_2 = No. of gallons of regular.

Objective function:

$$\text{Min } C = .80x_1 + .70x_2$$

$$\begin{array}{lll}
\text{s.t. constraints:} & x_1 + x_2 = 6{,}000 & \text{storage capacity} \\
& x_1 \leq 3{,}000 & \text{availability of premium} \\
& 4x_1 - 3x_2 \geq 0 & \text{weighted average of octane ratings} \\
& x_1, x_2 \geq 0 &
\end{array}$$

The third constraint is obtained by forming the weighted average of octane ratings, $\dfrac{95x_1 + 88x_2}{x_1 + x_2} \geq 91$, and clearing terms, yielding $95x_1 + 88x_2 \geq 91x_1 + 91x_2$.

The first constraint is an equation, and we first obtain the x_1 and x_2 intercepts. Both intercepts are 6,000, and the graph of the constraint is a straight line. Note that since this constraint is only a line, the feasible region will be a line segment and not an area of the plane.

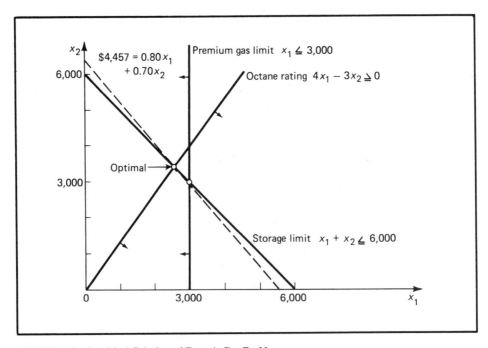

FIGURE 2-8   Graphical Solution of Rent-A-Car Problem

   The second constraint has an x_1 intercept of 3,000 and no x_2 intercept. Thus, the graph of $x_1 = 3,000$ is a vertical line.

   The third constraint passes through the origin and also the point 3,4. Plotting all three constraints, we obtain the following graph of the feasible region. Notice that the feasible region consists of only the thicker portion of the line segment $x_1 + x_2 = 6,000$. The slope of the objective function is found from $.70x_2 = C - .80x_1$, or $x_2 = C/.70 - 1.14x_1$. Thus, the slope is -1.14, and for every 1.14-unit decrease in x_2 there is a 1-unit increase in x_1. The dashed isocost line passes through the point of the feasible region, which occurs at the intersection of the lines $x_1 + x_2 = 6,000$ and $4x_1 - 3x_2 = 0$. Solving these two equations simultaneously, we get:

$$x_1 + x_2 = 6,000 \qquad 4x_1 + 4x_2 = 24,000$$
$$\underline{4x_1 - 3x_2 = 0} \quad \longrightarrow \quad \underline{-4x_1 + 3x_2 = 0}$$
$$7x_2 = 24,000, \text{ or } x_2 = 3,428.6$$
$$\therefore \ x_1 = 2,571.4$$

The minimal cost associated with this solution is $\$.80(2,571.4) + \$.70(3,428.6) = \$4,457.14$.

Problem Statement

The Yuba Manufacturing Co. is planning its aggregate production levels for the last quarter of the year and would like to minimize the combined cost of production and inventory. Production capacities for October, November, and December are 6,000, 6,000, and 4,000 respectively. The demand for the firm's product is expected to be 3,000, 7,000, and 5,000 during the last quarter. Given that per-piece production cost is $3.00 and storage cost per month is $1.00, find a low-cost production/inventory schedule.

Solution

The formulation of this problem can be a linear programming model, but it's even simpler as a transportation-type model. Let the plant capacity each month represent the supplies available, and the demand each month represent the demand at a "destination." We have the following 3×3 transportation model:

OCT. DEMAND	NOV. DEMAND	DEC. DEMAND	
3	4	5	6,000 Oct. capacity
M	4	5	6,000 Nov. capacity
M	M	5	4,000 Dec. capacity
3,000	7,000	5,000	

The cell in the first row, first column represents October production for October demand. The cell in the first row, second column represents October production for November demand. Notice that the cost increases by $1.00 for each month the unit is stored. The M's represent infinite costs in inadmissible cells.

We can obtain an effective heuristic (not necessarily optimal) solution by using the VAM heuristic. Since the column opportunity losses are all 0 in the example, we calculate only the row opportunity losses at each step. Note that the unusual cost structure of the example will cause the row opportunity losses to be the same. The sequence of VAM calculations is shown below. Ties between largest opportunity costs are broken arbitrarily. The solution stipulates that in October, Yuba should produce 3,000 units for demand in October and 3,000 units for storage to meet November demand. Likewise, November production would include 4,000 units for November demand and 1,000 units for storage. In December, Yuba should produce 4,000 units as partial fulfillment of December demand.

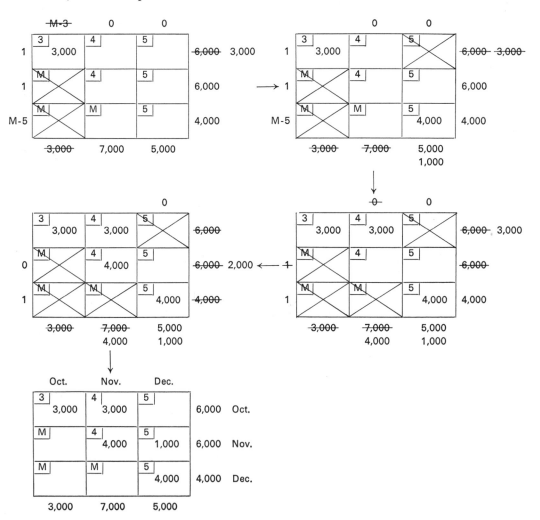

REVIEW QUESTIONS

1. What are some applications of linear programming in the area of production, government, and nonmanufacturing operations?
2. What specific properties must be satisfied in order for a mathematical model to be solvable by linear programming?
3. What are some of the limitations of linear programming?
4. What does every optimal LP solution correspond to geometrically?
5. Explain why the transportation model is a part of the category of network models.
6. What are the advantages and disadvantages of using heuristics rather than optimization procedures to solve transportation problems?
7. Can you name some applications of transportation models other than distribution of a commodity from plant to market?
8. Briefly discuss the idea underlying VAM.
*9. Explain how to minimize rather than maximize an objective function in LP.
*10. What is a shadow price?
*11. Discuss the kinds of questions management can answer in performing sensitivity analysis.

PROBLEMS

1. The Ace Manufacturing Company produces two lines of its product, the super and the regular. Resource requirements for production are given in the following table:

PRODUCT LINE	PROFIT CONTRI- BUTION	ASSEMBLY TIME (HR.)	PAINT TIME (HR.)	INSPEC- TION TIME (HR.)
Regular	50	1.2	.8	.2
Super	75	1.6	.9	.2

*These problems to be answered after studying the supplement to this chapter.

There are 1,600 hours of assembly man-hours available per week, 700 hours of paint time, and 300 hours of inspection time. Regular customers will demand at least 150 units of the regular line and 90 of the super. Formulate an LP model that will determine the optimal product mix on a weekly basis.

2. A farmer would like to determine what quantities of various grains to feed his cattle in order to meet minimum nutritional requirements at lowest cost. He is considering the use of corn, barley, oats, and wheat. The following table relates the relevant dietary information per pounds of grain:

NUTRIENT	CORN	BARLEY	OATS	WHEAT	MINIMUM DAILY REQUIREMENTS
Protein	10	9	11	8	20 mg.
Calcium	50	45	58	50	70 mg.
Iron	9	8	7	10	12 mg.
Calories	1,000	800	850	9,000	4,000
Cost/lb.	.55	.47	.45	.52	

Formulate an LP model to determine the dietary mix that minimizes cost.

3. Jiffy Job Shop would like to try a quantitative approach to its machine-loading problem. There are three machines in the shop, and they produce five different products. Each machine has an 8-hour time availability each working day. Today they have a demand of 6, 3, 2, 1, and 5 for products 1 through 5 respectively. The following table gives relevant cost and production time data:

PRODUCT \\ MACHINE	COST OF PRODUCING ONE UNIT OF PRODUCT j ON MACHINE i					TIME REQUIRED (IN HRS.) TO PRODUCE ONE UNIT OF PRODUCT j ON MACHINE i				
	1	2	3	4	5	1	2	3	4	5
1	12	10	13	9	8	1	.8	1.5	.5	.6
2	7	6	12	11	9	1.5	.9	.7	.4	.9
3	14	8	5	3	2	1.2	1.1	.9	.8	.5

6 3 2 1 5

Formulate an LP model to determine the amount of product j to be allocated for production on machine i.

Max Prod. = $x_1 + x_2 + x_3$

4. Solve the following problem graphically:

$$\text{Maximize } 6x_1 + 8x_2$$
$$\text{subject to: } x_1 \leq 12$$
$$x_2 \leq 10$$
$$2x_1 + 3x_2 \leq 36$$
$$x_1, x_2 \geq 0$$

5. Solve the following minimization problem by the graphical method:

$$\text{Minimize } x_1 + x_2$$
$$\text{subject to: } x_2 \geq 2$$
$$2x_1 - x_2 \geq 0$$
$$3x_1 + 2x_2 \leq 12$$
$$x_1, x_2 \geq 0$$

6. The Slik Oil Company produces two lines of motor oils and a special engine additive called motor honey. All three products are produced by blending two components. These components contribute various properties, including viscosity. The viscosity in the product is proportional to the viscosities of the blending components.

BLENDING COMPONENT	VISCOSITY	COST/BARREL	AVAILABILITY
Component 1	20	$ 6.50	10,000 barrels/wk.
Component 2	60	11.00	4,000 barrels/wk.

PRODUCT	VISCOSITY REQUIRED	PROFIT CONTRIBUTION/BARREL
30 W oil	30	$ 8.00
40 W oil	40	9.00
Motor honey	50	12.00

Assuming no limitation on the demand, determine how many barrels of each oil product Slik should produce each week.

7. The P & R company distributes its product from three plants to four regionally located warehouses. The monthly supplies and demands, along with per-unit

transportation costs, are given as:

TO\FROM	WAREHOUSE 1	WAREHOUSE 2	WAREHOUSE 3	WAREHOUSE 4	SUPPLY
Plant 1	2	12	6	10	20
Plant 2	14	6	2	12	10
Plant 3	18	8	10	8	25
Demand	11	13	17	14	55

Use Vogel's Approximation Method to find a feasible shipping pattern and total transportation cost.

8. The Continental Trailer Rental Co. has a problem in trying to relocate rented trailers. Currently, the supply exceeds the demand, and the firm needs to relocate trailers at minimum transportation cost. Currently, there are surplus trailers at locations 1, 2, 3, and 4, while trailers are demanded at locations 5, 6, and 7. The relevant data are:

	LOCATION						
	1	2	3	4	5	6	7
Surplus trailers	6	7	8	3			
Demanded trailers					5	4	9

Cost per Trailer Transported

TO\FROM	5	6	7
1	8	11	8
2	12	10	6
3	15	7	9
4	12	12	7

Determine an effective relocation of trailers.

9. The American Products Corporation must decide on its production schedule for the next four months. It has contracted to supply a special part for the months of October, November, December, and January at the rates of 12,000, 10,000, 15,000, and 17,000 units respectively. American can produce each part at a cost of $6 during regular time or $9 during overtime. Each month, American has a production capacity of 10,000 units during regular time and 6,000 units during overtime. The part can be stored at a cost of $2 per month; however, there is zero inventory on hand at the beginning of October, and there must be zero inventory at the end of January. American can thus overproduce in some months and store the excess to help meet future demand in other months. Construct a transportation model (tableau) to solve American's production scheduling/ inventory storage problem. *Hint:* Define the sources as the modes of production in each month, and define the destinations as the demand required during each month.

*10. Solve by the simplex method:

$$\text{Maximize } 8x_1 + 7x_2$$
$$\text{subject to: } 3x_1 + 4x_2 \leq 15$$
$$7x_1 + 5x_2 \leq 20$$
$$x_1, x_2 \geq 0$$

*11. A stereo mail-order warehouse has 8,000 square feet available for storage of loudspeakers. The jumbo speakers cost $295 each and require four square feet of space, the midsize speakers cost $110 and require three square feet of space, and the economy speakers cost $58 and require one square foot of space. The demand for the jumbo speakers is at most 20 per month. The wholesaler has $10,000 to invest in loudspeakers this month. Assuming that the jumbo speakers contribute $105 to profit, the midsize contribute $50, and the economy contribute $28, how many units of each type should the wholesaler buy and stock?

*12. The optimal simplex tableau for a maximization problem with all ($\leq$) constraints is given by:

c_j		4	2	0	0	0	
c_b	BASIC	x_1	x_2	s_1	s_2	s_3	SOLUTION
2	x_2	0	1	1	-1	0	4
4	x_1	1	0	$-\frac{1}{4}$	$\frac{3}{4}$	0	3
0	s_3	0	0	2	-4	1	8
	$c_j - z_j$	0	0	-1	-1	0	20

---

*From material in supplement to this chapter.

a. What is the optimal solution?

b. What are the shadow prices?

c. Suppose the resources could be obtained at no cost. Which right-hand side would you recommend for expansion, and why?

d. Which of the three resources are being fully utilized?

*13. Solve problem 4 by the simplex method.

*14. Transform the following problem to standard form by making all constraints equations:

$$\text{Min } 13x_1 + 17x_2$$

$$\text{s.t.:} \quad x_1 + x_2 \geq 1{,}700$$

$$3x_1 - 4x_2 = 0$$

$$x_1, x_2 \geq 0$$

Case: COASTAL STATES CHEMICALS AND FERTILIZERS*

In December 1975, Bill Stock, general manager for the Louisiana Division of Coastal States Chemicals and Fertilizers, received a letter from Fred McNair of Cajan Pipeline Company which notified Coastal States that priorities had been established for the allocation of natural gas. The letter stated that Cajan Pipeline, the primary supplier of natural gas to Coastal States, might be instructed to curtail natural gas supplies to its industrial and commercial customers by as much as 40 percent during the ensuing winter months. Moreover, Cajan Pipeline had the approval of the Federal Power Commission (FPC) to curtail such supplies.

Possible curtailment was attributed to the priorities established for the use of natural gas:

First Priority: Residential and commercial heating

Second Priority: Commercial and industrial users whereby natural gas is used as a source of raw material

Third Priority: Commercial and industrial users whereby natural gas is used as boiler fuel

---

*Iverstine and Kinard, *Cases in Production and Operations Management* (Columbus, Ohio: Charles E. Merrill Publishing Company, 1977.)

Almost all of Coastal States's use of natural gas was in the second and third priorities. Hence, its plants were certainly subject to brownouts, or natural gas curtailments. The occurrence and severity of the brownouts depended on a number of complex factors. First of all, Cajan Pipeline was part of an interstate transmission network which delivered natural gas to residential and commercial buildings on the Atlantic Coast and in northeastern regions of the United States. Hence, the severity of the forthcoming winter in these regions would have a direct impact on the use of natural gas.

Second, the demand for natural gas was soaring because it was the cleanest and most efficient fuel. There were almost no environmental problems in burning natural gas. Moreover, maintenance problems due to fuel-fouling in fireboxes and boilers were negligible with natural gas systems. Also, burners were much easier to operate with nautral gas as compared to the use of oil or the stoking operation when coal was used as fuel.

Finally, the supply of natural gas was dwindling. The traditionally depressed price of natural gas had discouraged new exploration for gas wells; hence, shortages appeared imminent.

Stock and his staff at Coastal States had been aware of the possibility of shortages of natural gas and had been investigating ways of converting to fuel oil or coal as a substitute for natural gas. Their plans, however, were still in the developmental stages. Coastal States required an immediate contingency plan to minimize the effect of a natural gas curtailment on its multiplant operations. The obvious question was, What operations should be curtailed and to what extent to minimize the adverse effect upon profits? Coastal States had approval from the FPC and Cajan Pipeline to specify which of its plants would bear the burden of the curtailment if such cutbacks were necessary. McNair, of Cajan Pipeline, replied, "It's your 'pie'; we don't care how you divide it if we make it smaller."

The Model

Six plants of Coastal States's Louisiana Division were to share in the "pie." They were all located in the massive Baton Rouge–Geismar–Gramercy industrial complex along the Mississippi River between Baton Rouge and New Orleans. Products produced at those plants which required significant amounts of natural gas were phosphoric acid, urea, ammonium phosphate, ammonium nitrate, chlorine, caustic soda, vinyl chloride monomer, and hydrofluoric acid.

Stock called a meeting of members of his technical staff to discuss a contingency plan for allocation of natural gas among the products if a curtailment developed. The objective was to minimize the impact on profits. After detailed discussion, the meeting was adjourned. Two weeks later, the meeting reconvened. At this session, the following data were presented:

Table 1   Contribution to Profit and Overhead

PRODUCT	$/TON
X_1 Phosphoric acid	60
X_2 Urea	80
X_3 Ammonium phosphate	90
X_4 Ammonium nitrate	100
X_5 Chlorine	50
X_6 Caustic soda	50
X_7 Vinyl chloride monomer	65
X_8 Hydrofluoric acid	70

Table 2   Operating Data

PRODUCT	CAPACITY (TONS/DAY)	PRODUCTION RATE (PERCENT OF CAPACITY)	NATURAL GAS CONSUMPTION (1,000 CU. FT./TON)
Phosphoric acid	400	80	5.5
Urea	250	80	7.0
Ammonium phosphate	300	90	8.0
Ammonium nitrate	300	100	10.0
Chlorine	800	60	15.0
Caustic soda	1,000	60	16.0
Vinyl chloride monomer	500	60	12.0
Hydrofluoric acid	400	80	11.0

Coastal States's contract with Cajan Pipeline specified a maximum natural gas consumption of 36,000 cu. ft. $\times 10^3$ per day for all of the six member plants. With these data, the technical staff proceeded to develop a model that would specify changes in production rates in response to a natural gas curtailment. (Curtailments are based on contracted consumption and not current consumption.)

Case Discussion Questions

1. Develop a contingency model and specify the production rates for each product for (a) a 20 percent natural gas curtailment, and (b) a 40 percent natural gas curtailment.

2. Explain which of the products in Table 2 should require the most emphasis with regard to energy conservation. ⇀

3. What problems do you foresee if production rates are not reduced in a planned and orderly manner? ⇁

4. What impact will the natural gas shortage have on company profits? ⇁

SUPPLEMENT TO CHAPTER 2

THE SIMPLEX METHOD

You may have discovered in Chapter 2 that it is impossible to use the graphical method of solution on problems that are at all complex. The greatest importance of the graphical method is as an aid to understanding the simplex method. We will discuss the simplex method in its basic form here. For large-scale, real-world applications of LP, more sophisticated variants of the simplex method are actually used; however, the principles are essentially the same.

The simplex method is similar to solving a system of linear equations. In fact, the simplex method does solve a system of equations, and the solution derived not only solves the equations but also optimizes an objective function. In this sense, the simplex method is a straightforward generalization of various methods for solving a system of equations.

The simplex method is an iterative technique. That is, it establishes an initial feasible solution, then repeats the solution process, making successive improvements, until the optimal solution is found. It is sometimes referred to as an adjacent extreme-point solution procedure, because it generally begins at an extreme point of the feasible region, then successively evaluates adjacent extreme points until the one representing the optimal solution is found.

Simplex Procedures

In order to use the simplex method, it is necessary to state all the constraints as equations rather than inequalities. Mathematically, it is easier to solve systems of equations than systems of inequalities. Therefore, we shall have to convert less-than-or-equal-to and greater-than-or-equal-to constraints into equations. First we shall learn how to convert $\leq$ constraints.

Suppose we have the constraint $x_1 + x_2 \leq 5$. We may convert this inequality to an equation by adding an additional variable, called a slack variable. Thus we have $x_1 + x_2 + s_1 = 5$, where $s_1 \geq 0$. A slack variable, as the name implies, represents unused resources. In the foregoing equation, if $x_1 = 2$ and $x_2 = 1$, then s_1 must equal

2. Thus, $x_1 + x_2 < 5$, and s_1 represents two units of the right-hand-side resource that are left over.

Notationally, we distinguish between slack and decision variables. The x_i represent decision variables and refer to actual activities; the s_i denote slack variables that represent unused capacity.

Let us refer back to the Electrovox problem of Chapter 2 in order to illustrate converting $\leq$ constraints to equations. Recall that the objective is to produce the appropriate number of hi-gain and standard CBs in order to maximize profit. Suppose that management has been able to procure additional hi-gain transistors, so that the constraint limiting transistor availability to 40 units per day no longer applies. Thus, the Electrovox problem (after dropping the transistor constraint) is written in standard form as:

$$\text{Maximize } 20x_1 + 50x_2 + 0s_1 + 0s_2$$

$$\text{s.t.: } 1.2x_1 + 4x_2 + s_1 \qquad = 240$$

$$.5x_1 + 1x_2 \qquad + s_2 = 81$$

$$x_1, x_2, s_1, s_2 \geq 0$$

We have thus transformed a system of inequalities into a system of equations ready to be solved by the simplex method. Notice that the slack variables are given an objective-function coefficient of zero.

The simplex method is concerned only with solutions that geometrically correspond to extreme points of the feasible region. These extreme-point solutions are also called basic feasible solutions. A complete mathematical definition of basic solutions is beyond the scope of this text. For our purposes, it will be sufficient to observe that a basic solution has exactly as many variables in solution as there are equations. Thus, a system of m equations in n unknowns will have m variables in solution for any basic solution. For example, the Electrovox problem above will have two variables in solution, since there are two constraint equations. This will leave two variables nonbasic or out of solution at a value of zero. The simplex method determines which two of the four variables are most profitable.

Basic Steps in the Simplex Procedure

Let us take a closer look at the computational steps involved with the simplex method. In successively examining adjacent extreme points, the simplex method continually finds improved solutions. That is, it only examines points that are not only feasible but yield at least as good a value in the objective function as the previous point. In short, the simplex method encompasses the following basic steps:

1. An initial basic feasible solution is established.
2. An optimality check is next performed to determine whether the solution is yet optimal. If the solution is optimal, stop, for no further calculations are needed.

However, if the solution is not optimal, a new variable must be found that will improve the solution. This new entering variable is always a nonbasic variable whose value is currently zero.

3. The value of the entering variable is increased until the value of some basic variable is forced down to zero. This basic variable is called the leaving variable.

4. The entering variable now takes the place of the leaving variable; at any iteration, there are only m variables that are in the solution. The next step is to update all relevant information required in the simplex procedure. This updating process is called pivoting. After updating, the procedure returns to step 2.

The Simplex Tableau

Each repetition of steps 2 through 4 is called an iteration in the simplex method. The computer can execute such iterations by merely storing the appropriate information and then operating on it whenever it is needed. When you execute the simplex method by hand, the calculations are more conveniently dealt with in tabular form. This table is called a simplex tableau; the form of the starting tableau for the Electrovox problem is shown in Tableau 2-1.

Tableau 2-1   Initial Simplex Tableau for Electrovox

Objective function
coefficients ———→ c_j 20   50   0   0

c_B	BASIC VARIABLE	x_1	x_2	s_1	s_2	SOLUTION
0	s_1	1.2	4	1	0	240
0	s_2	.5	1	0	1	81
	z_j	0	0	0	0	
Relative costs ———→	$c_j - z_j$	20	50	0	0	0

Total profit

The tableau shows the coefficients of the constraint equations as well as other useful information.

The c_j row at the top of the tableau shows the coefficients of the respective variables in the objective function. The next row down simply labels the various columns. The next two rows consist of the coefficients of the two constraint equations of the Electrovox problem. The bottom row of the tableau is very important, for this row indicates whether the solution is optimal. The $c_j - z_j$ numbers in the last row are called opportunity or relative costs. They indicate the per-unit increase in the value of the objective function for every unit of variable x_j brought into the solution. The

z_j numbers represent the amount of profit that is lost for each unit of variable x_j that is brought into solution.

Looking next at the columns of Tableau 2-1, the c_B numbers at the far left are the objective-function coefficients of the basic variables. They are currently all 0, as the slack variables in the initial solution all have 0 objective-function coefficients. The next column, labeled "Basic Variable," lists those variables that are in solution at this particular iteration. The last column on the far right gives us the solution values of each basic variable. In Tableau 2-1, we can see that the values of s_1 and s_2 are 240 and 81 respectively. The last entry in the solution column represents the total profit of the solution.

The Basic Steps Applied

Step 1: Establish initial basic feasible solution. To complete the initial tableau requires no calculation (except possibly the z_j values). The tableau always contains as many basic variables as there are constraints. To determine which variables are in the initial solution, we scan the original column of coefficients of the constraints in standard form and pick those variables that have a $+1$ coefficient and all other coefficients of 0. These starting variables are always either slack variables or artificial variables, which we shall discuss later. Setting up the initial tableau completes the first step of the simplex method.

Step 2: Check solution for optimality. In the lower right-hand corner of the initial Electrovox tableau (Tableau 2-1), the profit of the current solution is 0. This is because only slack variables are in solution. The solution column indicates that $s_2 = 81$—that is, we have 81 hours of inspection time left over—and s_1 is equal to 240. In the tableau, the decision variables x_1 and x_2 are nonbasic and equal to zero; thus, we are producing nothing and, consequently, making zero profit.

The $c_j - z_j$ opportunity costs indicate whether the current solution is optimal or not. In this case, they indicate that it is not optimal, because they are not all less than or equal to zero.

The z_j's represent the amount of profit that is given up for each unit of variable x_j that enters the solution. The c_j's indicate the amount of profit gained for each unit of x_j brought into solution. The $c_j - z_j$, then, represents the net profit for bringing x_j into solution. Thus, we can improve our profit by bringing in either x_1 or x_2. Normally, you will choose the variable whose $c_j - z_j$ is largest. This choice of entering variable gives the fastest rate of improvement, although not necessarily the greatest degree of improvement. Hence, x_2 is chosen as the entering variable.

The z_j's can be calculated by observing how much of each of the current basic variables must be given up in order for x_j to have its value increased and enter the solution. The coefficients in the column of the tableau that are directly under any variable x_j are called substitution rates or substitution coefficients. They indicate how much of the current solution must be changed for every unit of x_j brought into solution. Thus, from Tableau 2-1 we can see that if one unit of x_2 enters the solution (that is, if one hi-gain is produced), then we must give up four units of assembly slack and one unit of inspection slack time.

Furthermore, each of the two basic variables s_1 and s_2 is worth zero. It costs nothing to give them up! Thus, each $z_j = 0$. Each $c_j - z_j$ for the nonbasic variables is calculated:

$$c_1 - z_1 = 20 - [0(1.2) + 0(.5)] = 20$$

$$c_2 - z_2 = 50 - [0(4) + 0(1)] = 50$$

The $c_j - z_j$ for all basic variables is always zero.

For every unit of x_1 brought into solution, we can increase profits by 20; for every unit of x_2, we can increase profits by 50. Therefore, because when we are maximizing, we normally bring in the nonbasic variable that has the largest $c_j - z_j$ value, x_2 now enters the solution.

Step 3: Increase value of entering variable until some basic variable reaches zero.
Since only m variables can be basic (in this case, $m = 2$), we must now determine a variable to leave the basis. Our resources are limited; so increasing the value of x_2 forces at least some of the other basic variables to decrease in value. We must be careful not to increase x_2 so much that some basic variable becomes negative. Happily, there is a simple test to determine which variable should leave the solution and how much of x_2 should enter. This *ratio test* consists of dividing each number in the solution column by its associated coefficient in the column under x_2. This ratio is formed only for those rows in which the coefficient under x_2 is positive. Negative and zero coefficients are excluded. Hence, for row 1, we form the ratio 240/4, and for row 2, 81/1. As is shown in Tableau 2-2, we get 60 and 81, respectively. The row that has the smallest ratio shows the variable to leave the solution. Since row 1 has the smallest ratio, s_1 leaves the solution.

Tableau 2-2   Illustration of Ratio Test and Pivot Selection

		c_j	20	50	0	0		
	c_B	BASIC VARIABLE	x_1	x_2	s_1	s_2	SOLUTION	Ratio
→	0	s_1	1.2	④	1	0	240	240/4
	0	s_2	.5	1	0	1	81	81/1
		$c_j - z_j$	20	50	0	0	0	

Step 4. Bring new variable into solution and revise tableau for new iteration. In the last basic step of the simplex method, we must bring x_2 into the solution and revise all the numbers in the tableau so that we may return to step 2 and begin a new iteration. The procedure used to do this is called pivoting. All rows in the tableau, including the $c_j - z_j$, are updated by this procedure. After the initial tableau, we shall dispense with the z_j row at the bottom of the tableau. There are two steps to the pivoting process. In one step, we update the pivot row; this is the row in which the minimum ratio occurred. In the other step, we update all remaining rows.

The number in the tableau that occurs at the intersection of the leaving row and the entering column is called the pivot element. In Tableau 2-2, the circled number is the pivot element, and the arrows indicate the entering column and leaving row. The entire pivot row is updated by dividing all entries in the pivot row by the pivot element. Thus, we divide the pivot row by 4 yielding 1.2/4 4/4 1/4 0/4 240/4. Tableau 2-3 shows the partially completed tableau.

Tableau 2-3   First Iteration with Pivot Row Updated

C_B	c_j BASIC VARIABLES	20 x_1	50 x_2	0 s_1	0 s_2	SOLUTION
50	x_2	.3	1	.25	0	60
0	s_2					
	$c_j - z_j$					

For every row other than the pivot row, we can update by using the formula:

New row = Old row − Pivot intersection number × New pivot row

where the pivot intersection number is the number in the row that is in the pivot column. To demonstrate the formula, let's update the remaining rows in the tableau:

$$
\begin{array}{rrrrrr}
\text{New row 2} = & (.5 & 1 & 0 & 1 & 81) \\
& -(1)(.3 & 1 & .25 & 0 & 60) \\
\hline
= & .2 & 0 & -.25 & 1 & 21 \\
\text{New } c_j - z_j \text{ row} = & (20 & 50 & 0 & & 0) \\
& -(50)(.3 & 1 & .25 & & 0) \\
\hline
= & 5 & 0 & -12.5 & & 0
\end{array}
$$

In Tableau 2-4, the completed tableau for the second solution is presented. The current solution value in the lower right-hand side of the tableau is calculated by taking the c_B column times the solution column to yield: Profit $= 50(60) + 0(21) = 3,000$.

Tableau 2-4   Updated Tableau After First Iteration

c_j		20	50	0	0		
C_B	BASIC VARIABLES	x_1	x_2	s_1	s_2	SOLUTION	min. ratio
50	x_2	.3	1	.25	0	60	60/.3
0	s_2	②	0	−.25	1	21	21/.2
	$c_j - z_j$	5	0	−12.5	0	3,000	

The pivoting process merely involves multiplying one equation by a constant and adding it to another equation. However, certain rules involving elementary row operations are observed so that the solution to the updated system of equations is the same as the original LP model. Thus, the rows in Tableau 2-4 still represent equations.

Returning to our calculations, we can see that the second solution in Tableau 2-4 is not optimal, since $c_1 - z_1 = 5$. Thus, x_1 will be the entering variable, and the leaving variable is calculated by forming the minimum ratios 60/.3 and 21/.2. Row 2 yields the minimum ratio, and s_2 becomes the leaving variable. Thus, .2 becomes the pivot element.

In updating the rows of the tableau, we first calculate the new pivot row:

$$\left(\frac{.2}{.2} \quad \frac{0}{.2} \quad \frac{-.25}{.2} \quad \frac{1}{.2} \quad \frac{21}{.2} \right)$$
$$= (1 \quad 0 \quad -1.25 \quad 5 \quad 105)$$

The remaining rows are updated:

$$
\begin{array}{rccccc}
\text{New row } 1 = (.3 & 1 & .25 & 0 & 60) \\
- (.3)(1 & 0 & -1.25 & 5 & 105) \\
\hline
= 0 & 1 & .625 & -1.5 & 28.5 \\
\end{array}
$$

$$
\begin{array}{rcccc}
\text{New } c_j - z_j \text{ row} = (5 & 0 & -12.5 & 0) \\
(-5)(1 & 0 & -12.5 & 5) \\
\hline
= 0 & 0 & -6.25 & -25 \\
\end{array}
$$

The new solution value is $50(28.5) + 20(105) = 3,525$, which is optimal. The updated tableau is shown in Tableau 2-5.

Tableau 2-5   Optimal Tableau for Electrovox Problem

C_B	BASIC VARIABLES	c_j → 20 x_1	50 x_2	0 s_1	0 s_2	SOLUTION
50	x_2	0	1	.625	−1.5	28.5
20	x_1	1	0	−1.25	5	105
	$c_j - z_j$	0	0	−6.25	−25	3,525

The tableau indicates optimality, since all solution values are nonnegative and all $c_j - z_j$ are less than or equal to zero, which indicates that no higher profit can be achieved. The feasibility of the solution may be checked by substituting this tableau's values back into the original constraints of the model.

From Tableau 2-5, we can see that variables x_2 and x_1 are in the final solution at values 28.5 and 105, respectively. This corresponds to real conditions of producing 28.5 hi-gain sets and 105 standard sets. The optimal profit is found in the lower right-hand corner at a value of $3,525. This solution is precisely the same as that determined by the graphical method.

Which of the two resources is being fully utilized? From the optimal tableau, we can see that slack variables s_1 and s_2 are nonbasic and therefore have value zero. Consequently, there is no surplus assembly or inspection time, and these two resources are being fully utilized.

MINIMIZATION PROBLEMS AND OTHER TYPES OF CONSTRAINTS

So far, we have examined only maximization problems and constraints that were less-than-or-equal-to ($\leq$) type constraints. In LP analysis, it is necessary to handle minimization and equality ($=$), as well as greater-than-or-equal-to constraints ($\geq$).

There are two approaches we can use to solve a minimization problem. First, we can formulate the minimization problem, then change the signs of all coefficients in the objective function and solve the problem as a maximization problem. The resulting values of the decision variables will be correct, and changing the sign of the final objective function value yields the correct value. Many computer codes only maximize (or minimize), and the decision maker must sometimes use this reversing trick to solve an LP problem on the computer.

Another approach to minimization involves changing the simplex solution procedure. Again, the alteration is simple; it involves only a change in the selection criterion for the entering variable. Instead of picking the variable with the most positive $c_j - z_j$ to enter the solution, we simply pick the variable with the most negative $c_j - z_j$. The minimization terminates when all $c_j - z_j \geq 0$.

In solving either minimization or maximization problems, it is often necessary to include $=$ and $\geq$ type constraints. The problem with these constraints is in determining a starting feasible solution for the simplex method. For example, if we have the constraint $3x_1 + 5x_2 = 12$, then it is already in equation form. But what are the beginning values of the basic variables? To obtain an easy starting solution, we use an artificial variable, A_1, to obtain

$$3x_1 + 5x_2 + A_1 = 12$$

Now we can begin the simplex method with $A_1 = 12$ in the initial solution. In order for the final solution to be feasible, A_1 must equal zero. Thus, we must drive the artificial variables to zero value in the final solution. There is more than one way to do this; we can assign the artificial variables an arbitrarily low objective-function coefficient for a maximization problem or an arbitrarily high value for a minimization problem. Alternatively, we could solve the LP problem in two phases, the first of which is to drive the artificial variables to zero value.

The conversion procedure to $\geq$ type constraints involves subtracting a slack and adding an artificial. Thus, $3x_1 + 5x_2 \geq 12$ becomes:

$$3x_1 + 5x_2 - s_1 + A_1 = 12$$

Some commercial LP codes make these transformations for the user; others do not. Failure to drive all artificial variables to zero value in any LP problem means that the problem has no feasible solution; that is, it is impossible to find decision variable values that satisfy all the constraints. In this case, the analyst must remodel the problem to arrive at a feasible solution.

AFTER THE SOLUTION, THEN WHAT?

Some may argue that there is no such thing as a single optimum solution to a real-world LP problem. They may say that data are not precise or that parameters of the model are continually changing and possibly changing the optimal solution. They are probably right.

It is very seldom that an LP problem is analyzed and only one solution is derived.

c_j		2	3	0	0		
c_B	BASIC VARIABLES	x_1	x_2	s_1	s_2	SOLUTION	Ratio
3	x_2	1/2	1	1/2	0	3	$3/\frac{1}{2}$
0	s_2	(5/2)	0	$-1/2$	1	5	$5/\frac{5}{2}$
	$c_j - z_j$	1/2	0	$-3/2$	0	9	

$\uparrow$

c_j		2	3	0	0	
c_B	BASIC VARIABLES	x_1	x_2	s_1	s_2	SOLUTION
3	x_1	0	1	3/5	$-1/5$	2
2	x_2	1	0	$-1/5$	2/5	2
	$c_j - z_j$	0	0	$-7/5$	$-1/5$	10

The optimal solution is to produce two units of x_1 and x_2 with a total profit of 10.

Problem Statement

Convert the following problem to standard form (all equations):

$$\text{Min } 14x_1 + 9x_2 + 11x_3$$
$$\text{s.t.: } x_1 + x_2 + x_3 = 400$$
$$2x_1 + x_2 + 3x_3 \leq 1{,}000$$
$$7x_1 - 5x_2 + 8x_3 \geq 100$$
$$x_1, x_2, x_3 \geq 0$$

Solution

Using the appropriate slack and artificial variables, we convert to equations in the following manner:

$$\text{Min } 14x_1 + 9x_2 + 11x_3 + 0s_1 + 0s_2 + MA_1 + MA_2$$
$$\text{s.t.: } x_1 + x_2 + x_3 + A_1 = 400$$
$$2x_1 + 3x_2 + 3x_3 + s_1 = 1{,}000$$
$$7x_1 - 5x_2 + 8x_3 - s_2 + A_2 = 100$$
$$x_1, x_2, x_3, s_1, s_2, A_1, A_2 \geq 0$$

The M objective-function coefficients of the artificial variables A_1 and A_2 represent very large penalty numbers. Their purpose is to ensure that no artificial variable will appear in any optimal solution. If we were maximizing, the objective-function coefficients would be a $-M$.

REFERENCES

ADVANI, S., "A Linear Programming Approach to Air Cleaner Design," *Operations Research*, March–April 1974, pp. 295–97.

CHARNES, ABRAHAM, and W.W. COOPER, *Management Models and Industrial Applications of Linear Programming*. New York: John Wiley, 1961.

DAELLENBACH, HANS G., and EARL J. BELL, *User's Guide to Linear Programming*. Englewood Cliffs, N.J.: Prentice-Hall, 1970.

DANTZIG, GEORGE B., *Linear Programming and Extensions*. Princeton, N.J.: Princeton University Press, 1963.

DUTTON, R., G. HINMAN, and C.B. MILLHAM, "The Optimal Location of Nuclear Power Facilities in the Pacific Northwest," *Operations Research*, May–June 1974, pp. 478–87.

FELDSTEIN, M., and HAROLD LUFT, "Distributional Constraints in Public Expenditure Planning," *Management Science*, August 1973, pp. 1414–22.

GASS, SAUL I., *Illustrated Guide to Linear Programming*. New York: McGraw-Hill, 1970.

GLASSEY, C.R., and V.K. GUPTA, "A Linear Programming Analysis of Paper Recycling," *Management Science*, December 1974, pp. 392–408.

GRINOLD, RICHARD C., "Input Policies for a Longitudinal Manpower Flow Model," *Management Science*, Vol. 22 (1976), 570–75.

HEROUX, R.L., and W.A. WALLACE, "Linear Programming and Financial Analysis of the New Community Development Process," *Management Science*, April 1973, pp. 857–72.

LEE, SANG M., *Linear Optimization for Management*. New York: Petrocelli/Charter, 1976.

LYONS, D.F., and V.A. DODD, "The Mix-Feed Problem," *Operational Research*. Amsterdam: North-Holland Publishing, 1975.

MARCUSE, W., L. BODIN, E. CHERNIAVSKY, and YASUKO SANBORN, "A Dynamic Time Dependent Model for the Analysis of Alternative Energy Policies," *Operational Research*. Amsterdam: North-Holland Publishing Co., 1975.

NAYLOR, THOMAS H., EUGENE T. BYRNE, and JOHN M. VERNON, *Introduction to Linear Programming: Methods and Cases*. Belmont, Calif.: Wadsworth, 1971.

REVELLE, C., D. MARKS, and J. LIEBMAN, "An Analysis of Private and Public Sector Location Models," *Management Science*, Vol. 16 (1970), 692–707.

SAVAS, E., "Simulation and Cost-Effectiveness of New York's Emergency Ambulance Service," *Management Science*, Vol. 15 (1969), B608–27.

SMITH, V.E., "A Diet Model with Protein Quality Variable," *Management Science*, February 1974, pp. 971–80.

ZIERER, T.K., W.A. MITCHELL, and T.R. WHITE, "Practical Applications of Linear Programming to Shell's Distribution Problems," *Interfaces*, Vol. 6, No. 4 (August 1976), 13–26.

chapter 3

COMPUTER
SIMULATION

INTRODUCTION

In this chapter, we describe *computer simulation*, which is often referred to as *Monte Carlo simulation*. In general, simulation is a descriptive rather than an optimization technique and involves developing a model of some real phenomenon and then performing experiments on that model.

This broad definition applies to types of simulation other than computer simulation. A spacecraft simulator, a wind tunnel, a model airplane, and an analog simulation of some continuous process are all examples of simulations that differ fundamentally from computer simulation. To be more specific, computer simulation is a numerical technique that involves modeling a stochastic system on a digital computer with the intention of predicting the system's behavior. Experiments on the simulation model are, in effect, similar to observing the system over a significant period of time.

Of the three quantitative methods discussed in Part 2 of this book, simulation enjoys the widest application, owing to its greater flexibility. As we mentioned in Chapter 2, LP carries several assumptions that restrict its application; and the same type of restrictions apply to the application of queuing theory. As we shall see, however, simulation is more expensive and does not yield optimal solutions.

Reasons for Using Simulation

The many reasons why a manager uses simulation to solve a problem can be clustered into two major categories.

First, experimentation with the real system may be impractical or impossible. A hospital administrator may have difficulty justifying experimenting with the real coronary-care unit to determine the optimal number of beds and the best medical-team configuration, whereas experimentation on a surrogate system, a computer simulation model, would be totally acceptable.

Second, the real system may be too complex to permit mathematical representation or model solution. Often, if experimentation with the real system is impractical, an alternative would be to develop a mathematical model of the system or problem in question. A great majority of the time, however, the real system is too complex to model or solve mathematically, and simulation is used as the tool of last resort.

Simulation Applications

As can be inferred by the following list of applications, computer simulation is probably the most generally useful quantitative technique used by the operations manager. Its major utility is its ability to solve a wide range of operational problems.

Health-Care Applications. Simulation has been used to predict the effect of various physician mixes on the utilization of hospital resources, and to plan the configuration of emergency rooms, coronary-care units, and other hospital facilities. Staffing of nursing stations, primary-care teams, and scheduling operations and admissions are all problems that have been attacked using computer simulation. Even the optimal location of ambulances has been examined using simulation.[1]

Urban Applications. Cities have used simulation to solve some of their most pressing problems—problems such as police dispatching and beat design, the planning and design of transit systems, evaluation of operating alternatives at airports, planning for snow emergencies and garbage collection, the location of emergency vehicles, long-range financial planning, and many more.

Industrial Applications. Manufacturing organizations have used simulation to schedule their productive process, make inventory policy decisions, design productive systems, determine machine maintenance schedules, design distribution systems, and even test the effects of increased production on the operation of an overhead crane.

Financial Applications. The rapid growth in the use of simulation as a financial planning tool is evidenced by the more than 25 financial modeling software packages currently available commercially. All kinds of pro forma statements are produced using financial simulation packages. Portfolio selection models are common, as are capital budgeting models.

Military Applications. Large-scale military battles, as well as individual weapon systems, have been simulated to aid in the design both of weapon systems and of strategic and tactical operations.

Agricultural Applications. Simulation has been used to make decisions concerning equipment on a sugar plantation, to predict the effects of various policy alternatives on the Venezuelan cattle industry, and to aid in the design of regional grain collection, handling, and distribution in Canada.

The literature contains a wealth of diverse applications of computer simulation; the list above represents only a small sample of successful applications.

Manual Simulation

In order to give you some understanding of the technique of computer simulation, let's analyze a very simple problem. Two new ship-docking facilities are being finished this year, and a decision must be made regarding how many tugs will be necessary to service ships wishing to dock. Using data from similar ports and a great deal of subjective judgment, the time between ship arrivals is distributed as shown in

---

[1] For material detailing this and the other applications listed here, see the list of references at the end of this chapter.

Table 3-1. Time spent at the dock is estimated in similar manner; that probability distribution is shown in Table 3-2. Tugging time is fairly constant at one hour per tug, and ships are taken on a first-come, first-served basis, with ships being tugged to sea having priority over those being tugged to port. The flow of a ship through the port facility is shown in Figure 3-1. Notice that a tug is needed first to tow the ship to the berth, and it is then released while the ship is unloaded. Once the ship is ready to leave the berth, a tug is needed to tow the ship into the open water.

Table 3-1   Ship Interarrival Time Distribution

TIME BETWEEN SHIP ARRIVALS	PROBABILITY
1 hour	.30
2 hours	.25
3 hours	.15
4 hours	.15
5 hours	.05
6 hours	.05
7 hours	.05
	1.00

Table 3-2   Unloading Time Distribution

UNLOADING TIME	PROBABILITY
1 hour	.05
2 hours	.15
3 hours	.20
4 hours	.25
5 hours	.30
6 hours	.05
	1.00

The first step in developing the simulation is to develop a way of generating the two stochastic variables in the system, ship arrival times and unloading times. This is done using numbers from a uniform distribution whose parameters are 0 and 1. Remember that a uniform probability distribution is one in which the random variable is defined over a range from a to b. If the parameters of the uniform distribution are 0 and 1, then random $P(x \leq .25)$, for example, is equal to 0.25, and $P(.25 \leq x \leq .75) = .5$. Figure 3-2 depicts the uniform distribution in graphic form.

The process of generating stochastic variables is basic to computer simulation; it is accomplished by defining a function that relates a uniformly distributed random variable to a random variable distributed in another manner. Remember that once this function, known as a *process generator*, has been developed, it is easy to sample

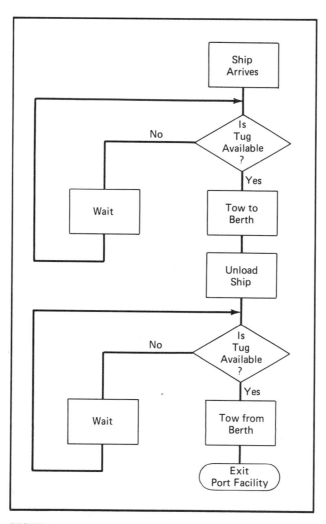

FIGURE 3-1 **Ship Flow through Port Facility**

from a uniform distribution and transform that uniformly distributed random variate into an arrival time or an unloading time. In our problem, both stochastic variables are treated as discrete variables. The function describing arrival times and unloading times can be found by defining the cumulative probability distributions of the two variables and relating that distribution to a uniform random variable between 0 and 1. Because a number chosen from a uniform distribution with parameters 0 and 1 will 30 percent of the time fall in the range of 0 to .3, approximately 30 percent of the ships generated according to the function described in Table 3-3 will arrive one hour after the preceding ship. Similarly, approximately 15 percent of the arrivals will come just four hours after the preceding ship.

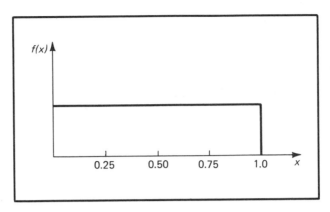

FIGURE 3-2   **Uniform Distribution**

Table 3-3   Ship Interarrival Time Generating Function

UNIFORM RANDOM VARIABLE	TIME BETWEEN ARRIVALS
.00– .30	1 hour
.30– .55	2 hours
.55– .70	3 hours
.70– .85	4 hours
.85– .90	5 hours
.90– .95	6 hours
.95–1.00	7 hours

Generation of unloading times is accomplished in a similar manner. If a random number is chosen between 0 and .05, the generated unloading time is one hour. If the random number is between .4 and .65, the generated unloading time is four hours. See Table 3-4 for the unloading time generating function.

You must remember, however, that we are describing a random process, and it would take a large number of ship arrivals for these percentages to be considered very

Table 3-4   Unloading Time Generating Function

UNIFORM RANDOM VARIABLE	UNLOADING TIME
.00– .05	1 hour
.05– .20	2 hours
.20– .40	3 hours
.40– .65	4 hours
.65– .95	5 hours
.95–1.00	6 hours

accurate. In other words, if only 50 arrivals were generated, it would not be unreasonable for 12 or 13 ships to take three hours to unload even though the expected number of ships taking three hours to unload is 10 (.2 times 50).

Having defined the system and the process generators, we are now ready to simulate the harbor operation. First, we must decide what experiments we are interested in running. For the sake of illustration, let's run two experiments, one with one tug and the other with two tugs. The critical output variable from the simulator is the average time spent by a ship waiting for a tug. Let's simulate 48 hours and assume an around-the-clock operation. Let us also assume that the random numbers needed to generate ship arrivals are chosen from the random numbers in Table 3-5, starting in the upper left-hand corner. Random numbers to generate unloading times are chosen from the same table, starting in the upper right-hand corner. In a computer simulation, these random numbers would be generated by a random-number generating function and not chosen from a table.

Looking at Table 3-6, because the random number .445282 falls between .3 and .55, the first ship is simulated to arrive two hours into the simulated time period. The next ship arrives only one hour later, because its random number, .066257, falls between 0 and .3. Since a tug is available at two hours into the simulation, it is assigned immediately to the first ship, and one hour later the ship is ready for unloading. Unloading time for ship number 1 is generated at two hours, because .106182 is between .05 and .20. The one tug is assigned to ship 2 immediately after servicing ship 1 but is idle for an hour waiting for ship 1 to be unloaded. To make sure you understand how the simulation is working, you should verify the numbers in Tables 3-6 and 3-7.

Upon examination of Tables 3-6 and 3-7, it is apparent that if the object were to minimize ship waiting time, then two tugs should be employed, since the average waiting time is reduced from .5 hours (Hours spent waiting/No. of ships) to 0 hours. If, however, the objective is to minimize the cost of waiting plus the cost of operating the port, then costs of waiting and the cost of operating a tug would have to be determined.

Table 3.8 is a listing of a GPSS computer program that simulates the harbor problem. The experiments described in Tables 3.6 and 3.7 were run on the computer for a simulated time of 4800 hours instead of 48 hours. It took a medium sized third generation computer less than 5 CPU seconds to simulate 4800 hours of harbor operation. The GPSS program took less than one hour to write and debug. During that simulated time 1748 ships arrived at the port facility. A summary of the results of the two experiments are summarized in Table 3.9. Although the correlation between the manual and computer simulations is quite close for the two-tug configuration, the computer simulation of the one-tug configuration gives an average waiting time of more than twice that given by the manual simulation. It should be clear that the reason we include an example of a manual simulation in this chapter is to give you a deeper understanding of what computer simulation is, not to suggest that real problems are solved using manual simulation.

Table 3-5 Random-Number Table

.445282	.353333	.112460	.494758	.956412	.285648	.106182
.066257	.441906	.055118	.353555	.625270	.569627	.790333
.615352	.579120	.936548	.407208	.014319	.421038	.397360
.594821	.992685	.602720	.682154	.668440	.871255	.211575
.428152	.664736	.135047	.827656	.750516	.054190	.570499
.935282	.477204	.445679	.379244	.264349	.172899	.658255
.393437	.436322	.077000	.535109	.517650	.289920	.080668
.874724	.522334	.261491	.867939	.854214	.313831	.195065
.345906	.319852	.805962	.957102	.488950	.319787	.518168
.230927	.722047	.253941	.025220	.865850	.968126	.016103
.383484	.155976	.484498	.503207	.658759	.423696	.613343
.866792	.680668	.282878	.571261	.881661	.148613	.956734
.402887	.806714	.214300	.025378	.223563	.112981	.665817
.978072	.876081	.453834	.838279	.945164	.126478	.252390
.376035	.984704	.523906	.281099	.971441	.298754	.049552
.608526	.205187	.754386	.679630	.288311	.613193	.084362
.987430	.165323	.105069	.142509	.909431	.174001	.859131
.588776	.800478	.503880	.818984	.378979	.903020	.007307
.916667	.434235	.355410	.224342	.147361	.865086	.864270
.399848	.620655	.125302	.165914	.867769	.713384	.470383
.401840	.177596	.449017	.095737	.533275	.338016	.228617
.329558	.919797	.552755	.038363	.255378	.187000	.823605
.258627	.139314	.508244	.795636	.199622	.037007	.425445
.219602	.488609	.955238	.333945	.406528	.433665	.943236
.786436	.049489	.489014	.488679	.530948	.787576	.946926
.593372	.037899	.887044	.981170	.903624	.591212	.414656
.167034	.270299	.118483	.278210	.602910	.113570	.255230
.509250	.758433	.967347	.978183	.162974	.174195	.578402
.902657	.210320	.138008	.935174	.368968	.797242	.462741
.601267	.442931	.246182	.490711	.728634	.955403	.174712
.449643	.125448	.705902	.106384	.285185	.753657	.955278
.948750	.094997	.031238	.332454	.713580	.289390	.314123
.280228	.854264	.603533	.932821	.165132	.595403	.086226
.158733	.176363	.629582	.190230	.475139	.138766	.556342
.089161	.527890	.364889	.438324	.345949	.130772	.671094
.849617	.057854	.700570	.682735	.791279	.603053	.496812
.553393	.849053	.113780	.041200	.223180	.968275	.801036
.091737	.341098	.220956	.255856	.546529	.976471	.940064
.852144	.652287	.244428	.595987	.376065	.892506	.970457
.790186	.007002	.930339	.519015	.741036	.775080	.981155
.911208	.636852	.620241	.989783	.356524	.231102	.177894
.987448	.323640	.054813	.416119	.003391	.275281	.621161
.249438	.906181	.192145	.997242	.254147	.549703	.010896
.118046	.610211	.598851	.101210	.217602	.394718	.409892
.906891	.752321	.351903	.340528	.876046	.191524	.264726
.864643	.805323	.050154	.053020	.866732	.723211	.538683
.723195	.491027	.437407	.205195	.294510	.920305	.871236
.944672	.826904	.459380	.314145	.750449	.675389	.298291
.711250	.582876	.096009	.330172	.116949	.730150	.328360
.398807	.437603	.036349	.279671	.350884	.588266	.371640

Table 3-6   Harbor Simulation, One-Tug Configuration

SHIP NO.	RANDOM NO.	ARRIVAL TIME IN HOURS	TIME WHEN TUG WAS ENGAGED (TO BERTH)	ARRIVAL TIME AT BERTH	RANDOM NO.	TIME UNLOADING IS FINISHED	TIME WHEN TUG WAS ENGAGED (FROM BERTH)	TIME TUG WAS RELEASED	TIME SPENT WAITING
1	.445282	2	2	3	.106182	5	5	6	0
2	.066257	3	3	4	.790333	9	9	10	0
3	.615352	6	6	7	.397360	10	10	11	0
4	.594821	9	11	12	.211575	15	15	16	2
5	.428152	11	12	13	.570499	17	17	18	1
6	.935282	17	18	19	.658255	24	24	25	1
7	.393437	19	19	20	.080668	22	22	23	0
8	.874724	24	25	26	.195065	28	28	29	1
9	.345906	26	26	27	.518168	31	31	32	0
10	.230927	27	27	28	.016103	29	29	30	0
11	.383484	29	30	31	.613343	35	35	36	1
12	.866792	34	34	35	.956734	41	41	42	0
13	.402887	36	36	37	.665817	42	42	43	0
14	.978072	43	43	44	.252390	47	47	48	0
15	.376035	45	45	46	.049552	47	48	49	1
16	.608526	48	49	50	.084362	52	52	53	1

Table 3-7 Harbor Simulation, Two-Tug Configuration

SHIP NO.	RANDOM NO.	ARRIVAL TIME IN HOURS	TIME WHEN TUG WAS ENGAGED (TO BERTH)	ARRIVAL TIME AT BERTH	RANDOM NO.	TIME UNLOADING IS FINISHED	TIME WHEN TUG WAS ENGAGED (FROM BERTH)	TIME TUG WAS RELEASED	TIME SPENT WAITING
1	.445282	2	2	3	.106182	5	5	6	0
2	.066257	3	3	4	.790333	9	9	10	0
3	.615352	6	6	7	.397360	10	10	11	0
4	.594821	9	9	10	.211575	13	13	14	0
5	.428152	11	11	12	.570499	16	16	17	0
6	.935282	17	17	18	.658255	23	23	24	0
7	.393437	19	19	20	.080668	22	22	23	0
8	.874724	24	24	25	.195065	27	27	28	0
9	.345906	26	26	27	.518168	31	31	32	0
10	.230927	27	27	28	.016103	29	29	30	0
11	.383484	29	29	30	.613343	35	35	36	0
12	.866792	34	34	35	.956734	41	41	42	0
13	.402887	36	36	37	.665817	41	41	42	0
14	.978072	43	43	44	.252390	47	47	48	0
15	.376035	45	45	46	.049552	47	47	48	0
16	.608526	48	48	49	.084362	51	51	52	0

Table 3-8 GPSS Simulation Model—Harbor Problem

```
1       FUNCTION    RN1,D7
.3,1/.55,2/.7,3/.85,4/.9,5/.95,6/1.0,7
2       FUNCTION    RN1,D6
.05,1/.2,2/.4,3/.65,4/.95,5/1.0,6
TUG     STORAGE     1
BERTH   STORAGE     2
        SIMULATE
1       GENERATE    FN1
2       QUEUE       TUGLN
3       ENTER       TUG
4       DEPART      TUGLN
5       ADVANCE     1
6       LEAVE       TUG
7       ENTER       BERTH
8       ADVANCE     FN2
9       LEAVE       BERTH
10      QUEUE       TUGLN
11      ENTER       TUG
12      DEPART      TUGLN
13      ADVANCE     1
14      LEAVE       TUG
15      TERMINATE
16      GENERATE    4800
17      TERMINATE   1
        START       1
        END
```

Table 3-9 Harbor Simulation Results

	TOTAL NUMBER OF SHIPS GENERATED	AVERAGE TUG UTILIZATION	AVERAGE BERTH UTILIZATION	AVERAGE TIME SPENT WAITING FOR A TUG
1 Tug Configuration	1,745	.727	.676	1.172 hours
2 Tug Configuration	1,745	.363	.671	.03 hour

STEPS IN A SIMULATION STUDY

The harbor situation introduced you to simulation as an idea and a technique. In the rest of this chapter, we shall reinforce this intuitive understanding by describing the various stages or tasks in a simulation study. First you formulate the problem, then collect and analyze the data. Then you formulate a model, submit it to computer processing, and analyze the results.

Problem Formulation

You can't arrive at the right answer if you are working on the wrong problem. Therefore, the first step is to formulate the problem properly. Often the manager has only a vague idea of what the problem is. This vague idea must be translated into an explicit, written statement of the objectives of the study. The explicit original statement of the problem should not be considered sacrosanct, however, for this reason: As the simulation study progresses, the simulator becomes more knowledgeable about the system being simulated and about the objectives of the organization. Consequently, it is sometimes necessary to modify the objectives as the nature of the problem becomes clearer. Usually, the statement of objectives takes the form of questions to be answered, hypotheses to be tested, and effects to be estimated. Obviously, it is also necessary to identify the criteria to be used to evaluate these questions. In the harbor situation, the problem was simply how many tugs should be employed, and the evaluation criteria should probably be the cost of ships waiting and the cost of providing the tug service.

Data Collection

The second task, and possibly the most time-consuming step in a simulation study, is the job of collecting data. Quantitative data are necessary for several reasons. First, data are required to describe the system being simulated. If you don't understand the real system thoroughly, it isn't very likely that you will simulate the system properly. Second, data must be gathered as the foundation for generating the various stochastic variables in the system. For example, in the harbor system, real data concerning arrivals and unloading times were gathered and analyzed to determine the proper probability distributions and their parameters. Finally, data are necessary to test and validate the model. In order to use a simulation model to make decisions, the decision maker must be confident that the real-world phenomenon has been adequately and accurately represented. Often, the best way to accomplish this validation is to compare simulator output with historical data. To adequately model the harbor situation, data concerning arrivals, tow times, unloading times, waiting costs, tug costs, tug downtime, and other variables would need to be collected.

Data Analysis

Once the data have been collected, they must be analyzed and the proper generating functions must be developed. In the harbor example, the stochastic variables—ship arrival times and unloading times—were generated using cumulative probability distributions. These were estimated subjectively. Actually, subjective probability distributions are somewhat atypical; probability distributions based on empirical data usually yield more reliable simulation results and thus are preferable.

Two basic tasks must be accomplished in order to generate random variables. First, the raw data of a stochastic variable must be analyzed to determine how that random variable is distributed. Then, a function must be derived to generate the stochastic variable, using a uniformly distributed random number between 0 and 1. The following procedure is typically used to determine how a random variable is distributed:

1. The data are grouped into a frequency distribution.
2. This frequency distribution is depicted graphically as either a histogram or a frequency polygon.
3. From the shape of the histogram, a probability distribution is hypothesized.
4. Probability distribution parameters are estimated using sample statistics.
5. The hypothesis is tested, using one of several nonparametric statistical tests such as the *chi-square* or *Kolomogorov-Smirnov test*.
6. If the hypothesis is rejected, distribution parameters can be changed slightly, and the new hypothesis tested.
7. If no known probability distribution can be found to fit the sample data, the simulator is often forced to use the cumulative probability distribution of the sample data.

The next step in analyzing the data is to develop the functions necessary to generate a nonuniformly distributed random variable from a uniform random number between 0 and 1. If the random variable is discrete, it is easy to use the cumulative probability distribution, as we did in the manual simulation of the harbor.

To derive a generating function for continuous random variables, you must use the integral calculus, but the basic idea is the same. The object is to define the stochastic variable in terms of a uniformly distributed random number. For example, the process generator for a random variable distributed according to a negative exponential distribution is:

$$x = -\frac{1}{\lambda} \ln (r)$$

where x = an exponentially distributed random variable
r = uniform random number between 0 and 1
$\frac{1}{\lambda}$ = mean of the distribution
$\ln$ = natural logarithm

Formulate the Model

A simulation model is an abstraction—usually mathematical—of some real phenomenon or system. Model building is a very difficult step in the simulation process, because the model builder must strike a balance between model realism and the cost of developing that model. If a crucial variable or functional relationship is omitted, the model does not accurately predict the behavior of the real system. If the model is too close to the real-world system, it can easily be too expensive to collect data for, or to program and execute. The goal of the model builder is to build a model that adequately describes the real system at a minimum cost of human and computer resources. You can imagine that model building is an art rather than a science.

Write and Test the Program

To solve a real problem using simulation, the computer is an absolute necessity. The computer language you use is, therefore, a matter of some consequence.

Computer programming languages can actually be thought of in a hierarchy. The assembler languages of the various computer manufacturers are at the lowest level, and they are almost never used in simulation studies for several reasons. First, they are machine-dependent, which means that an assembler language program will not run on a machine other than the model for which it was created. An IBM 370 assembler language program, for example, can only be run on an IBM 360 or IBM 370 series computer. Secondly, it is excessively complex to write a simulation program in assembler language. An assembler program to simulate the harbor problem might take as many as 10,000 assembler language instructions and as long as 200 hours to write and debug.

Compiler languages, the next level of programming languages, are often used for simulation. FORTRAN, BASIC, PL1, and ALGOL are the most popular computer languages used for this purpose. Compiler languages are machine-independent, and because they are more sophisticated than assembler languages, a programmer has far less detail to be concerned with; so the programming effort is reduced. To simulate the harbor problem might take 300–400 FORTRAN statements and 30–40 hours programming time.

Special-purpose simulation languages, such as SIMSCRIPT, GPSS, DYNAMO, and GASP, simplify programming even more. As mentioned earlier in this chapter, a GPSS program for the harbor problem took only 24 statements and less than one hour to program and debug. The reason for the reduction in programming effort with a simulation language like GPSS is that each GPSS statement or block can be thought of as a FORTRAN subroutine (a small program in itself); and such things as the simulation clock and next-event logic are preprogrammed into the GPSS software. An additional benefit is that the probability of creating a valid program is increased.

Why, then, are most simulators written in compiler languages such as FORTRAN and BASIC? One reason is that special-purpose simulation languages such as GPSS and SIMSCRIPT are not as widely available as the compiler languages. All but the very smallest computers have FORTRAN, COBOL, or BASIC compilers in their software packages. Often, a simulation language such as GPSS is not used because the person conducting the simulation study does not know a special-purpose language and is unwilling to invest the time needed to learn one. Clearly, an organization that uses simulation techniques to aid in its decision process should consider acquiring a simulation processor such as GPSS or SIMSCRIPT, and then train its staff in the use of the simulation language.

Validating the Simulation Model

Perhaps the most difficult step in a simulation study is validating the simulation model. It is foolish to use simulation results in the decision-making process unless you are quite confident that the simulation model represents the real-world situation accurately. Absolute validation is probably unattainable, but it is possible to gain confidence in a simulation model by making certain verifications.

Program testing. One aspect of a simulation that must be validated is whether the programmer has instructed the computer properly. It is possible that a simulation model is valid as designed but invalid as implemented on the computer. Standard program-testing techniques should be employed to ensure congruence between simulator design and simulator program. These techniques include manual calculations, program traces, and so on. It is necessary to verify the absence of programming errors when you are validating a simulation, but this step alone is not sufficient. The program can be perfect and the simulation model still be totally invalid.

Variable generation test. Earlier in this chapter, we mentioned that nonparametric goodness-of-fit tests could be applied to hypotheses concerning the distributions of the various stochastic variables. These same tests should be applied to the output from the various generating functions to ensure that the real-world variables and simulated variables are distributed in the same manner. For example, if the interarrival time in a real queuing system is normally distributed with a mean of five minutes and a standard deviation of two minutes, then the random variable of interarrival times being generated in the simulation program should also be normally distributed with $\mu = 5$ and $\sigma = 2$.

Subjective validation. The design as well as the output of the simulation model ought to be reviewed by the people who are most familiar with the real system. This subjective validation should properly be done by people not directly involved in the simulation study.

Historical validation. If the simulator is designed to simulate an existing system, it is often possible to simulate the system as it is currently configured and then compare actual historical data to simulation output. For example, if the real system is a harbor operation, vital statistics such as the average waiting time of a vessel and the average time a vessel spends in the harbor should be compared to the distribution of various output variables. The absence of significant differences between simulated results and historical results may tend to validate the simulator; but it does not guarantee that the simulator will accurately predict the behavior of the real system under different conditions.

Confidence in the validity of a simulation model is crucial to the successful use of simulation. For this reason, no stone should be left unturned when performing the validation step of a simulation study.

Experimental Design

Once a simulation model has been implemented and validated, it can be used for its original purpose, experimentation. Simulation, you will recall, is a means of providing information necessary for decision making when a real-world system cannot be sufficiently manipulated. A simulation model synthetically gathers the information necessary to describe the system under study. The object is to gather the information necessary for decision making—at the lowest possible cost. Usually, real-world experiments are more costly than simulation experiments, and thus one can experiment with a greater number of alternatives when using a simulation model. For example, if the system under study is a harbor and the decision variables are the number of tugs and the number of berths, management can experiment with many combinations of decision variables to determine the optimal harbor configuration using simulation. If, however, experiments were made on the real system, far fewer alternatives could be evaluated.

The questions of the length of simulation runs, initialization periods, sample sizes, and optimization procedures are beyond the scope of this text. Many of the answers are contained in the traditional literature concerning experimental design.

Analysis of Simulation Results

If the simulation model is valid and the simulation experiments have been designed properly, analysis of simulation output is fairly straightforward. Often, certain statistical techniques, such as analysis of variance, can be helpful in analyzing simulation results.

WHEN TO SIMULATE

Once the problem has been formulated, the manager must decide whether or not to attempt to solve the problem using computer simulation. This decision process is depicted in Figure 3-3.

As we said earlier, the problem should be formulated explicitly in terms of hypotheses to be tested and questions to be answered. After the problem has been formulated, a solution technique other than simulation is often judged to be more appropriate. The important point is that choosing a solution methodology must succeed, not precede, the problem-formulation phase of any scientific study. If an analytical technique or model is available or can be adapted to the problem, it should probably be used. If an analytical technique such as classical inventory theory, which is discussed in Chapter 10, or queuing theory, discussed in Chapter 4, cannot be applied, then the manager must make the decision between simulating and making an intuitive, seat-of-the-pants decision. This judgment, in turn, depends on the nature of the individual decision. In other words, is the decision important enough to justify the estimated cost of developing, validating, and experimenting with a simulation model?

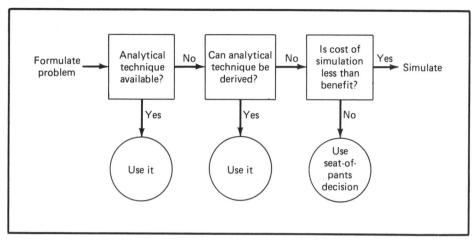

FIGURE 3-3   When to Simulate

Advantages of Simulation

In deciding whether or not to simulate, the manager must weigh the advantages of the technique.

1. The greatest advantage is that simulation allows the management scientist to model complex and dynamic phenomena that otherwise could not be dealt with in a scientific way.
2. Simulation permits experimentation that might be impossible or infeasible otherwise. "What-if"–questions can be asked using simulation.
3. By simulating the system, the management scientist gains valuable insight into the system and into the relative importance of the different variables.
4. Simulation allows for the compression of real time. To predict the behavior of a system over the period of a year may take only a few seconds or minutes using computer simulation.
5. Simulation is often used to test a proposed analytical solution.

Disadvantages of Simulation

Naturally, there are some significant disadvantages to using simulation to solve operational problems.

1. Simulation is not an optimization technique. Typically, different system configurations are experimented with to find a good, but *not* guaranteed best, solution.
2. Simulation is an expensive way to solve a problem. In addition to the cost of building and validating a simulation model, experimentation using computer simulation can be quite costly.

3. Because of the nature of simulation, sampling error exists in all output from simulation models. Of course, this sampling error can be reduced by increasing the sample size or by lengthening the computer run time.

4. A real disadvantage is that simulation is often misused because many people who are qualified to write a simulation program are not qualified to perform a total simulation study. In other words, many programmers do not possess the necessary statistical background.

5. Probably the most serious shortcoming of simulation is that it is a tool of solution evaluation and thus does not generate problem solutions. Therefore, the decision maker has to develop proposed solutions; then, simulation can be used to test the relative desirability of those solutions.

The Future of Simulation

At the beginning of this chapter, we indicated that simulation was widely used in the management of a wide variety of operations. There are four major reasons why computer simulation will continue to expand into almost every imaginable area of application.

1. Simulation is probably the most powerful of management science techniques, because many different kinds of problems can be solved using simulation.

2. The cost of computing has been decreasing and will continue to do so at a very rapid rate.

3. Simulation languages will continue to evolve and, indeed, to be invented, thus making it less expensive and less time-consuming to solve problems by means of this technique.

4. Finally, as more managers are made aware of the power of simulation as a tool for the decision-making process, the more popular simulation will become.

SUMMARY

Computer simulation is probably the most potent, most flexible, and consequently one of the most common quantitative tools used today to solve operational problems. Computer simulation is to the social scientist what a laboratory is to the chemist or physicist. Its major contribution is that it allows the decision maker to predict the behavior of a system under various circumstances and configurations.

There are eight basic phases in a simulation study. These are problem formulation, data collection, data analysis, model formulation, program formulation and testing, model validation, experimental design, and finally, the analysis of results.

The application of simulation to the solution of operational problems is on a steep growth trend. Simulation is being applied to a rapidly increasing variety of problems, mainly because of its ability to model complex and dynamic systems that could otherwise not be modeled. Another reason for the recent explosion in simulation applications is that the major disadvantages of simulation, cost and the unavailability of necessary data, are being mitigated by the rapid advances that have been made and are being made in computer hardware and software technology.

SOLVED PROBLEM

Problem Statement

A car-wash chain is planning to build another car-wash facility and is trying to decide how many stalls to build. Past experience has shown that the time between arriving customers is exponentially distributed. The mean of the distribution depends on the traffic count per hour going by the facility. Based on city traffic engineering data, the mean time between arrivals is estimated to be ten minutes. The time required to wash a car is ten minutes and constant. Also, it has been established that people generally do not get in line if there are more than two cars waiting. If management wants to build a facility such that there is a low probability of losing customers because of the length of the line but at the same time doesn't want to overbuild, how many stalls should be built? Simulate for eight hours, or 480 minutes.

Solution

The process generator for the exponential distribution is:

$$x = -\frac{1}{\lambda} \ln(r)$$

Therefore, in order to calculate the time between arrivals, merely plug the random number into the function above. For example:

$$r = .494$$
$$x = -10 \ln(.494)$$
$$= (-10)(-.7052)$$
$$= 7.052, \text{ rounded to 7 minutes}$$

The time until the next arrival is $7 + x$. Let

$$r = .353$$

then,

$$x = -10 \ln(.353)$$
$$= (-10)(-1.04)$$
$$= 10 \text{ minutes rounded}$$

Therefore, the second customer arrives at 17 minutes into the simulation. The rest of the solution tables merely keep track of the system as simulated time progresses.

1 Stall

RANDOM NO.	TIME OF ARRIVAL	TIME IN	TIME OUT	NO. IN LINE	LOST CUSTOMER?
.494	7	7	17	0	No
.353	17	17	27	0	No
.407	26	27	37	0	No
.682	30	37	47	0	No
.827	32	47	57	1	No
.379	42	57	67	1	No
.535	48	67	77	1	No
.867	49	—	—	2	Yes
.957	49	—	—	2	Yes
.025	86	86	96	0	No
.503	93	96	106	0	No
.571	99	106	116	0	No
.025	136	136	146	0	No
.838	138	146	156	0	No
.281	151	156	166	0	No
.679	155	166	176	1	No
.142	175	176	186	0	No
.818	177	186	196	0	No
.224	192	196	206	0	No
.165	210	210	220	0	No
.095	234	234	244	0	No
.038	267	267	277	0	No
.795	269	277	287	0	No
.333	280	287	297	0	No
.488	287	297	307	0	No
.911	288	307	317	0	No
.278	301	317	327	1	No
.978	301	—	—	2	Yes
.935	302	—	—	2	Yes
.490	309	327	337	1	No
.106	331	337	347	0	No
.332	342	347	357	0	No
.932	343	357	367	1	No
.190	360	367	377	0	No
.438	368	377	387	0	No
.682	372	387	397	1	No
.041	404	404	414	0	No
.255	418	418	428	0	No
.595	423	428	438	0	No
.519	430	438	448	0	No
.989	430	448	458	1	No
.416	439	458	468	1	No
.997	439	—	—	2	Yes
.101	462	468	478	0	No
.340	473	478	488	0	No
.053	502	—	—		

2 Stalls

RANDOM NO.	TIME OF ARRIVAL	STALL NO.	TIME IN	TIME OUT	NO. IN LINE	LOST CUSTOMER?
.494	7	1	7	17	0	No
.353	17	1	17	27	0	No
.407	26	2	26	36	0	No
.682	30	1	30	40	0	No
.827	32	2	36	46	0	No
.379	42	1	42	52	0	No
.535	48	2	48	58	0	No
.867	49	1	52	62	0	No
.957	49	2	58	68	0	No
.025	86	1	86	96	0	No
.503	93	2	93	103	0	No
.571	99	1	99	109	0	No
.025	136	1	136	146	0	No
.838	138	2	138	148	0	No
.281	151	1	151	161	0	No
.679	155	2	155	165	0	No
.142	175	1	175	185	0	No
.818	177	2	177	187	0	No
.224	192	1	192	202	0	No
.165	210	1	210	220	0	No
.095	234	1	234	244	0	No
.038	267	1	267	277	0	No
.795	269	2	269	279	0	No
.333	280	1	280	290	0	No
.488	287	2	287	297	0	No
.911	288	1	290	300	0	No
.278	301	1	301	311	0	No
.978	301	2	301	311	0	No
.935	302	1	311	321	0	No
.490	309	2	311	321	1	No
.106	331	1	331	341	0	No
.332	342	1	342	352	0	No
.932	343	2	343	353	0	No
.190	360	1	360	370	0	No
.438	368	2	368	378	0	No
.682	372	1	372	382	0	No
.041	404	1	404	414	0	No
.255	418	1	418	428	0	No
.595	423	2	423	433	0	No
.519	430	1	430	440	0	No
.989	430	2	433	443	0	No
.416	439	1	440	450	0	No
.997	439	2	443	453	0	No
.101	462	1	463	473	0	No
.340	473	1	474	484	0	No
.053	502					

If management were to use the simulation to make a decision concerning the number of stalls, the profit lost from customers' not stopping would have to be weighed against the cost of the second stall. Another important statistic might be the average time a customer spent waiting. Obviously, the prudent operations manager would run the simulation for more than eight hours, so that the sampling error inherent in a simulation study could be significantly reduced.

REVIEW QUESTIONS

1. Define *computer simulation.*
2. How does simulation differ from LP?
3. Discuss two major reasons for using simulation for solving decision problems.
4. Why is a computer necessary when simulating a real system?
5. What are the major phases in a simulation study?
6. What is a process generator?
7. What are uniform random numbers used for in simulation?
8. Why aren't assembler languages used to code simulation models?
9. Why is FORTRAN the most popular language used for simulation?
10. Why should one use a special-purpose simulation language?
11. List two advantages GPSS has over FORTRAN as a simulation language.
12. Why is validation an important step in any simulation study?
13. How does historical validation differ from subjective validation?
14. List three advantages of using simulation.
15. List three disadvantages of using simulation.
16. Why is the application of simulation likely to increase significantly in the near future?

PROBLEMS

1. The Page Milk Company has a large gallon-bottling machine that occasionally breaks down owing to bearing failure. The machine has two bearings of this type. In order for one of the bearings to be replaced, the machine must be shut down. This machine shutdown costs the company approximately $30 per hour. The bearings are relatively inexpensive, at $5 per bearing. At present, a bearing is replaced only when it fails. The time between bearing failures is distributed as shown in the table below. The time it takes to replace a bearing is fairly deterministic at one hour. An employee has suggested that, since it is as easy to replace both

B.S. #   R.#   B.S. time in hours   time B Ro?l. Time B@7.@n   ti(#h. ms D

bearings as one, the company should try a new policy of replacing both bearings when either one fails. Limited experience with similar bearings has yielded the following probability distribution of bearing failures when both bearings are replaced:

HOURS BETWEEN BEARING FAILURES (1 REPLACEMENT BEARING)	PROBABILITY	PmF	cdF	un R.V.
20	.05	.05	0 – .05
40	.07	.12	.05 – .12
60	.13	.25	.12 – .25
70	.35	.60	.25 – .60
80	.30	.90	.60 – .90
90	.07	.97	.90 – .97
100	.03	1.00	.97 – 1.00
	1.00		

HOURS BETWEEN BEARING FAILURES (2 REPLACEMENT BEARINGS)	PROBABILITY		
40	.05	.05	0 – .05
75	.10	.15	.05 – .15
100	.15	.30	.15 – .30
125	.25	.55	.30 – .55
150	.20	.75	.55 – .75
180	.15	.90	.75 – .90
200	.10	1.00	.90 – 1.00
	1.00		

Use manual or computer simulation to solve this policy problem. If you simulate manually, simulate for the period of one month. Assume a 24-hour workday and a 7-day workweek. *for 1 mo.   24×30 = 720 hours*

Fri. 2. The Checkmate Barbershop now has only one barber. Business is quite good, and the proprietor is trying to decide whether to hire an additional barber. Customers arrive at the barbershop at a rate of three per hour (interarrival times are distributed exponentially, with a mean of 20 minutes). The time it takes to give a haircut is exponentially distributed, with a mean of 15 minutes. The barber has noticed that when two customers are waiting for a haircut, a new customer generally will not join the queue. Haircuts cost $4, and a new barber would cost the shop $100 per week plus $1 for each haircut. Use simulation to help in the decision of whether or not to hire the additional barber. *for 8 hours ×60m = 480 min.*

3. Dr. Williams has the appointment schedule shown in the following table. Based

60° /*48°*

R.# | rime of rerival | Time in | Time out | No. waiting | Lost customers?

Dr. Williams's Appointment Schedule

APPOINTMENT TIME	PATIENT	EXPECTED APPOINTMENT DURATION
9:00	Dupont	30
9:15	Austin	20
9:45	Stratman	20
10:00	Rief	30
10:30	Lawrence	20
11:00	Cook	30
11:30	Suess	20
11:45	Collins	30

on his past experiences, Dr. Williams's estimate of arrival times is:

10% chance of a patient arriving 15 minutes early
20% chance of a patient arriving 5 minutes early
45% chance of a patient arriving on time
15% chance of a patient arriving 10 minutes late
5% chance of a patient arriving 20 minutes late
5% chance of a patient failing to arrive

The duration of each patient's appointment is a stochastic variable that, from past experience, is estimated to be distributed as follows:

10% chance that it will take 80% of the expected time
15% chance that it will take 90% of the expected time
40% chance that it will take 100% of the expected time
25% chance that it will take 110% of the expected time
5% chance that it will take 120% of the expected time
5% chance that it will take 130% of the expected time

Dr. Williams is due in surgery at 1:30 P.M. and must leave the office by 12:15 in order to make it. Dr. Williams would like to know the probability of his not having to cancel any appointments and being on time for surgery. Assume Dr. Williams gets to the office at 9:00 and sees patients on a first-come, first-served basis. Use manual or computer simulation to answer Dr. Williams's question. If you simulate manually, simulate five mornings.

4. A ski shop carries a particularly popular pair of skis that sells for $150 and wishes to know how many pairs to order and when to order. Demand is not known with certainty (see the following table). Lead time is seven days. The cost of the skis, which depends on the quantity ordered, is shown in the second table. It costs $25 to place an order, and a stockout is assumed to cost $25 per unit. Cost of carrying inventory is 20% of the value of inventory per year (.055% per day).

Historical Frequency of Demand

DEMAND PER DAY	NO. OF OBSERVATIONS
0	20
1	26
2	41
3	50
4	38
5	13
6	8
7	3
8	1
	200

Price Schedule

ORDER	PRICE PER PAIR OF SKIS
Less than 25	$100
25 or more	95
50 or more	90
100 or more	80

a. Simulate the following two inventory policies for one month (assume a 30-day month and a beginning inventory of 15 pairs with no skis on order).
   i. Order 15 pairs when inventory reaches 10 pairs.
   ii. Order 25 pairs when inventory reaches 20 pairs.
b. Which of the policies above is better? Explain.
c. What other experiments should be run?

5. The owner of a large laundromat is considering the opening of a second store. The location he has in mind can accommodate 20 washers and 10 dryers. At peak times, he has found time between arrivals to be exponentially distributed with a mean of 10 minutes. The number of washers used by one customer is random and distributed according to the table below.

NUMBER OF WASHERS	RELATIVE FREQUENCY
1	.20
2	.35
3	.20
4	.15
5	.05
6	.03
7	.01
8	.01
	1.00

Dryers can accommodate two loads of washing. Both washers and dryers take 30 minutes. The owner has found that in order for him to make a profit, the washers must be operated at 40% capacity during peak hours. Simulate manually for two hours. Should the new laundromat be installed at the proposed location? Assume that there are five customers waiting when the doors are opened for business.

6. Consider a parts department in an auto dealership. At the present time, one clerk operates the parts department, but the owner-manager of the dealership has noticed rather long lines of mechanics waiting for parts. Interarrival times of mechanics are exponentially distributed with a mean of six minutes. Service times are also exponential with a mean of five minutes. By simulating 25 arrivals, analyze the desirability of adding a second parts clerk.

7. A machine shop has two machine centers. Jobs arrive at the shop according to the following distribution:

NO. OF JOBS PER 8-HOUR DAY	RELATIVE FREQUENCY
0	.40
1	.20
2	.20
3	.10
4	.05
5	.05
	1.00

A given job can take one of the following four possible paths through the machine shop, with the indicated relative frequencies:

Machine Center 1 only—25%
Machine Center 2 only—10%
Machine Center 1, then Machine Center 2—50%
Machine Center 2, then Machine Center 1—15%

Amounts of time required for jobs on each machine center range according to the following probability distributions:

Machine Center 1

TIME IN HOURS	RELATIVE FREQUENCY
1	.10
2	.10
3	.15
4	.20
5	.10
6	.10
7	.08
8	.07
9	.07
10	.03
	1.00

Machine Center 2

TIME IN HOURS	RELATIVE FREQUENCY
1	.10
2	.15
3	.20
4	.20
5	.15
6	.10
7	.03
8	.03
9	.02
10	.02
	1.00

Simulate the machine shop for ten 8-hour days using the following machine-loading rules:

1. First come, first served.
2. Priority based on the amount of processing time left for the job. For example, if two jobs are waiting for machine center 2, and one has 5 hours of processing left and the other has 7 hours left, the job with 5 hours left would have priority.

Case: EMERGENCY AMBULANCE SERVICE*

The City of New York has been providing emergency ambulance service to residents, visitors, and transients since 1870. In 1967, the Department of Hospitals provided round-the-clock service with 109 ambulances, and responded to over a half-million calls.

---

*This case is based on a report prepared for the Mayor of New York by Dr. E.S. Savas, Deputy City Administrator. The report is entitled, "Emergency Ambulance Service," March 8, 1968. The case was prepared by Richard J. Gill, Management Analysis Center, Inc., Washington, D.C. under the supervision of Graeme M. Taylor, on behalf of the Ford Foundation and the State-Local Finances Project, George Washington University. This case is intended for class discussion only, and certain names and facts may have been changed which, while avoiding the disclosure of confidential information, do not materially lessen the value of the case for educational purposes. This case is not intended to represent either effective or ineffective handling of an administrative situation, nor does it purport to be a statement of policy by the city involved. Reprinted with the permission of Richard J. Gill.

Distributed by the Intercollegiate Case Clearing House, Soldiers Field, Boston, Mass. 02163. All rights reserved to the contributors. Printed in USA.

Organization

The city was traditionally divided into 49 hospital districts for the purpose of emergency ambulance operation.

In each of 17 districts, emergency ambulance service was operated by a municipal hospital, while in the remaining 32 districts, private hospitals operated the service under contract to the Department of Hospitals. The organization of the Department of Hospitals's ambulance service is indicated in Figure 3-4. Table 3-10 summarizes ambulance deployment.

The ambulances in each district were based at the hospital, with the ambulance attendants reporting to the head of nursing, and the drivers to the garage foreman. Until 1942, a hospital intern was assigned to each ambulance, but since then, trained attendants have been used. Ambulance attendants were typically nurse's aides who were given additional training and paid an extra $240 per month for duty on ambulances. The position was noncompetitive and did not require an examination. In 1967, 40 percent of the ambulance attendants were female.

The drivers normally had no medical training and were classified as "motor-vehicle operators" in the city's civil service scheme. They were permanently assigned to a specific garage (i.e., hospital), although they reported to the Department of Hospitals rather than to any specific hospital administrator. Their work schedule differed from the attendants' schedule. Neither attendants nor drivers were paid overtime.

Table 3-10   Emergency Ambulance Service (A): Operation of Emergency Ambulances in New York City

	HOSPITALS (DISTRICTS)		AMBULANCES		ACTUAL REPORTED TOURS* PER WEEK	
	PRIVATE	MUNICI-PAL	PRIVATE	MUNICI-PAL	PRIVATE	MUNICI-PAL
Manhattan	10	4	18	15	394	294
Bronx	1	4	1	14	21	259
Brooklyn	10	6	15	23	301	392
Queens	8	2	11	6	224	126
Richmond	3	1	4	2	84	42
Subtotal	32	17	49	60	1,024	1,113
Grand Total	49		109**		2,137	

*A tour is an operational ambulance for 8 hours (one ambulance can operate $3 \times 7 = 21$ tours/week).
**109×3 tours/day $\times 7$ days/week $= 2,289$ possible tours per week. (*Note:* "actual reported tours" do not agree with this theoretically possible figure.)

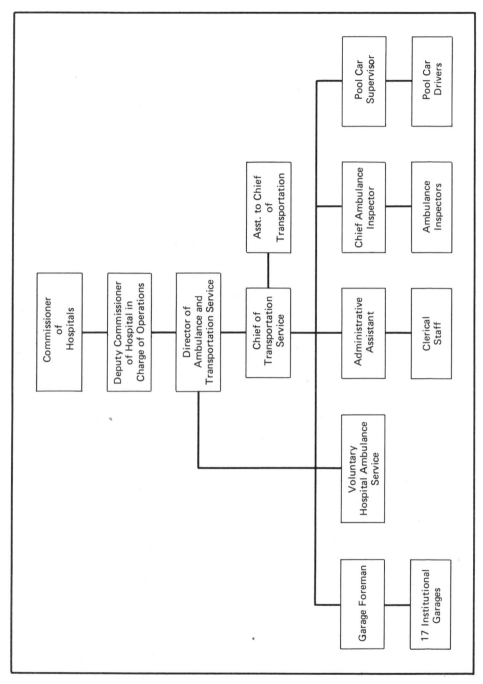

FIGURE 3-4 Emergency Ambulance Service (A)

Operation

A typical call for service originated with the police department. The police dispatcher determined the hospital district in which the emergency was located, and contacted the hospital garage by telephone. At the same time, he also dispatched a police officer to the scene. The police officer's main role was to render emergency aid prior to arrival of the ambulance, and to gather necessary information regarding the incident. In cases of illness, he sometimes assisted in moving the patient into the ambulance.

At the hospital garage, the ambulance dispatcher (foreman) assigned the call to a particular ambulance. The ambulance could communicate with the police dispatcher by radio to report its status and receive information; there was no radio communication with the hospital. (Sometimes an ambulance would be reassigned to a more urgent call while en route.)

Upon arrival at the scene, the ambulance either picked up the patient to be taken to the hospital (after necessary first aid was administered), or it was determined that no action was necessary, in which case the driver notified the police dispatcher of the ambulance's availability for assignment to another call.

The patient was taken to the hospital's emergency facilities, where appropriate treatment was administered. Upon completion of a standard form (requiring such information as patient's age, nearest relative, address, and telephone number), the patient was formally accepted by the hospital and the ambulance was released.

Table 3-11 summarizes emergency ambulance calls in 1967.

Costs

The Department of Hospitals annually entered into contracts with voluntary (i.e., private) hospitals to supply emergency ambulance service. The hospitals were paid on the basis of the number of calls handled. In 1967, the city contracted for 49 ambulances from 31 hospitals at a cost of approximately $1.87 million. All operating costs, including purchase of the ambulance(s), were borne by the private hospitals; they were reimbursed $35,000 annually for up to 3,500 calls, $37,500 for 3,501 to 5,000 calls, and $40,000 for over 5,000 calls.

The city spent approximately $4.3 million in 1967 to operate emergency ambulances attached to municipal hospitals.

Case Discussion Questions

As a systems analyst assigned to recommend improvements in the emergency ambulance service in New York City:

Table 3-11 Emergency Ambulance Service (A) : 1967 Emergency Ambulance Calls (000)

	EMERGENCY ROOM ONLY	ADMISSIONS	UNNECESSARY	DOA	OTHER HOSPITAL	NOT REMOVED	OTHER	TOTAL CALLS*
Manhattan								
Municipal	31.7	16.3	10.6	2.3	10.8	3.6	1.2	75.4
Private	38.1	10.8	12.7	3.6	23.7	4.1	0.8	88.8
Total	69.8	27.1	23.3	5.9	34.5	7.7	2.0	164.2
Bronx								
Municipal	42.1	10.6	12.6	2.2	12.1	2.9	0.3	81.1
Private	1.3	0.6	0.5	0.3	1.6	0.3	0.0	3.9
Total	43.4	11.2	13.1	2.5	13.7	3.2	0.3	85.0
Brooklyn								
Municipal	53.9	18.3	14.1	2.8	10.2	4.8	1.0	102.0
Private	35.7	7.4	11.4	2.7	17.5	3.6	1.6	75.1
Total	89.6	25.7	25.5	5.5	27.7	8.4	2.6	177.1
Queens								
Municipal	12.9	7.0	3.5	1.4	1.5	1.2	0.1	27.1
Private	14.7	3.5	4.2	2.0	15.2	2.4	0.2	39.2
Total	27.6	10.5	7.7	3.4	16.7	3.6	0.3	66.3
Richmond								
Municipal	0.0	0.0	0.0**	0.0**	0.2	0.0**	0.0	0.2
Private	2.9	2.4	0.7	0.5	1.8	0.9	0.1	8.6
Total	2.9	2.4	0.7	0.5	2.0	0.9	0.1	8.8
Whole City								
Municipal	140.6	52.2	40.7	8.7	34.9	12.6	7.5	285.8
Private	92.7	24.7	30.1	9.1	59.9	11.3	2.0	215.7
Total	233.3	76.9	70.8	17.8	94.8	23.9	9.4	501.5

*Totals may not add up, due to rounding.
**Less than 51.

1. Define the system and/or systems involved.
2. Specify possible objectives and output measures.
3. Formulate alternative ways of achieving the objectives.
4. Suggest the analytic approach you would use to evaluate each alternative.

REFERENCES

BLUMENTHAL, RALPH, "For Conrail, Model Railroad is Computer," *New York Times*, December 1, 1975, 54, 59.

BRYANT, J.W., "A Simulation of Retailer Behavior," *Operations Research Quarterly*, Vol. 26, No. 1 (April 1975), 133–49.

COHEN, KALMAN J., and E.J. ELTON, "Inter-Temporal Portfolio Analysis Based on Simulation," *Management Science*, Vol. 14 (September 1967), 5–18.

CONWAY, R.W., "An Experimental Investigation of Priority Dispatching," *Journal of Industrial Engineers*, Vol. 11 (1960), 221–30.

COOK, THOMAS M., and BRADLEY S. ALPRIN, "Snow and Ice Removal in an Urban Environment," *Management Science*, Vol. 23, No. 5 (November 1976), 227–35.

———, THOMAS M., and LAWRENCE J. GITMAN, "Cash Budgeting—A Simulation Approach," *Journal of the Midwest Financial Association*, 1973, 87–94.

———, THOMAS M., and ROBERT OGLE, "Forecasting Hospital Utilization." A paper presented at the Tenth Annual Conference of the Health Services Division of the AIIE. 1979.

———, THOMAS M., and ROBERT A. RUSSELL, "A Simulation and Statistical Analysis of Stochastic Vehicle Routing with Timing Constraints" *Decisions Sciences*, Vol. 9, No. 4 (October 1978), 673–87.

DAVIS, K. ROSCOE, "Some Aspects of Price Strategy," *OMEGA, International Journal of Management Science*, Vol. 2, No. 4 (1974), 515–22.

DeMAIRE, J. DOUGLAS, "The Overhead Crane," *Industrial Engineering*, Vol. 6, No. 3 (March 1974), 12–17.

EDEN, COLIN L., "Rules for Scheduling Semi-Automatic Machines with Deterministic Cycle Times," *International Journal of Production Research*, Vol. 13, No. 1 (January 1975), 41–55.

EILOART, TIM, and NIGEL SEARLE, "Business Games off the Shelf," *New Scientist*, September 28, 1972, 575–79.

EILON, SAMUEL, and STEPHEN MATHEWSON, "A Simulation Study for the Design of an Air Terminal Building," *IEEE Transactions on Systems, Man and Cybernetics*, SMC-3, No. 4 (July 1973), 308–17.

FETTER, R.B., and J.D. THOMPSON, "The Simulation of Hospital Systems," *Operations Research*, September–October 1965, 689–711.

GARDINER, CHRISTOPHER, and PETER W. WARD, "A Long Range Financial Resource Planning Model for a Local Authority," *Operations Research Quarterly*, Vol. 25, No. 1 (March 1974), 55–64.

GORDON, GEOFFREY, *The Application of GPSS V to Discrete System Simulation.* Englewood Cliffs, N.J.: Prentice-Hall, 1975.

———, *System Simulation.* Englewood Cliffs, N.J.: Prentice Hall, 1969.

HANNAN, EDWARD, "Planning an Emergency Department Holding Unit," *Economic Planning Science*, Vol. 9, No. 5 (October 1975), 179–88.

HERSHAUER, JAMES C., and RONALD G. EGERT, "Search and Simulation Selection of a Job-Shop Sequencing Rule," *Management Science*, Vol. 21, No. 7 (March 1975), 833–43.

HERTZ, D.B., "Risk Analysis in Capital Budgeting," *Harvard Business Review*, Vol. 42 (January–February 1964), 95–106.

HESPOS, RICHARD F., and PAUL A. STRASSMAN, "Stochastic Decision Trees for the Analysis of Investment Decisions," *Management Science*, Vol. 11, No. 10 (August 1965), B244–59.

JURECKA, W., and H. STAUBLE, "A Deterministic Simulation of the Concrete Construction of a Dam," *Operations Research*, Vol. 19, No. 6 (December 1975), B195–B207.

KWAK, N.K., P.J. KUZDRALL, and HOMER H. SCHMITZ, "The GPSS Simulation of Scheduling Policies for Surgical Patients," *Management Science*, Vol. 22, No. 9 (May 1976), 982–89.

LARSON, RICHARD C., "Decision-Aiding Tools in Urban Public Safety Systems," *Sloan Management Review*, Vol. 14, No. 2 (Winter 1972–73), 55–73.

LASDON, GAIL S., "Planning the Delivery of Outpatient Services Using Simulation," *IEEE Transactions on Systems, Man, and Cybernetics*, SMC-3, No. 5 (September 1973), 508–13.

LEGRANDE, E., "The Development of a Factory Simulation System Using Actual Operating Data," *Management Technology*, Vol. 3, No. 1 (May 1963), 1–19.

LEVENE, S.M., and J.G. WATSON, "An Assessment of the Application of On-Line Computers to Control of an Underground Railway—A Simulation Study," *Transportation Research*, Vol. 8, No. 2 (April 1974), 123–35.

MARTIN, FRANCIS F., "*Computer Modeling and Simulation.* New York: John Wiley, 1968.

MILLER, PETER J., and JAMES S. BURGESS, JR., "Simulating a Municipal Problem," *Journal of Industrial Engineering*, Vol. 7, No. 6 (June 1975), 10–14.

MILLER, S.F., "Systems-Simulation in a Practical Policy-Making Setting: The Venezuelan Cattle Industry," *American Journal of Agricultural Economics*, Vol. 55, No. 3 (August 1973), 920–32.

NANDA, R., "Simulating Passenger Arrivals at Airports," *Industrial Engineering*, Vol. 4, No. 3 (March 1972), 12–19.

NAYLOR, THOMAS H., et al., *Computer Simulation Techniques*. New York: John Wiley, 1966.

NELSON, ROSSER T., "Labor and Machine Limited Production Systems," *Management Science*, Vol. 13 (May 1967), 648–71.

NEW, C.C. "Matching Batch Sizes to Machine Shop Capabilities: An Example in Production Scheduling," *Operations Research Quarterly*, Vol. 23, No. 4 (December 1972), 561–72.

NOLAN, RICHARD L., "Productivity Estimates of the Strategic Airlift System by the Use of Simulation," *Naval Research Logistics Quarterly*, Vol. 19, No. 4 (December 1972), 737–52.

OFFENSEND, FRED L., "A Hospital Admission System Based on Nursing Work Load," *Management Science*, Vol. 19, No. 2 (October 1972), 132–38.

PACKER, ARNOLD H., "Simulation and Adaptive Forecasting as Applied to Inventory Control," *Operations Research*, Vol. 15, No. 4 (July–August 1967), 660–79 (CR 13,997).

PETERSEN, CLIFFORD C., "Simulation of an Inventory System," *Industrial Engineering*, Vol. 5, No. 6 (June 1973), 35–44.

RAPP, MATTHIAS H., "Man-Machine Interactive Transit System Planning," *Socio-Economic Planning Science*, Vol. 6, No. 1 (February 1972), 95–123.

ROCHETTE, RENE, and RANDALL P. SADOWSKI, "A Statistical Comparison of the Performance of Simple Dispatching Rules for a Particular Set of Job Shops," *International Journal of Production Research*, Vol. 14, No. 1 (1976), 63–75.

SCHMIDT, J.W., and RICHARD E. TAYLOR, *Simulation and Analysis of Industrial Systems*. Homewood, Ill.: Richard D. Irwin, 1970.

SCHRIBER, THOMAS J., *Simulation Using GPSS*. New York: John Wiley, 1974.

SHANNON, ROBERT E., *Systems Simulation: The Art and Science*. Englewood Cliffs, N.J.: Prentice-Hall, 1975.

SISSOURAS, A.A., and B. MOORES, "The 'Optimum' Number of Beds in a Coronary Care Unit," *OMEGA, International Journal of Management Science*, Vol. 4, No. 1 (1976), 59–65.

SORENSON, ERIC E., and J.F. GILHEANY, "A Simulation Model for Harvest Operations under Stochastic Conditions," *Management Science*, Vol. 16, No. 8 (April 1970), 549–65.

SWOVELAND, C., D. UYENO, I. VERTINSKY, and R. VICKSON, "Ambulance Location: A Probabilistic Enumeration Approach," *Management Science*, Vol. 20, No. 4 (December 1973), 686–98.

TYRCHMEWICZ, EDWARD W., "A Model for Rationalizing the Canadian Grain Transportation and Handling System on a Regional Basis," *American Journal of Agricultural Economics*, Vol. 55, No. 5 (December 1973), 805–13.

UYENO, DEAN H., "Health Manpower Systems: An Application of Simulation to the Design of Primary Care Teams," *Management Science*, Vol. 20, No. 6 (February 1974), 981–89.

WELLS, GARY R., "A Sensitivity Analysis of Simulated River Basin Planning for Capital Budgeting Decisions," *Computers and Operations Research*, Vol. 2, No. 1 (April 1975), 49–54.

WYMAN, F. PAUL, and GERALD CREAVEN, "Experimental Analysis of a GPSS Simulation of a Student Health Center," *Socio-Economic Planning Science*, Vol. 6, No. 5 (October 1972), 489–99.

chapter

4

QUEUING THEORY

INTRODUCTION

Queuing theory is a branch of operations research that enables the operations manager to describe the behavior of systems that involve waiting lines. For example, the decision maker charged with the responsibility of designing a ski resort could utilize queuing theory to decide on the location, number, and type of ski lifts, and the location and number of beginner, intermediate, and advanced ski runs. The objective in designing the skiing system would be to balance the cost of construction and operation of the system with the cost of waiting experienced by those staying at the resort. Queuing theory could yield the expected waiting times for the various lifts, as well as the expected lengths of the lines, utilization of facilities, and so on.

Successful applications of queuing theory can easily be found in the management science literature. For example, in the August 1976 issue of *Interfaces*, several students reported using elementary queuing models to assist a bank in making a decision on how to expand its drive-in facilities.[1] Two basic options were available: a "robo-window" system (remote tellers connected by pneumatic tubes to customer cars), and a traditional expansion of the current system that involved 8-foot-by-8-foot teller stations located on a traffic lane. The major concern of bank management was the quality of customer service and not the relative costs of the two alternatives. Data were gathered concerning arrivals and service times, and the appropriate queuing model was used to determine the distribution of waiting time. As shown in Figure 4-1, the final configuration of the drive-in banking system included the addition of two robo-windows. Bank management testifies that the system was built based on the study and that waiting times for customers had been predicted with a high degree of accuracy.

Queuing theory is often used by the manager of operations to schedule production and services. Its role in production and service scheduling is discussed in more detail in Chapter 12.

Queuing theory is different in nature from linear programming, which is treated in Chapter 2. Queuing theory does not find optimal solutions. Rather, it uses elements of statistics and mathematics for the construction of models that describe the important descriptive statistics of a queuing system. This statistical description then becomes part of the data upon which optimization decisions are based. The queuing-system descriptive statistics include such factors as the expected waiting time of the calling units, the expected length of the line, and percentage of idle time for the *service facility* (the source of goods or services for which the calling units wait).

---

[1]B.L. Foote, "A Queuing Case Study of Drive-In Banking," *Interfaces*, Vol. 6, No. 4 (August 1976), 31–37.

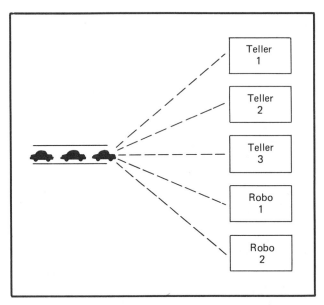

FIGURE 4-1 Approved Drive-in Banking System

When queuing theory is applied, management's objective is usually to minimize two kinds of costs: those associated with providing service and those associated with waiting time. After queuing theory has generated its statistical interpretation of the queuing system, the analyst assesses the various costs of providing service versus the costs of customer waiting in order to design the system that best meets the objectives of the organization.

THE QUEUING SYSTEM

As you can see in Figure 4-2, there are four parts of any queuing system—the calling population, the queue, the service facility, and the served calling units. Three of these entities have certain properties and characteristics that must be considered before

FIGURE 4-2 Queuing System

appropriate modeling schemes can be formulated. We shall describe the calling population, the queue, and the service facility in some detail. In general, served calling units merely leave, or exit, the system.

The Calling Population

The *calling population*, often referred to as the *input source*, has three characteristics that are important to consider when deciding on what type of queuing model to apply:

1. The size of the calling population
2. The pattern of arrivals at the queuing system
3. The attitude of the calling units

Size of the calling population. This factor has a dramatic effect on the choice of queuing models. (Compare the number of alternatives associated with infinite versus finite calling populations in Figure 4-3.) Queuing systems in which the calling population can be considered *infinite* in size are generally more likely to be amenable to analytical modeling. Examples of infinite calling populations in queuing systems are cars on a toll road and patients at the emergency room of a hospital. It is much more difficult to derive queuing models that can be applied to systems in which the calling populations are very limited. Examples of *finite*, or *limited-source, queuing systems* would include three in-house computers that must be serviced by a customer engineer if they break down, and students who may take advantage of a professor's office hours for help in a specific course.

The key to determining whether you can assume an infinite calling population is whether the probability of an arrival is significantly changed when a member or members of the population are receiving service and thus cannot arrive to the system. If there are only three calling units in a calling population and one is receiving service, the probability of another arrival is significantly reduced, because the size of the calling population is cut by 33.3 percent.

Pattern of arrivals. Calling units arrive at the queuing system either according to some predetermined schedule or in a random fashion. If arrivals are scheduled, as patients at a dentist's office are, analytical queuing models are usually inappropriate. If arrivals are random, it is necessary to determine the probability distribution of the time between arrivals. It has been shown mathematically that if the probability density function of the interarrival times is exponential, calling units arrive according to a so-called *Poisson process*. Poisson arrivals are very common in queuing systems. They generally exist in situations where the number of arrivals is independent of how many arrivals have occurred in previous time intervals. This basic property states that the conditional probability of any future event depends only on the present state of the system and is independent of previous states of the system. The *Poisson probability density function* gives the probability on k arrivals in a given time period. The mathe-

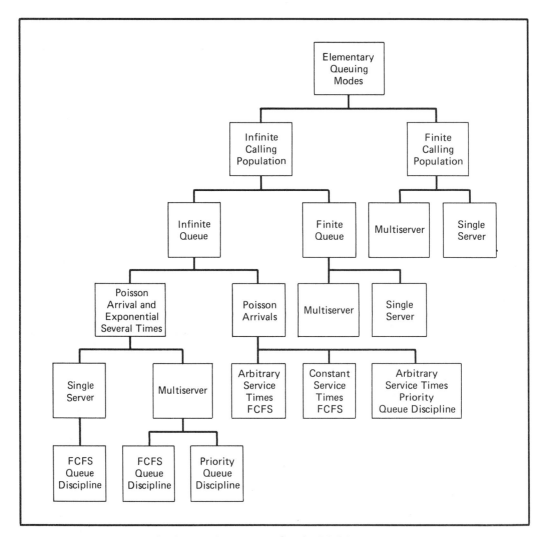

FIGURE 4-3   A Representative Sample of Elementary Queuing Models

matical form of the Poisson probability function is:

$$P(x = k) = e^{-m}m^k/k! \text{ for } m > 0; k = 0, 1, 2 \dots$$

where

e = the base of natural logarithms with a value approximately equal to 2.71828

m = mean number of events occurring in a given time period

k = number of events

Although many queuing systems have random arrivals that behave according to a Poisson process, it is possible for the interarrival times to be distributed in a nonexponential fashion. Therefore, it is necessary to determine the distribution and parameters of the interarrival time distribution statistically before deciding on how to approach any queuing problem.

Attitude of the calling units. The final characteristic of the calling population that must be considered is the attitude of the calling unit. In other words, can you assume that a calling unit will enter the queuing system regardless of the status of the system? For example, would everybody who wants to buy gas at a particular service station stop at that station if there were 15 cars waiting for service? Then, too, can you assume that a calling unit will remain in the system until served? A customer may tire of waiting and leave. Generally, most analytical queuing models assume a very patient calling unit.

The Queue

The property of queue length. This characteristic of queues is related in a sense to calling-population size and, sometimes, to calling-population attitude. In applying models, the queue is characterized by its maximum length, which can be *limited* or *unlimited*. Limitation is usually attributable either to customer attitude or to the space available for the queue. There are few choices for queuing systems that have finite queues. Generally, if you can assume that calling units join the queue regardless of its length, the probability of applying an analytical queuing model is greatly increased.

The Service Facility

The three basic properties of the service facility that we must analyze are:

1. The structure of the queuing system
2. The distribution of service times
3. The service discipline

Queuing-system structure. This characteristic is classified in part as single-phase or multiphase. A *single-phase* system is one in which the calling unit receives service from only one type of server. A pay telephone, for example, is a single-phase queuing system. A *multiphase* system exists when the calling unit must obtain the services of several different types of server. Imagine a freighter pulling into the harbor to unload its cargo: First, that freighter must obtain the services of a tugboat; then it must obtain a berth; then it must be unloaded; and after it is unloaded, the tug's services are needed again for the freighter's return to the open water.

In addition to multiphase versus single-phase structure, queuing systems can also be described as single-channel or multichannel. A *single-channel* system is a system with only one server. A *multichannel* system, on the other hand, has more than one server performing the same service. A drive-in bank facility is a single-channel system when there is only one teller on duty and a multichannel system when more than one teller is working. Obviously, queuing systems can represent any combination of phases and channels. An example of a multiphase, multichannel system is a harbor that has more than one tug and more than one berth. Figure 4-4 depicts schematics of several different queuing structures.

The great majority of queuing models are single-phase models. It is possible, nonetheless, to view a multiphase system as separate single-phase systems in which the output from one server becomes the input for another server.

Distribution of service times. Service times can be constant or random in nature. If service time is a random variable, it is necessary for the analyst to determine how that random variable is distributed. In many cases, service times are exponentially distributed; when this is the case, the probability of finding an applicable model is increased.

As you can see in Figure 4-5, if service times are exponentially distributed, the probability of relatively long service times is small. For example, the length of telephone calls has been shown to be exponentially distributed.

The important point is that you should not make assumptions concerning either the service times of the various servers in the system or, equally important, the arrival pattern of calling units without using the appropriate nonparameteric statistical tests.

Service discipline. This characteristic is the decision rule that determines which calling unit in the queuing system receives service. A service discipline (or *queue discipline*, as it is sometimes called), can be classified in one of two ways:

1. First come, first served (FCFS)
2. Priority

Most queuing systems that involve people operate with FCFS service discipline, even though it has been shown to be somewhat inefficient, simply because people usually do not tolerate other systems. Priority disciplines can be divided into two categories—preemptive priority and nonpreemptive priority. Preemptive priority disciplines allow calling units that arrive at the queuing system to replace units already receiving service. For example, consider an emergency room of a hospital when only one doctor is on duty. Obviously, if, at the time a critically ill patient arrives, that doctor is treating a patient whose condition is not critical, the patient who was being served is preempted, because a calling unit with a higher priority has arrived at the system.

Nonpreemptive priority simply causes the units in the queue to be arranged so that when a service facility becomes available, the calling unit with the highest priority receives service first. There is no displacement of units in service. Computer systems frequently use priority scheduling.

It is also possible for a queuing system to have no formal queue discipline, in which case the server selects calling units at random. Random selection often exists at the candy and popcorn counter in a movie theater or at European ski resorts.

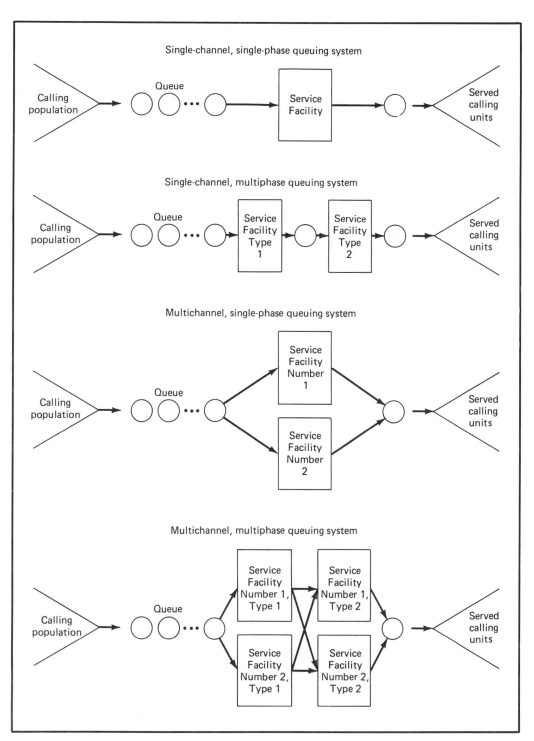

FIGURE 4-4 A Representative Sample of Elementary
Queuing-System Characteristics

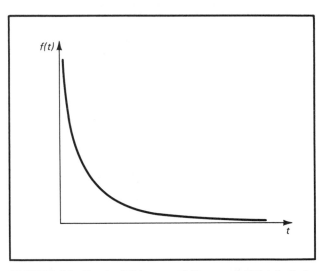

FIGURE 4-5   Graph of $f(t) = \mu e^{-\mu t}$ (**Exponential Distribution**)

Descriptive Statistics of a Queuing System

Now that we have described certain properties of its major components—the calling population, the queue, and the service facility—you should have a good notion of the nature of the queuing system itself. Before we go on to the specific subject of queuing models, you should be aware that almost all such mathematical models reveal information about the operating characteristics of a queuing system in a *steady state*. The steady-state condition exists when a system's behavior is not a function of time. Typically, a queuing system goes through a stage in which queuing statistics do not reflect long-term expected values (that is, the system does not exhibit the values you would expect it to show over the long run). This stage often occurs at a system's "start." For example, when a grocery store opens its doors in the morning, no customers are present in the system; therefore, there is a period of time when a statistic such as the expected time spent waiting in line would be understated.

ELEMENTARY QUEUING MODELS

In this section, we get down to defining some of the queuing models you first saw in Figure 4-3, and to showing the functions that describe various queuing statistics. Because the mathematics necessary to derive most queuing models is beyond the scope of this text, we have omitted model derivations. The emphasis, instead, is on identifying the assumptions of each model and on explaining how these models are used.

Notation and Definitions

In order to help you understand the specific queuing statistics that are available from most queuing models, we must first define certain queuing terms and introduce a limited amount of notation. You should become familiar with the following list of notations and definitions before you read further in this chapter:

L_q = expected or mean length of the queue (number of calling units in the queue)

L_s = expected number of calling units in the system (number in the queue plus number being served)

W_q = expected or mean time spent waiting in line

W_s = expected or mean time spent in the system (including waiting time and service time)

λ = mean arrival rate (number of calling units per unit of time)

μ = mean service rate (number of calling units served per unit of time)

$1/\mu$ = mean service time for a calling unit

s = the number of parallel (equivalent) service facilities in the system

$P(n)$ = the probability of having n units in the system

ρ = server utilization factor (that is, the proportion of time the server can be expected to be busy)

Models That Have an Infinite Calling Population

All queuing models can be classified as either infinite-source models or finite-source models. Infinite-source models are much more numerous and varied than models with finite calling populations. All queuing statistics given are steady-state statistics.

The basic single-server model. The assumptions of this model are:

1. Poisson arrival process
2. Exponential service times
3. Single server
4. FCFS service discipline
5. Infinite source
6. Infinite queue

The functions necessary to calculate the queuing statistics for the basic single-server model are given below:

$$P(0) = 1 - (\lambda/\mu)$$
$$P(n) = P(0)(\lambda/\mu)^n$$
$$\rho = \lambda/\mu$$
$$L_s = \lambda/(\mu - \lambda)$$
$$L_q = \lambda^2/[\mu(\mu - \lambda)]$$
$$W_s = 1/(\mu - \lambda)$$
$$W_q = \lambda/[\mu(\mu - \lambda)]$$

Example: The production supervisor of a large factory has decided to locate an additional tool crib geographically removed from the existing tool crib, so that production workers will have to spend less time walking to get tools. The plans are to make the tool crib a one-man operation, and the production supervisor would like to know the expected queuing statistics. From data gathered at the main tool crib, it is believed that employees will arrive at the new one at a rate of 20 per hour, and it takes an average of two minutes to service a tool request. Arrivals are believed to be Poisson and service times are exponentially distributed. First, it is necessary to determine the units of time for λ and μ. Obviously, λ and μ must be expressed in the same time units. Let's choose hours. Therefore, $\lambda = 20$ employees per hour, and $\mu = 30$ employees per hour.

The probability of an empty system is:

$$P(0) = 1 - \lambda/\mu = 1 - 20/30$$
$$= 1/3$$

The expected utilization of the tool crib is:

$$\rho = \lambda/\mu = 2/3 = .667$$

The number of employees expected to be waiting and in the process of being served is:

$$L_s = \lambda/(\mu - \lambda)$$
$$= 20/10$$
$$= 2 \text{ employees}$$

The number of workers expected to be waiting for service is:

$$L_q = \lambda^2/[\mu(\mu - \lambda)]$$
$$= 20^2/[30(30 - 20)]$$
$$= 400/300$$
$$= 1.33 \text{ workers}$$

The time an employee is expected to spend getting a tool, not counting walking time, is:

$$W_s = 1/(\mu - \lambda)$$
$$= 1/(30 - 20)$$
$$= .1 \text{ hours}$$
$$= 6 \text{ minutes}$$

The time an employee is expected to spend waiting, not counting service time, is:

$$W_q = \lambda/[\mu(\mu - \lambda)]$$
$$= 20/[30(30 - 20)]$$
$$= 20/300$$
$$= .0667 \text{ hours}$$
$$= 4 \text{ minutes}$$

Multiserver model with Poisson arrivals and exponential service times. The assumptions of this model are identical to those of the basic single-server model described previously, except that the number of servers is assumed to be greater than 1. There is an additional assumption: All servers have the same rate of service. Formulae for the basic queuing statistics are given below. The mean service rate μ in the following model refers to each server's service rate.

$$P(0) = \cfrac{1}{\sum_{n=0}^{s-1} \cfrac{(\lambda/\mu)^n}{n!} + \cfrac{(\lambda/\mu)^s}{s!}\left(1 - \cfrac{\lambda}{s\mu}\right)^{-1}}$$

$$P(n) = \frac{(\lambda/\mu)^n}{n!} P(0) \qquad \text{for } 0 \leq n \leq s$$

$$= \frac{(\lambda/\mu)^n}{s! \, s^{n-s}} P(0) \qquad \text{for } n \geq s$$

$$\rho = \lambda/s\mu \qquad \text{(assuming each server has the same mean service rate of units per time period)}$$

$$L_q = \frac{P(0)(\lambda/\mu)^s \rho}{s!(1 - \rho)^2}$$

$$W_q = L_q/\lambda$$

$$W_s = W_q + (1/\mu)$$

$$L_s = L_q + (\lambda/\mu)$$

Because $P(0)$ is difficult to calculate without making an error, tables such as Table 4-1 are often used to find the probability of an empty queuing system.

Table 4-1 Multiserver Poisson-exponential queuing system: Probability that the system is idle, p_0

$\dfrac{\lambda}{s\mu}$	2	3	4	5	6	7	8	10	15
.02	.9608	.9418	.9231	.9048	.8869	.8694	.85214	.81873	.74082
.04	.9231	.8869	.8521	.8187	.7866	.7558	.72615	.67032	.54881
.06	.8868	.8353	.7866	.7408	.6977	.6570	.61878	.54881	.40657
.08	.8519	.7866	.7261	.6703	.6188	.5712	.52729	.44933	.30119
.10	.8182	.7407	.6703	.6065	.5488	.4966	.44933	.36788	.22313
.12	.7857	.6975	.6188	.5488	.4868	.4317	.38289	.30119	.16530
.14	.7544	.6568	.5712	.4966	.4317	.3753	.32628	.24660	.12246
.16	.7241	.6184	.5272	.4493	.3829	.3263	.27804	.20190	.09072
.18	.6949	.5821	.4866	.4065	.3396	.2837	.23693	.16530	.06721
.20	.6667	.5479	.4491	.3678	.3012	.2466	.20189	.13534	.04979
.22	.6393	.5157	.4145	.3328	.2671	.2144	.17204	.11080	.03688
.24	.6129	.4852	.3824	.3011	.2369	.1864	.14660	.09072	.02732
.26	.5873	.4564	.3528	.2723	.2101	.1620	.12492	.07427	.02024
.28	.5625	.4292	.3255	.2463	.1863	.1408	.10645	.06081	.01500
.30	.5385	.4035	.3002	.2228	.1652	.1224	.09070	.04978	.01111
.32	.5152	.3791	.2768	.2014	.1464	.1064	.07728	.04076	.00823
.34	.4925	.3561	.2551	.1821	.1298	.0925	.06584	.03337	.00610
.36	.4706	.3343	.2351	.1646	.1151	.0804	.05609	.02732	.00452
.38	.4493	.3137	.2165	.1487	.1020	.0698	.04778	.02236	.00335
.40	.4286	.2941	.1993	.1343	.0903	.0606	.04069	.01830	.00248

Number of Channels, s

Table 4-1 (*Continued*)

.42	.4085	.2756	.1834	.1213	.0800	.0527	.03465	.01498	.00184
.44	.3889	.2580	.1686	.1094	.0708	.0457	.02950	.01226	.00136
.46	.3699	.2414	.1549	.0987	.0626	.0397	.02511	.01003	.00101
.48	.3514	.2255	.1422	.0889	.0554	.0344	.02136	.00820	.00075
.50	.3333	.2105	.1304	.0801	.049	.0298	.01816	.00671	.00055
.52	.3158	.1963	.1195	.0721	.0432	.0259	.01544	.00548	.00041
.54	.2987	.1827	.1094	.0648	.0831	.0224	.01311	.00448	.00030
.56	.2821	.1699	.0999	.0581	.0336	.0194	.01113	.00366	.00022
.58	.2658	.1576	.0912	.0521	.0296	.0167	.00943	.00298	.00017
.60	.2500	.1460	.0831	.0466	.0260	.0144	.00799	.00243	.00012
.62	.2346	.1349	.0755	.0417	.0228	.0124	.00675	.00198	.00009
.64	.2195	.1244	.0685	.0372	.0200	.0107	.00570	.00161	.00007
.66	.2048	.1143	.0619	.0330	.0175	.0092	.00480	.00131	.00005
.68	.1905	.1048	.0559	.0293	.0152	.0079	.00404	.00106	.00004
.70	.1765	.0957	.0502	.0259	.0132	.0067	.00338	.00085	.00003
.72	.1628	.0870	.0450	.0228	.0114	.0057	.00283	.00069	.00002
.74	.1494	.0788	.0401	.0200	.0099	.0048	.00235	.00055	.00001
.76	.1364	.0709	.0355	.0174	.0085	.0041	.00195	.00044	
.78	.1236	.0634	.0313	.0151	.0072	.0034	.00160	.00035	
.80	.1111	.0562	.0273	.013	.0061	.0028	.00131	.00028	
.82	.0989	.0493	.0236	.0111	.0051	.0023	.00106	.00022	
.84	.0870	.0428	.0202	.0093	.0042	.0019	.00085	.00017	
.86	.0753	.0366	.0170	.0077	.0035	.0015	.00067	.00013	
.88	.0638	.0306	.0140	.0063	.0028	.0012	.00052	.00010	
.90	.0526	.0249	.0113	.0050	.0021	.0009	.00039	.00007	
.92	.0417	.0195	.0087	.0038	.0016	.0007	.00028	.00005	
.94	.0309	.0143	.0063	.0027	.0011	.0005	.00019	.00003	
.96	.0204	.0093	.0040	.0017	.0007	.0003	.00012	.00002	
.98	.0101	.0045	.0019	.0008	.0003	.0001	.00005	.00001	

Example: Because tool-crib clerks earn considerably less than skilled workers, the production supervisor in the previous example would like to analyze the effect of hiring two clerks for the proposed new tool crib. Remember, λ is expected to be 20 employees per hour, and service time is expected to be two minutes. In order to help the production supervisor make a decision concerning the staffing of the tool crib, we must analyze the queuing system using two clerks and compare the pertinent descriptive statistics. Although not all queuing statistics are important to the production supervisor, we will calculate them for illustration purposes.

The probability of an empty system is:

$$P(0) = \frac{1}{\sum\limits_{n=0}^{1} \frac{(20/30)^n}{n!} + \frac{(20/30)^2}{2!}\left(1 - \frac{20}{60}\right)^{-1}}$$

$$= \frac{1}{\frac{(20/30)^0}{0!} + \frac{(20/30)^1}{1!} + \frac{(20/30)^2}{2!}\left(1 - \frac{20}{60}\right)^{-1}}$$

$$= \frac{1}{1 + 2/3 + (2/9)(3/2)}$$

$$= \frac{1}{1 + 2/3 + 1/3}$$

$$= \frac{1}{2}$$

$$= .50$$

$P(0)$ can also be found in Table 4-1 since, $\lambda/s\mu = .33$ it is necessary to interpolate between .32 and .34.

The average utilization of the tool-crib personnel is:

$$\rho = \lambda/s\mu$$

$$= \frac{20}{(2)(30)}$$

$$= .333$$

The number of workers expected to stand in line is:

$$L_q = \frac{P(0)(\lambda/\mu)^s\rho}{s!(1 - \rho)^2}$$

$$= \frac{(.5)(2/3)^2 1/3}{2!(1 - 1/3)^2}$$

$$= 1/12 \text{ workers}$$

The expected waiting time is:

$$W_q = L_q/\lambda$$
$$= \frac{1/12}{20}$$
$$= .00417 \text{ hours}$$
$$= .25 \text{ minutes}$$

The total time an employee can be expected to stay at the tool crib is:

$$W_s = W_q + 1/\mu$$
$$= .25 + 2.0$$
$$= 2.25 \text{ minutes}$$

The expected number of workers standing in line and being served at any one time is:

$$L_s = L_q + \lambda/\mu$$
$$= .25 + 20/30$$
$$= .9167 \text{ workers}$$

Now, back to the production manager's problem: whether to staff the new tool crib with one or two clerks. The pertinent queuing statistic is expected waiting time. Expected waiting time for the single-server case was 4 minutes as opposed to .25 minutes for the tool crib with two clerks. The per-worker difference in expected waiting time is, therefore, 3.75 minutes. If we expect 20 workers per hour, then the per-hour working time lost owing to having one tool crib clerk rather that two is 75 minutes [(20)(3.75)]. If tool-crib clerks make less money per hour than does the average worker, the production manager might be well advised to employ two tool clerks even though expected utilization (33.3 percent) is quite low.

Single-server model with arbitrary service times.   If the analyst has determined that arrivals to the system are Poisson-distributed but cannot accept the hypothesis that service times are exponentially distributed, it is quite possible that a valid model does exist. Specifically, the assumptions of this model are:

1.   Poisson arrival process
2.   Infinite calling population
3.   Infinite queue
4.   FCFS queue discipline
5.   Single server
6.   The distribution of service time is unknown, but it has a mean, $1/\mu$, and a variance, σ^2. These parameters are known.

The steady-state results are:

$$L_q = (\lambda^2\sigma^2 + \rho^2)/[2(1 - \rho)]$$
$$\rho = \lambda/\mu$$
$$L_s = \rho + L_q$$
$$W_q = L_q/\lambda$$
$$W_s = W_q + (1/\mu)$$
$$P(0) = 1 - \rho$$

It is interesting to note that as σ^2 increases, L_q, L_s, W_q, and W_s all increase. This means that the performance of the queuing system is not dependent solely on mean service time but on the variance in service time as well. Consequently, a server with a higher mean service time may still be the more productive if it is also the more consistent.

When service times are constant, as might be the case in a process such as a car wash, the foregoing model can be applied. The only difference is that the variance σ^2 is equal to zero. Therefore, $L_q = \rho^2/[2(1 - \rho)]$. The other relationships remain unchanged.

Example: A savings and loan association is opening a branch in a nearby suburb. This branch is expected to need one savings counselor, but management wants to have descriptive queuing statistics to confirm an intuition that only one savings counselor is actually necessary. Plans are to transfer one savings counselor from the main office. Data concerning this particular counselor's time spent with a customer have been collected, but goodness-of-fit tests indicate that these service times are not exponentially distributed. It is further estimated that the mean service time is 15 minutes and variance is 10 minutes. Customers are expected to arrive in a Poisson manner at a rate of two per hour.

$$\lambda = 2 \text{ customers per hour}$$
$$\mu = 4 \text{ customers per hour}$$
$$\sigma^2 = 1/6 \text{ hour}$$
$$L_q = \frac{4(1/6) + (1/2)^2}{2[1 - (1/2)]}$$
$$= \frac{11/12}{1}$$
$$= 11/12$$
$$= .9166 \text{ customers}$$
$$\rho = 2/4$$
$$= 1/2$$
$$L_s = 1/2 + 11/12$$
$$= 17/12$$
$$= 1.4166 \text{ customers}$$

$$W_q = \frac{11/12}{2}$$

$$= 11/24 \text{ hours}$$

$$= 27.5 \text{ minutes}$$

$$W_s = 11/24 + 6/24$$

$$= 17/24 \text{ hours}$$

$$= 42.5 \text{ minutes}$$

$$P(0) = 1 - 1/2$$

$$= 1/2$$

The foregoing queuing statistics suggest that either the savings and loan customers are going to have to be very patient or the firm will lose savings customers if it carries out its plan to have only one savings counselor.

Example: The manager of a small, coin-operated car wash is thinking about adding a vacuum cleaner to the business so that customers can vacuum the insides of their automobiles. Service time for the vacuum is constant at five minutes, and arrivals are Poisson at a rate of ten per hour. For this example, assume an infinite queue and calling population. Before investing in the vacuum, the manager wishes to know what to expect with respect to customers waiting to use it.

$$\lambda = 10 \text{ customers per hour}$$

$$1/\mu = 1/12 \text{ hour per customer}$$

$$\sigma^2 = 0$$

$$\mu = 12 \text{ customers per hour}$$

$$\rho = 5/6$$

$$= .833$$

$$L_q = \frac{(5/6)^2}{2(1/6)}$$

$$= 2.08 \text{ customers}$$

$$L_s = 5/6 + 25/12$$

$$= 2.92 \text{ customers}$$

$$W_q = \frac{25/12}{10}$$

$$= .208 \text{ hours}$$

$$= 12 \text{ minutes}$$

$$W_s = 12 + 5$$

$$= 17 \text{ minutes}$$

With these results, the manager might want to seriously consider two vacuums, since the probability of a customer's joining the queue when there are two or more cars waiting is low.

Single-server model with a finite queue.   Often, queue length constitutes a constraint on the queuing system. If queue length is limited either by customer attitude or the physical facilities, it is not possible to use any of the models previously described. The model we present in this section has assumptions identical to the first basic single-server model we developed in this chapter, except that the restriction of an infinite queue length can be dropped. The steady-state results that have been derived are as follows:

$$P(0) = \frac{1 - (\lambda/\mu)}{1 - (\lambda/\mu)^{M+1}}$$

where

$M =$ maximum number of calling units in the system and the maximum queue length is $M - 1$

$$P(n) = P(0)(\lambda/\mu)^n \qquad \text{for } n = 0, 1, \ldots M$$

$$L_s = \frac{\lambda/\mu}{1 - (\lambda/\mu)} - \frac{(M + 1)(\lambda/\mu)^{M+1}}{1 - (\lambda/\mu)^{M+1}}$$

$$L_q = L_s + P(0) - 1$$

$$W_q = \frac{L_q}{\lambda[1 - P(M)]}$$

$$W_s = W_q + 1/\mu$$

The foregoing results require that $\lambda < \mu$.

Example. Consider a one-chair barbershop. At the present location, a barber has, on the average, ten customers per day. The average haircut takes 20 minutes. Cutting time has been shown to be exponentially distributed. It has been this barber's experience that customers do not wait for a haircut if two people are already waiting. A move to a new location is possible. The new location would probably increase the number of customers per day to 15. What are the queuing statistics for the proposed new location?

$$\lambda = 15 \text{ customers per day}$$

$$\mu = 24 \text{ customers per day}$$

The probability of no one's being in the shop is:

$$P(0) = \frac{1 - \dfrac{15}{24}}{1 - \left(\dfrac{15}{24}\right)^4}$$

$$= \frac{.375}{.847}$$

$$= .443$$

The expected number of customers in the shop is:

$$L_s = \frac{\frac{15}{24}}{1 - \frac{15}{24}} - \frac{(4)\left(\frac{15}{24}\right)^4}{1 - \left(\frac{15}{24}\right)^4}$$

$$= \frac{.624}{.375} - \frac{.610}{.847}$$

$$= .947 \text{ customers}$$

The expected number of customers waiting for a haircut is:

$$L_q = .947 + .443 - 1 = .390 \text{ customers}$$

The probability of two people waiting, hence turning away customers, is:

$$P(3) = (.443) \cdot \left(\frac{15}{24}\right)^3$$

$$= .108$$

The expected waiting time is:

$$W_q = \frac{.390}{15(1 - .108)}$$

$$= .029 \text{ days}$$

$$= 13.92 \text{ minutes}$$

The total expected time for a customer to get a haircut is:

$$W_s = 13.92 + 20$$

$$= 33.92 \text{ minutes}$$

Model That Has a Finite Calling Population

In some queuing systems, the size of the calling population is so small that to assume it to be infinite would seriously degrade the usefulness of a queuing model. Some results that have been derived for a limited-source model are presented in this section. The model described next assumes a Poisson arrival process and exponentially distributed service times. It can be applied to a multiserver queuing system or a single-server system whose queue discipline is FCFS. The steady-state descriptive statistics are:

$$P(0) = \frac{1}{\left[\sum_{n=0}^{s-1} \frac{N!}{(N-n)!\,n!}\left(\frac{\lambda}{\mu}\right)^n + \sum_{n=s}^{N} \frac{N!}{(N-n)!\,s!\,s^{n-s}}\left(\frac{\lambda}{\mu}\right)^n\right]}$$

where

N = the number of calling units in the calling population
λ = mean arrival rate for each individual unit

$$P(n) = \begin{cases} P(0)\dfrac{N!}{(N-n)!\,n!}\left(\dfrac{\lambda}{\mu}\right)^n & \text{for } 0 \leq n \leq s \\[2mm] P(0)\dfrac{N!}{(N-n)!\,s!\,s^{n-s}}\left(\dfrac{\lambda}{\mu}\right)^n & \text{for } s \leq n \leq N \\[2mm] 0 & \text{for } n > N \end{cases}$$

$$L_s = \sum_{n=1}^{N} nP(n)$$

$$W_s = L_s/\lambda_e$$

where
$$\lambda_e = \lambda(N - L_s)$$

$$\begin{cases} W_q = W_s - (1/\mu) \\ L_q = \lambda_e W_q \end{cases}$$

Example: In a certain manufacturing facility are three large, numerically controlled (NC) milling machines. These three machines are repaired by two repair technicians. Each NC machine breaks down in a Poisson manner on the average of every four hours. Repair times are exponentially distributed, with a mean of three hours. Determine the steady-state queuing statistics. Let's choose hours as our unit of time. Therefore:

$$\lambda = .25 \text{ per hour} \qquad \text{and}$$

$$\mu = .33 \text{ per hour}$$

The probability of all machines being operational is:

$$P(0) = \cfrac{1}{\left[\dfrac{3!}{(3-0)!\,0!}\left(\dfrac{25}{33}\right)^0 + \dfrac{3!}{(3-1)!\,1!}\left(\dfrac{25}{33}\right)^1 + \dfrac{3!}{(3-2)!\,2!\,2^0}\left(\dfrac{25}{33}\right)^2 + \dfrac{3!}{(3-3)!\,2!\,2^1}\left(\dfrac{25}{33}\right)^3\right.}$$

$$= .177095$$

The probability of one machine being down is:

$$P(1) = .177095\left(\dfrac{3!}{2!\,1!}\right)\left(\dfrac{25}{33}\right)^1$$

$$= .402489$$

The probability of two machines being down is:

$$P(2) = .177095\left(\dfrac{3!}{1!\,2!}\right)\left(\dfrac{25}{33}\right)^2$$

$$= .304916$$

The probability of all three machines being down at one time is:

$$P(3) = .177095\left(\frac{3!}{0!\,2!\,2'}\right)\left(\frac{25}{33}\right)^3$$

$$= .115498$$

The expected number of NC machines broken is:

$$L_s = .402489 + 2(.304916) + 3(.115498)$$

$$= 1.3588 \text{ NC milling machines}$$

The effective arrival rate is:

$$\lambda_e = (.25)(3 - 1.3588)$$

$$= .4103 \text{ breakdowns per hour}$$

The expected total time it takes for a machine to become operational is:

$$W_s = 1.3588/.4103$$

$$= 3.31172 \text{ hours}$$

The expected time spent waiting for a repair technician is:

$$W_q = 3.31172 - 3.0$$

$$= .31172 \text{ hours}$$

$$= 18.7 \text{ minutes}$$

The number of NC machines expected to be waiting in line is:

$$L_q = (.4103)(.31172)$$

$$= .127899 \text{ NC machines}$$

An economic analysis of this queuing system would be possible, since the cost of waiting could conceivably be computed, as could the cost of additional repairmen. Consequently, the queuing model could be used to make a very rational decision regarding the optimal number of repairmen.

APPLICATION OF QUEUING THEORY

So far in this chapter, we have described the structure and characteristics of queuing systems and have defined several representative queuing models. By now, it is obvious to you that before a queuing model can be applied, the actual queuing system must be carefully analyzed.

Such an analysis of the queuing system should include the identification and verification of the system characteristics we described earlier. Once the system has been analyzed, the analyst must identify the decision variables. In simple queuing systems, these variables are usually the number of servers and, often, the type of server. The queue discipline often constitutes another controllable variable. Having identified decision variables, each of which is generally discrete in nature, the analyst must determine the criteria for a good set of decision variables. These criteria are usually economic in nature. The cost of the queuing system must be weighed against the waiting time of the calling units.

Two approaches to the problem of applying queuing theory to making decisions are common. One approach is to explicitly define the cost of one calling unit waiting one unit of time and then minimize an objective function such as:

$$Z = C_q + C_w$$

where

C_q = cost of the queuing system
C_w = cost of waiting

This approach is best if the cost of waiting can be explicitly defined; however, it is often very difficult to do so. If you are trying to decide on how many teller windows to have open in a bank, or how many checkout counters to have open in a super-market, the loss of goodwill caused by long lines and long waits is difficult to measure. If, however, you are trying to decide on the number of repairmen to have available to fix your productive machinery, these costs can be reasonably estimated.

The second approach to applying queuing theory is to seek to minimize a cost function subject to a set of constraints about the line length and expected waiting times. Although this approach is not so clear-cut or objective as explicitly estimating the cost of waiting, it is often more acceptable to management.

Once the queuing system has been analyzed and the criteria for decision making have been defined, the analyst must decide on the solution methodology. Either an analytical queuing model, such as one of the models presented in this chapter, can be applied, or a computer simulation model can be written. The advantages of using an analytical model as opposed to a simulation model are computational efficiency and the absence of sampling error. Although queuing theory has advanced considerably in recent years and many models have been derived, real-world queuing systems often do not have a mathematical counterpart. Rather than force a real queuing system to fit a mathematical model by simplifying the assumptions about system properties, one should use computer simulation. This relatively new tool was discussed in detail in the preceding chapter. In addition to having the flexibility to model any queuing system, simulation is not restricted to a few steady-state operating characteristics. For example, the frequency distribution of waiting times can be determined, not just the mean or expected value of waiting time.

Regardless of whether an analytical or simulation model is used to evaluate the different sets of decision variables, you should realize that determining the "best" set of decision variables is a trial-and-error process. Queuing theory is not an optimization technique; it is a descriptive tool.

SUMMARY

Queuing systems exist everywhere in the real world, and queuing theory can play an important role in the design of systems involving waiting lines and the scheduling of many services. The importance of *properly* applying analytical queuing models cannot be overstated. In order to avoid misapplication, system properties must be carefully analyzed before an appropriate model can be selected.

We have examined only a small fraction of the queuing models that have been derived, but you should realize that there is a large probability that an analytical queuing model that fits the real-world system you are interested in may not exist and may be impossible to derive mathematically. If such is the case, simulation is often used to analyze queuing systems that are too complex to be described using an analytical queuing model.

When analyzing queuing systems, it is important to understand that queuing theory, like computer simulation, is a descriptive tool that yields expected operating characteristics of the queuing system under differing configurations. Decision variables such as queue discipline, number of servers, speed of the server, and so on, must be supplied to the model and are not output from the model. Typically, the output from queuing models becomes an input to a judgmental decision concerning the configuration of the queuing system.

SOLVED PROBLEMS

Problem Statement

The city council of a small town has decided to build a tennis court in the central park. An average of ten sets of players are expected to arrive per twelve-hour day. Playing time is exponentially distributed, with a mean of one hour. Arrivals are Poisson. What are the expected queuing statistics, assuming the basic single-server model?

Solution

If we let hours be the time unit,

$$\lambda = 10/12 \text{ arrival per hour}$$

$$\mu = 1 \text{ departure per hour}$$

The probability of no one using the tennis court is:

$$P(0) = 1 - \frac{\lambda}{\mu} = 2/12 = .1667$$

The expected utilization of the tennis court is:

$$\rho = \frac{\lambda}{\mu} = 10/12 = .8333$$

The number of groups expected to be waiting for a court is:

$$L_q = \frac{\lambda^2}{[\mu(\mu - \lambda)]} = \frac{(10/12)^2}{1(1 - 10/12)} = 4.167 \text{ groups}$$

The number of groups expected to be waiting and playing tennis is:

$$L_s = \frac{\lambda}{\mu - \lambda} = \frac{10/12}{2/12} = 5 \text{ groups}$$

Expected waiting time is:

$$W_q = \frac{\lambda}{\mu(\mu - \lambda)} = \frac{10/12}{2/12} = 5 \text{ hours}$$

The expected time for waiting and playing is:

$$W_s = \frac{1}{\mu - \lambda} = \frac{1}{2/12} = 6 \text{ hours}$$

Problem Statement

Given the steady-state queuing statistics found in the preceding example, the city council wants to investigate the effect of building two tennis courts rather than one.

Solution

$$\lambda = \frac{10}{12} \qquad \mu = 1 \qquad s = 2$$

The probability of empty tennis courts is:

$$P(0) = \frac{1}{\displaystyle\sum_{n=0}^{s-1} \frac{(\lambda/\mu)^n}{n!} + \frac{(\lambda/\mu)^s}{s!}\left(1 - \frac{\lambda}{s\mu}\right)^{-1}}$$

$$= \frac{1}{\dfrac{\left(\dfrac{10}{12}\right)^0}{0!} + \dfrac{\left(\dfrac{10}{12}\right)^1}{1!} + \dfrac{\left(\dfrac{10}{12}\right)^2}{2!}\left(1 - \dfrac{\dfrac{10}{12}}{2}\right)^{-1}}$$

$$= \frac{1}{1.83 + .59523}$$

$$= \frac{1}{2.425} = .4123$$

The average utilization of the tennis courts is:

$$\rho = \frac{\lambda}{s\mu} = \frac{10/12}{2} = .4167$$

The number of groups expected to be waiting for a court is:

$$L_q = \frac{P(0)(\lambda/\mu)^s \rho}{s!\,(1-\rho)^2}$$

$$= \frac{(.4123)\left(\frac{10}{12}\right)^2 (.4167)}{2!\,(1-.4167)^2}$$

$$= \frac{.1193}{.6805}$$

$$= .1753 \text{ groups}$$

The number of groups expected to be waiting and playing is:

$$L_s = L_q + \frac{\lambda}{\mu}$$

$$= .1753 + 10/12$$

$$= 1.009 \text{ groups}$$

The expected waiting time is:

$$W_q = L_q/\lambda$$

$$= \frac{.1753}{10/12}$$

$$= .21 \text{ hours, or } 12.6 \text{ minutes}$$

The average time spent playing and waiting is:

$$W_s = W_q + \frac{1}{\mu}$$

$$= 12.6 \text{ minutes} + 60 \text{ minutes}$$

$$= 72.6 \text{ minutes}$$

Problem Statement

If the assumption about exponential service times is dropped from the single-tennis-court problem and the variance is 30 minutes, what would the queuing statistics be? Remember, $\lambda = .8333$ groups per hour, and $\mu = 1$ group per hour.

Solution

The expected length of the queue is:

$$L_q = \frac{\lambda^2\sigma^2 + \rho^2}{2(1 - \rho)}$$

$$L_q = \frac{(.8333^2)\left(\frac{1}{2}\right)^2 + .8333^2}{2(1 - .8333)}$$

$$= 2.6 \text{ groups waiting}$$

The expected utilization of the tennis courts is:

$$\rho = \lambda/\mu$$

$$= \frac{10/12}{1} = .8333$$

The average number of groups playing and waiting is:

$$L_s = \rho + L_q$$

$$= .8333 + 2.6$$

$$= 3.4333 \text{ groups}$$

The average waiting time is:

$$W_q = L_q/\lambda$$

$$= 2.6/.8333$$

$$= 3.12 \text{ hours}$$

The average time spent waiting and playing is:

$$W_s = W_q + 1/\mu$$

$$= 3.12 + 1$$

$$= 4.12 \text{ hours}$$

Finally, the probability of the court's not being used is:

$$P(0) = 1 - \rho$$

$$= 1 - .8333$$

$$= .1667$$

Problem Statement

Because of budget restrictions, city managers feel that only one tennis court can be built at the present time. Someone has suggested limiting play to one hour for each group in order to reduce waiting time and lines. How would this suggestion change the queuing statistics?

Solution

With the limitation of one hour playing time, the problem reduces to a single-server model with constant service times. The expected queuing statistics are as follows.
The expected utilization of the court remains:

$$\rho = \lambda/\mu = .8333$$

The average number of groups waiting to play is:

$$L_q = \frac{\rho^2}{2(1-\rho)}$$
$$= \frac{.8333^2}{2(1-.8333)}$$
$$= 2.08 \text{ groups}$$

The average number of groups playing and waiting is:

$$L_s = \rho + L_q$$
$$= .8333 + 2.08$$
$$= 2.9133 \text{ groups}$$

The average waiting time is:

$$W_q = L_q/\lambda$$
$$= 2.08/.8333$$
$$= 2.496 \text{ hours}$$

The average time spent playing and waiting is:

$$W_s = W_q + 1/\mu$$
$$= 2.496 + 1$$
$$= 3.496 \text{ hours}$$

Therefore, it looks as though some improvement can be made by restricting play to one hour.

Problem Statement

One member of the city council has challenged the validity of the assumption of an infinite queue. He contends that people will not wait for the court if two groups are already waiting. What effect does the omission of the infinite queue have on the queuing statistics?

Solution

The maximum number of calling units in the system is 3. The probability of the tennis court's being idle is:

$$P(0) = \frac{1 - \lambda/\mu}{1 - (\lambda/\mu)^{M+1}}$$

$$P(0) = \frac{1 - .8333}{1 - (.8333)^4}$$

$$= .3219$$

The probability of the court's being used but no line is:

$$P(1) = P(0)(\lambda/\mu)^1$$
$$= (.3219)(.8333)$$
$$= .2682$$

The probability of one group waiting is:

$$P(2) = (.3219)(.8333)^2$$
$$= .2235$$

The probability of two groups waiting, or probability of a group arriving and not staying, is:

$$P(3) = (.3219)(.8333)^3$$
$$= .1863$$

The expected number of groups playing and waiting is:

$$L_s = \frac{\lambda/\mu}{(1 - \lambda/\mu)} - \frac{(M + 1)(\lambda/\mu)^{M+1}}{1 - (\lambda/\mu)^{M+1}}$$

$$= \frac{.8333}{1 - .8333} - \frac{(3 + 1)(.8333)^4}{1 - (.8333)^4}$$

$$= 4.9988 - 3.7246$$

$$= 1.2742 \text{ groups}$$

The expected number of groups waiting is:

$$L_q = L_s + P(0) - 1$$
$$= 1.2742 + .3219 - 1$$
$$= .5961$$

The expected time spent waiting is:

$$W_q = \frac{L_q}{\lambda[1 - P(M)]}$$
$$= \frac{.5961}{.8333(1 - .1863)}$$
$$= .8791 \text{ hours}$$

The expected time spent waiting and playing is:

$$W_s = W_q + 1/\mu$$
$$= .8791 + 1$$
$$= 1.8791 \text{ hours}$$

REVIEW QUESTIONS

1. Define what is meant by the term *queuing theory*.
2. How does queuing theory differ from linear programming?
3. What are the two major costs involved in any queuing system?
4. What are the basic elements of a queuing system?
5. What characteristics of the calling population must be analyzed when applying a queuing model to a real queuing system?
6. What three basic properties of the service facility must be analyzed when applying queuing models?
7. What is meant by steady-state queuing statistics?
8. Explain two basic approaches used in applying queuing theory to decision making.
9. How would you classify the structure of a hospital's emergency room?
10. What is meant by queue discipline?

PROBLEMS

1. Analyze the following queuing systems by describing their various system properties:
   a. Barber shop
   b. Bank
   c. Machine repairman
   d. Traffic light
   e. Grocery-store checkout counter
   f. Tugs in a harbor
   g. Airport runway
   h. Computer system
   i. Hospital emergency room
   j. Gas station
   k. Car wash
   l. Tool crib
   m. Laundromat

2. A large domestic airline employs one reservation clerk in a local office during the day. The reservation clerk has suggested that another clerk be hired so that customers calling for reservations will not have to wait an inordinate amount of time. Management has decided that the average customer should not have to wait more than two minutes. In order to study the desirability of adding another reservation clerk, a study was done to determine the distribution of arrival times and service times. Calls arrived in a Poisson manner on the average of 30 per hour. The time it took to make a reservation was exponentially distributed with a mean of 1.5 minutes. Given the company's policy of an average waiting time of less than two minutes, what should the manager of the local office do with regard to hiring an additional reservation clerk?

3. The Toll Road Authority wants to know how many toll booths to design into its Main Road exit. Naturally, an objective is to minimize cost, but there is also a stipulation that the expected line length during peak hours should not exceed five cars. From data taken from other toll-road exits, it has been determined that interarrival times and service times are exponentially distributed. The peak arrival rate is expected to be ten cars per minute. The average service time is 15 seconds. How many toll booths should be designed into the system?

4. At Disneyland, plans are being made to install a new ride. Management would like to get a feel for the length of lines and the expected waiting times for this ride so that a decision can be made on whether to have one or two such installations. People arrive in a Poisson manner, but the time the ride takes is constant. Estimates are that people will arrive at a rate of one every two minutes. The ride takes 1.75 minutes. Analyze the queuing system.

5. The local supermarket has the policy that checks are cashed by the store manager only. Customers wishing to cash checks arrive in a Poisson manner at an average rate of 45 customers per hour. The manager takes, on the average, one minute to cash a check. This service time has been shown to be exponentially distributed.

  a. Compute the percentage of time that the manager spends cashing checks.

  b. Compute the average time a customer is expected to wait.

  c. Compute the number of customers waiting to get checks cashed.

  d. Compute the probability of the manager's attending to some other function, assuming that check cashing is the manager's first priority.

  e. Explain to the manager how you would analyze the effect of adding the assistant manager to the check-cashing function.

6. Two lawyers are in partnership. Each lawyer has a secretary. Jobs arrive for each secretary in a Poisson manner at a rate of three per hour, on the average. It takes either secretary an average of 15 minutes to accomplish each individual job. This service time is exponentially distributed.

  a. Assuming that each secretary does only the work of one lawyer, what is the expected waiting time for each job?

  b. What would be the effect of pooling the secretaries?

7. A certain computer company has five identical computers. Each machine fails on the average of ten times per week, and it takes a customer engineer an average of 2.5 hours to fix a machine. Historical data indicate a Poisson arrival process and exponential service times. Because of serious scheduling consequences, management does not want a machine down for more than three hours. For this reason, it has been decided that expected waiting time should not exceed $\frac{1}{2}$ hour. Assume the facility operates 24 hours per day and seven days per week.

  a. What are the expected times a machine will have to wait with one customer engineer on duty? With two customer engineers on duty?

  b. What is your recommendation to management?

  c. What options do you think management has in addition to increasing the number of customer engineers?

8. An administrator at a small hospital is contemplating a relocation of the hospital's X-ray facility. Currently, the X-ray department is so located that only two patients can be waiting for the X-ray machine at one time, with the result that emergency patients are sent back to emergency and inpatients sent back to their rooms. The potential new location would double the amount of waiting space available. Arrivals at X-ray occur in a Poisson manner at a rate of six per hour. On the average, it takes about eight minutes to service an X-ray request. These service times have been shown to be exponential. Analyze the administrator's decision problem, using queuing theory.

9. Ships arrive at a harbor in a Poisson fashion at a rate of five per 8-hour day. It takes the one tug servicing the harbor an average of one hour per ship. Tugging has been shown to be normally distributed with a variance of 16 minutes. Compute the steady-state queuing statistics for the harbor tug operation.

10. A free one-doctor outpatient clinic of a hospital takes patients without appointments from 1:00 to 5:00 in the afternoon. Patients arrive according to a Poisson process at a rate of five per hour. Service times are exponential, with a mean of ten minutes. Patients are taken on a first-come, first-served basis. Apply the appropriate queuing model and calculate pertinent queuing statistics. What assumptions did you make about the outpatient clinic?

11. Can employing two doctors be justified, in your judgment, for the outpatient clinic described in problem 10?

12. A one-pump service station has room for only two cars waiting. Cars arrive at the station in a Poisson manner at a rate of ten cars per hour. It takes, on the average, four minutes to service a customer. These times are thought to be exponential. What are the expected queuing statistics for the service station? What specifically are the assumptions of your queuing model?

13. A flying club is contemplating the construction of its own private airport. Plans are to build one landing strip. Demand for the landing strip is estimated by club members to be seven planes per hour. Landing times are known to be normally distributed, with a mean of five minutes and standard deviation of two minutes. If arrivals are assumed to be Poisson, what are the expected queuing statistics?

14. The manager of a large department store has noticed long customer lines in the catalog sales department. At present, the department has two clerks. The manager has asked you to do a study and recommend changes in the system to decrease customer waiting time and the length of the lines. You have collected arrival and service time data and have found that arrivals are Poisson-distributed and service times are exponentially distributed. Customers arrive at an average rate of 20 per hour, and the average catalog sale takes five minutes. Analyze the problem and make your recommendation to the store manager.

Case: PIERCE AND PIERCE PUBLIC WAREHOUSE*

Jerry and John Pierce are making plans for their new public warehouse in Memphis, Tennessee. Presently, the Pierce brothers own and operate a public warehouse in Tulsa, Oklahoma. Their father, Sinclair Pierce, built it in 1948 and financed it by an inheritance received in 1946. Prior to the inheritance, Sinclair Pierce managed a supply depot for one of the major oil-drilling companies in Tulsa. The idea for a public warehouse originated because the drilling company received numerous requests from area industrial firms to store equipment and supplies in its large, well-secured depot warehouses. The oil-drilling company issued storage permits as a favor to area firms, but permits were always temporary and were quickly rescinded if the storage space was required by the drilling company. Hence, Sinclair Pierce had a "readymade" market for his warehouse in 1948.

Pierce's sons, Jerry and John took over the management of the warehouse in 1967 when Sinclair retired after a minor heart attack. Jerry directs the opera-

---

*This case was reprinted by permission of The Charles E. Merrill Publishing Co., from *Cases in Production and Operation Management* by Iverstine and Kinard.

tions of the warehouse, and John is primarily responsible for customer relations. Although each owns 50 percent of the company, their father appointed the elder son, Jerry, to the position of president and as the ultimate decision maker in the company's operations. Under this arrangement, the warehouse has enjoyed a great deal of success. The Tulsa warehouse was expanded by 50 percent in 1970. Clients are both private firms and public organizations, including the Tulsa County School Board and the City of Tulsa Streets and Parks Commission.

Because of the success of the Tulsa warehouse, the Pierce brothers have decided to build another facility in Memphis. The site was selected because Memphis is located at the intersection of Interstate Highways 55 and 40 and is located on the Mississippi River. Also, Memphis is one of the main hubs of the Illinois Central Railroad. Hence, in 1973, land was purchased to build the new facility on a spur of the ICRR in southeast Memphis.

A major factor in planning the new warehouse is the determination of the number of docking platforms to service the incoming and outgoing trucks. The Pierce brothers do not own any trucks, so the warehouse schedule is to be almost totally dependent upon the arrival of customer trucks and common carriers for receipt and shipment of equipment and supplies. (The warehouse will also receive and ship materials by rail, but this activity can be accurately scheduled by working closely with the Illinois Central Railroad yard in Memphis.)

The frequency of arrival of customer trucks and common carriers, together with the time required to service these trucks, will determine the number of docking platforms and the number of docking crews that will be required. The number of docking platforms will determine the warehouse configuration and roadway design. The number of docking crews will dictate staffing requirements and the number of forklift trucks. (Typically, a forklift truck is used by each docking crew, and one or more are used for general warehouse operations.)

From market forecasts in the Memphis area and data from the Tulsa warehouse, four trucks per hour are expected to arrive for loading or unloading during the planned warehouse hours of 7:00 A.M. to 5:00 P.M. (Monday through Friday). The time required for servicing the trucks is expected to average 50 minutes, with a standard deviation of 15 minutes. With this information, the Pierce brothers believe that they can make docking and servicing plans.

Case Discussion Questions

1. How many docking platforms and servicing crews would you recommend for the new warehouse?
2. What nonquantitative factors would you include in this analysis?
3. What additional information would be helpful? How might you obtain this information?

REFERENCES

CHASE, R.B., and H.J. AQUILANO, *Production and Operations Management*. Homewood, Ill.: Richard D. Irwin, 1977.

COX, DAVID R., and WALTER L. SMITH, *Queues*. Agincourt, Ont.: Methuen Publications, 1961.

HILLIER, FREDERICK S., and GERALD J. LIEBERMAN, *Introduction to Operations Research*, 2nd ed. San Francisco: Holden-Day, Inc., 1974.

MORSE, PHILIP M., *Queues, Inventories and Maintenance*. New York: John Wiley, 1958.

SAATY, THOMAS L., *Elements of Queuing Theory*. New York: McGraw-Hill, 1961.

TAHA, HAMDY A., *Operations Research: An Introduction*. New York: Macmillan, 1971.

TRUEMAN, RICHARD E., *An Introduction to Quantitative Methods for Decision Making*. New York: Holt, Rinehart & Winston, 1977.

part THREE

design
of productive
systems

chapter 5

PROCESS DESIGN AND FACILITIES

In Chapter 1, we viewed operations management as the management of an operational system in which inputs are transformed into outputs. In this chapter, we explore the design of the transformation process that converts inputs to outputs. The effective design of the transformation process is critical to the subsequent operation and control of the operational system.

Examples of transformation processes are common in service as well as manufacturing industries. Process design at General Motors assembly plants involves the design of a system that will convert raw materials to automobiles; process design at hospitals relates to the transformation of sick patients to healthy ones; and process design at universities involves the design of curricula and faculty to convert entering students to knowledgeable graduates. Even though manufacturing process design tends to be more complicated technically than service process design, certain similarities exist between the two.

Process design may involve a completely new design for a new product or service, or a redesign of an existing procedure. In either case, the design must completely specify the equipment that is to be used, the technical procedures, and the type of personnel. A poor design can result in higher production costs and future design adjustments, as well as uncompetitive levels of services. Large capital outlays are often required in obtaining the equipment necessary for process design. Thus, the need for an effective design is apparent.

The research and engineering phases of process design entail a great deal of creative art. There are few quantitative models that can be used to generate an effective process. A knowledge of the latest scientific and technological advancements is important, but the general experience and firsthand knowledge of the process designer is an indispensable ingredient for successful design. Communication and information exchange between the process designer and operating management must take place to ensure a design that is not only technically correct but flexible and economically sound. Effective design is an ongoing procedure in which technical improvements or new products dictate a frequent reexamination of current processes.

Historically, the criteria by which process design has been measured are productivity and economic considerations such as cost minimization. Since the early days of the Industrial Revolution and Taylor's scientific management heyday, a mechanistic point of view has greatly influenced the nature of process and job design. The principles of division of labor, automation, and specialization have been applied to the design of man–machine systems. These principles, coupled with technological advancements, have enabled man to increase his productivity by over 600 percent since the turn of the century.

These principles, however, do not remain the sole means of structuring modern man–machine systems in order to accomplish goals or work tasks. The harmonious interworkings of men, machines, and physical facilities are recognized now as depending on certain human needs and values as well as automation and economic criteria. A new sociotechnical school of thought calls for the incorporation of human and social-system needs as well as technological considerations in process and job design. However, the best technical design devoid of human considerations or the best social-system design may not in either case represent the best overall design. Figure 5-1 illustrates the notion that a best overall design must incorporate technical and social needs.

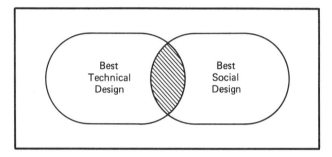

FIGURE 5-1 **Effective Process Design Incorporates Technical and Social Needs**

The recognition of certain psychological job requirements was evident earlier in the job enlargement and job enrichment schools of thought. These approaches to job and process design will be further discussed in the next chapter. The sociotechnologists feel that a systems perspective that views both technical and social factors improves the designs suggested by both the job enrichment and job enlargement approaches. Contrasting examples of designs based on automation and psychological factors, respectively, are the U.S. auto industry and the Volvo plant in Sweden. U.S. auto manufacturing is a highly technical assembly-line production process that is largely influenced by productivity. The Volvo plant in Kalmar, Sweden, has undertaken significant changes whereby a team of 15 to 25 workers now assembles an entire automobile. So far, productivity has remained approximately the same, but worker absenteeism is down significantly. It may be several more years before the success of the Volvo experiment can be measured. One thing is certain, the operations manager of the future will have to make decisions regarding the tradeoffs between mechanistic designs and worker sociopsychological needs or preferences.

In the remainder of this chapter, we shall examine product design as a necessary input to process design. Next, we shall consider some of the important aspects of process design. Even though process design is primarily a creative art, there are certain principles that apply. Closely tied to the process design problem is the plant or facilities layout problem. In this chapter, we study both product- and process-oriented layout problems. In particular, we will focus on assembly-line balancing and effective computer programs to aid in the layout design.

PRODUCT DESIGN

Product design serves as an input to process design and in many cases dictates the nature of the process design. The responsibility for product design usually lies with the marketing and engineering groups within a firm. However, these groups must interact with process designers in order to ensure the production feasibility, maintenance, and reliability of the final product. The marketing function generally initiates the search for a new product, and estimates consumer needs. Several alternatives may be considered, and a market analysis may be carried out to forecast sales and set pricing policies. Given a desired end product, it is necessary to determine the feasibility of actually producing the item. Preliminary decisions must be made regarding product attributes such as reliability, maintainability, and service life. If the "product" is actually a service, then decisions regarding quality, speed, cost, and reliability of the service are required. Product specifications are also key inputs to the associated process design. For example, food weights or volumes would be important specifications in the processed-foods industries, whereas blueprints and metallurgical constraints may be important for a manufacturing operation.

Preliminary product design requires an information exchange between the product and process designers. It must be established whether the firm currently has the capability of producing a given product. If not, then production capability must be obtained from an outside source, or else process research and development must be undertaken. Cost estimates for various process alternatives must be determined, and if R&D is involved, interaction between R&D and the product development group must take place. If an acceptable design can be created that will satisfy product specifications and cost limitations, then the final product design stage is entered. See Figure 5-2 for an illustration of the simplified steps of product design.

In the final design stage, potential shortcomings of the product should be reduced through the analysis of prototype models. The final product should be sound from the standpoint of both the production engineer and the consumer. The final design itself will include complete technical or physical specifications, required components, and assembly or "gozinto" charts. In some cases, a product testing program is initiated during the final design stage. Sample usage or test marketing may reveal minor modifications in the design phase that would improve the final product.

Purchasing: Make-or-Buy Decisions

A key issue in product design is whether to produce required materials in-house or buy from outside suppliers. This decision usually rests with the purchasing department or materials manager in conjunction with design personnel. The purchasing function is becoming an increasingly important aspect of operations management as prices escalate and material resources become more scarce. Total purchases by a manufacturing firm sometimes add up to 75 percent of sales revenues.

Design and production personnel must supply the purchasing department with accurate information concerning the materials needs of new products and quality

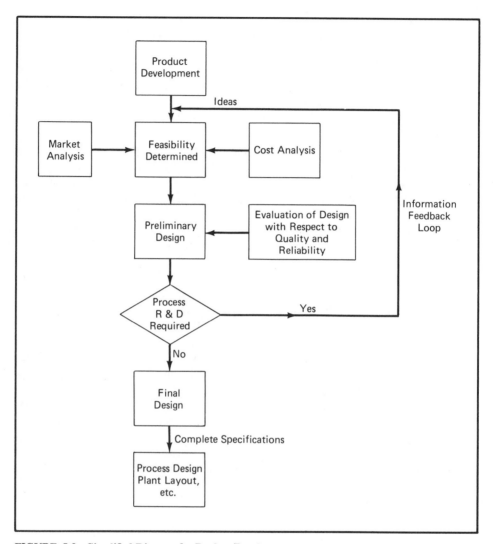

FIGURE 5-2   Simplified Diagram for Product Development

changes in current products. The production process depends on purchasing to supply the required materials at the right time. It is important to avoid shortages and the disruption of the production process. In addition to supplying materials for production, purchasing departments are responsible for buying required services and paying the proper prices.

Effective operations management requires close cooperation not only between production and marketing and engineering, but also with purchasing. Purchasing and production design should work together to achieve standardization and product simplification. Costs can be reduced by minimizing the variety of items purchased and the differences between items. An accurate estimate of monthly or annual materials requirements can sometimes enable purchasing to utilize quantity discounts by buying larger quantities. Also, blanket purchase orders can sometimes be set up to secure a certain price while receiving shipments on an "as-needed" basis. Purchasing should also be aware of market prices and materials availabilities to ensure smooth and cost-effective production. If the product design personnel are also well informed, new products will be more likely to incorporate widely available materials with lower overall costs.

Joint decisions between purchasing and design must sometimes be made as to whether a particular item should be made or bought. Such decisions may be made primarily on the basis of economic feasibility; however, noneconomic factors should also be considered. For example, patents or legal restrictions may prevent a company from manufacturing certain parts. Also, the desire to have more direct control over the quality and availability of parts may force certain firms to produce in-house. Seasonal fluctuations may call for making the part during times of low demand in order to use idle facilities, and buying the part during times when there is high competition for in-house productive resources.

Many make-or-buy decisions can also be analyzed on an economic basis. What costs can be avoided if the part is bought instead of produced? What increased production costs are incurred if the part is produced in-house? One standard type of analysis involves the use of a breakeven chart considering fixed versus variable costs of production. Assuming a linear purchase cost (no quantity discounts), the purchase costs are related to volume of parts ordered. Line A in Figure 5-3 reflects a proportional increase in costs per increase in volume. To produce in-house, however, usually involves a fixed cost that reflects a sunk cost for productive resources committed to producing the particular product. Fixed costs include machine setup costs and plant overhead. Assuming that the variable or per-piece manufacturing cost is linear, we obtain line B in Figure 5-3. The variable cost is normally less than the purchase cost of the part, but the fixed-cost component must be "covered" before it is profitable to

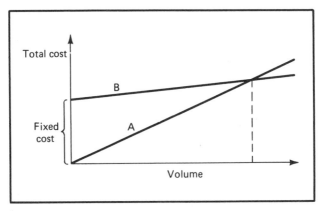

FIGURE 5-3 Breakeven Analysis

produce in-house. As the graph in Figure 5-3 suggests, a certain volume of output is required before it would be profitable to produce in-house. This volume is precisely where lines A and B cross. Expected volumes less than the breakeven point would economically favor buying, whereas volumes greater than the breakeven point would favor producing in-house. These economic factors should be ranked with noneconomic factors for the final decision.

PROCESS DESIGN

Process design has already been touched upon as a necessary forethought in the product design stage. Specifically, however, process design involves choice of processing system, specific equipment to be used, and choice of work flow. We assume at this point that the technology exists to produce the desired product and that the projected process costs are within economic reason. These questions should be answered during the product design stage.

Choice of Processing System

There are two basic types of processing systems: the intermittent or job-shop type of system, and the continuous or assembly-line type. In the intermittent system, general-purpose machines are grouped by their inherent function. The intermittent system is capable of operating on many different types of jobs at any one time. No single product has demand that is high enough to warrant continuous processing. Particular jobs may be in process at several different times during a week or month. Some examples of intermittent-type processing systems are job shops, hospital emergency rooms, insurance claim processing, restaurant kitchens, and computer systems.

Continuous or assembly-line-type processing systems are characterized by a high volume of output. Generally, a single product is processed continually by a group of special-purpose machines that are designed for a specific function and have little or no productive capability outside that function. Continuous-type processing systems are typical in automobile manufacturing, appliance manufacturing, petroleum and chemical processing, electronics industries, and many situations in which a high volume of a standardized product is desired. The advantages of continuous systems are primarily higher output and greater product consistency. Disadvantages include a greater initial investment required and lack of flexibility to accommodate product changes.

Some productive systems occur in a mixed form of the intermittent and continuous type. For example, one stage of a plant may fabricate component parts, with machines such as lathes, drill presses, and milling machines grouped together for this purpose. On the other hand, a continuous assembly-line operation may be used to assemble the parts into a final product. Even though the plant may comprise several mixed systems, each production stage usually falls into either the intermittent or continuous category. The final decision as to the type of system to be used in the entire plant or in a single stage depends upon several factors, such as output level, space restrictions, labor costs, capital investment costs, materials-handling costs, and the maintenance and reliability of the equipment. These factors, along with human and social factors, form the basis for the final decision as to the nature of the productive system.

Equipment Selection and Work Flow

Once the nature of the processing system has been determined, the remaining aspects of process design relate to the selection of specific equipment and the choice of work-flow patterns through the selected machines. In selecting equipment, whether it is special-purpose or general-purpose, a primary consideration is cost minimization. Factors such as initial capital cost, fixed and variable operating costs, and depreciation schedules are relevant. A thorough financial analysis is wise in making most capital investments. The major steps in a capital budgeting process include the generation of alternatives, estimation of costs and benefits, and finally the selection of alternatives. Several methods exist for selecting the most effective alternative. The one probably used most by practitioners is the payback method, in which the number of years required to recover the initial investment is calculated. A more effective procedure, which considers the time value of money, is the present-value method, in which future cash flows are discounted to the present and then compared to the cost of the investment. Ratios of benefits to costs can then be used to rank various alternatives. Finally, linear and 0-1 integer programming models can be used to apply an optimization approach to the capital budgeting decision process. These mathematical approaches would be useful primarily when many alternatives exist and several restrictions or constraints apply.

In addition to the financial aspects, other factors management should consider include:

1. Precision and engineering tolerances of output
2. Speed of operation
3. Flexibility in product input and output
4. Maintenance and reliability
5. Availability of replacement parts
6. Safety
7. Level of skill required of operator

Following the selection of equipment, one of the last considerations in process design is the flow of the product or parts through the productive system. Process flow is normally given some thought in earlier design stages, such as initial product design and capacity planning. It is difficult to determine appropriate equipment and output volume limitations without some idea of the flow of work through the system. In work-flow analysis, we begin to leave the physical design aspects of the transformation process and focus more on the means by which the product is processed. Work-flow analysis then overlaps with process planning, which phases in the daily operations aspects of production.

Process-flow choices deserve careful consideration, because they can affect the size of waiting lines at various facilities, storage area requirements, and the needed amount of in-process inventory required for smooth production. Continuous systems with more standard operations are easier to analyze than intermittent systems with widely differing job mixes. In job shops, some products require a unique flow routing, and thus it is difficult to estimate future process flows. The most common type of decision aids used in process planning is schematic charts. The nature of the product to be processed must be known before flow process charts can be used. The charts are a visual illustration of the logical sequence of a process and thus provide a means of examining and improving the process. An *assembly chart* shows the component parts of a product, the sequence of assembly, and the materials for flow pattern. Figure 5-4 illustrates an assembly chart for an energy economizer unit for commercial water-heating systems.

The assembly chart is more useful for preliminary design plans prior to manufacture. Operation process charts are more complete and are used to plan the exact manufacturing processes. The operation process charts specify tolerances, location and sizes of holes to be drilled for each part, and so on. Figure 5-5 illustrates a more detailed operation process chart for the economizer of Figure 5-4. This information, along with demand quantities, can be used to assign equipment and determine the sequence of operations in the process.

A common goal in the design of work flow is to avoid delays and the necessity for storage operations, as these are nonproductive stages. Intermittent processes, because of the lack of standardization, have more delays in production and transportation. Continuous processes often have fixed flows that are governed by assembly lines or overhead conveyor systems. In the plant layout section of this chapter, we shall examine some procedures for minimizing transportation and production delays. Also, in Chapter 12 on scheduling, we will study sequencing rules that aid in minimizing processing time and maximizing output from the system.

In both continuous and intermittent systems, the choice of materials-handling equipment can affect both the cost and the efficiency of transporting raw materials, parts, and finished products. We have already mentioned some common fixed materials-handling systems, such as conveyor systems. In intermittent systems as well as some continuous systems, variable-path equipment such as forklift trucks, hand trucks, electric trucks, and overhead cranes play an important part in transportation. The final selection hinges upon the type of product to be moved, layout of the plant, and costs. A financial analysis is recommended for selection of any capital equipment. Some of the more progressive production firms have implemented computer-assisted materials-handling systems. For example, at American Airlines, they have developed the DOCS (Distribution Operational Control System) for moving small to moderate-sized parts from the warehouse to the main production shop. Parts are requested in the shop by personnel who present an ID badge for clearance on a remote computer terminal processor (RTP). The message for a specified number of parts is sent imme-

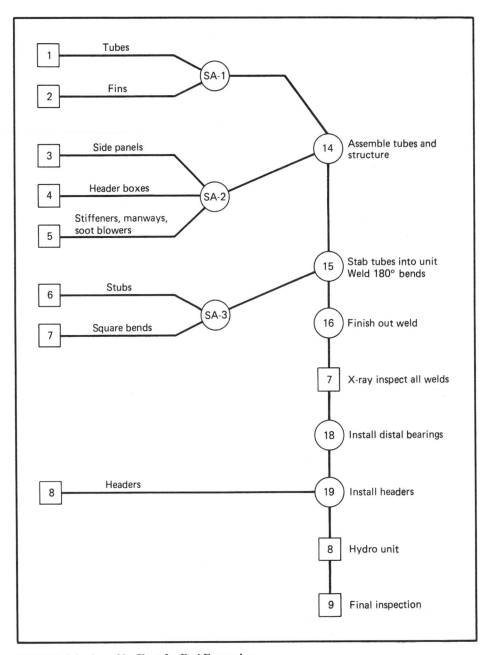

FIGURE 5-4   Assembly Chart for Fuel Economizer

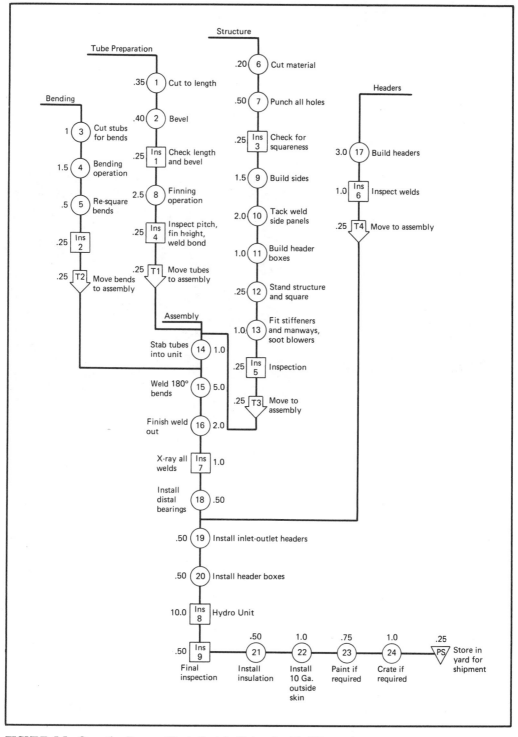

FIGURE 5-5 Operation Process Chart, Kentube Retromiser Fuel Economizer

SOURCE: Kentube Division, Tranter, Inc., Tulsa, Oklahoma.

diately to a computer-directed remote vehicle processor (RVP), or "auto-picker, which automatically selects the correct shelf in the warehouse and, with the aid of human operator, loads the required parts in a pneumatic tube system that transport the parts in a matter of minutes. Figure 5-6 depicts the remote terminal processor an remote vehicle processor for a "state-of-the-art" computerized materials-handlin system.

FIGURE 5-6 Remote Terminal Processor and Remote Vehicle Processors for State of the Art Computerized Materials Handling System

SOURCE: Reproduced courtesy of Clay Bernard Systems International.

Process Design Example

We have concentrated primarily on the process design of productive systems rather than service systems. Let us now consider the process design of a computer time-sharing system. We assume that the computer facilities are to be offered to interested users on a commercial basis. The objective is to design a system that will maximize job throughput and thus revenue.

Clearly, the technology exists (from many computer companies) to design a commercial time-sharing system. Assuming that the computer hardware is not already available, it will be necessary to purchase or lease a computer central processing unit and required peripheral equipment such as magnetic tape drives, central memory storage units, and disk drives for storage of user files and operating system software. The purchase or lease decision should be analyzed carefully, since sophisticated computer equipment costs millions of dollars and new technology renders some systems obsolete in relatively short periods of time. The choice of computer make and model depends not only on cost considerations but also such factors as systems support personnel and compatible software packages offered by the vendor. Capacity decisions regarding the speed of the CPU and size of the core memory will affect the nature of the service offered. Smaller capacity will limit not only the number of users who can process jobs on the system simultaneously, but also the size of any particular job a user can run on the system.

For large time-sharing systems, a front-end processor may be used to edit line control and the scheduling of messages between user and computer. Smaller systems can do without a front-end processor but must supply a time-sharing port for each user. The nature of the computing service to be offered will also be affected by the types of computer programs or software capability mantained by the time-sharing service. For example, the service may provide scientific programs for aid in solving problems in the physical sciences. Software packages for linear programming and many of the techniques covered in this course may also be offered, along with certain data-processing functions. Each of the services, however, incurs an additional cost for the system.

Once the computer hardware and supporting software have been selected, the remaining decisions concern the flow of jobs through the system. The computer job-flow problem is similar to the intermittent job-shop production problem, in that many jobs will possess unique characteristics. To improve throughput, most time-sharing systems process small jobs, requiring little CPU time and little memory, ahead of larger jobs. Really huge jobs are usually processed at night or at other non-prime-time hours. However, priorities can be built into the computer scheduling of jobs.

Given the hardware, software, and job-flow patterns, the computer time-sharing service is designed. However, later changes in user needs or demand pattern will require a redesign of certain aspects of the system. This is consistent with the notion that good process design is an ongoing activity.

LAYOUT DESIGN

Layout problems occur in a variety of enterprises—manufacturing plants, job shops, computer systems, fast-food restaurants, offices, and retail department stores, to name just a few. The basic nature of the layout design affects the efficiency with which the system can operate. For example, layout in a retail store can affect not only the capacity of the system relative to customers, but also the salability of various items. In this section we address some of the guidelines and techniques for layout design.

Layout is a continuation of process design. Layout decisions are closely tied to the earlier process design decisions regarding type of equipment, work flow, and choice of materials-handling systems. These earlier decisions depended on a tentative plan for the layout of the physical facility. Final decisions regarding layout may require some changes in earlier design choices. The entire process is an iterative process in which information and details gained at later stages of design are fed back to the earlier stages to arrive at a more effective and compatible system.

The layout decision concerns the most effective placement or arrangement of components within the productive or service system. These components may include machines, aisles, desks, conveyor systems, and sources of inventory. The objective may be to maximize output, minimize inventory costs, or minimize transportation delays between work stations. The overall objective may include some combination of these goals; in any case, the objectives must be clearly understood before layout decisions are made. The needed capacity of the system must also be estimated. Capacity decisions should reflect future capacity needs as well as those of the present. It is less costly to design a system once than to redesign it several times to accommodate future changes in product or service demand. For this reason, a good layout should be adaptable to accommodate variations in existing products or future developments of new products. A flexible design would also be able to respond to technological improvements in processes and equipment.

Another major consideration involves the building or site where the layout is to be located. A new building can be designed for any capacity or layout configuration. An existing building actually constrains the nature of the layout, although remodeling can provide additional space or configuration alternatives. Once the layout planner has studied the aforementioned details, he must select from a particular layout format. The two major formats we study in this chapter are product layout and process layout. We now turn to the basic issues involved in these types of layout.

Product Layout

Product layout is a type of layout in which the components are arranged according to the production stages of a particular product. The nature of the production steps of the product dictate the form of the layout; the components and work stations are devoted exclusively to the production of the single product. The equipment is special-purpose and the process is relatively inflexible. The degree of specialization required in product layout often necessitates a high fixed cost. A high volume of output is a characteristic of product layout, because it is necessary to cover the fixed cost of the special-purpose equipment. Product layout is typified in the automobile industry, appliance manufacturing, food processing, and chemical processing.

Product layout is not always capital-intensive. Sometimes it involves labor-intensive assembly lines; in this case, workers assemble the product in a sequence of work stations, and the final product emerges from the final station. Product layout, whether it is capital- or labor-intensive, is usually simpler than process layout. The layout decisions are mostly defined by the required production stages of the product to be produced. Once the special-purpose equipment is selected, little discretion is left as to the location of the equipment and work stations; these decisions are partly determined by the technological aspects of the production process. Graphic aids, such as two- or three-dimensional replicas, can be used to help in planning the layout.

Assembly-line balancing. The most challenging aspect of product layout is the achievement of a smooth product flow through the production process. The problem of smoothing the assembly process and minimizing worker or machine idle time is called the *assembly-line balancing* problem. Once the general form of the line has been established, it is necessary to break the line into work stations and determine the work content of each station. At this point, the process design problem has shifted from the macro aspects of the overall problem to the micro apsects of individual work-station content. Line balancing is really more of a scheduling problem than a layout problem; however, determining the number of work stations required can affect the layout of the line.

In line balancing, we have to divide the work to be done along the line into work elements. Work elements are small tasks that must be performed on every component passing through the line. Associated with each work element is an estimated or standard time that represents an average time required by most people or processes to complete the work element. (More will be said in Chapter 6 on establishing these standard times.)

Given the work elements and their standard times, we must group the work elements into work stations. Usually, a work station is assigned to one worker; however, more than one worker may be assigned. The problem is called a line-balancing problem, since the basic idea is to balance the work load between work stations. In line balancing, the objective is usually to (1) determine the minimum number of work stations required, given a specified cycle time; or (2) determine the minimum cycle time, given a specified number of work stations. The *cycle time* is the length of time between completed products coming off the line; it is also the length of time that the partially completed product is available at each work station. Normally, the desired level of output will determine the needed cycle time and hence the minimum number of work stations in objective 1. However, both objectives are usually considered in a line-balancing analysis. Minimizing the number or work stations is basically a layout problem, whereas determining the minimum cycle time is more of a scheduling problem.

Given the work elements and their standard times, line balancing requires that the precedence relationships between work elements be specified. *Precedence relationships* specify which work elements must precede others in order to successfully assemble the product.

To illustrate the line-balancing problem, let us consider that of the Accusound Company. In Table 5-1, we present the work elements, times, and precedence relationships for the Accusound standard bookshelf speaker. The assembly data presented in Table 5-1 can be further illustrated through the use of a precedence graph as shown in Figure 5-7. The precedence graph visually depicts the precedence relationships between work elements. Thus we can see from Figure 5-7 that tasks c and e must be completed before task f can be started.

In order to perform a line-balancing analysis, we need to know the desired cycle time. Suppose management has forecasted a demand of 400 bookshelf speakers per day. Given an eight-hour workday, this means that the company must produce 50 speakers per hour. Thus, the available cycle time is calculated as:

$$\text{Cycle time } C = \frac{60 \text{ sec./min.} \times 480 \text{ min.}}{400 \text{ speakers}} = \frac{28,800}{400} = 72 \text{ seconds}$$

Table 5-1   Assembly Tasks, Times, and Precedence Relationships for Accusound Speaker
of Figure 5-7

TASK	PERFORMANCE TIME IN SECONDS	DESCRIPTION	TASK THAT MUST PRECEDE
a	48	Wrap wire for voice coil	—
b	6	Position spider	a
c	12	Center spider in voice coil	b
d	22	Cement paper cone to surround	—
e	16	Fasten voice coil to paper cone	c, d
f	21	Attach cone and surround to frame	c, e
g	6	Position magnet and voice coil assembly	f
h	9	Tighten nut and bolt on magnet	g
i	12	Drill four 5-mm holes in frame	—
j	20	Solder lead wires to terminals	g, i
k	35	Test frequency response in anechoic chamber	h, j
	207 Total seconds		

If Accusound can produce a speaker every 72 seconds, the desired output of 400 speakers per eight-hour day can be realized.

If only one worker is used to assemble the speaker, then the least amount of time in which a speaker could be produced is 207 seconds, the total time of all tasks. This assumes that no extra time is required for operator tool changing or additional movements. Obviously, to produce a speaker in 72 seconds or less, Accusound needs more than one work station. To calculate the theoretical minimum number of work stations required to output 50 speakers per hour, we can calculate SMIN, the theoretical minimum, as:

$$\text{SMIN} = T/C = 207/72 = 2.875 \approx 3$$

where T denotes the total of all work-element times, and the value of SMIN is rounded up to the next whole number. SMIN represents only a theoretical minimum; owing to precedence relationships, the actual minimum number of work stations may exceed SMIN.

Assuming that the minimal number of work stations has been achieved, the next objective is to maintain the cycle time and distribute work loads evenly throughout the work stations. An ideally balanced line would assign the exact same total of task performance times to each work station. In the Accusound balance problem, a perfectly balanced line would consist of three work stations each having the same total work time, say, 69 seconds. However, perfectly balanced lines rarely (if ever) exist in practice.

The line-balancing problem is a combinatorial problem, in that many possible sequences exist for assigning tasks to work stations. If we let N = the total number of tasks to be performed, then without precedence relationships there are $N!$ possible ways to sequence the N steps. Precedence relationships reduce the possible number of feasible sequences to approximately $N!/2^p$, where p denotes the number of precedence relationships. In the Accusound example of Figure 5-7, there are 11 tasks and 12 precedence relationships, for approximately $11!/2^{12} = 39,916,800/4,096 = 9,745$ possible sequences. For large-scale line-balancing problems, the number of possible sequences becomes astronomically large. A systematic procedure is clearly needed to determine a good sequence that effectively balances the line.

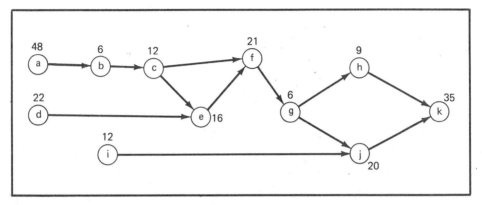

FIGURE 5-7   **Precedence Graph for Accusound Speakers**

Computational studies have shown that the dynamic programming approach of Held, Karp, and Sharesian, and the biased sampling approach of Arcus, are currently the most effective methods for balancing assembly lines.[1] However, both these techniques require significant amounts of computer computation. One relatively effective procedure, which is also easy to calculate, is the rank positional weight technique by Helgeson and Birnie.[2] This technique assigns each task a "weight" based on the sum of the time to perform that task plus the performance times of all the tasks that follow it in the precedence chart. The rule may be stated as: *Assign those tasks with the largest weights first, taking into account allowable cycle time and precedence constraints.* Thus, the ranked positional weight procedure assigns the tasks with the largest weights to the first work station (in conjunction with precedence relationships) until the sum of task times fills the cycle time. The remaining tasks are assigned in order of descending weights to work stations 2, 3, and so on.

To illustrate the procedure, let's apply it to the Accusound line-balancing problem. Referring to Figure 5-7, we can add up the performance times of all tasks and their successors. These resulting "weights" are shown in Table 5-2. Allocating tasks

[1]M. Held, R.M. Karp, and R. Sharesian, "Assembly-Line Balancing: Dynamic Programming with Precedence Constraints," *Operations Research*, Vol. 11, No. 3 (May–June 1963); A.L. Arcus, "COMSOAL: A Computer Method for Sequencing Operations for Assembly Lines," *International Journal of Production Research*, Vol. 4, No. 4 (1966).

[2]W.B. Helgeson and D.P. Birnie, "Assembly Line Balancing Using the Ranked Positional Weight Technique," *Journal of Industrial Engineering*, Vol. 12, No. 6 (November–December 1961).

Table 5-2 Ranked Weights of Tasks

TASK	*TIME OF TASK PLUS FOLLOWING TASKS*
a	173
d	129
b	125
c	119
e	107
f	91
g	70
i	67
j	55
h	44
k	35

according to the ranked positional weight rule, we obtain the work-station assignments shown in Table 5-3.

Notice at work station 2 in Table 5-3 that tasks *i* and *j* could not follow *g*, since the total time assigned to work station 2 would then exceed the cycle time of $C = 72$ seconds. The work-station configuration would appear as the sequence of steps shown in Figure 5-8.

The actual cycle time achieved for the Accusound balancing problem is $C = 70$ seconds. This is the largest total performance time at any one station. Under ideal conditions, an Accusound speaker would roll off the assembly line every 70 seconds.

One measure of the balance of an assembly line is called the balance delay factor.

Table 5-3 Ranked Positional Weight Assignments of Tasks to Work Stations

	TASK	TASK TIME	*REMAINING FEASIBLE TASK WITH HIGHEST RANK*
Work station 1	a	48	d
	d	22	—
		70 total	
Work station 2	b	6	c
	c	12	e
	e	16	f
	f	21	g
	g	6	h
	h	9	—
		70 total	
Work station 3	i	12	j
	j	20	k
	k	35	—
		67 total	

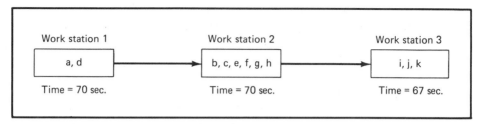

FIGURE 5-8 Work-Station Layout Along Line

This factor measures the percentage of idle time along the line. From Figure 5-8 we can see that work station 3 is idle three seconds for every speaker produced. If we let $\sum_{i=1}^{N} t_i$ denote the sum of all the task performance times and n the total number of work stations, then the balance delay factor is calculated as:

$$\text{Balance delay } d = 100 \times \frac{n \times C - \sum_{i=1}^{N} t_i}{n \times C}$$

In the Accusound example, the balance delay is:

$$d = 100 \times \frac{3 \times 70 - 207}{3 \times 70} = 100 \times \frac{210 - 207}{210} = 1.43\%$$

Any delay percentage under 10 percent is considered a relatively good balance. The balance delay factor depends upon not only the technique used to balance the line, but also the specified cycle time. Some cycle times will have a higher balance delay factor even when the line is optimally balanced. For example, if Accusound wants to produce 600 speakers a day, the required cycle time is 48 seconds. Rebalancing the line with $C = 48$, we obtain a 4-station layout as in Figure 5-9. In this solution by the ranked positional weight technique, we obtain an actual cycle time of 48 seconds and a balance delay of:

$$d = 100 \times \frac{5 \times 48 - 207}{5 \times 48} = 100 \times \frac{240 - 207}{240} = 13.75\%$$

Each station except the first will have a significant amount of idle time.

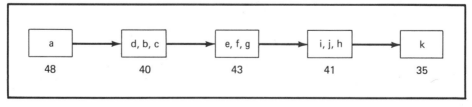

FIGURE 5-9 Line Layout with Cycle Time $C = 48$

Further considerations. Line-balancing problems involving people will undoubtedly incur operator or worker variability. The actual task performance times will vary somewhat between operators and by the same operator at different points in time. Thus, the idea of a perfectly balanced line is never a reality. One implication of operator variability is the need for in-process inventory. If the line is semipaced and the input of one station depends upon the output of the preceding one, a slow output may cause the next station to wait unnecessarily unless some in-process inventory exists to keep the next station busy. Determining an appropriate amount of in-process inventory to maintain is difficult, but computer simulation can be used as a tool in analyzing this problem. For example, the production line could be simulated with various levels of in-process inventory, and the level that provided the most production output for the cost of inventory would be selected.

Some factors in actual practice may prove to be more important to output than balance in the line. In a paced line, in which work is paced by a conveyor or machine, Conrad has found that the critical factor was how long the part or work piece was available to the operator. He found that if parts were fixed to the moving line, the operator would occasionally miss the part and reduce output. Full line capacity was utilized, however, when parts were allowed to form queues or waiting lines at the work station. Under these conditions, the operator could balance his short cycle against his long cycles to achieve the desired average output.[3]

A final consideration in line balancing concerns the human element. Thus far, the product layout analysis has been from a mechanistic point of view. The sociotechnical aspects of production lines sometimes create the problem of a choice between achieving high output and worker morale or satisfaction. Monotonous assembly-line jobs can sometimes be made more satisfying by enlarging the scope of the job at each station. This process requires that the cycle time be increased. One possible solution is to employ multiple production lines. Thus, a single line with cycle time of $C = 48$ would be equivalent to two lines with $C = 96$, or three lines with $C = 144$. Multiple lines obviously require a different layout and may impose different restrictions in terms of work flow and materials handling. One benefit of multiple lines is that the longer cycle time generally allows greater flexibility in assigning tasks to work stations, and consequently a better balance delay. Also, reliability may be improved, in that the breakdown of a single machine or line will not affect production along the other lines. The operating flexibility of multiple lines may be further backed by human considerations. What good is a theoretically balanced line if absenteeism is high or workers are on strike?

Process Layout

Process layout is characteristic of intermittent systems just as product layout is more common in continuous systems. In process layout, no one product dominates the layout scheme. Department or work areas are grouped together according to similarity

---

[3]R. Conrad and B.A. Hille, "Comparison of Paced and Unpaced Performance at a Packing Task," *Occupational Psychology*, Vol. 20, No. 1 (January 1955), 15–28.

of function. Thus, in a job shop, a deburring machine might be located near a drilling machine, and in a hospital, the nursery might be located near the labor/delivery room. The objective in locating manufacturing departments is to minimize materials-handling costs or transportation costs. In office layout, the objective may be to minimize cost-weighted employee trips between departments. A similar application in engineering office layout may attempt to locate close together work areas that have a high number of face-to-face contacts over a period of time.

Whether the process layout problem involves a manufacturing, hospital, or office system, the idea is to locate departments relative to each other in order to optimize a chosen criterion. Since intermittent systems are not restricted to fixed paths, the layout of departments must strive to be effective for the overall combination of departmental interactions. Thus, the best relative location of departments may be excellent or good for some paths in the system but poor for some others. What we need is a systematic procedure to help achieve the best overall locations.

Several quantitative models have been developed to aid in the layout decision process. Some of these are available as computer programs and have been used many times in practice. However, these quantitative models have their limitations and quite often have to be improved by human refinements on the part of the layout designer. Practical aids such as two- and three-dimensional scale models are also helpful in arriving at an effective layout. With the aid of templates or three-dimensional scale models, the designer can experiment with various layouts without actually implementing them.

To gain further insight into the nature of process layout, let's consider the following example, in which we want to arrange six hospital departments. Figure 5-10

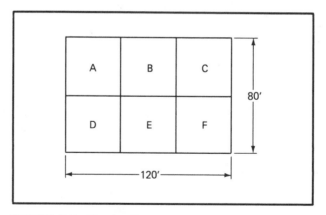

FIGURE 5-10   Hospital Floor Plan

depicts an idealized hospital floor plan in which each department is assumed to have the same dimensions. Our objective is to assign six departments to the six locations so as to minimize the sum of the products of distance and number of patient trips. Table 5-4 displays the average number of patient trips per week between the departments. This type of data could be determined from existing hospital records or collected over

Table 5-4   Patient Trips per Week

FROM DEPARTMENT		TO					
		OB/GYN 1	NURSERY 2	X-RAY 3	LAB 4	OR 5	ICU/CCU 6
OB/GYN	1		80	10	20	15	
Nursery	2.	95		5	10		
X-ray	3		15		100		8
Lab	4	20		90		25	
OR	5		20				40
ICU/CCU	6		35		60		

a period of time. If the hospital was not yet built, the interdepartmental traffic data would have to be estimated.

One objective in our layout could be to minimize the number of nonadjacent departments. However, it seems more meaningful to weight the distance of patient trips between departments by the frequency of those trips. Measuring the distances between the centers of the respective department areas, we obtain the distance matrix in Table 5-5.

Table 5-5   Distances Between Department Areas

	A	B	C	D	E	F
A	—	40	80	40	57	90
B	40	—	40	57	40	57
C	80	40	—	90	57	40
D	40	57	90	—	40	80
E	57	40	57	40	—	40
F	90	57	40	80	40	—

We can use the numbers in Tables 5-4 and 5-5 to calculate a weighted distance or "cost" for each assignment of departments to locations. These weighted distances are the distances between areas, weighted by the traffic flow between departments. For example, suppose we assign departments 1 and 2 (OB/GYN and Nursery) to areas A and B respectively. The distance between A and B is 40 feet, the traffic flow from department 1 to department 2 is 80 patients per week, and the traffic flow from department 2 to department 1 is 95 per week. Thus, the weighted distance is:

$$\text{Weighted distance} = \text{Distance} \times \text{Total traffic flow}$$
$$= 40 \times (80 + 95)$$
$$= 40 \times 175$$
$$= 7000$$

Using weighted distances emphasizes the importance of placing departments with a large amount of traffic close together. With this reasoning, it would seem from Table 5-4 that departments 1 and 2 should be close together, as well as 3 and 4, and 5 and 6. Thus, a layout designer may come up with the layout as presented in Figure 5-11.

The complex interactions between departmental distance and traffic flow make it difficult to visualize further improvement in the layout. Fortunately, quantitative models are available to aid in this decision process.

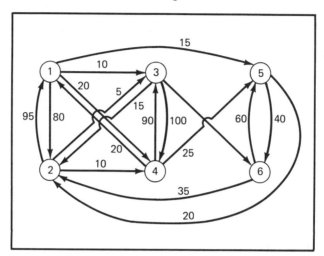

FIGURE 5-11   Flow Graph of Initial Solution

CRAFT. Computational studies have shown that one of the most effective tools is the CRAFT algorithm. CRAFT stands for Computerized Relative Allocation of Facilities Technique. CRAFT is a heuristic algorithm that was developed by G. C. Armour and E. S. Buffa.[4] Being a heuristic, CRAFT does not guarantee an optimal layout but generally yields an effective solution. The CRAFT algorithm requires a starting layout from which it tries to make improvements by exchanging the locations of two (or three) departments. For each possible exchange, the computer program calculates the net change in total weighted distance. The best exchange is kept at each trial and serves as the starting point for the next trial of exchanges. The procedure terminates when no two (or three) departmental exchanges yield a reduction in total weighted distance.

Let us apply the CRAFT heuristic to the hospital layout problem. Since there are six departments, there are 6! = 720 possible arrangements. Limiting the exchanges to only pairwise exchanges greatly reduces the number of arrangements to 15. For brevity, let's consider only pairwise exchanges of the first department with all other departments. This yields the six possible layouts shown in Table 5-6. The initial assignment of Figure 5-11 is shown with a total weighted distance of 30,501. This was

---

[4]G.C. Armour and E.S. Buffa, "A Heuristic Algorithm and Simulation Approach to Relative Location of Facilities," *Management Science*, Vol. 9, No. 1 (1963), 294–309.

Table 5-6

AREA	A	B	C	D	E	F	TOTAL WEIGHTED DISTANCE
Assigned	1	3	5	2	4	6	30,501
Departments	3	1	5	2	4	6	33,550
	5	3	1	2	4	6	43,251
	2	3	5	1	4	6	30,121
	4	3	5	2	1	6	30,731
	6	3	5	2	4	1	37,055

obtained by computing the distance times total flow between departments. Given six departments taken two at a time, there are $\binom{6}{2} = \frac{6!}{4!\,2!} = 15$ pairs of weighted distances to calculate. These are broken down as:

DEPARTMENT PAIRS	WEIGHTED DISTANCE
1–3	400
1–5	1,200
1–2	7,000
1–4	2,280
1–6	0
3–5	0
3–2	1,140
3–4	7,600
3–6	456
5–2	1,800
5–4	1,425
5–6	4,000
2–4	400
2–6	2,800
4–6	0
	30,501 Total

The fourth pair of exchanges yields a slight improvement in total weighted distance. The location of 2–A, 3–B, 5–C, 1–D, 4–E, and 6–F yields a weighted distance of 30,121. This arrangement is depicted in Figure 5-12. Whether or not this solution is optimal is not yet established. The CRAFT heuristic would proceed with another trial of paired exchanges, and so on until no improvement was found. But another improved solution, if found, still may not be optimal. Generally, however, it will be better than a manually derived layout. The vast number of calculations for even moderate-sized problems dictates the use of a computer for the CRAFT algorithm.

The actual CRAFT computer program can solve layout problems with up to 40 departments. The program requires an initial feasible layout from which it tries to make improvements. Unlike those in our simple example, the departments can be of different sizes, and they can be specified as fixed in a particular location. This feature

Area A Dept. 2	Area B Dept. 3	Area C Dept. 5
Area D Dept. 1	Area E Dept. 4	Area F Dept. 6

FIGURE 5-12 Improved Solution Layout

of the program is very useful in evaluating layouts where some of the departments are already established. Some sample computer output from the CRAFT computer program is shown in Figure 5-13.

```
      1  2  3  4  5  6  7  8  9  10 11 12 13 14 15 16 17 18
 1    A  A  A  A  B  B  B  B  B  B  B  E  E  E  D  D  D  D
 2    A        A  B              B  E     E  D           D
 3    A  A  A  A  B  B  B  B  B  B  B  E     E  D           D
 4    I  I  I  I  I  I  E  E  E  E  E  E     E  D  D  D  D  D
 5    I           I  E                          E  G  G  G  G  G
 6    I           I  E                    E  E  G           G
 7    I           I  E                    E  G  G           G
 8    I           I  E                    E  G           G
 9    I           I  E  E  E  E  E        E  G           G
10    I           I  C  C  C  C  E  E  E  G           G
11    I           I  C        C  C  E  E  G           G
12    I           I  C        C  E  E  G           G
13    I           I  C        C  E  E  G  G  G  G  G  G
14    I           I  C  C  C  C  C  E  E  G  G  H  H  H  H
15    I  I  I  I  I  I  I  I  I  I  I  I  I  I  H           H
16    I  F  F  F  F  F  F  F  F  H  H  H  H  H  H  H           H
17    F  F                    F  H                          H
18    F                       F  H                          H
19    F  F  F  F  F  F  F  F  F  H  H  H  H  H  H  H           H
20    J  J  J  J  J  J  J  J  J  J  J  J  J  J  H           H
21    J                                         J  H           H
22    J  J  J  J  J  J  J  J  J  J  J  J  J  J  H  H  H  H

TOTAL COST: 1847.90
```

FIGURE 5-13 Final Output from CRAFT for an Energizing-Office Layout

SOURCE: E.S. Buffa, *Modern Production Management*, 4th ed. (New York: John Wiley, 1973).

Other computerized layout techniques have also been developed. ALDEP and CORELAP use preference ratings instead of weighted distances between the centers of locations as the goal to be achieved. Both techniques utilize subjective managerial preferences as to the importance that locations be close together. In some cases, it may be advantageous to incorporate subjective preferences, but in several different studies, CRAFT has proved to be the most effective tool for generating layouts that achieve low materials-handling or departmental interaction costs.

Although useful, CRAFT is not without limitations. It assumes that distances between departments are always measured from the centers, and sometimes it will produce oddly shaped departments (although of the appropriate square footage). CRAFT also assumes that cost varies linearly with distance. Thus, solutions generated by CRAFT serve mainly as input to the final decision process. The layout designer has the freedom and insight to refine the computer-generated layout that is restricted by assumptions. This designer will need to consider restrictions on the locations of heavy equipment, nearness of transportation means to receiving facilities, limited access to various departments, and the confines of the facility if it already exists. The final layout should thus be the product of not only an objective analysis but also human refinements and, in some cases, managerial preferences.

SUMMARY

In this chapter, we have considered the basic issues of process design and facilities layout. We have focused upon the series of decisions that must be made in order to effectively design the transformation process. From product design to process design, an information feedback loop is necessary in order for tentative designs to be refined into final designs. The cost of appropriate forethought is far less than the potential costs of future redesigns.

We considered the macro aspects of process design, such as choice of equipment and work flow, as well as the micro aspects pertaining to the tasks at individual work stations. Facilities layout is a continuation of process design. In both product and process layout, computerized models are available to aid in the planning process. Although valuable, these computer models have their limitations, and potential users should be aware of the assumptions and limitations. Final layouts result from a blend of subjective and objective inputs.

Many of the design problems we have considered depend upon the creative insight and experience of the designer more than on a quantitative decision model. However, certain principles do exist as guidelines for design and layout problems. Most of the principles extend to service industries as well as manufacturing industries. Service industries are characterized by simpler technologies than manufacturing industries, and hence their design problems require less technical expertise.

The systems approach is the most effective approach to any type of decision problem. In process design and facilities layout, the systems approach involves the incorporation of sociotechnical as well as economic considerations. Current productive systems are dominated by economic criteria, but future systems will need to be designed with adequate consideration given to worker satisfaction and the meaningfulness of jobs.

SOLVED PROBLEMS

Problem Statement

Telcomp Co. is getting ready to produce a new line of cathode-ray-tube (CRT) computer terminals. A decision is needed on whether to produce the power supply or to purchase it from an outside supplier. The per-piece manufacturing cost would be about $47 per unit after a fixed cost of $18,000. Purchase price of the power supply is $65. Telcomp anticipates sales of 2,000 units over the next two years. How should the firm proceed?

Solution

Since variable costs appear to be proportional to units made or purchased, we can apply a breakeven analysis. The graph below shows the costs for the volume considered. For a volume of 2,000 units, the nondiscounted cost of producing the power supply is $112,000, whereas the cost of purchasing is $130,000. If Telcomp has the available production capacity and no other production alternatives are more profitable, it should produce the power-supply unit.

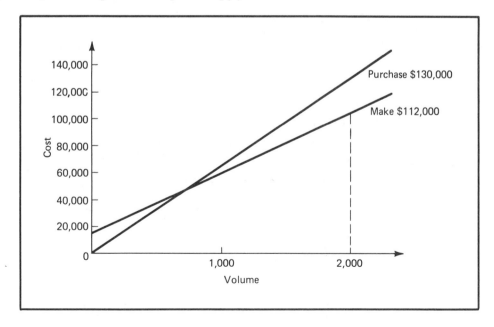

Problem Statement

A Chicago toy manufacturer produces a toy with the following precedence graph. The times associated with the tasks are in minutes.

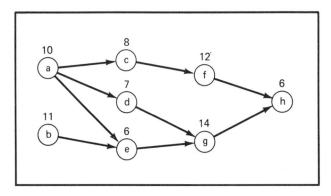

1. What is the minimum cycle time?
2. How many of these toys could the company make per 8-hour (480-min.) workday with one assembly line?
3. Given a cycle time of 20 minutes, find the minimum number of work stations and balance the line.

Solution

1. Since the maximum task time is 14 minutes, the minimum cycle time possible is 14 minutes.
2. Given one assembly line and a maximum cycle time of 14 minutes, the number of toys produced per day would be:

$$\frac{\text{time available}}{\text{cycle time}} = \frac{480}{14} = 34.28 \approx 34 \text{ toys per day}$$

3. The minimum number of work stations needed is:

$$\text{SMIN} = T/C = 74/20 = 3.7 \approx 4$$

Using the ranked positional weight heuristic, we obtain the following assignment of tasks to work stations:

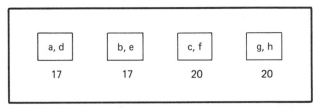

The balance delay d is only:

$$100 \times \frac{4 \times 20 - 74}{4 \times 20} = 7.5\%$$

Problem Statement

Consider a CRAFT heuristic that exchanged the location of departments three at a time. How many possible exchanges are there for 50 departments?

Solution

Taking 50 things three at a time, we obtain:

$$C_3^{50} = \binom{50}{3} = \frac{50!}{3!\,47!} = \frac{50 \cdot 49 \cdot 48}{3 \cdot 2 \cdot 1} = 19{,}600 \text{ possible exchanges}$$

Problem Statement

Figby Co. is a manufacturing concern with six main departments. The plant is broken into six main areas, as shown below.

Area 1	Area 2	Area 3
Area 4	Area 5	Area 6

The work flow between departments is shown in the following table:

			TO			
FROM	A	B	C	D	E	F
A			6	5	2	
B					3	6
C	4				7	1
D	3				8	
E		5				4
F		7	2			

How should the departments be arranged?

Solution

The main objective is usually to arrange the departments so that departments having traffic flow between them are adjacent or as close as possible. The following arrangement was obtained by inspection, but it is very effective, since all departments with flow between them are adjacent.

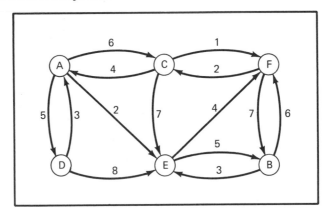

REVIEW QUESTIONS

1. What are some differences in process design between manufacturing and service industries?
2. What are some primary considerations in product design?
3. Why is it important to have an information feedback exchange between product and process design?
4. Briefly explain the sociotechnical view of process design.
5. What are the two basic types of processing systems?
6. Explain the difference between assembly and operation process charts.
7. What are the relevant factors in a make-or-buy decision?
8. How is facilities layout a continuation of process design?
9. What are two basic layout formats, and what are the likely objectives of each?
10. What conditions should exist in order for an assembly line to be justified?
11. Under which of the following conditions would you expect a worker to perform best on an assembly line? (a) Work pieces are spaced 5 feet apart on a paced line moving 5 feet per minute; or (b) work pieces are spaced $2\frac{1}{2}$ feet apart on a paced line moving $2\frac{1}{2}$ feet per minute.
12. How can you enlarge the scope of jobs on assembly lines?
13. What computerized procedures are available for process layout? How do they differ?

14. Explain how assembly-line balancing and process layout are combinatorial problems.

15. Why is a heuristic used for large-scale process layout problems?

16. What are some limitations of the CRAFT algorithm for process layout?

PROBLEMS

1. Construct an assembly chart for a pair of eyeglasses.

2. What process design problems would you expect in the following?
   a. Bank
   b. Cafeteria
   c. Hospital emergency room

3. A valve is needed to complete a particular subassembly. The Ajax Company is trying to decide whether to make the valve or buy it from an outside supplier. The valve would cost $10 from an outside supplier and $5 to produce in-house. If the fixed costs of producing the valve are $2,000 and the expected demand for the valves is 500, what should the company do?

4. Suppose that in problem 3, the demand for valves is not really certain. Management estimates that there is a 40% chance of needing 300 valves and a 60% chance of needing 600 valves. How would you approach the problem?

5. The purchasing department of Haley Manufacturing Co. is trying to decide whether to make or buy a blower motor for its new line of gas furnaces. A purchased unit would cost $110, whereas Haley could make one for $70. Assuming that the fixed costs of gearing up for production of the motor are $15,000, how large would total demand have to be in order to justify manufacturing the motor?

6. Maxwell Supply Co. orders a particular product on a monthly basis. Orders are placed at the beginning of the month and arrive at the end of the month for sale in the following month. The firm has no problem selling all available units, but its small warehouse limits storage to 120 units of the product. The firm is trying to decide on a purchasing strategy for the next quarter. Purchase and selling prices vary each month and are shown below:

MONTH	PURCHASE PRICE BEGINNING OF MONTH	SELLING PRICE DURING MONTH
Jan.	70	78
Feb.	75	80
Mar.	80	95

Fifty units of inventory are on hand before January, and none is desired after March. Formulate a linear programming model to determine how many units to buy and sell in each month in order to maximize profits.

7. Balance the Accusound speaker problem of Figure 5-7 for a cycle time of $C = 90$ seconds.

8. Solve the following line-balancing problem for a cycle time of $C = 15$.

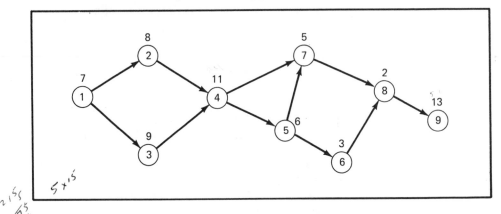

9. Consider the hospital layout problem of Table 5-4. See if you can find a layout with a lower total weighted distance than 30,121.

10. The Hartwell Electronics Co. wants to produce a microprocessor, with the work broken down into the following steps:

TASK	PERFORMANCE TIME IN SECONDS	IMMEDIATE PREDECESSORS
1	18	–
2	10	1
3	9	1
4	7	2
5	12	2, 3
6	14	4, 5
	70 sec.	

a. If Hartwell would like to produce 1,000 microprocessors per day, what is the minimal cycle time?

b. What is the theoretical minimum number of work stations required?

c. Balance the line.

d. Calculate the balance delay.

11. For a large layout problem with 25 departments, how many possible combinations of layouts are there if we consider exchanging locations only a pair at a time? three at a time?

12. Use the CRAFT heuristic rule to solve the following process layout problem. Assume the objective is to minimize total weighted distance.

Distances

To Location *j*

From Location *i*	1	2	3	4
1	—	4	7	5
2	4	—	9	5
3	7	9	—	4
4	5	5	4	—

Work Volume Between Machines

To Machine *s*

From Machine *r*	A	B	C	D
A	—	9	4	7
B	8	—	6	6
C	11	8	—	10
D	9	4	5	—

Assume that the initial layout is D–1, B–2, C–3, and A–4.

13. Develop your own solution to the layout problem presented in problem 12. Use trial and error or your own method.

14. Consider the following initial layout for six departments:

1 Receiving	2 Saw	3 Lathe
4 Mill	5 Assembly	6 Shipping

60′

90′

Below is the average interdepartmental load summary for one month:

		TO				
FROM	*REC. 1*	*SAW 2*	*LATHE 3*	*MILL 4*	*ASS. 5*	*SHIP 6*
Receiving 1		300	50	50		
Saw 2			150	100	50	
Lathe 3				250	150	
Mill 4					300	100
Assembly 5						300
Shipping 6						

Each department is 30′ × 30′ in size; estimate the distance between locations and try to find a better layout that will minimize weighted total distance between departments. Use the CRAFT heuristic.

15. Without using the CRAFT heuristic, develop your own solution to the layout example in problem 14.

Case: OTHELLO PRODUCTS, INCORPORATED*

Othello Products, Incorporated, consisted of a plant and office area of 60,000 square feet and employed 150 hourly and 32 salaried employees. Othello had been primarily a job-shop operation producing various-sized lots of medium- to high-quality precision parts for a large number of local consumer goods manufacturers. For many years, the volume of work in the shop had fluctuated widely from period to period. Consequently, Othello employees were either operating under "make work" or "get it out at any cost" conditions. This constant alternation between feast and famine caused numerous supervisory and managerial problems. To combat high costs and excessive employee turnover, the management of Othello initiated two new major programs. The first of these was a work standards program, and the second a program directed toward finding kinds of work that would provide some long-term stability to Othello's volume of business.

The work standards program was designed to provide a method for placing valid production rates on every operation of every work order issued to Othello's manufacturing organization. As an initial step, stopwatch time studies of over 800 basic operations performed on Othello's facilities were made. After the task of collecting the time studies was completed, the individual operational elements from these studies were sorted, classified, and cross-referenced. The final step was to develop a set of predetermined standard times particularly applicable to Othello's operation. It was hoped that this information would provide a means for making economical and accurate cost estimates, for setting shop production standards, and for controlling overall manufacturing costs.

*© Copyright 1977, Graduate School of Business Administration, University of Washington, Seattle, Washington 98195.

SOURCE: From Cases in Manufacturing Management by Schrieber et al., © 1965 by McGraw Hill, Inc.. Used with permission of McGraw Hill Book Company.

This adaptation will appear in *Case Book in Production and Operations Management* by Johnson et al. to be published by Prentice-Hall, Inc.

The second program consisted of an all-out effort to find one or more long-term products or contracts. An ideal product was believed to be one that was compact, easy to store, labor-intensive, and yet relatively simple to manufacture. It was felt that if the product could be manufactured for inventory during slack periods, it could provide one means of leveling the overall production rate and labor force required by the firm. After approximately a year, one such product was identified. A sketch of this product is shown in Figure 5-14.

FIGURE 5-14   Sketch of Proposed Reducer (Overall dimensions 18 × 18 × 16 inches high)

The product was a compact, variable-speed gear reducer used by a large manufacturer for whom Othello had previously made numerous experimental parts. The reducer appeared ideal in that the components required a considerable amount of medium-precision machining using equipment that Othello currently had available. Over 85 percent of the reducer's finished cost (excluding overhead and profit) consisted of direct labor. The manufacturer had issued an invitation for bids for the first production lot to a group of selected suppliers who were known to be competent in this kind of work.

Since Othello had made most of the parts for the experimental model, it had relatively complete information regarding the raw material cost and machining requirements of the component parts. Actual stopwatch time studies on many of the machine operations required had been made. It was believed that it would be easy to obtain accurate estimates of the remaining machining operations by applying the standard time data, which were scheduled to be available well ahead of the final date for submitting the bid. The major unsolved problem was to determine the assembly costs.

Table 5-7 Gear Reducer Assembly Requirements

ACTIV-ITY CODE	ACTIVITY	QUAN-TITY[1]	UNIT TIME[2]	HAN-DLING TIME[3]	CAN-NOT PRE-CEDE	TOOLING COST[4]
a[5]	Start	..	.00	.00	....	$ 0
b	Press main bearings	2	.59	.21	a	3,500
c	Press grease seals	2	.32	.15	a	1,500[6]
d	Insert welsh plugs	4	.13	.08	a	375(ab)[9]
e	Mount on chain conveyor	1	.17	....	b,c,d	......
f	Assemble main drive gear	1	1.19	.17	e	1,250(k)[9](q)[9]
g	Insert main drive gear assembly	1	.63	.07	f	......
h	Position main drive gear bearing block	1	.30	.07	g	75
i	Insert and engage bolts	4	.04	.02[7]	h	......
j	Tighten bolts with torque wrench	4	.06	.04[8]	i	225
k	Assemble reduction gear	1	.63	.17	e	(f)[9]
l	Insert reduction gear	1	.33	.09	k	......
m	Position reduction gear bearing block	1	.16	.07	l	25
n	Insert and engage bolts	4	.04	.02[7]	m	......
o	Shim for end play	1	.18	.06	m	85
p	Tighten bolts with torque wrench	4	.06	.04[8]	n,o	(j)[9]
q	Assemble idler shaft	1	.23	.17	e	(f)[9]
r	Insert idler shaft	1	.49	....	q	......
s	Position idler shaft bearing block	1	.20	.05	r	95
t	Insert and engage bolts	4	.04	.02[7]	s	......
u	Tighten bolts with torque wrench	4	.06	.04[8]	t	(j)[9]
v	Place gasket	1	.08	.02	e	......
w	Place base plate	1	.29	....	j,p,u,v	......
x	Insert and engage bolts	12	.04	.02[7]	w	......
y	Tighten bolts with torque wrench	12	.05	.04	x	(j)[9]
z	Insert pressure and lubricant fittings	4	.15	.04	e	35
aa	Fill lubricant	1	.51[10]	....	y,z	3,800
ab	Plug lubricant holes	2	.10	.05	aa	(d)[9]
ac	Pressure test	1	3.80[11]	....	ab	1,800
ad	Remove pressure fittings and plug holes	2	.29	.04	ac	60
ae	Dynamometer test	1	1.87[12]	....	ab	4,800
af	Attach name and instruc-tion plate	1	.30	.08	e	900
ag	Wipe clean	1	.26	.03	ad,ae	......
ah	Attach test results	1	.08	....	af,ag	......
ai	Release from conveyor	1	.08	....	ah	......

To obtain accurate assembly costs, several workers and a process engineer were assigned the task of devising an appropriate assembly procedure. Data in Table 5-7 are the result of these efforts. To obtain these data, each worker was allowed, uninstructed but under the surveillance of the process engineer, to assemble and disassemble a reducer. The experience gained was pooled, and from the best method used by the various workers, 34 basic assembly operations were defined. Each of these operations was then time-studied using stopwatch techniques. The times shown in Table 5-7 represent the standard unit times.

The time-study standards were based on 100 percent performance, this being the output that was expected from an average experienced worker having reasonable skill in the type of operation performed and working at a natural rate of speed. Since the time studies were made on employees who were considered to be relatively inexperienced in assembly work, an 85 percent skill rating was assigned to all operations. Because of the highly cooperative spirit of the employees, however, practically all operations were rated for effort at or above 115 percent. Thus, in almost all cases, the stopwatch standards determined were met or exceeded in the actual assembly trials.

The only remaining task with regard to estimating the assembly cost was to lay out the assembly process in terms of specific work stations and determine the equipment and labor costs. It was a company policy to maintain good

---

[1]Number of cycles or repetitions of basic operation to complete the specified activity for each unit.

[2]Time in minutes to complete a single cycle of operation included in the specified activity.

[3]Time in minutes to pick up, position, lay aside tools, etc., if more than one activity is assigned to a specific work station. For example, if activities "b" and "c" are assigned to independent work stations, the performance time is 1.18 and .64 minutes, respectively. If they are assigned to a single work station, the performance time is 2.18 minutes (1.18 + .64 + .21 + .15 = 2.18).

[4]Cost of company-supplied tools and special equipment to perform specified activity. Must be included for every work station at which all or any part of the specified activity is performed.

[5]Dummy operation. Requires no time or manpower. Assumes main castings are positioned on belt conveyor.

[6]Can substitute tool use for operation "b." Can use common tool if this operation is performed at the same work station as operation "b."

[7]Activities "i," "n," "t," and "x" can be combined without incurring handling time, since they contain identical elements and require common tools.

[8]Activities "j," "p," and "u" can be combined without incurring handling time, since they contain identical elements and require common tools.

[9]Requires identical tooling as activity shown in parentheses. Can use common set of tooling if operations are performed at the same work station.

[10]Activity completely automatic, no operator required.

[11]Activity completely automatic except for operator who must visually check for leaks. One operator can oversee the testing of up to four units simultaneously. Operator cannot perform any other function regardless of how many units he oversees.

[12]Activity completely automatic except for operator who connects hydraulic dynamometer coupling, records test results, and shuts down test equipment in case of an emergency. One operator can process up to two units simultaneously. Operator cannot perform any other function regardless of the number of units he oversees.

working conditions, and thus it was felt that the design of work stations should provide each employee with a minimum of 5 linear feet of work space along the assembly line. This was considered possible, since an area 85 feet in length and 25 feet in width was available for the placement of the line and for in-process parts storage areas. It was felt that the entire line should be conveyorized, as this would substantially reduce the problem of maintaining efficient performance. Estimates of conveyor costs indicated that the belt conveyor required for activities "a" through "d" of Table 5-7 would cost about $6,600, plus $300 per lineal foot of conveyor. This was essentially a belt conveyor from which parts could be removed for processing and replaced for transporting to the next work station.

A chain conveyor was suggested for activities "e" through "ai" of Table 5-7 and was estimated to cost approximately $9,500 plus $525 per lineal foot. This was a conveyor upon which the housing would be clamped and thus not removable at the work stations. This type of a conveyor would pace the line and allow completely automatic testing of the assembly, as the unit would be accurately and positively located at each work station.

"Banking" facilities capable of holding up to 10 parts at any given work station were available for the belt conveyor at an additional cost of $300 per station. No such facility was available for the chain conveyor. One of the conveyor firms that had been contracted quoted a price of $4,200 plus $175 per lineal foot for small feeder conveyors that could serve as feeders to the main conveyor line for parts or subassemblies.

The contract upon which Othello was bidding was for 1,800 reducers a week for a period of six months. The invitation to bid provided that if the winning bidder wished to absorb all equipment and tooling costs, he would be free to build and sell the reducer in the open market under his own trade name. To Othello management, this appeared to be an excellent opportunity for Othello to develop a new product line, and it was decided that if the contract was received, an initial 8-hour single-shift 5-day-week capacity would be installed that was 10 percent in excess of the contract demand. Since Othello was currently operating on a one-shift 5-day-week basis, this plan would comply with current operations and allow for up to a 200 percent increase in production by going to two shifts of ten hours each on a 6-day-week basis.

Case Discussion Questions

1. Sketch an approximate assembly line designating specific work stations and the operations and activities performed at each work station. At what speed should the conveyor be designed to operate?

2. What are the approximate capital and labor costs per unit associated with the line you sketched? Assume that direct labor costs average $9.65 per hour.

REFERENCES

ARCUS, A.L., "COMSOAL: A Computer Method for Sequencing Operations for Assembly Lines," *International Journal of Production Research*, Vol. 4, No. 4 (1966).

ARMOUR, G.C., and E.S. BUFFA, "A Heuristic Algorithm and Simulation Approach to Relative Location of Facilities," *Management Science*, Vol. 9, No. 1 (1963), 294–309.

BUFFA, E.S., G.C. ARMOUR, and T.E. VOLLMANN, "Allocating Facilities with CRAFT," *Harvard Business Reivew*, Vol. 42, No. 2 (March–April 1964), 136–59.

CONRAD, R., and B.A. HILLE, "Comparison of Paced and Unpaced Performance at a Packing Task," *Occupational Psychology*, Vol. 20, No. 1 (January 1955), 15–28.

COOK, THOMAS M., "Job Scheduling in a Multiprogrammed Computer," *Proceedings of the 1974 Winter Simulation Conference*, Vol. 2, 675–87.

DAVIS, L.D., and E.L. TRIST, "Improving the Quality of Work Life: Experience of the Socio-Technical Approach," in *Work in America*. Cambridge, Mass.: M.I.T. Press, June 1972.

ENGLESTAD, P.H., "Socio-Technical Approach to Problems of Process Control," in *Design of Jobs*, eds. L.E. Davis and J.C. Taylor. Middlesex, England: Penguin Books, 1972.

FRANCIS, R.L., and J.A. WHITE, *Facility Layout and Location: An Analytical Approach*. Englewood Cliffs, N.J.: Prentice-Hall, 1974.

HELD, M., R.M. KARP, and R. SHARESIAN, "Assembly-Line Balancing: Dynamic Programming with Precedence Constraints," *Operations Research*, Vol. 11, No. 3 (May–June 1963).

HELGESON, W.B., and D.P. BERNIE, "Assembly Line Balancing Using the Ranked Positional Weight Technique," *Journal of Industrial Engineering*, Vol. 12, No. 6 (November–December 1961).

MASTOR, A.A., "An Experimental Investigation and Comparative Evaluation of Production Line Balancing Techniques," *Management Science*, Vol. 16, No. 11 (July 1970), 728–46.

MOORE, J.M., *Plant Layout and Design*. New York: Macmillan, 1962.

RITZMAN, L.P., "The Efficiency of Computer Algorithms for Plant Layout," *Management Science*, Vol. 18 No. 5 (January 1972) 240–48.

chapter

6

JOB DESIGN AND WORK MEASUREMENT

As stated in the preceding chapter, one of the primary design functions of management is the designing of the man–machine system that is to be used in the transformation process. As depicted in Figure 6-1, the nature of man–machine systems has been evolving since primitive man. Not too many years ago, man performed the majority of the work of most man–machine systems. Today, except in some of the less-developed countries of the world, man's work role in general is changing. In today's sociotechnical system, man is called upon to do less physical labor and perform more of a machine-supervisory role.

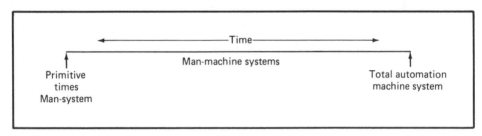

FIGURE 6-1 Evolution of Work

Obviously, in many man–machine systems, man still performs the dominant work role. One could cite many sectors of the American economy in which machines still perform only as an aid, helping man perform a work function. For example, the construction industry remains a labor-intensive industry where machines are employed to do the demanding physical tasks, but man still plays a dominant role. The health-care industry employs many sophisticated machines but remains a labor-intensive industry. At the other extreme are process control plants, such as oil refineries, which employ only a few people for the purpose of supervising the machines that actually do the work.

Herbert Simon predicted in 1960 that in 25 years the technology would exist for machines to perform any and all tasks in an organization. Although Simon may have missed his prediction by a few years, it is clear that sometime in the relatively near future, technology will have advanced to the stage he predicted. Does this mean that wide-scale unemployment will exist? Does it mean that people will be replaced by machines as soon as it is technically feasible? The answer to these questions is obviously no. Today, it is technically feasible to accomplish many human tasks with machines, but for many of these tasks, it is not economically feasible to replace man with a machine. Since total automation is in the somewhat distant future, and man's role in the transformation process will remain critical for many years, it is important to study job design and job measurement in an effort to design a more efficient and humanely satisfying productive system.

Job design is simply the structuring of work activities for an individual or a team. Good job designs must answer the following job-related questions:

1. What work is to be performed?
2. Who is to perform the work?
3. Where is the work to be done?
4. When is the work to be done?
5. Why is the job necessary?
6. How should the work be accomplished?

The majority of this chapter is devoted to answering these questions.

For organizational purposes, we divide job design into two basic elements, a human element and a work element. Important human factors relating to job design include physiological considerations, social considerations, and psychological considerations. In studying the work element of a job, the questions of what is to be done, how it is to be accomplished, and how the work is to be measured are all important considerations.

THE HUMAN ELEMENT IN JOB DESIGN

When discussing the human element in job design, it is convenient to organize the discussion into two sections, physiological or physical considerations and psycho-sociological considerations. Both areas are extremely important to the sound design of any job in an organization.

Physiological/Physical Considerations

Generally, machines have been shown to have definite comparative advantage over human beings when it comes to tasks that involve applying a great amount of force, doing repetitive tasks, and storing and processing data. It does not follow, however, that these types of tasks are consistently assigned to machines to perform. On the contrary, millions of people are employed to do jobs that machines could do better. Therefore, determining the physical and physiological limitations with respect to a job is an important segment of the job design function. If a job is designed that is physically impossible for a person to perform consistently well, then the psychological and social considerations of the job design have little meaning. In other words, the physical and physiological considerations help define the feasible region of the appropriate job design.

One way of describing work would be to identify a continuum of work as shown in Figure 6-2. Regardless of whether the task involves the strenuous use of large

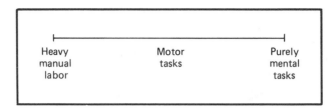

FIGURE 6-2   Work Continuum

muscles or the use of small muscles, or is purely mental in nature, there are limits concerning fatigue within which a job must be constrained. Work physiology aids the job designer by identifying the physiological limits of a job. These limits are identified by developing physiological indexes such as heartbeat rate, perspiration rate, body temperature, and oxygen-consumption rate. The basic methodology for a work physiology study is depicted in the flow chart in Figure 6-3. Let us illustrate, using an example.

The job being designed is that of lifting hot sheets of aluminum coming off the assembly line and stacking them. Different configurations would have two or three men on each side of the sheets of aluminum. Other decision variables are how many extra workers to employ for relieving purposes. The first step would be to test average workers to find their physiological indexes, such as heartbeat at rest and calorie consumption per minute. Then, take the four-man configuration with one extra man

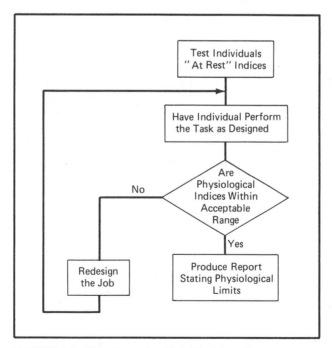

FIGURE 6-3   Flow Chart of a Work-Physiology Study

and perform the job for a period of time with the proper measuring instruments. If this configuration showed that the work load was too demanding, other configurations could be tried until the job came within normally accepted physiological limits.

Although most of the research of work physiology has been concerned with strenuous jobs using large muscle groups, the same principle of finding the physiological limits of a job can be followed for less strenuous tasks. The difference is in the measurement of fatigue. In some instances, other physiological indexes can be used; in other instances, it is necessary to observe the individual and infer that fatigue has set in when response rates fall or error rates increase.

Often, the physiological limits of a job depend on the environment in which the job is to be performed. If a worker is asked to do a strenuous task in a non-air-conditioned plant where temperatures sometimes exceed 100°, he can't be expected to do as much work as if the plant had a constant temperature of 75°. Similarly, the expectations of output from a design engineer should increase when he or she is provided with a private office, free from distractions.

It should be obvious that analyzing the environment in which a job must be done is of critical importance in designing the job. The job designer should ask questions such as, What is the best physical environment in which to accomplish this task? Is the best physical environment economically feasible? What compromises can be made in the environmental setting? Given an environment, what are the physiological constraints of the job?

To illustrate, take the job of a worker banding together bales of scrap aluminum in the cast house of an aluminum factory. The air in the cast house is dusty, the lighting is poor, the temperature ranges from 95° to 110°, the humidity is high, and so is the noise level. The job designer might have decided that the optimal environment would be a well-lighted, air-conditioned room, but the machine is located in the cast house and those are the conditions that exist there. A fan might be installed as a compromise, but the adverse conditions would be only slightly improved. Other changes in the environment might require an unacceptable capital expenditure. Therefore, all the job designer can hope to accomplish from a physical standpoint is to define an acceptable pace for the worker so that he will have time to recover from physiological fatigue.

Since Congress passed the Occupational Safety and Health Act (OSHA) in 1970, many operations managers have less flexibility in designing jobs. Jobs that are considered unsafe from an accident viewpoint or that entail environmental hazards under the law must be redesigned to meet safety and health standards.

Psychological Considerations

In the preceding chapter, we described a relatively new school of thought that defines the productive system as a sociotechnical system that has social and technical subsystems. Historically, the productive system has been largely thought of as a technical system, and consequently, the designers of processes and jobs have used productivity and economic considerations as the primary criteria in the design process. With productivity as the yardstick for success, jobs have become more and more specialized.

As shown in Figure 6-4, jobs that had been accomplished by one master craftsman have now been divided into many small work elements to be done by many workers with significantly lower skill levels.

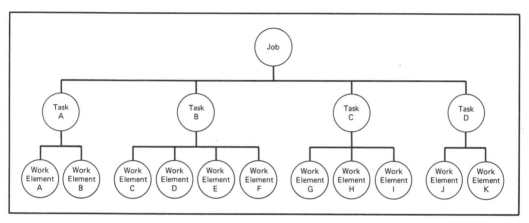

FIGURE 6-4   Job Specialization

In the late eighteenth century, Adam Smith articulated three major advantages of the division of labor. First, he stated, the worker develops a higher level of skill when a task is performed repetitively. Second, time is saved that is normally lost when a worker changes from performing one task to performing another. Finally, as men or women specialize in specific tasks or work elements, they will develop tools and machines to aid in the performance of, or to completely perform, the task. The results of the principle of division of labor have been impressive. Indeed, our present high standard of living is the direct result of mass production.

Since the early 1930s, operations managers and researchers in the field of management have proposed another goal for the design of processes and jobs: job satisfaction. A recent movement in the management literature, the job enlargement movement, proposes a reversal in the trend of increased specialization of labor. Advocates of job enlargement feel that specialization has been carried too far and that the trend toward specialization must be reversed for the good of society as well as for the good of the worker.

Job enlargement involves adjusting or enlarging a job in one or two dimensions. Horizontal job enlargement usually means a greater variety of tasks for the worker. A keypuncher's job might be enlarged horizontally by increasing the number of applications to be punched by a single operator. In other words, an operator who had been keypunching only payroll data from one source document could be given other applications with other source documents, thus increasing the scope of his or her job. Vertical job enlargement, often referred to as job enrichment, refers to giving the worker increased responsibility with respect to a given task. If the keypunch operator were involved in the design of the source document he or she was punching from and was responsible for the verifying operation, the job would have been enlarged vertically in two aspects.

There are many advantages and disadvantages of job enlargement, both to productivity and to the worker. First, the advantages of job enlargement to productivity, or the technical side of the sociotechnical system, often include the following:

1. Increased quality of the good or service that is produced
2. Decreased absenteeism
3. Decreased tardiness
4. Decreased turnover of personnel
5. Fewer labor grievances

The disadvantages of job enlargement to productivity include:

1. Lower productivity, due to less repetitive work
2. Higher training costs, due to increased skill levels and responsibility
3. Higher wages, due to the increased difficulty of finding suitable replacements
4. Higher recruiting and hiring costs

The advantages of job enlargement to the individual worker often include:

1. Increased gratification from the work itself, due to increase in variety and responsibility
2. Increased control over the work flow, which often decreases frustration and fatigue
3. Increased opportunity to affect the productive system through developing new work methods
4. Increased growth opportunities, so that an individual's organizational role can be expanded
5. Decreased in boredom, caused by less repetition of tasks
6. Increased in social benefits, due to necessary change in the layout of the work area and the increased contact with other workers
7. Decreased localized muscle fatigue, due to less repetitive tasks

What are advantages to some workers are disadvantages to others, owing to the variability in personalities and the psychosociological needs an individual requires from his work. In other words, some workers would list increased responsibility as an advantage of job enlargement, whereas others, with different utility functions, would list it as a disadvantage. Other commonly accepted worker advantages, like increased mental effort required or increased educational background, are disadvantages to those without a surplus of mental capacity or education.

One might ask, What is wrong with viewing the productive system from a purely technological point of view if giant strides in productivity have resulted historically from such a strategy? The answer lies in how the objectives of productive organization are defined. If the sole objective of the productive system is production, then any concession made to the goals of the coexisting social system must be rationalized by their positive effect on production. Although many have tried to justify the concepts and ideas of job enlargement and job enrichment by alluding to increases in productivity and other economic measures, to date no study has conclusively shown that increased productivity results from the job enlargement process. There have been many reports describing a job enlargement or job enrichment process that conclude that subsequent increases in productivity and product quality have resulted. Unfortunately, these studies have almost universally suffered from inadequate experimental design that invalidates the cause-and-effect relationship, making it impossible to say that increased production wasn't caused by some factor other than the simple enlargement of the job. Therefore, at present the jury is still out, and there are many who feel that job enlargement has a detrimental effect on productivity and that its only justification is in terms of job satisfaction on the part of the individual worker. The unanswered questions are, Is the law of diminishing returns applicable to the continuing increase in specialization? Is there a point at which continued increase in specialization has a detrimental effect on production, and if so, have we as an industrialized nation already passed that point in many industrial and service organizations?

As we approach the job design function of the operations manager, however, we must reconcile the goals of the sociotechnical system we are working within. Earlier in this chapter, we said that the goals and objectives of the technical systems differ dramatically from the goals of the social system present in an organization. If we assume that the goals of the social system are relevant goals of the organization, then it is not necessary to justify all job design decisions in terms of increased productivity. Changes in existing jobs or the design of new jobs can be made considering the human in the man–machine system as an individual and not merely a factor of production. His or her goals, self-actualization needs, social needs, and the like should be seriously considered during the job design process. Tradeoffs between productivity and human needs must be made. Merely optimizing either the technical system or the social system is an unsatisfactory answer to the job design problem.

THE WORK ELEMENT IN JOB DESIGN

The remaining portion of this chapter deals with work methods and work measurement techniques. Historically, work methods have been considered the domain of the worker. No one told the eighteenth-century blacksmith precisely how to accomplish a given task. As the trend toward specialization of jobs continued, many jobs and work methods have been designed by experts in methods engineering or methods analysis. Today, it is common for input concerning work methods to come from specialists in methods engineering as well as from the workers themselves. Regardless of who performs the analysis, the primary goal remains increased efficiency through either decreased cost or increased productivity.

Work Methods

Tools.   In the detailed definition of work methods, the analyst has a number of tools at his or her disposal. In this section, we describe the most commonly used tools and indicate their sphere of application. Then the major steps taken in a methods improvement study will be described.

Regardless of the type of job being analyzed, the analyst can take advantage of the numerous principles of motion study that have evolved over many years. A complete list of motion-study principles is outside the scope of this text, but Moore suggests an appropriate abridged list:

I.   *Rules for minimizing human movements.* Never do a job the hard way if there is an easier way.

    1.   Don't do jobs by hand if machines can do them. Transfer everything possible to machines. In particular, try to design machines which not only will do the operation but will first place the product in position and then eject it after the operation.

    2.   Eliminate handling. Bring materials as close as possible to the point of work and remove them by gravity if possible; if this cannot be done, do it mechanically. If materials must be handled by a man, handle as many as possible at one time. Design machines to do two or more operations once the material has been put in position.

    3.   Use the fewest motions possible. Move as little of the body as is necessary to do the job; in fact, move only the fingers if finger motion will do. Don't reach; put things where little reaching is necessary.

    4.   Use fixed positions for all materials and tools. Put them close to and in front of the operator to reduce searching as well as reaching for them. Motions then become automatic.

II.   *Rules for making the best use of men.* A whole man produces more than part of a man.

    5.   Use two hands but avoid using hands purely as holding devices. Idle hands do no work. If both are not busy, redistribute the work between them. On light assembly jobs, mechanical holding devices can often make a job into a one-handed job, in which case an identical job can be done with the other hand. The man will not do twice as much work as with one hand, but he is likely to do half as much more. Working with two hands may take practice, but it is quite possible. Typists do it all the time.

    6.   Use the feet as well as the hands if they can be used to push a pedal or do some useful movement. Hands and feet can both be used at the same time. Does it sound impossible? Fifty million of us do this every day when we drive our cars.

    7.   Study and analyze all hesitations and short delays within jobs and eliminate them when possible.

    8.   Where unavoidable delays occur, give men other work to keep working.

    9.   The time an expert takes is possible for everyone. Try to get all men to do as well.

III. *Rules for saving energy.* Tiring movements waste energy.
   10. Transfer all heavy lifting to mechanical lifting devices.
   11. Use momentum where possible, rather than force. A man cannot, for example, *push* a nail into a board even with a hammer. But if he *swings* the hammer, its momentum does the job. Avoid momentum, however, if muscular effort has to be used to stop it.
   12. Continuous, curved motions are easier and less tiring than motions involving sharp changes in direction.
   13. Assign all work to the body member best suited for it; in typing, for example, don't do it all with the little finger.
   14. Use the body to the best advantage mechanically. If force must be exerted, exert it at heights and in positions where the body can employ the most force.
   15. Eliminate working conditions which add to fatigue. Use power-driven tools. Get rid of poor lighting, poor ventilation, fumes, dusty conditions, temperature extremes, and humidity. If possible, provide a comfortable chair and arrange work so the operator can stand or sit as he wishes.
   16. On fatiguing jobs, allow rest periods. The heavier the task, the more necessary are frequent (but short) rest periods. Many short rest periods are better than a few long rest periods.
   17. On monotonous jobs, provide an occasional break; monotony and fatigue are related. Consider job enlargement to lessen monotony.

IV. *Rules for placing men.* Use manpower to its best advantage in view of the jobs to be filled and the men available.
   18. Where several workers do the same job day after day, cut the job up into small tasks and let each worker specialize. Each will acquire greater proficiency, and the group will produce more.
   19. Put workers on jobs well suited to them, and place only well-suited men on the jobs. Put women on jobs where they are better than men, usually light, fast jobs requiring finger dexterity. Put men on heavier jobs.
   20. Avoid using high-priced labor on low-price work even if this work is but a small part of a high-priced man's job. Divide the job and assign work to the grade of worker required.[1]

In addition to these principles of motion economy, there exist various charting techniques that are extremely valuable when properly applied to work methods design. The various charts are used under different conditions and circumstances, and as we describe the different types of charts, the appropriate application areas are indicated.

Flow diagrams and process charts similar to those found in Figures 6-5 and 6-6 are helpful in eliminating or combining unnecessary steps, shortening transportation distances, or identifying unnecessary delays in a productive process. Once the present mode of operation has been documented using a flow diagram or process chart or

---

[1]Franklin Moore, *Production Management*, 6th ed. (Homewood, Ill.: Richard D. Irwin, © 1973).

FIGURE 6-5 Example of Flow Diagram

SOURCE: Marvin E. Mundel, *Motion and Time Study*, 4th edition (Englewood Cliffs, New Jersey: Prentice-Hall, Inc., 1970).

194

Type of chart	PROCESS CHART – MAN ANALYSIS		
Method	ORIGINAL	Machine no.	D - GROUP
Operation	INSPECT DRAWN COPPER WIRE	Operation no.	I - 3
		Part no.	—
Part name	ALL DRAWN COPPER	Chart by	C.W. Mc.
Operator	SIMON GREEN	Date charted	6/4/

DIST.	SYMBOL	DESCRIPTION
24'	○	To next finished spool
	○	Take spool
24'	○	To inspection bench
	○	Place spool on bench
	○	Strip and cut outer layer which is always damaged in drawing
15'	○	To scrap container
	○	Dispose of scrap
15'	○	To inspection table
	○	Cut 2' from end, then 2" sample from 2' piece
	◇	O.D. with box micrometer
	○	Pick up spool
24'	○	To machine's "inspection" rack
	○	Place spool

SUMMARY	
○	7
□	0
◇	1
○	5
▽	0
Dist.	102' AVG.

FIGURE 6-6 Example of Process Chart

SOURCE: Marvin E. Mundel, *Motion and Time Study*, 4th edition (Englewood Cliffs, New Jersey: Prentice-Hall, Inc., 1970).

both, questions such as the following can be asked to improve the existing design:

What work is to be performed? Is it necessary? Can it be refined?

Who is to perform the work? Can others perform the work who are less skilled or less experienced?

Where is the work to be done? Can it be done elsewhere?

When is the work to be done? Can it be done earlier or later?

Why is the individual job element necessary? Can it be eliminated? Can it be combined?

How is the work being done? Are there alternatives?

Figures 6-7 and 6-8 reflect an alternative, improved work method to the method documented in Figures 6-5 and 6-6.

An operations chart divides the functions of each hand into components of reach, grasp, transport, position, and so on. As shown in Figure 6-9, each hand is analyzed in parallel often on a time scale so that the manner in which the hands work together can be analyzed. Operations charts are primarily used to analyze tasks that have short cycles and are of a repetitive nature.

If the task were a repetitive, short-cycle task that had a high volume, it might be economically feasible to analyze it using a micromotion study, in which the task is filmed using a high-speed camera and then each frame of film is analyzed to develop a simo (simultaneous motion) chart. The difference between an operations chart and a simo chart is the level of detail and the relative costs. For many low- to medium-volume applications, a simo chart cannot be shown to be cost-effective. See Figure 6-10 for an example of a simo chart.

When both the man and machine components of the man–machine system are important parts of the task being studied, man–machine charts are often a useful device. Like the one shown in Figure 6-11, these reflect each job element and depict what the machine part of the system is doing and what the human part of the system is doing at all times. Therefore, human idleness and machine idleness are readily discernable and rational decisions based on resource cost can be made concerning methods design. Obviously, if a machine cost five times per hour more than the human operating it, operator idle time is far less critical than machine idle time.

When the transformation process involves the coordinated efforts of a team, activity charts or multiman process charts are useful in documenting the activities of each team member on a time scale. See Figure 6-12 for an example of an activity chart.

Steps in work methods improvement study. The first step in any methods improvement study is to identify the job to be improved. Monks suggests that jobs that have the following characteristics often offer more potential than others for cost reduction or improved industrial relations:

1. High labor content
2. Large demand and are frequently occurring

Type of chart _PROCESS CHART – MAN ANALYSIS_

Method _PROPOSED_   Machine no. _D-GROUP_

Operation _INSPECT DRAWN COPPER WIRE_   Operation no. _I-3_

_____   Part no. _~_

Part name _ALL DRAWN COPPER_   Chart by _C. W. Mc_

Operator _BASED ON GREEN_   Date charted _6/4/_

DIST.	SYMBOL	DESCRIPTION
20'	⊙	To next finished spool with bench
	◯	Take spool
	◯	Place on bench
	◯	Strip, cut and sample
	◯	Dispose of scrap in container attached to bench
	◇	O.D. with box micrometer
4'	⊙	Bench to "inspected" rack
	◯	Pick up spool
	◯	Place spool

SUMMARY AND RECAPITULATION

	PROPOSED	ORIG.	SAVED
◯	6	7	1
□	0	0	0
◇	1	1	0
○	2	5	3
▽	0	0	0
DIST	24' AVG.	102' AVG.	78' AVG.

FIGURE 6-7 Proposed Process Chart

SOURCE: Marvin E. Mundel, _Motion and Time Study_, 4th edition
(Englewood Cliffs, New Jersey: Prentice-Hall, Inc., 1970).

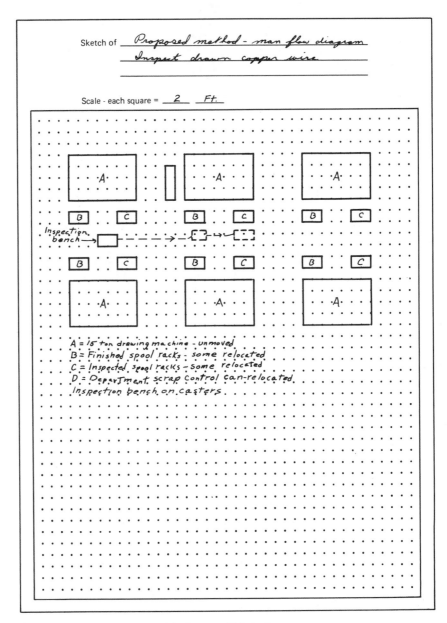

FIGURE 6-8   Process Chart of the Improved Method

SOURCE: Marvin E. Mundel, *Motion and Time Study*, 4th edition
(Englewood Cliffs, New Jersey: Prentice-Hall, Inc., 1970).

198

RIGHT AND LEFT HAND OPERATION CHART
Page 2 of 2

Improved _____ Method
Assembly _____ Operation
Bench _____ Mach. No.
a-321 Opr. No.
GG Part No.
Hand-hole Cover Part _____ W.H. Chart by _____ 3/4 Date
R. Allen Operator

SUMMARY /2 /PER. PC.	Right Hand		Left Hand		Both Hands		Saved	Pc.
	ORIG	IMP	ORIG	IMP	ORIG	IMP		
○	16		12	14	14	14		0
▽	17		14	14	15.5	15.5		-1.5
	1		6	16	3.5	12.5		
	0		2	0	1			-1
TOTAL	34		34	44	34	34		10

#	Left hand description	Right hand description
1	To left side assem.	To left side assem.
2	Assem. cotter	Left side assem.
3	Left side assem.	To pliers
4		Pick up pliers
5		To assembly
6		Bend left cotter
7	To right side assem.	To right side assem.
8	Right side assem.	Bend right cotter
9	For right hand	To aside pliers
10		Place pliers
11	To left assembly	To right assembly
12	Pick up assem.	Pick up assem.
13	To finished parts	To finished parts
14	Place assembly	Place assembly
15		
16		
17		
18		
19		
20		

RIGHT AND LEFT HAND OPERATION CHART
Page 1 of 2

Improved _____ Method
Assembly _____ Operation
Bench _____ Mach. No.
a-321 Opr. No.
GG Part No.
Hand-hole Cover Part _____ W.H. Chart by _____ 3/4 Date
R. Allen Operator

SUMMARY /2 /PER. PC.	Right Hand		Left Hand		Both Hands		Saved	Pc.
	ORIG	IMP	ORIG	IMP	ORIG	IMP		
○	16		12	14	14	14		0
▽	17		14	14	15.5	15.5		-1.5
	1		6	16	3.5	12.5		
	0		2	0	1			-1
TOTAL	34		34	44	34	34		10

#	Left hand description	Right hand description
1	To bolt	To bolt
2	Pick up bolt	Pick up bolt
3	To work area	To work area
4	Assem. bolt to jig	Assem. bolt to jig
5	To washer	To washer
6	Pick up washer	Pick up washer
7	To assembly	To assembly
8	Assem. washer	Assem. washer
9	To cover plate	To cover plate
10	Pick up plate	Pick up plate
11	To assembly	To assembly
12	Assem. Plate	Assem. plate
13	To bar	To bar
14	Pick up bar	Pick up bar
15	To assembly	To assembly
16	Fit and spin on	Fit and spin on
17	To cotter pin.	To cotter pin.
18	Pick up cotter	Pick up cotter
19	To right side assem.	To right side assem.
20	Rights	Assem cotter

FIGURE 6-9 Example of an Operations Chart

SOURCE: Marvin E. Mundel, *Motion and Time Study*, 4th edition (Englewood Cliffs, New Jersey: Prentice-Hall, Inc., 1970).

SIMO – CHART

Method _Original_   Film no. _A-6-CC_

Operation _Assembly_   Operation no. _DT 27A_

Part no. _27_

Part name _Battle dropper top_   Chart by _Ross_

Operator _Armstrong - 157_   Date charted _2/22/_

Left Hand Description	Symbol	Time	Total Time in Winks	Time	Symbol	Right Hand Description	Clock
			0				
Finished part to tray	TL	8					120
	RL	2		20	TE / UO	To rubber tops	
							130
To bakelite caps	TE	16	20				
				10	G	Rubber tops	140
Bakelite caps	G	8					
To work area	TL	4		12	TL	To work area	150
	P	2	40				
				8	P	To bakelite	160
For assembling	H	18					
				6	A		170
For RH to grasp top	P	2		2	RL	Rubber tops	
			60	4	TE	To top of rubber	
For RH to pull rubber top	H	14		2	G	Top of rubber	180
				8	A	Pull rubber thru	
For glass	P	4		2	RL		190
				6	TE	To glass rods	
			80	8	G	Glass rod	200
For assembly of glass	H	32		8	TL	To cap	210
				2	P		
			100	10	A	Insert glass	220
			110	2	RL		
							230
LH Summary						RH Summary	
58.2%	H	64		24	A	21.8%	
14.6%	TE	16		20	TE	18.2%	
11.0%	TL	12		20	G	18.2%	
7.2%	G	8		20	TL	18.2%	
7.2%	P	8		10	P	9.1%	
1.8%	RL	2		10	UO	9.1%	
				6	RL	5.4%	

FIGURE 6-10 Example of a Simo Chart

SOURCE: Marvin E. Mundel, *Motion and Time Study*, 4th edition (Englewood Cliffs, New Jersey: Prentice-Hall, Inc., 1970).

Type of chart **Man and machine operation chart**

Method **Improved** Machine no. **G 14**

Operation **Centerless grind** Operation no. **12**

Part no. **B-2**

Part name **Bearing** Chart by **Wren**

Operator **T. Silles** Date charted **4/4/**

Left hand description	Symbols	Right hand	Grinder
To finished bearing		To supply	
Take out		Pick up bearing	
For gaging		To grinder	
		Place in grinder	
		To feed	
		Engage feed	
		To gage	
		Pick up gage	
		To bearing	
		Gage	
To finished parts box		Gage to bench	
Place in box		Lay on bench	
		To feed lever	
		Take hold	
		Finish grind	
		Back off	

Summary and Recap

	IMP R LH	RH	BH	Mach.	Orig. Mach.	Orig. BH	
○	2	9	11	9	2	11	Saving expected
○	2	7	9	−		8	because move
▽	8	0	8	−		3	steps take place
▽	4	0	4	7	12	6	during machine
Total	16	16	32	16	14	28	on and fewer
							during machine
							down time

FIGURE 6-11 Example of a Man-Machine Chart

SOURCE: Marvin E. Mundel, *Motion and Time Study*, 4th edition (Englewood Cliffs, N.J.: Prentice-Hall, Inc., 1970).

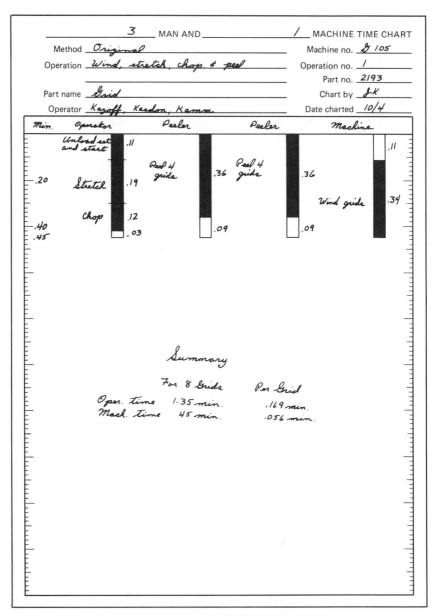

FIGURE 6-12   Example of an Activity Chart

SOURCE: Marvin E. Mundel, *Motion and Time Study*, 4th edition
(Englewood Cliffs, New Jersey: Prentice-Hall, Inc., 1970).

3. Present quality control problems
4. Are bottlenecks in the productive system
5. Are unsafe, unpleasant, or fatiguing
6. Offer excessively low or high earnings
7. Have never been studied before[2]

The second step in any methods improvement study is to document and analyze the present method. This step can take advantage of the principles of motion economy and the various charting methods discussed earlier in this chapter. In documenting and analyzing the present system, it is essential to obtain input from those who are closest to the job, the workers themselves. Not only will involving the workers result in a better understanding and analysis of the present system, but it will aid immeasurably in the implementation of the new work methods.

After the present system or work method has been documented and analyzed, alternative designs can be developed. Once a discrete number of alternatives have been identified, they must be analyzed and measured against the present work method and each other. Based on measures of efficiency such as time, cost, output, quality, and/or social benefits, a method for performing the task must be selected. Again, when defining and selecting alternatives to the present work method, it is important to continue worker involvement in the process. Having a number of workers involved could be achieved through assigning some representative worker to the methods improvement team and through an employee suggestion system.

Once the improved method has been selected for implementation, it is necessary to convince line management that there is a better way than the way they have been doing a given task. In addition, it is important to sell the idea to the individual workers. If either line supervision or the workers themselves oppose the change, there is little hope for an effective transition, and it is quite possible that the entire methods improvement study could fail in its goal of increased efficiency through improved work methods.

It is important to realize that no job or work method has been designed optimally; all jobs can be improved in one aspect or another. Therefore, once the improved method has been implemented, it is important to maintain control over it to ensure that workers haven't regressed to the original work method. In addition, it is necessary to allow work methods to evolve by analyzing and implementing small changes.

To summarize, there are five basic steps in any methods improvement study:

1. Identify the job to be studied.
2. Document and analyze the existing work method.
3. Develop alternative work methods and choose the best.
4. Implement the new method.
5. Maintain control and supervise additional change of the improved work method.

---

[2]Joseph G. Monks, *Operations Management: Theory and Problems* (New York: McGraw-Hill, 1977).

WORK MEASUREMENT

Measurement of work is a necessary function of the operations manager. The output resulting from work measurement is in the form of labor standards that seek to establish norm production rates for workers or standard times required to complete a given job. All organizations need labor standards in one form or another. Often, these standards have been derived in a very informal way, owing to the type of job or perhaps the type of organization. Some jobs do not lend themselves to strict standards because of the variable nature of the work activity; and in some very small organizations, even though formal labor standards could be derived, they haven't been, owing simply to the size of the firm or relative lack of sophistication on the part of management personnel.

Regardless of whether labor standards have been developed in a scientific way and formally written into the procedures of an organization, or just exist rather vaguely in the mind of supervisory personnel, they are often necessary raw data that management must use in making a variety of decisions. Decisions upon which labor standards have a direct impact include:

1. Pricing decisions
2. Budgeting decisions
3. Hiring decisions
4. Firing decisions
5. Wage increase decisions
6. Wage incentive plan decisions
7. Inventory decisions
8. Bidding decisions
9. Scheduling decisions

Because of the widespread influence of labor standards, several formal, rather scientific methods of determining labor standards have been developed. A description of these formal methods makes up the remainder of this chapter.

Time Study

Time-study methods for measuring short, repetitive jobs were first developed by Frederick Taylor in the late nineteenth century. Today, time-study methods are the most commonly used of the formal techniques for deriving labor standards. By analyzing and timing one worker's performance of the task to be measured, the time-study procedure generalizes or infers a standard time for that task for all workers.

To derive a labor standard using time-study methods, the following procedure is followed. First, the worker is selected, and the purpose and procedure of the time study is explained to him or her. The job in question must then be broken into elements or distinct operations, each taking a matter of several minutes or a number of seconds. The next step is to time a number of cycles for each distinct operation. This is done using a stopwatch or, if the cycle time is extremely short, a high-speed camera. The number of cycles that should be timed is a function of the amount of confidence the analyst wishes to have in the mean cycle time and the variance. Rather than devote a great deal of space to sample-size calculation, let us use Table 6-1 as a guide to the

Table 6-1   Guide to Number of Cycles to be Observed in a Time Study

	MINIMUM NUMBER OF CYCLES TO STUDY (ACTIVITY)		
WHEN TIME (HOURS) PER CYCLE IS MORE THAN:	*OVER 10,000 PER YEAR*	*1,000 TO 10,000*	*UNDER 1,000*
8.000.................	2	1	1
3.000.................	3	2	1
2.000.................	4	2	1
1.000.................	5	3	2
0.800.................	6	3	2
0.500.................	8	4	3
0.300.................	10	5	4
0.200.................	12	6	5
0.120.................	15	8	6
0.080.................	20	10	8
0.050.................	25	12	10
0.035.................	30	15	12
0.020.................	40	20	15
0.012.................	50	25	20
0.008.................	60	30	25
0.005.................	80	40	30
0.003.................	100	50	40
0.002.................	120	60	50
under 0.002.................	140	80	60

From Benjamin W. Niebel, *Motion and Time Study,* 6th ed. (Homewood, Ill.: Richard D. Irwin, 1976,) p. 325.

number of cycles to be observed. After the appropriate number of cycles has been observed, the average cycle time can be computed as shown in equation 6.1 below:

$$\bar{t} = \frac{\sum_{i=1}^{N} t_i}{N} \qquad\qquad 6.1$$

where $\bar{t}$ = average cycle time
                 t_i = an individual observation
                 N = sample size or number of observations

After all job elements are timed and their respective average times computed, the average time for the job being measured can be computed by merely adding the average job-element times. This sum, which is shown in equation 6.2, is known as the observed operator performance time.

$$PT = \sum_{j=1}^{m} \bar{t}_j \qquad 6.2$$

where
$$PT = \text{observed operator performance time}$$
$$\bar{t}_j = \text{average cycle time for job element } j$$
$$m = \text{number of job elements}$$

The next step is to modify the observed operator performance time by multiplying it by a subjective estimate of the operator's performance rating. This performance rating represents the analyst's estimate of how much slower or faster the worker is working in relation to a normal pace. If he or she is working 25 percent faster, the performance rating would be 1.25. The modified operator performance time is called normal time and is computed as shown in equation 6.3:

$$NT = PT \cdot PR \qquad 6.3$$

where
$$NT = \text{normal time}$$
$$PT = \text{performance time}$$
$$PR = \text{performance rating}$$

The final step is to calculate a standard time for the job by adding an allowance time to the normal time for personal needs of the worker and for unavoidable delays such as machine breakdowns. This allowance for personal time is often included in union contracts and typically varies from 10 to 15 percent. The standard time is calculated using equation 6.4:

$$ST = NT(1 + A) \qquad 6.4$$

where
$$ST = \text{standard time}$$
$$NT = \text{normal time}$$
$$A = \text{allowance}$$

To illustrate the procedure just described, let's consider the following example. The operation is to bore a 1.5-centimeter hole in a round metal disk. To perform the operation accurately, it is necessary to place the disk in a jig before drilling. The job can be broken into two elements, positioning the disk in the jig and drilling the hole. The company annually produces more than 10,000 final assemblies for which the disk is a part. Since cycle time for placing the disk in the jig is approximately 3 minutes (.05 hours) and the drilling time is about 1.2 minutes (.02 hours), Table 6-1 indicates sample sizes of 25 and 40 for the two operations respectively. These times are reflected in Tables 6-2 and 6-3 respectively.

Table 6-2   Jig Positioning Times in Minutes

OBSERVATION NO.	TIME	OBSERVATION NO.	TIME
1	2.95	14	3.01
2	2.93	15	2.86
3	3.50	16	3.05
4	2.71	17	3.21
5	2.92	18	3.21
6	3.11	19	2.42
7	3.02	20	2.97
8	3.05	21	2.79
9	2.97	22	3.15
10	2.83	23	3.03
11	2.99	24	2.97
12	2.89	25	3.06
13	2.87		

Table 6-3   Drilling Times in Minutes

OBSERVATION NO.	TIME	OBSERVATION NO.	TIME
1	1.11	21	1.20
2	1.12	22	1.22
3	1.21	23	1.12
4	1.09	24	1.09
5	1.31	25	1.31
6	1.21	26	1.22
7	1.22	27	1.21
8	1.40	28	1.20
9	1.15	29	1.19
10	1.11	30	1.17
11	1.13	31	1.23
12	1.21	32	1.15
13	1.20	33	1.14
14	1.23	34	1.24
15	1.21	35	1.27
16	1.18	36	1.26
17	1.25	37	1.30
18	1.27	38	1.10
19	1.17	39	1.21
20	1.16	40	1.17

The average jig positioning time is:

$$\bar{t}_1 = \frac{2.95 + 2.93 + \ldots + 3.06}{25}$$

$$= \frac{74.47}{25}$$

$$= 2.9788 \text{ minutes}$$

The average drilling time is:

$$\bar{t}_2 = \frac{1.11 + 1.12 + \ldots + 1.17}{40}$$

$$= \frac{47.94}{40}$$

$$= 1.1985 \text{ minutes}$$

The performance time of the job is found by adding the two component performance times:

$$PT = 2.9788 + 1.1985$$

$$= 4.1773$$

Let us assume that the analyst's subjective rating was that the worker was working just a little faster than normal pace, let's say 5 percent. Then, the normal time for the job could be calculated as follows:

$$NT = (4.1773)(1.05)$$

$$= 4.386$$

The final step is to calculate the standard time for the job using equation 6.4. Let's assume an allowance for personal time of 10 percent.

$$ST = (4.386)(1 + .10)$$

$$= 4.825 \text{ minutes}$$

Predetermined Time Standards

Another way to determine a time standard for a job is to break the job into minute elements for which published standards exist. When using predetermined time standards (PTS), the analyst is forced to break the job into very small elementary movements, such as "reach 3 inches," or "grasp," or "handle." Typically, one minute of work is divided into several hundred elementary movements.

Using published time standards offers several advantages over the time-study methods previously described. First, predetermined time standards are less subjective than time-study methods, because no performance rating is required. Therefore, PTS is widely accepted as being a fair way of determining standards. Second, if the job is currently being performed, there is no necessity to disrupt operations to time it. Third, PTS can be applied to jobs before they have been installed in the productive system. Fourth, setting labor standards using PTS is less expensive than time-study methods.

The major disadvantage to using PTS to set labor standards is theoretical problems that adversely affect the accuracy of the procedure. Much of the accuracy depends on the expertise of the analyst in breaking the job down properly and upon the implicit assumption that the total time for the job is found by merely adding the times required to accomplish the minute elements of the job. Often, if it is cost-effective, a job's standard time is computed using both time-study methods and PTS.

Some companies use the data base they develop by time-study methods to compile their own published or predetermined time standards. The major difference between internally developed and externally published predetermined standards is in the level of detail. Externally published predetermined standards relate to functions taking less than half a second, whereas internally predetermined standards typically relate to job elements taking 20–30 seconds.

Work Sampling

About 50 years after Taylor applied his time-study methods, work sampling was introduced. Work sampling involves drawing a sample of random observations of a particular job to determine what proportion of the worker's time is spent on various job functions. Experience has shown that work sampling is best applied to jobs that have long cycle times or are infrequent. Repetitive short-interval jobs are still best analyzed using time-study methods or some form of predetermined labor standards.

Work sampling has several advantages over time-study methods:

1. Work sampling is generally less expensive, because the study can be performed by less-skilled and therefore less-expensive personnel.
2. Jobs having longer cycle times can be studied economically.
3. Work sampling studies are less disruptive to the productive system.
4. Since the study period is longer, there is less chance of biasing the results with the effect of short-term variations.

The application of work sampling to the calculation of standard times can be divided into seven steps:

1. Identify the job or jobs that are to be the subject of the work sampling study.
2. Describe the job in writing by listing the activities of the workers.
3. Inform the affected workers.
4. Determine the number of observations required. Given a desired degree of accuracy, it is possible to statistically determine the appropriate sample size using equation 6.5 below:

$$N = \frac{Z_\alpha^2 pq}{a^2} \qquad\qquad 6.5$$

where N = sample size
Z_α = the standard normal deviate for a given α level
p = value of the sample proportion
$q = 1 - p$
a = absolute error desired

5. Prepare a tour schedule that ensures random selection of the sample observations. This can be done using a random-number table to assign observation times.
6. Make and record the data necessary to compute standard time.
7. Compute the standard time using equation 6.6:

$$ST = \left(\frac{T \cdot W \cdot I}{P}\right) \cdot \left(\frac{1}{1-A}\right) \qquad\qquad 6.6$$

where ST = standard time per unit
T = total time spent by the operator (working time and idle time)
W = working time proportion
I = performance index
P = total number of units produced
A = allowances expressed in decimal form

To illustrate the work sampling methodology, let us consider the following example. A large oil company has a credit-card processing center. Gas tickets are mailed into the center, where they are read by optical scanning equipment. Approximately 15 percent of the tickets are rejected and sent to a key-to-disk operation. Trays of tickets are manually keyed into a record stored on a magnetic disk. The job to be studied is the keying of one tray of cards. Specifically, the activities of the operators are idle or busy keying in data. After informing the operators of the study, it is necessary to determine the number of observations. Let us assume we wish to be 95 percent confident that our estimate of busy time will be within ± 3 percent. Suppose we estimate the percentage of time an average operator is busy at 75 percent. Using a level of significance of .05:

Table 6-4   Standard Normal Deviate

α	Z_α
.01	2.58
.05	1.96
.10	1.64
.15	1.44

Table 6-4 shows that Z_α is 1.96. Using equation 6.5, the number of observations can be calculated in the following manner:

$$N = \frac{(1.96)^2(.75)(.25)}{.03^2}$$

$$= 800.33$$

The next step is to design a random tour schedule. This can be done by dividing the workweek into 2,400 minutes (40 hours $\times$ 60 minutes); then, taking a four-digit random-number table and eliminating all numbers greater than 2,400, select 800 random numbers from the shorter list, each of which would represent a time of the week an observation should be taken.

Once the data have been collected and recorded, it is time to compute the standard time. Assume that the working time percentage of the sample is 80 percent and the subjective estimate of the performance index is 1.05. Also assume that the number of boxes processed in a week by the worker being studied was 48 and that the union contract stipulates an allowance of 15 percent. Standard time is computed using equation 6.6, as shown below:

$$ST = \left(\frac{(2400)(.8)(1.05)}{48}\right) \cdot \left(\frac{1}{1 - .15}\right)$$

$$= 49.41 \text{ minutes/tray}$$

SUMMARY

In this chapter, we have seen that the function of job design and work measurement is an extremely important and demanding function of the manager of a productive system. Extremely complex behavior problems exist that obviously could not be dealt with here. It is safe to say, however, that the job design process should be viewed in terms of the sociotechnical system and that an operations manager who seeks to maximize either the goals of the technical system or those of the social system to the exclusion of the other is ill-advised and will ultimately fail.

We have attempted here to highlight some of the more commonly used tools for improving work methods. These include the principles of motion study that have evolved over many years and the various charting techniques. The rationale for and the importance of labor standards has been described, and the three most common methods of determining labor standards have been developed. Like all introductory chapters, this chapter should serve as a jumping-off place for further investigations into the area of job design and work measurement.

SOLVED PROBLEMS

Problem Statement

Consider the job of making hot fudge sundaes at the local ice cream parlor. The job can be broken into two elements, filling the dish with ice cream and providing the topping (hot fudge, whipped cream, nuts, and a cherry). Using the time-study technique, develop a standard time for making hot fudge sundaes.

Solution

The first step in the time study is to take the appropriate number of stopwatch measurements. To determine the appropriate number of measurements of each job element, the store manager was asked how many hot fudge sundaes were sold each year and his estimate of cycle times for the two job elements. He said that about 75 hot fudge sundaes were made per day and it took about 30 seconds for each job element. With this information, Table 6-1 indicates that a set of 60 observations is appropriate for each job element. (Use the first column, because 75 sundaes per day is more than 10,000 per year and 30 seconds is approximately .008 hours.)

The next step is to take our time measurements. After the data has been collected let us assume that the average time to put ice cream in the dish was 37 seconds, and average topping time was 29 seconds. Therefore, the operator performance time is:

$$PT = \sum_{i=1}^{2} \bar{t}_i$$
$$= 37 \text{ seconds} + 29 \text{ seconds}$$
$$= 66 \text{ seconds}$$

It was perceived that the worker making the study was working about 10 percent faster than normal, and hence the performance rating is 1.10. To calculate normal time, merely multiply the performance time by the performance rating.

$$NT = PT \cdot PR$$
$$= (66 \text{ seconds})(1.1)$$
$$= 72.6 \text{ seconds}$$

Allowance for personal needs is 15 percent. Standard time for making a hot fudge sundae, therefore, is:

$$ST = NT(1 + .15)$$
$$= 72.6(1 + .15)$$
$$= 83.49 \text{ seconds}$$

Problem Statement

The job to be studied is that of a lumberjack team cutting down a tree. The following information must be ascertained.

1. Estimate of the proportion of time spent on the task of cutting down a tree. (Assume 70%.)
2. The absolute range of error. In other words, given a confidence level, what is the width of the confidence interval? (Assume 5% absolute error and a confidence level of 95%.)

3. An allowance for personal time. (Assume 10%.)
4. The number of trees cut per day. (Assume 20 trees per day.)
5. The performance index. (Estimated to be 1.0.)

Solution

First we must calculate the sample size by using the following formula:

$$N = \frac{Z_\alpha^2 pq}{a^2}$$

$$= \frac{(1.96)^2(.7)(.3)}{.05^2}$$

$$= \frac{.807}{.0025}$$

$$= 322.7$$

If 323 observations are taken randomly and the sample working time percentage was 65, then the standard time can be computed as follows:

$$ST = \frac{T \cdot W \cdot I}{P} \frac{1}{1 - A}$$

$$= \frac{(8 \text{ hours})(.65)(1.0)}{20} \frac{1}{1 - .1}$$

$$= .2889 \text{ hours}$$

$$= 17.33 \text{ minutes}$$

REVIEW QUESTIONS

1. What is the major reason that all productive systems of the 1990s will *not* be totally automated?
2. Distinguish between physiological and psychological considerations in job design.
3. Why is work physiology applied to strenuous physical tasks rather than mental tasks?
4. Briefly describe the methodology of a work physiology study.
5. List four important environmental factors in job design.
6. What relevance does OSHA have to job design?
7. List five major advantages of the division of labor.
8. What is the major premise of the "job enlargement" school of thought?
9. Distinguish between vertical and horizontal job enlargement.
10. List five important advantages of job enlargement accruing to productivity.

11. List four disadvantages of job enlargement with respect to productivity.
12. List five advantages to workers of job enlargement.
13. What is the present consensus regarding job enlargement's effect on productivity?
14. Briefly, what is the major contention of the sociotechnical school of thought?
15. List what you believe to be the five most important motion-study principles suggested by Moore.
16. Distinguish between a flow diagram and a process chart.
17. Distinguish between an operations chart and a man–machine chart.
18. What is a simo chart?
19. List five characteristics that could make a job a good candidate for a methods study.
20. What are the basic steps in a work methods study?
21. Give two reasons for involving workers in a methods improvement study.
22. List five decisions for which management needs labor standards data.
23. Distinguish between time-study methods and work sampling.
24. What are predetermined time standards?
25. How does the use of PTS differ from a time study?
26. List two advantages of using published time standards.
27. List two disadvantages of using published standards.
28. List two important advantages of work sampling.
29. To what kind of applications is work sampling best applied?
30. What are the seven steps to setting labor standards through work sampling?

PROBLEMS

1. The standard time for a particular hospital task was 10 minutes. Owing to a change in the system, unavoidable delays have increased and a new standard must be developed. The appropriate work sampling was performed, with the results reflected in Table 6-5.

Table 6-5 Work Sampling Results

ACTIVITY	NUMBER OF OBSERVATIONS	% OF OBSERVATIONS
Working	576	82.3
Idle	124	17.7
Total	700	100.0

Thirty-five patients per 8-hour day are processed. If the union contract has a personal allowance of 10%, what is the new standard time? Assume a performance index of 1.0.

2. The average for the five elementary tasks of a given job were calculated as:

$$\bar{t}_1 = 27 \text{ seconds}$$

$$\bar{t}_2 = 43 \text{ seconds}$$

$$\bar{t}_3 = 15 \text{ seconds}$$

$$\bar{t}_4 = 29 \text{ seconds}$$

$$\bar{t}_5 = 21 \text{ seconds}$$

The worker being timed was judged to be working at a normal pace. What is the difference in the standard time for the job using a 10% allowance for personal time as opposed to a 15% allowance?

3. If α is equal to .05, and the absolute error desired for a work sampling study is $\pm 5\%$, compute the sample size if the proportion of busy time is 70%.

4. If you want to be 95% confident in your prediction using work sampling techniques and you can afford to sample only 100 observations, what degree of error must be tolerated if p is 75%?

5. Given the following random numbers, design a tour schedule for taking 25 observations for a work sampling study. Assume an 8-hour observation period.

131	375	124	043	225
311	005	834	621	197
117	152	420	907	527
420	319	254	183	500
817	339	664	298	603
616	153	801	461	721
028	174	395	972	636
306	500	854	386	702
212	054	713	494	190
904	497	154	454	773

6. Make the following charts for jobs of which you have firsthand knowledge:
    a. Flow diagram
    b. Process chart
    c. Operations chart
    d. Simo chart
    e. Man–machine chart
    f. Activity chart

7. Make a time study for any short-cycle repetitive job you have access to.

8. Make a work sampling study of any long-cycle repetitive job you have access to.

9. If you work, select a job you perform and apply the tools in this chapter to improve that job. Write up a complete report of your study.

Case: AMERICAN ADHESIVES COMPANY*

The management of the American Adhesives Company in its Adhesive, Resin, and Chemical Division strives to develop the optimal combination of all variables of the job. With this in mind, the management has been observing and timing the packaging operation of dry adhesives, including the palletizing of the material at the packer. The operation involves the sacking, sewing, and palletizing of 100-pound sacks of dry adhesives for shipment to the plywood industry.

Several different types of mixtures are packaged for shipment during the course of a day. Production is intermittent and by batch, based on the orders received. Ten thousand pounds of material constitute a batch.

The packaging operation is essentially a two-man operation. One worker completes the two phases of sacking and sewing, and the second worker palletizes the filled sacks. A third man operates a lift truck that transports the palletized sacks directly to the loading station. Since all three men often trade jobs to alleviate boredom, management timed each of them in the performance of the sacking, sewing, and palletizing phases. Figure 6-13 shows the flow process chart of the operation under study. The schematic representation of the working area is illustrated in Figure 6-14.

The Working Environment

Management realized that it could not measure the effectiveness of a job design without a knowledge of the working environment in which it was placed. Investigated were:

1. Placement of materials
2. Lighting
3. Ventilation

---

*This case was prepared by Professor Raymond J. Ziegler, President, James Stamp Co., Lakeland, Florida, and was reprinted with his permission.

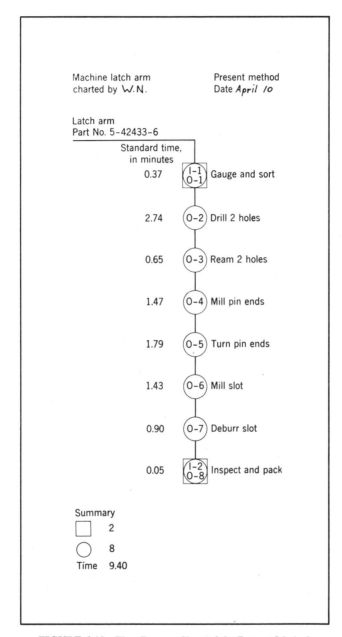

FIGURE 6-13   Flow Process Chart of the Present Method

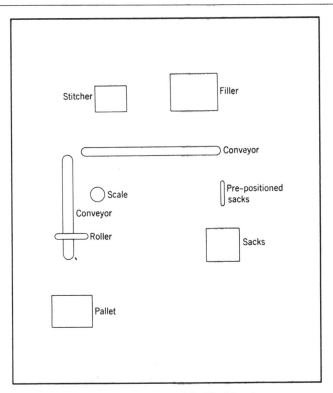

FIGURE 6-14   Layout of the Working Area

4. Heating
5. Cleanliness of the working area
6. Noise

The unfilled sacks were located well within the reach of the average worker. Placed on a reclining stand, they required a minimum of effort to grasp. The dry glue base material was gravity-fed from a hopper located above the filling machine.

The lighting practice was 30 footcandles (on task, or 30 inches above floor); however, there was no fixture directly above the palletizing phase of the operation.

The average condition of air movement was 25 feet per minute. Occasionally the workers were troubled by dust from the powder-dry material being handled.

Although the working area was quite comfortable for summer work, there appeared a possibility that it might be rather cold and drafty during the winter months.

The working area was swept clean during the slack periods in production, and was never allowed to become untidy or dirty enough to hamper production.

Unwanted sound did not appear to be excessive. It was moderated by the music piped into all sections of the plant and played all day long.

The Sacking Phase

This phase of the work was broken down into the following elements:

1. Reach
2. Grasp
3. Transport empty
4. Position
5. Fill (machine time)

The reach element begins the sacking phase of the operation. The worker has just moved from the stitching machine back to the pre-positioned sacks. The pre-positioning of empty sacks was not timed, since it is completed during the delay between lot orders.

The grasp element begins as soon as the worker touches the empty sack and ends when he secures a firm hold and moves the sack. The operator must be careful to grasp only one sack.

The operator then transports the empty sack to the filler. The element ends when the operator begins to place the sack in position. The distance from the stand to the filler is approximately 3.5 feet.

The positioning element involves fitting the sack to the filler and securing the clamps, which hold the sack in position.

Filling is a machine-controlled element. The machine is started by a foot-operated lever and automatically stops when the predesignated amount of material is gravity-fed from a hopper located above the machine. Agitation of the sack during filling is provided by a carrier on which the sack rests.

Each of the three operators was timed five times on each element and, when averaged, this value was used to obtain a grand average for each element. The summation of the grand average elemental values resulted in a total average sacking time of 0.2537 minutes.

The Sacking Phase

	OPERATOR 1	OPERATOR 2	OPERATOR 3	GRAND AVERAGE
Total Time	0.2455	0.2413	0.2742	0.2537
Reach	0.0220	0.0198	0.0247	0.0222
Grasp	0.0055	0.0058	0.0095	0.0069
Transport empty	0.0300	0.0282	0.0400	0.0327
Position	0.0280	0.0275	0.0400	0.0319
Fill	0.1600	0.1600	0.1600	0.1600

The Sewing Phase

This phase of the work was broken down into the following elements:

1. Grasp
2. Inspect
3. Position
4. Stitch
5. Inspect
6. Transport loaded and release

When the sacks are automatically released from the filler, they are transported approximately 3 feet on a conveyor belt, toward the stitching machine.

The flow process chart of the present method shows a delay at this point. When the operator is performing the elements of transport empty and position in the sacking cycle, the sack is awaiting handling. The delay in production caused by the waiting sack averages 0.0320 of a minute per sack.

The grasp element begins when the operator touches the sack, and ends when he holds the sack firmly in both hands.

Inspection consists of a quick eye check of the filled sack. Although minute in time, it is classified separately.

Positioning of the sack involves the placing of the top of the sack in such a manner as to facilitate feeding into the stitcher. The sack is manually positioned and started into the machine. The element ends when the machine begins the actual stitching.

The rate of stitching is partially controlled by the operator as he guides the moving sack through the machine, and this accounts for the variation in the times for each man.

An inspection of the stitching is performed at this point.

The sewing phase of the operation ends when the worker transports the sack from the first conveyor to the second. The worker must lift the 100-pound sack approximately 4 inches from the level of the first conveyor, turn to his left, walk approximately 3 feet, lower the sack to the second conveyor, and release it. The release is accomplished so that the sack's label is turned up and the top of the sack proceeds up the conveyor first. Management made no attempt to separate the transport loaded and release elements.

Upon completion of the release element, the worker returns to the pre-positioned sack area, a distance of 4 feet.

The Sewing Phase

	OPERATOR 1	OPERATOR 2	OPERATOR 3	GRAND AVERAGE
Total Time	0.1647	0.1649	0.1598	0.1631
Grasp	0.0259	0.0122	0.0190	0.0190
Inspect	0.0142	0.0090	0.0100	0.0111
Position	0.0325	0.0466	0.0326	0.0372
Stitch	0.0523	0.0565	0.0526	0.0538
Inspect	0.0023	0.0026	0.0026	0.0025
Transport loaded and release	0.0375	0.0380	0.0430	0.0395

The Palletizing Phase

This phase of the work was broken into the following elements:

1. Stamp
2. Hold
3. Grasp
4. Transport loaded
5. Stack
6. Transport return

After the sack has been placed on the second conveyor by the worker, it travels upward at an approximately 30-degree angle, moving constantly over the rubber-surfaced belt. It passes through a roller, which prepares the sack for later stacking by pressing it. The elapsed time between the sewing and palletizing phases of the operation averaged 0.1870 of a minute. American preferred to keep this time separate, but included it as part of the total operation time.

The palletizing phase begins when the sack reaches the worker and is stamped with the lot number. Since the conveyor is constantly moving, the worker must hold the sack firmly to keep it from running off the end of the belt while he places the stamp.

The grasp element begins when the worker places both hands on the sack, and ends as soon as movement takes place.

The sack must be transported at least 3 feet and in some instances 5 feet, depending on the placement of the pallet. This factor caused significant variations in the time for this element.

Stacking of the bag was dependent on the placement of previous sacks, and varied greatly, affecting the worker's average time.

Transport return includes the travel time of the worker from the pallet to the conveyor preparatory to performing another stamp element.

A lift truck removes the palletized stacks upon the completion of each stack. Occasionally the worker is required to start a second stack if the lift truck is in use in some other part of the plant.

The Palletizing Phase

	OPERATOR 1	OPERATOR 2	OPERATOR 3	GRAND AVERAGE
Total Time	0.3618	0.3113	0.3517	0.3416
Stamp	0.0295	0.0225	0.0272	0.0264
Hold	0.0115	0.0180	0.0119	0.0138
Grasp	0.0156	0.0112	0.0176	0.0148
Transport loaded	0.1080	0.0488	0.0900	0.0823
Stack	0.0142	0.0168	0.0160	0.0157
Transport return	0.1830	0.1940	0.1890	0.1886

Total Operational Time

Sacking phase	0.2537
Sewing phase	0.1631
Transitional travel time	0.1870
Palletizing phase	0.3416
Total Average Time	0.9454

American was prepared to reexamine all aspects of its initial observation and timing of the packaging operation of dry adhesives, including the palletizing of the material at the packer. Its managers were instructed to be on the lookout for changes that would improve job design and could be supported in practice.

Case Discussion Questions

What recommendations for improvement would you propose to the management of American Adhesives Company?

REFERENCES

ABRUZZI, A., *Work Measurement*. New York: Columbia University Press, 1952.

BARNES, RALPH M., *Motion and Time Study: Design and Measurement of Work*, 6th ed. New York: John Wiley, 1968.

BUFFA, ELWOOD SPENCER, *Operations Management: The Management of Productive Systems*. New York: John Wiley, 1976.

CHAPANIS, ALPHONSE, *Man-Machine Engineering*. Belmont, Calif.: Wadsworth, 1965.

CHASE, RICHARD B., and NICHOLAS J. AQUILANO, *Production and Operations Management*, rev. ed. Homewood, Ill.: Richard D. Irwin, 1977.

DAVIS, L.E., "Job Satisfaction Research: The Post-Industrial View," *Industrial Relations*, Vol. 10 (1971), 176–93.

————, and A.B. CHERNS, eds., *Quality of Working Life: Cases*, Vol. II. New York: Free Press, 1975.

————, and J.C. TAYLOR, eds., *Design of Jobs*. Middlesex, England: Penguin Books, 1972.

DICKSON, PAUL, *The Future of the Workplace*. New York: Weybright and Talley, 1975.

FOY, N., and H. GORDON, "Worker Participation: Contrasts in Three Countries," *Harvard Business Review*, Vol. 54, No. 3 (May–June 1976), 71–83.

HACKMAN, J.R., and E.E. LAWLER III, "Employee Reactions to Job Characteristics," *Journal of Applied Psychology*, Vol. 55, (1971), 265–68. Also in Davis and Taylor, *Design of Jobs*.

HERBST, P.G., *Socio-technical Design, Strategies in Multidisciplinary Research*. London: Tavistock, 1974.

HERZBERG, FREDERICK, "One More Time: How Do You Motivate Employees?" *Harvard Business Review*, January–February 1968.

MAYER, RAYMOND R., *Production and Operations Management*, 3rd ed. New York: McGraw-Hill, 1975.

MONKS, JOSEPH G., *Operations Management: Theory and Problems*. New York: McGraw-Hill, 1977.

MOORE, FRANKLIN, *Production Management*. Homewood, Ill.: Richard D. Irwin, 1973.

NADLER, G., *Work Design*, rev. ed. Homewood, Ill.: Richard D. Irwin, 1970.

NIEBEL, BENJAMIN W., *Motion and Time Study*, 5th ed. Homewood, Ill.: Richard D. Irwin, 1972.

THORSRUD, E., and F. EMERY, "Industrial Democracy in Norway," *Industrial Relations*, Vol. 9, No. 2 (February 1970), 187–96.

TRIST, E.L., G.W. HIGGIN, H. MURRAY, and H.P. POLLACK, *Organizational Choice.* London: Tavistock, 1963.

VAN DER ZWAAN, A.H., "The Sociotechnical Systems Approach: A Critical Evaluation," *International Journal of Production Research*, Vol. 13, No. 2 (1975), 149–63.

VROOM, V.H., *Work and Motivation.* New York: John Wiley, 1964.

chapter 7

FACILITY LOCATION

One of the important factors influencing the effectiveness of distribution or services is the location of production, warehouse, and service facilities. The number and relative location of key facilities has a direct effect on the cost of product distribution and services. In many industries, transportation and distribution costs are one of the largest expenses of doing business. One survey indicated that physical distribution costs absorb between 10 and 25 percent of net sales income.[1]

But although the costs of distributing products and providing services have become increasingly important, only a few companies have been really successful in controlling these costs; these successful companies seem to have in common the fact that they use the available scientific methods and computer technology for analysis of distribution problems and long-range planning of facilities. For example, one U.S. corporation has reduced distribution costs from 9 percent to less than 6 percent of the total cost of goods sold.[2] Standard Oil Company of New Jersey recently saved $5 million through the use of a mathematical model for planning distribution and manufacturing operations.[3]

The rationale for delving into a location analysis is not limited to benefitting only manufacturing-oriented distribution systems. Many benefits have been derived from applying location models to hospitals, ambulances, fire engines, police protection, sewage treatment plants, and nuclear power plants. In this chapter, we first examine the location of manufacturing plants and warehouses for product distribution; then we look at some examples of locating nonmanufacturing service functions.

PLANT LOCATION

A need for locating additional production plants can have several possible causes: Increased product demand may necessitate increased production capacity. Emerging markets or new products may require another production location to facilitate distribution. Changes in the cost or availability of required resources may also precipitate a location analysis.

Many plant location questions are ultimately decided by political factors or the personal preferences of top management. However, it has been demonstrated that

---

[1]R. Shannon and T. Ignizio, "A Heuristic Programming Algorithm for Warehouse Location," *AIIE Transactions*, Vol. II, No. 4 (December 1970), 334–39.

[2]R.J. Atkins and R.H. Shriver, "New Approach to Facilities Location," *Harvard Business Review*, May–June 1968, pp. 70–79.

[3]*Ibid.*

the difference in results between a good scientific solution and a manual "seat-of-the-pants" solution can easily be a reduction of at least 5 to 15 percent in total distribution costs. In this chapter we shall consider some procedures that analytically determine effective locations for reducing relevant costs.

Factors Influencing Plant Location

In actual plant location analysis, many factors other than least-cost distribution influence the final location decision. Since plant and other facility location problems represent large resource commitments, their analysis must be consistent with the long-range goals of the organization. The capital assets that are tied up in plant facilities can be enormous for manufacturing organizations. Furthermore, plant location and capacity decisions can have significant effects on gaining market access, satisfying customer needs, and accruing net revenue for the organization.

Another factor influencing the final location of plants is zoning regulations. Site selection must satisfy city or area zoning regulations with respect to structural characteristics and type of industry.

Technological factors such as availability of power, raw materials, or transportation systems may dictate the unique location of a particular plant. Energy-dependent activities such as aluminum reduction need to be located near relatively inexpensive and plentiful sources of energy. Mining operations have to be located near the origin of the raw resources. Also, the processing plants for these types of resources are generally located near rivers or railway systems for economical transportation.

Intangible factors affecting future costs of a plant can include the tax structure of the local community and the community's attitude toward the type of enterprise. Local land and construction costs are tangible factors that must be compared between communities. Also, the quality and availability of the local labor supply can have significant effects on wage rates and training costs. Some plants have located labor-oriented plants in the southern United States or even foreign countries to take advantage of cheaper labor. However, wage rates can change with unionization, and they are not always commensurate with productivity. The trend of U.S. firms to locate outside this country has lessened with rapidly increasing wages in foreign countries, but some industries with high labor content can still lower costs by locating abroad.

Development of pollution-control standards has added a new dimension to the location analysis of plants that emit any type of air or water pollution. Standards vary within states or communities and thus can be a decisive factor in choosing a location. Urban areas such as New York and Los Angeles have particularly stringent air-emission standards. In some cases, these standards have not been enforced, in the interest of a productive economy. However, the pollution-control problem is a relatively new one and should continue to pose problems for management not only in location studies, but also in increased plant costs to meet emission standards.

Capacity Considerations

Once a plant has been located, its productive capacity still remains to be determined. Questions exist as to the time frame from which to judge capacity requirements. Should the plant be adequate for the next five, ten, or 20 years? Forecasting future capacity needs is a worthwhile but inexact endeavor. Top-level management must base its decisions on its own visions as well as scientific forecasts. Larger plants require a larger investment but sometimes offer advantages. Larger plants with perhaps more automatic equipment allow a higher volume of output and sometimes a lower unit cost of production. Rapidly rising construction costs can also mean that a large plant that is underutilized in its first few years may offer the least-cost alternative in the long run. In some cases, government tax benefits are created to stimulate capital investment in productive capacity. These incentives may lower plant development costs during periods of planned economic recovery.

Decisions regarding present and future plant capacity should be carried out with a thorough financial analysis of the investment alternative. A net present-value analysis or other means of measuring future cash inflows and outflows should be calculated and considered along with budget limitations and need for future productive capacity.

Locating a Single Plant

The decision regarding the location of a plant may be determined by one of the previously discussed factors, such as energy needs or managerial preference. However, even the consideration of these factors alone usually results in several feasible alternatives for plant location. The final decision then is normally based on cost considerations, although other criteria, such as proximity to market and speed of distribution, may be relevant. Once a set of feasible locations has been determined, an optimization model or a heuristic can then be used to find the alternative that results in the minimum production and distribution costs. Assuming that management's objective is to minimize the total cost of production and distribution, let us consider an example problem in locating an additional plant to an existing system. We use the transportation method of linear programming to minimize distribution costs.

Take the Electrovox problem of Chapter 2. We assume that demand for CB radios has increased 20 percent, and this is reflected in increased demand at each warehouse. Let us further assume that management has limited the choice of new plant locations to St. Louis and Atlanta. Figure 7-1 depicts the geographic nature of the distribution problem. Table 7-1 updates the Electrovox problem to include the increase in demand.

The plants at Washington, D.C., Denver, and Los Angeles have monthly production capacities of 50, 80, and 120 respectively. The monthly customer demands at regional warehouses are now 108 at New York, 84 at Chicago, 48 at Dallas, and 60 at San Francisco. The matrix of per-unit shipping costs is presented in Table 7-1.

In Chapter 2, we solved the distribution problem (with reduced demand) by

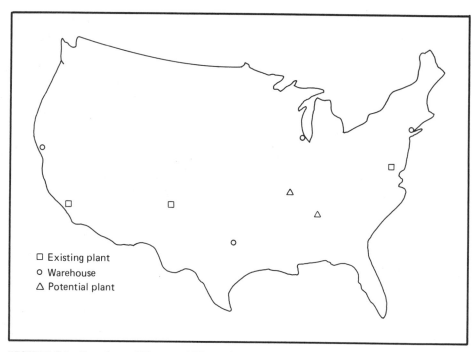

FIGURE 7-1   Locations of Plants and Warehouses, and Potential Plant Locations for Electrolux

Table 7-1   Data for Electrovox Location Problem

	UNIT SHIPPING COSTS				
	TO WAREHOUSE				PLANT CAPACITY (1,000s)
FROM PLANT	*NEW YORK*	*CHICAGO*	*DALLAS*	*SAN FRANCISCO*	
Washington, D.C.	.80	.90	1.10	1.60	50
Denver	1.20	.70	.50	.80	80
Los Angeles	1.40	1.00	.60	.70	120
?					100
Demand (1,000s)	108	84	48	60	350 / 300

Vogel's Approximation Method. This heuristic reached a final distribution cost of $203,000, an amount only .49 percent more than the optimal cost of $202,000. Let us assume in our analysis that we have an optimization procedure for transportation models at our disposal. We can use this procedure to determine the minimum distribution costs when either the St. Louis or Atlanta alternative is considered.

The management at Electrovox has decided that the new plant should have a capacity of 100 per month. This represents 50 units of unused capacity in order to accommodate future demand. Because of differences in local wage rates and overhead, the per-unit production costs of the three existing plants are $9, $10, and $8 respectively, at Washington, D.C., Denver, and Los Angeles. It is estimated that differential production costs would amount to $9 at St. Louis and $8 at Atlanta. The monthly overhead for plant and equipment costs is estimated to be $6,000 at St. Louis and $8,000 at Atlanta over the life of the plant. We are now ready to analyze the location problem on a cost basis. Table 7-2 reflects the combined per-unit shipping and production costs when the St. Louis location is considered; we arrived at the estimated combined costs of shipping and production for St. Louis by adding $9 to each of the shipping costs from St. Louis to New York ($1.00), Chicago ($.50), Dallas ($.60), and San Francisco ($1.10).

Table 7-2   Combined Shipping and Production Costs

<table>
<tr><td colspan="6" align="center">TOTAL COSTS</td></tr>
<tr><td rowspan="3">FROM PLANT</td><td colspan="4" align="center">TO WAREHOUSE</td><td rowspan="3">PLANT CAPACITY (1,000s)</td></tr>
<tr><td></td><td></td><td></td><td>SAN</td></tr>
<tr><td>NEW YORK</td><td>CHICAGO</td><td>DALLAS</td><td>FRANCISCO</td></tr>
<tr><td>Washington, D.C.</td><td>9.80</td><td>9.90</td><td>10.10</td><td>10.60</td><td>50</td></tr>
<tr><td>Denver</td><td>11.20</td><td>10.70</td><td>10.50</td><td>10.80</td><td>80</td></tr>
<tr><td>Los Angeles</td><td>9.40</td><td>9.00</td><td>8.60</td><td>8.70</td><td>120</td></tr>
<tr><td>St. Louis</td><td>10.00</td><td>9.50</td><td>9.60</td><td>10.10</td><td>100</td></tr>
<tr><td>Demand (1,000s)</td><td>108</td><td>84</td><td>48</td><td>60</td><td>350 / 300</td></tr>
</table>

Using the MODI method or some other procedure that optimizes standard transportation models, we can determine the optimal production/distribution schedule. In Table 7-3 we present the optimal solution.

The numbers in the upper left-hand corner of the cells in Table 7-3 are the unit production and shipping costs, whereas the numbers in the middle of the cells represent amounts produced and shipped. Thus, the optimal strategy is to produce and ship according to the following plan:

Washington D.C.	to New York	50
Denver	to New York	30
Los Angeles	to New York	12
Los Angeles	to Dallas	48
Los Angeles	to San Francisco	60
St. Louis	to New York	16
St. Louis	to Chicago	84

The total monthly distribution and production cost for this strategy is 50,000(9.80) + 30,000(11.20) + 12,000(9.40) + 48,000(8.60) + 60,000(8.70) + 16,000(10.00) + 84,000(9.50) = \$2,831,600.

Table 7-3   Optimal Production/Distribution Strategy for St. Louis Location

FROM \ TO	NEW YORK	CHICAGO	DALLAS	SAN FRANCISCO	PLANT CAPACITY (1,000s)
Washington, D.C.	9.80 \ 50	9.90	10.10	10.60	50
Denver	11.20 \ 30	10.70	10.50	10.80	80
Los Angeles	9.40 \ 12	9.00	8.60 \ 48	8.70 \ 60	120
St. Louis	10.00 \ 16	9.50 \ 84	9.60	10.10	100
Demand (1,000s)	108	84	48	60	300 \ 350

To evaluate the Atlanta alternative, we again use a linear programming optimization procedure to determine the best production/distribution strategy. The optimal solution for this alternative is presented in Table 7-4. When the Atlanta

Table 7-4   Optimal Production/Distribution Strategy for Atlanta Location

FROM \ TO	NEW YORK	CHICAGO	DALLAS	SAN FRANCISCO	PLANT CAPACITY (1,000s)
Washington, D.C.	9.80 \ 50	9.90	10.10	10.60	50
Denver	11.20	10.70 \ 30	10.50	10.80	80
Los Angeles	9.40	9.00 \ 12	8.60 \ 48	8.70 \ 60	120
Atlanta	9.00 \ 58	8.70 \ 42	8.60	9.30	100
Demand (1,000s)	108	84	48	60	300 \ 350

location is used, the optimal production distribution plan is:

Washington D.C.	to New York	50
Denver	to Chicago	30
Los Angeles	to Chicago	12
Los Angeles	to Dallas	48
Los Angeles	to San Francisco	60
Atlanta	to New York	58
Atlanta	to Chicago	42

The total monthly production distribution cost for the plan is 50,000(9.80) + 30,000(10.70) + 12,000(9.00) + 48,000(8.60) + 60,000(8.70) + 58,000(9.00) + 42,000(8.70) = $2,741,200.

We can now compare the two alternatives on an overall cost basis. We assume here that differences in total cost will result only from differences between distribution, production, and building and equipment costs. For the St. Louis location, the overall costs may be summarized as:

Production costs	$2,610,000
Distribution costs	221,600
Building and equipment costs	6,000
Total costs	$2,837,600

For the Atlanta location, we have:

Production costs	$2,510,000
Distribution costs	231,200
Building and equipment costs	8,000
Total costs	$2,749,200

Based on cost criteria alone, it appears that Atlanta is the more effective location for a new plant.

You may wonder what happened to the additional 50,000 units of production capacity. From Tables 7-3 and 7-4 we can see that the Denver plant absorbed all 50,000 units of slack for either locational alternative. This in reality may not be an acceptable production schedule. To bring the Denver plant down from 80,000 to 30,000 units of production may have negative consequences that are not directly measurable in monetary terms. Later we shall discuss decision making with multiple-criteria objectives.

MULTIPLE WAREHOUSE LOCATION

In the preceding section, we considered the location of an additional plant to meet demand and minimize production/distribution costs. We can generalize that same problem to consider more than one plant. In this section, however, we apply the multiple facility location analysis to warehouses; there are usually more warehouses than plants in a distribution system, and warehouses are less subject to the intangible decision factors often associated with plants.

Many approaches have been developed to solve warehouse location problems. Exact optimization procedures such as branch and bound have been developed by Effroymson and Ray and Khumawala; these have been successfully applied in actual practice.[4] Computer simulation is a valuable tool in evaluating various warehouse system configurations. However, simulation is not capable of generating solutions; rather, it evaluates them. Simulation is particularly effective in analyzing complex systems in which distribution decisions interact with other operations, such as inventory. Markland used simulation to evaluate field warehouse location configurations and inventory levels for the Ralston Purina Company.[5] Another common approach to warehouse location involves heuristic decision rules. Heuristics are necessary for solving really large-scale problems, since exact optimization techniques are not computationally practical. To give you an idea why less efficient optimization procedures cannot always be used in the analysis of real-world problems, consider a warehouse location problem presented by Khumawala and Whybark.[6] The following characteristics pertain to a medium-sized manufacturing firm that distributes only in the United States:

5,000	customers or demand centers
100	potential warehouse locations
5	producing plants
15	products
4	shipping classes
100	transportation-rate variables

In warehouse location problems, we are usually concerned with how many warehouses to have and where to locate them. Other relevant issues are modes of transportation and appropriate inventory levels to maintain between plant, warehouse, and customer. In our initial analysis here, we will consider the problem of how many warehouses to open and where to locate them. At first we assume that each

[4]M.A. Effroymson and T.A. Ray, "A Branch-Bound Algorithm for Plant Location," *Operations Research*, Vol. 14 (May–June 1966), 361–68; B.M. Khumawala, "An Efficient Branch and Bound Algorithm for the Warehouse Location Problem," *Management Science*, Vol. 18 (August 1972), 718–31.

[5]R.E. Markland, "Analyzing Geographically Discrete Warehousing Networks by Computer Simulation," *Decision Sciences*, Vol. 4 (April 1973), 216–36.

[6]B.M. Khumawala and D.C. Whybark, "A Comparison of Some Recent Warehouse Location Techniques," *The Logistics Review*, Vol. 7 (1971).

warehouse has sufficient capacity to serve all customers; thus we have to open only one warehouse. Other warehouses will only be opened in order to further reduce distribution costs. The basic tradeoffs involve variable transportation costs versus fixed costs of operating a warehouse. This particular problem is called the simple warehouse location problem. Let's look at a simple but effective heuristic by Khuma-wala for solving it.[7]

Warehouse Location Example

Consider the Automotive Parts Supply Co., which distributes car parts to five major customer demand centers in Los Angeles, Cleveland, San Antonio, New York, and Atlanta. The firm is considering four potential warehouse locations to facilitate distribution: Salt Lake City, Philadelphia, Chicago, and Dallas. In order to open a warehouse, the company must pay a fixed cost that includes the amortized cost of building the warehouse, inventory, taxes, insurance, and wages. The variable warehouse-to-customer costs include FOB cost at the warehouse, warehouse handling cost, and the warehouse-to-customer transportation costs. Figure 7-2 illustrates the geographical nature of the problem.

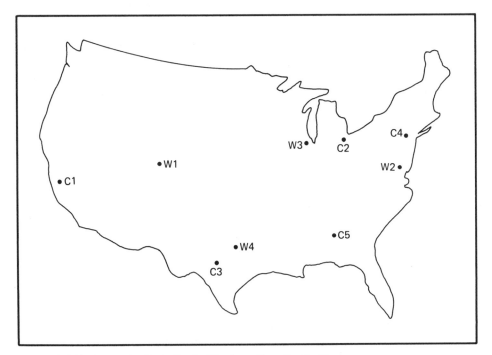

FIGURE 7-2   Automotive Parts Supply Warehouse Location Problem

[7]B.M. Khumawala, "An Efficient Heuristic Procedure for the Uncapacitated Warehouse Location Problem," *Naval Research Logistics Quarterly*, Vol. 20, No. 1 (March 1973), 109–21.

In Table 7-5, we present the fixed warehouse costs and distribution costs from warehouse to customer. The distribution costs in the table each represent the total yearly distribution cost if supplied entirely from the warehouse in the particular row. Note that each customer will receive all his supply from the single warehouse that is the cheapest open alternative.

Table 7-5 Fixed Costs and Warehouse Distribution Costs to Each of 5 Customers

		DISTRIBUTION COSTS FROM WAREHOUSE TO CUSTOMER				
FIXED COSTS PER YEAR		LOS ANGELES	CLEVE-LAND	SAN ANTONIO	NEW YORK	ATLANTA
9,000	Salt Lake City	6,000	20,000	16,000	36,000	28,000
6,000	Philadelphia	24,000	12,000	20,000	8,000	16,000
6,000	Chicago	18,000	8,000	12,000	10,000	10,000
8,000	Dallas	16,000	12,000	10,000	24,000	18,000

The heuristic procedure we consider is called by Khumawala the largest omega rule. The heuristic is based on the concept of opening and closing various warehouses based on some minimum and maximum savings calculations. The heuristic is quite effective, as it often yields the optimal solution. On large, real-world problems, the error (if it exists) is usually no more than 1 or 2 percent.

Steps of the Heuristic. First we calculate a lower bound on the savings that could be achieved by opening any single warehouse. If this lower bound is greater than zero, we automatically fix that warehouse open. The minimum distribution savings for opening a warehouse can be calculated by comparing the distribution cost with those of all other warehouses. For the Salt Lake City location, we calculate the minimum savings by looking down each column in Table 7-5 to see how much (if any) the distribution cost to each customer could be reduced if supplied by Salt Lake City. In column 1, we save at least $10,000 ($16,000 − $6,000) if a warehouse at Salt Lake City is opened. In the other four columns, no savings is found above the other best choice for each customer. Thus we may find the net minimum savings by subtracting the fixed costs of operating the warehouse at Salt Lake City. The lower bound or minimum savings is:

$$\text{MINSAV (1)} = [10{,}000 + 0 + 0 + 0 + 0] - \$9{,}000 = \$1{,}000$$

Calculating the minimum savings for the other three potential warehouses, we obtain:

$$\text{MINSAV (2)} = [0 + 0 + 0 + 2{,}000 + 0] - 6{,}000 = -4{,}000$$

$$\text{MINSAV (3)} = [0 + 4{,}000 + 0 + 0 + 6{,}000] - 6{,}000 = \$4{,}000$$

$$\text{MINSAV (4)} = [0 + 0 + 2{,}000 + 0 + 0] - 8{,}000 = -\$6{,}000$$

Since the minimum savings for warehouses 1 and 3 are both greater than zero, we fix both of them open. In case all minimum savings are less than zero, we open the one warehouse whose savings is largest.

In step 2, we calculate a maximum savings for these warehouses that have been neither opened nor closed (free). The maximum savings is calculated by comparing the distribution costs of the free warehouse with those of the ones that have been fixed open. Other warehouses that are free or fixed closed are ignored. Thus, the maximum savings for warehouses 2 and 4 are calculated as:

$$\text{MAXSAV (2)} = [0 + 0 + 0 + 2{,}000 + 0] - 6{,}000 = -\$4{,}000$$
$$\text{MAXSAV (4)} = [0 + 0 + 2{,}000 + 0 + 0] - 8{,}000 = -\$6{,}000$$

In this example, the MAXSAV and MINSAV calculations yielded the same results, but this will not normally be the case. In step 2, we open the warehouse with the largest positive MAXSAV value (if any exist). Likewise, we fix closed any warehouses whose maximum savings is negative. Step 2 is then repeated until a decision is reached on each potential warehouse location.

In this example, we are finished, for MAXSAV (2) and MAXSAV (4) are both negative; thus, we close them both. The final solution is to open the Salt Lake City and Chicago warehouses. Los Angeles is supplied by Salt Lake City; all other customers are supplied by the Chicago warehouse. The minimum annual cost is $61,000 and is broken down as:

Fixed costs	9,000 + 6,000	= 15,000
Transportation costs	6,000 + 8,000 + 12,000 + 10,000 + 10,000	= 46,000
Total costs		$61,000

Extensions

The simple plant location model has several applications, especially when fixed costs and distribution costs are the main concerns. However, many real-world location problems require generalizations of the model. The most obvious generalization is the case where the warehouses actually have limited capacity and cannot uniquely satisfy all customer demand. The problem is known as the capacitated warehouse location problem and has been studied by Khumawala and others.[8] The solution procedures are in most cases adaptations of the procedures for the simple plant location problem.

[8]See G. Sã, "Branch-and-Bound and Approximate Solutions to the Capacitated Plant-Location Problem," *Operations Research*, Vol. 17, No. 6 (November–December 1969), 1005–15.

Multiple Objectives

So far, we have assumed that managerial objectives were to minimize costs. In actual location problems, however, cost minimization is usually not the only objective sought by management. Other objectives may include stabilized employment at plants, contract requirements, minimizing inventories, balanced workloads at plants or warehouses, and special treatment of particular customers.

Research is in progress to develop methods that will help achieve multiple and, in some cases, conflicting objectives. One successful approach has been *goal programming*. Goal programming is a type of mathematical programming in which constraints are defined and various goals are stated and ranked according to priority. Keeping within the constraints, highest-priority goals are satisfied first. Lower-priority goals are satisfied only if higher-priority goals are not sacrificed. Thus, in location problems, we may first attempt to achieve stable employment, second cost minimization, and third minimal inventories. Lee and Moore have developed a goal programming model for distribution problems.[9]

Long-Range Warehouse Location Analysis

We have thus far considered the location of plants or warehouses under static conditions. That is, we have determined the best locations at a given point in time. Since plants and warehouses represent a long-term commitment, it would be helpful to analyze locations over extended periods of time. Emerging markets and changing demand patterns can cause shifts in the desired locations of warehouses. Sweeney and Tatham have developed a computerized procedure that uses mixed integer programming combined with dynamic programming to determine the optimal sequence of warehouse configurations over multiple periods.[10]

Let us examine an example problem from Sweeney and Tatham, which consists of two plants, five possible warehouse locations, 15 customer zones, and a five-year planning horizon. The demand forecasts for the customer zones are presented in Table 7-6. These demand forecasts reflect the company plans to begin marketing its product in the northern and western regions at the beginning of period 2. Throughout the planning horizon, demand is expected to increase slightly in the southern regions and heavily in the new market areas of Chicago and Milwaukee. The warehouse and plant capacities are shown in Table 7-7, and warehouse fixed costs in Table 7-8. The variable shipping costs were taken to be \$.006 per mile between plant and warehouse, and \$.01 per mile between warehouse and customer. The variable costs of storing and

---

[9]S.M. Lee and L.J. Moore, "Optimizing Transportation Problems with Multiple Objectives," *AIIE Transactions*, Vol. 5 (December 1973), 333–38.

[10]D. Sweeney and R. Tatham, "An Improved Long-Run Model for Multiple Warehouse Location," *Management Science*, Vol. 22, No. 7 (March 1976), 748–58.

Table 7-6 Demand Forecasts

	PERIOD				
CUSTOMER ZONE	1	2	3	4	5
Milwaukee, Wisc.	0.0	433,235	866,471	1,299,710	1,732,940
Chicago, Ill.	0.0	2,145,070	4,290,140	6,435,200	8,580,270
Bloomington, Ill.	0.0	35,074	70,148	105,223	140,297
Detroit, Mich.	4,459,800	4,459,800	4,459,800	4,459,800	4,459,800
Lansing, Mich.	353,426	353,426	353,426	353,426	353,426
Kalamazoo, Mich.	283,870	283,870	283,870	283,870	283,870
Cleveland, Ohio	2,756,360	2,756,360	2,756,360	2,756,360	2,756,360
Columbus, Ohio	1,142,360	1,142,360	1,142,360	1,142,360	1,142,360
Toledo, Ohio	1,264,290	1,264,290	1,264,290	1,264,290	1,264,290
Cincinnati, Ohio	1,445,380	1,589,920	1,734,450	1,878,990	2,023,530
Dayton, Ohio	881,624	969,786	1,057,950	1,146,110	1,234,270
Akron, Ohio	859,025	859,025	859,025	859,025	859,025
Benton Harbor, Mich.	0.0	62,668	125,337	188,005	250,673
Indianapolis, Ind.	1,166,790	1,283,470	1,400,150	1,156,830	1,633,510
Ft. Wayne, Ind.	388,384	388,384	388,384	388,384	388,384

SOURCE: D. Sweeney and R. Tatham, "An Improved Long-Run Model for Multiple ware-house Location," *Management Science*, Vol. 22, No. 7 (March 1976), 748–58.

Table 7-7 Warehouse and Plant Capacities (lbs. × 1,000)

WAREHOUSE		PERIOD				
LOCATION	NO.	1	2	3	4	5
Toledo	1	10,000	10,000	10,000	10,000	10,000
Chicago	2	7,000	7,000	10,000	10,000	10,000
Detroit	3	8,500	8,500	8,500	8,500	8,500
Cleveland	4	7,500	7,500	7,500	7,500	7,500
Cincinnati	5	12,000	12,000	12,000	12,000	12,000
PLANT						
LOCATION	NO.					
Akron	1	12,000	12,000	—	—	—
Indianapolis	2	18,000	18,000	18,000	18,000	18,000
Toledo	3	—	—	12,000	12,000	12,000

handling goods were taken to be constant and equal for all warehouses, and thus were not included in the analysis.

Assuming it costs $100,000 to close a warehouse and $200,000 to open a new

Table 7-8   Fixed Costs for Warehouses

WAREHOUSE LOCATION NO./YEAR		FIXED COST (× 1,000)				
		1	2	3	4	5
Toledo	1	300	300	300	300	300
Chicago	2	300	300	300	400	400
Detroit	3	300	300	300	300	300
Cleveland	4	320	320	320	320	320
Cincinnati	5	360	360	360	360	360

site, the Sweeney and Tatham model produces the following solution over the five years:

YEAR	CONFIGURATION
1	(1, 5)
2	(1, 5)
3	(1, 2, 5)
4	(1, 2, 5)
5	(1, 2, 5)
Total cost	$10,569,000

Thus, the optimal configuration consists of warehouses at Toledo and Cincinnati for the first two years, with the Chicago warehouse being opened for the last three. The analysis in the problem was for a single product, but the general methodology can be extended to include multiple products.

LOCATION MODELS IN THE PUBLIC SECTOR

Location models in the public sector are mainly based on providing services rather than distributing a physical product. Some of the techniques for locating service facilities are similar to distributional location methods but focus more on the geographic concentration of users and their needs.

The location of service-oriented facilities has been much discussed in the literature. The location of hospitals and regional health services has been studied by several researchers, including Abernathy and Hershey.[11] Kolesar and Walker have studied the dynamic relocation of fire companies in New York City in order to provide fire protection to each region at all times.[12] Other public location models include the

---

[11]W.J. Abernathy and J.C. Hershey, "A Spatial-Allocation Model for Regional Health-Services Planning," *Operations Research*, Vol. 20 (May–June 1972), 629–42.

[12]P. Kolesar and W.E. Walker, "An Algorithm for the Dynamic Relocation of Fire Companies," *Operations Research*, Vol. 22 (March–April 1974), 249–74.

locating of police protection, sewage treatment plants, and public parks and recreation facilities.[13] These types of location models can be more difficult to analyze in many cases, since multiple objectives and political constraints exist. Optimal location of public facilities depends on several demographic characteristics as well as required response times and priorities of service. In order to demonstrate the nature of locating service facilities, we take a brief look at applications involving ambulance services, nuclear power plants, and cash management services.

Location of Emergency Ambulance Services

The location of ambulances has been studied in major U.S. cities such as Los Angeles (Fitzsimmons)[14] and New York (Savas).[15] Let's consider the problem of improving ambulance service in New York City. Prior to the Savas study, New York's policy had been to station 109 ambulances at a total of 49 hospitals. Each hospital was in a designated district and sent out ambulances in response to requests only from within that district. In order to improve the ambulance response times, the city decided to try satellite garages for the ambulances. Any analytical procedure had to consider where the ambulance satellite garages should be located, the locations of hospitals, the geographic distribution and frequency of calls within each district, and finally, the number of ambulances.

In order to analyze this complex problem, the city used a computer simulation model to estimate actual response times and thus the performance of various location alternatives. The analysis was restricted to the Kings County Hospital district in Brooklyn, as shown in Figure 7-3. The average response time with the old system (housing ambulances at the hospital) was 13.5 minutes. Various location alternatives were designed and simulated. Finally, the analysts tried an entirely new approach, in which the hospital districts were ignored. Ambulances located at satellite garages would simply proceed to the nearest available hospital after picking up a patient. This system required a central dispatch facility to coordinate the status of requests with each ambulance and hospital. The simulation model predicted the best overall results for the system. If ten ambulances were located at demand centers in the Kings County district, response times were shown to drop 30 percent.

Nuclear Power Plant Location

Nuclear power plant location differs significantly from manufacturing plant location in that the main objective is to provide energy for nearby users. Decisions as to where to build nuclear power plants are to a large extent determined by political realities and

---

[13]C. Revelle, D. Marks, and J. Liebman, "An Analysis of Private and Public Sector Location Models," *Management Science*, Vol. 16, No. 11 (July 1970), 692–707.

[14]J.A. Fitzsimmons, "A Methodology for Emergency Ambulance Deployment," *Management Science*, Vol. 19 (February 1973), 627–36.

[15]E. Savas, "Simulation and Cost-Effectiveness Analysis of New York's Emergency Ambulance Service," *Management Science*, Vol. 15 (August 1969), B608–27.

FIGURE 7-3   Map of Brooklyn, Showing Hospital District and Areas near Hospital and Satellite

SOURCE: E. Savas, "Simulation and Cost-Effectiveness Analysis of New York's Emergency Ambulance Service," *Management Science*, Vol. 15 (August 1969), B608–27.

the willingness of a community to accept such a plant. However, the state of Washington, through its Energy Research Group, wanted to determine the most economically viable alternatives for nuclear plant location.

By 1981, available hydropower resources in the Pacific Northwest and all known area resources for coal-fired thermal plants will have been developed. Historical growth in demand for power in the Pacific Northwest has occurred at rates of 6 to 7 percent annually, and it appears that the incremental demand growth arising between 1981 and 1992 will have to be met by nuclear thermal plants.

Dutton, Hinman, and Millham have developed a model that optimizes nuclear power plant location with respect to capital-construction, operating, and transmission costs.[16] Their procedure uses the simplex method in conjunction with a branch-and-bound process to ensure integer solutions. In Figure 7-4, the layout of the problem studied is presented. The squares designate current power sources, the large circles are demand centers, and the small numbered circles represent potential 1,000-megawatt nuclear plant locations. In analyzing the problem starting and construction costs were annualized at 14 percent; variable operating costs are measured in mills per kilowatt hour. The model is essentially a two-product model, as peak and average annual power requirements are model constraints. Optimal plant locations are developed for future demand growth rates of 4, 5, 6, and 7 percent. For the 6 percent

---

[16]R. Dutton, G. Hinman, and C.B. Millham, "The Optimal Location of Nuclear-Power Facilities in the Pacific Northwest," *Operations Research*, Vol. 22, No. 3 (May–June 1974), 478–87.

FIGURE 7-4   The Projected Power–Supply Demand–Distribution Pattern for 1981, and the Locations of 13 Proposed 1,000–Megawatt Power Plants

SOURCE: R. Dutton, G. Hinman, and C.B. Millham, "The Optimal Location of Nuclear-Power Facilities in the Pacific Northwest," *Operations Research*, Vol. 22, No. 3 (May–June 1974), 478–87.

growth rate, the projected optimal solution is to build plants at all 13 locations except number 4. The combined annual site-dependent operating, transmission, and amortized capital-construction costs amounted to $75,700,000.

Cash Management

Our last location example applies location theory to making the best use of monetary resources. The first problem we consider is called the lockbox problem and involves the effective placement of receiving locations for large payments received. Consider a large firm that receives large payments from customers on a monthly basis. The checks are normally mailed by a given deadline. However, several days can elapse before the U.S. mail system and bank clearing system bring the check to be deposited in the recipient's account. Several days of interest on millions of dollars represents a significant amount of lost interest. The question then becomes where to locate lockboxes throughout banks in the United States in order to credit payments to the receiver's accounts as quickly as possible. Relevant data include the speed of the U.S. mail, cost of maintaining a lockbox, check clearing times, and total dollars involved.

Diametrically opposed to the lockbox problem is the cash disbursement problem.[17] Here, it is the objective of the payee to get his payment postmarked by the deadline but then take the maximum amount of time to clear his account. Maximizing day-dollar float requires data pertaining to check-clearing times between major U.S. banks. Such data are available from certain cash management services. These commercial services also perform a location analysis for clients. The costs for considering 100 potential bank account locations runs as high as $5,000; interestingly, one of the authors has performed a similar analysis with a heuristic, resulting in a total computer cost of less than $2. Some of the quantitative techniques used in solving these cash management problems are very similar to uncapacitated warehouse location problems, as any single account can handle all transactions. The cash disbursement location analysis offers a sophisticated way to generate more revenue for the firm, but only as long as the Federal Reserve System continues to absorb the float.

SUMMARY

In this chapter we have considered location models for a wide variety of applications. In the addition of a single manufacturing plant, we found the transportation method of linear programming to be useful in determining minimal distribution costs. Combining distribution costs with plant fixed and operating costs and subjective factors, we can select the best plant location.

For locating multiple plants or warehouses, several optimization procedures exist. We studied an effective heuristic for solving the uncapacitated warehouse location problem. Generalizations of the problem include the capacitated warehouse location problem and location problems with multiple objectives. We also considered a model that determines the optimal warehouse system configuration over a long-range period of time.

Location theory has many uses in the location of services or public facilities; health services, public parks, and recreation areas are prime examples. We examined three widely diverse applications in ambulance location, nuclear power plant location, and cash management.

All models and procedures studied require accurate data, which are often difficult to obtain. Finally, these procedures provide a rational basis from which to

---

[17]G. Cornuejols, M. Fisher, and G.M. Nemhauser, "Location of Bank Accounts to Optimize Float: An Analytic Study of Exact and Approximate Algorithms," *Management Science*, Vol. 23 (April 1977), 789–810.

make location decisions; the final location decisions incorporate not only these results but extraneous factors and the subjectivity of the decision maker.

SOLVED PROBLEMS

Problem Statement

The Zoro Lawn Mower Co. is planning to build a new plant to manufacture a new type of weed trimmer. Potential plant sites have been narrowed down to Oklahoma City and Mobile. The fixed costs of debt, utilities, and taxes are $275,000 for the Oklahoma City site and $255,000 for the Mobile location. The variable costs, which involve labor, materials, and transportation, are $16 and $18 per unit respectively.

1. If the Zoro Co. anticipates sales of 15,000 units, which location should it choose?
2. Suppose that the marketing department projects the following probabilities for annual sales:

SALES VOLUME	PROBABILITY
12,000	.10
15,000	.40
20,000	.30
25,000	.20

Which site would you select?

Solution

1. At a volume of 15,000 units, the annual costs are:

$$\text{Oklahoma City:} \quad \$275,000 + 16(15,000) = \$515,000$$
$$\text{Mobile:} \quad \$255,000 + 18(15,000) = \$525,000$$

Choose Oklahoma City based on cost criteria alone.

2. The solution to part 2 depends upon the company's attitude toward risk. However, calculating the expected volume yields:

$$\text{Expected volume} = .10(12,000) + .40(15,000) + .30(20,000) + .20(25,000)$$
$$= 1,200 + 6,000 + 6,000 + 5,000$$
$$= 18,200 \text{ units}$$

Probabilistically, 18,200 units are expected to sell. Based on this figure, the Oklahoma City site should be selected.

Problem Statement

A firm is considering the establishment of some warehouses to reduce distribution costs and time delays in getting its products from a central plant to their four primary markets. Questions arise as to how many warehouses to establish and where to locate them. The table below reflects fixed annual operating costs and total transportation costs for supplying a given customer entirely from a given warehouse. Which warehouses should be established?

POTENTIAL WAREHOUSES	FIXED COSTS	CUSTOMERS			
		A	B	C	D
St. Louis	50,000	75,000	50,000	55,000	20,000
Memphis	45,000	80,000	45,000	60,000	30,000
Jacksonville	48,000	100,000	35,000	70,000	40,000

Solution

Using the savings calculations of Khumawala's heuristic, we find:

MINSAV (St. Louis) $= [5,000 + 0 + 5,000 + 10,000] - 50,000 = -\$30,000$

MINSAV (Memphis) $= [0 + 0 + 0 + 0] - 45,000 = -\$45,000$

MINSAV (Jacksonville) $= [0 + 10,000 + 0 + 0] - 48,000 = -\$38,000$

Since the St. Louis warehouse yields the largest MINSAV value, we open it.

Next we calculate maximum savings of the Memphis and Jacksonville warehouses, given that the St. Louis warehouse is open:

MAXSAV (Memphis) $= [0 + 5,000 + 0 + 0] - 45,000 = -\$40,000$

MAXSAV (Jacksonville) $= [0 + 15,000 + 0 + 0] - 48,000 = -\$33,000$

Since both remaining warehouses have maximum benefits less than zero, both are closed, and the best solution is to open only the St. Louis warehouse at an annual cost of $250,000.

REVIEW QUESTIONS

1. What is the main purpose of using the transportation method of linear programming in locating a simple plant?
2. Besides distribution and fixed and operating costs, what other factors should be considered in locating plants?
3. Computer simulation can be useful in analyzing location problems, but what must you provide the simulator?

4. In multiple-objective problems, what are some of the more likely managerial objectives in addition to cost minimization?

5. How is goal programming useful in facility location?

6. When might it be advantageous for a firm to locate a plant in a foreign country?

7. In what ways does warehouse location differ from plant location?

8. In what ways does the location of service facilities differ from the location of manufacturing facilities?

9. Explain how the MINSAV and MAXSAV calculations of Khumawala's heuristic can be used to open and close warehouses.

10. What is the difference between static and dynamic plant location problems?

11. List the quantitative techniques (those we have mentioned in this chapter) that apply in analyzing location problems.

12. Sometimes the most rational or economical location as calculated by a quantitative model is not chosen. Explain.

13. Discuss the advantages of locating a large, centralized manufacturing facility as opposed to several decentralized facilities. Discuss the disadvantages.

14. Which factors do you think would play a prominent role in the location of each of the following?
    a. A large plant for the manufacture of washers and dryers
    b. Nuclear power plants
    c. Oil company headquarters
    d. A retail outlet for exclusive men's clothing

PROBLEMS

1. The Continental Co. currently has three production plants, which ship to its three regional warehouses monthly. Increased demand necessitates a new plant. Given the following data, use a rational means to determine whether the firm should open plant 4 or plant 5.

Distribution Costs

PLANT	WAREHOUSE A	B	C	PRODUCTION CAPACITY
1	10	18	4	45
2	6	14	2	30
3	4	12	8	50
Demand	40	55	80	

The variable per-unit production costs at all plants are approximately the same, but plant 4 would have an estimated per-year building and equipment cost of $23,000, whereas plant 5 would have a $25,000 cost. The two new plants would have capacities of 80 and transportation costs to the warehouses as follows:

WAREHOUSE

PLANT	A	B	C
4	11	10	7
5	12	8	5

2. The Parker Co. specializes in the manufacture of oil-rig equipment. It is considering three potential locations for a single new plant. The new plant will have the capacity to produce 5,000 units annually, and is expected to operate at 85 percent capacity. The north, west, and south plants would have annual fixed costs of $480,000, $430,000, and $400,000 respectively. Their variable production costs in the same order would be $100, $110, and $120 per unit. Based on economic criteria, would you select the north, west, or south plant site?

3. Using Khumawala's heruristic, determine which of the following potential warehouses should be opened. The costs under the customer represent per-unit transportation costs times total units demanded.

Total Costs of Supplying Customers

POTENTIAL WAREHOUSES	FIXED COSTS	CUSTOMERS				
		A	B	C	D	E
1	70	5	300	100	20	6
2	130	10	150	300	120	11
3	165	15	120	60	90	45
4	100	20	45	360	100	35

4. Consider a public-park location problem in which it is desired to locate exactly three parks among four communities. The state budget has appropriated money for three similar facilities, and fixed costs are not considered. In the first table below, we have distances from proposed park areas to communities, along with community population sizes.

PARK AREA	COMMUNITY				
	A	B	C	D	E
1	1	10	16	20	24
2	9	2	8	12	16
3	17	8	2	4	10
4	24	15	11	5	1
Population (1,000s)	75	171	153	137	805

When the population factors are used as weights, we obtain the following weighted table of distances:

PARK AREA	COMMUNITY				
	A	B	C	D	E
1	75	1,710	2,448	2,740	19,320
2	675	342	1,224	1,644	12,880
3	1,275	1,368	306	548	8,050
4	1,800	2,565	1,683	685	805

Which three areas should be opened to minimize the total weighted distance from park to community?

5. Suppose that a company is planning to expand its warehouse capacity. The company can either build a new warehouse or expand its current facility. Adding a new warehouse will reduce transportation costs by bringing the distribution point closer to the western market. However, the new warehouse will cost $1,000,000 to build, whereas expanding the old one will cost $600,000. Transportation optimization models indicate that the company will save $100,000 per year in distribution costs if the new warehouse is built. Given a 5-year planning horizon and a 10% cost of capital, which alternative should be undertaken? Does the decision change with a 10-year planning horizon?

6. The Smelly Oil Company pays $1 million monthly to suppliers in five major cities. Smelly would like to select cash disbursement points so as to maximize the float times on clearing checks. Below is a table reflecting three of their best options and the check-clearing times between the banks in each city.

DISBURSING BANKS	AVERAGE CLEARING TIMES IN DAYS				
	HOUS-TON	LOS ANGELES	NEW YORK	WICHITA	CHI-CAGO
Phoenix	2.7	3.1	4.2	2.9	3.3
Tucson	3.2	2.9	4.1	2.6	3.4
Helena	4.5	3.3	4.9	3.8	3.0
Payments	$200,000	$200,000	$400,000	$100,000	$100,000

At a 10% cost of capital, the interest on $1 million is about $275 per day. To maintain an account at any of the three banks costs $150 per month. In which of the three cities should disbursing accounts be established?

7. The management of Ancient Times Production Company prefers to solve plant location problems subjectively. One of the firm's new managers has suggested coming up with a single quantified measure for each of the two plant locations the company is considering. The following table reflects the decision factors and importance weighting factors. Each location is ranked on a scale from 1 to 10 with respect to each factor. Ten is a perfect rating.

Rating of Alternatives

FACTOR	% WEIGHTING	LOCATION 1 RATING	LOCATION 2 RATING
1. Transportation cost	40	8	7
2. Labor cost	15	6	6
3. Building cost	20	5	6
4. Cost of utilities	10	6	5
5. Community attitude	10	7	9
6. Labor attitude	5	6	7

What is your final rating for locations 1 and 2?

8. In problem 3, suppose that location 3 is an already-existing warehouse. Determine the best warehouse configuration with warehouse 3 in the solution. Is it a different solution?

9. A&T Food Distributors currently has warehouses in Chicago and Dallas. It plans to expand from two to four warehouses and to select two new sites out of three possibilities. The potential locations include Salt Lake City, Atlanta, and Philadel-

phia. The table below reflects fixed operating costs and variable transportation costs to A&T's five main distribution centers. Which two sites should be selected?

	WARE-HOUSES	FIXED COSTS	AVERAGE PER-UNIT TRANSPORTATION COSTS TO DISTRIBUTION CENTERS				
			A	B	C	D	E
Established	Chicago	200,000	5	7	4	3	1
	Dallas	190,000	4	6	7	1	5
Potential	Salt Lake City	200,000	2	9	9	5	8
	Atlanta	180,000	6	3	6	4	7
	Philadelphia	210,000	8	4	2	6	5
	Regional Demand		90,000	70,000	100,000	50,000	80,000

10. Suppose that in problem 2, the new plant may not necessarily operate at 85 percent efficiency. In fact, the marketing department has developed the following annual market volume forecast:

SALES	PROBABILITY
3,500	.20
4,000	.25
4,250	.35
4,750	.20

In view of the uncertainty, which plant would you open?

11. The Radex Company is interested in locating not only two new plants but also three new warehouses. The company would like to design an integrated distribution system that minimizes distribution and fixed and operating costs. It is considering three possible plant locations and five possible warehouse locations. Outline a systematic approach for solving this problem.

Case: THE FIBERTEX
PLASTIC CORPORATION*

The management of the Fibertex Plastic Corporation of Bellevue, Washington, a suburb of Seattle, faced the problem of planning for the proper location of the company. The existing lease on the building used as their factory was due to expire within the coming year. The management was considering five possible courses of action:

1. Remain in the present location
2. Move to a new location within the Seattle metropolitan area
3. Move to a new location within the Pacific Northwest
4. Move into the Middle West
5. Move to California

The Fibertex Corporation manufactured translucent building panels made from polyester resins reinforced with fiberglass mat. The paneling was made as flat or corrugated sheets varying in width from 24 to 42 inches and in length from 8 to 14 feet. There were six different corrugations, such as sine-wave form, shiplap form, hat section form, etc. Up to 14 different colors could be used for each corrugation, although most items were limited to four or six colors. The intensity of the color could be varied from completely opaque to as much as 80 percent light transmission. Surface finish could also be varied to produce either a smooth finish or a crinkle finish. The panels were manufactured in light weight of 6 ounces per square foot or in heavy weight of 8 ounces per square foot.

The corporation had pioneered the development of a new method of manufacture. At the Bellevue plant, the paneling was made in a continuous process in which the raw materials were inserted at one end of a 150-foot-long machine and emerged from the other end completely processed. The method of manufacturing involved the impregnating of the fiberglass mat with the polyester

*From *Cases in Manufacturing Management* by Schrieber et al., © 1965 by McGraw Hill, Inc. Used with permission of McGraw Hill Book Company.
This adaptation will appear in *Case Book in Production and Operations Management* by Johnson et al., to be published by Prentice-Hall, Inc.

resin between sheets of cellophane and passing the material through an oven containing platens that guided the material into the proper configuration. The heat in the oven caused the resin to cure into a hard, permanent material. Upon emerging from the oven, the panel was trimmed on the sides and cut to proper length ready for inspection and shipment. The continuous-process machine had been designed and patented by the owners of the company.

Other companies generally manufactured paneling by the batch method, in which the mat was impregnated by hand and molded on caul plates, which were piled one on top of another and rolled on a rack into an oven for curing. The continuous-process machine at Bellevue produced a superior panel at lower cost than could be made by the batch method. The batch method, however, had the advantage of greater flexibility for small runs, in that it permitted easier changeover between colors and configurations than the continuous-process machine.

Translucent plastic paneling was introduced to the market shortly after the end of World War II. Since that time, it had received enthusiastic acceptance by the public. The paneling had the characteristics of light weight, great strength, corrosion resistance, transmission of light, and case of handling. The material could be sawed, nailed, and handled in a rather rough manner without any damage. In contrast to glass, it was highly resilient to impact.

The major home market for translucent plastic paneling was in patio roofs and enclosures, over breezeways, for skylights, for awnings, for greenhouses, and for carports. In addition, it was used for interior partitions and other decorative effects. In industry, the material was used in roofs, windows, and partitions. There also appeared to be a potential market in such applications as truck bodies and fabricated parts, but this market had not yet been fully explored.

Although the price of the plastic paneling had been greatly reduced during the past several years, it was still considered a relatively expensive building material item. Lightweight paneling sold in the retail market at about 75 cents per square foot, and the heavyweight material sold at about 95 cents per square foot.

The Fibertex Corporation distributed its translucent plastic paneling through the Panelette Distributing Company of Santa Monica, California. Panelette had succeeded in building up a national market for paneling under its trade name.

The management of Panelette had urged Fibertex to move its manufacturing plant to some location in the Middle West or in California. They felt the potential market in California or in the Middle West was so much larger than in the Pacific Northwest that it would be more economical to locate manufacturing facilities in the large market areas and ship to the small market areas.

The management of the Fibertex Plastic Corporation felt that the growing market in the Pacific Northwest justified a machine in this area, although they recognized the desirability of production facilities close to the large market areas. The senior executives of Fibertex had lived in the Pacific Northwest for many years, and they and their families had a strong preference for remaining in the area.

The Bellevue plant was operated by a crew of five men that consisted of an engineer who also managed production operations, three men who worked on the continuous machine, and an inspector who also handled shipping and receiving. These men were paid the average going rate in the community. Mat was received by rail at an average cost of 69 cents per pound. Approximately $1\frac{3}{4}$ ounces of mat was used per square foot for the light paneling, and $2\frac{1}{2}$ ounces of mat was used per square foot for the heavy paneling. Practically all the balance of the paneling was resin, which was trucked from the Seattle warehouse of a national chemical manufacturer. Mat was purchased FOB Huntington, Pennsylvania, while the resin was sold nationally by the chemical companies at a uniform delivered price of 32 cents per pound. Freight charges on mat shipped to the West Coast were $6.07 per hundredweight in carload quantities.

The resin was normally shipped in 475-pound barrels. Near the manufacturing plants of the resin companies, it was possible to obtain bulk shipments of the resin at a savings of approximately 3 cents per pound. Fibertex bought resin from manufacturing plants located in Azusa, California, and in Cleveland, Ohio. Other materials used in the manufacturing process averaged 3 cents per square foot. The value of the machine at Bellevue was upwards of $200,000 and was depreciated on a 5-year basis on the assumption that it would be obsolete by that time. It had a capacity ranging from 2 to 15 linear feet per minute, averaging about 6 feet per minute on most types of paneling.

Dealers received a 25 percent markup on the paneling that they handled. Regional distributors had a 15 percent markup for their operation, and Panelette as the general distributor had a markup of 20 percent. Manufacturers' prices were quoted FOB at shipping point. Approximately six major companies were attempting to sell the paneling on a national basis and had forced prices down to where the margins were considered very thin. In addition, there were a large number of regional or local manufacturers operating on very small volume using the hand-batch methods in very simplified form. In the Seattle metropolitan area, there were two such small local manufacturers.

Some manufacturers had made very lightweight panels, down to 5 ounces and even 4 ounces per square foot, in order to offer a very low-priced product. These panels were sold for a little as 25 cents per square foot. Fibertex had refused to produce such panels because they felt the sacrifice in quality made very lightweight panels a poor buy for the customer even at very low prices.

Transportation charges for shipping the finished paneling between the Pacific Northwest and southern California were $9.94 per hundredweight for small quantities by truck, down to $4.65 per hundredweight for full carload quantities by rail. Transportation charges from the West Coast to east of the Mississippi River were approximately double the rates between the Pacific Northwest and southern California.

The Fibertex Plastic Corporation had most of its funds tied up in equipment and working capital requirements for raw inventory, accounts receivable, and current cash needs. As a result, it found it necessary to rent its building. An offer had been made by a local investor to provide it with a building of its own choosing anywhere within the Seattle metropolitan area, which would be rented to the corporation on the basis of $1\frac{1}{2}$ percent per month of the cost of the building. The company anticipated that it needed for manufacturing operations 12,000 square feet at an average building cost of about $35 per square foot. At the present time, the company was renting a building in Bellevue, 50 feet wide by approximately 160 feet long. Rail facilities were considered to be important, although not absolutely necessary. One of the problems the company faced in building in the city of Seattle was the restrictions contained in the zoning code, the building code, and the regulations of the fire department. The company operated on a nonunion basis, although the management had expressed its willingness to work with any union that the employees desired to have as their representative. Four unions had already attempted to organize the workers, but the employees of the corporation had felt that the enlightened personnel policies of the company did not make the cost and obligation of union affiliation desirable.

Although all the marketing problems at the present time were taken care of by the Panelette Distributing Company, the management of the Fibertex Corporation anticipated that it might have to handle its own marketing problems at some future date. This would require a capital investment in finished inventory, as well as 8,000 square feet of additional space for warehousing. At the present time, all finished paneling was shipped as rapidly as manufactured, in lots of 10,000 to 15,000 pounds. Most shipments left the Bellevue plant by rail, although a small number were shipped by truck. Over 80 percent of the production of the Bellevue plant was sent to the southern California market. The balance was largely consumed in the Pacific Northwest, with a small volume of drop shipments being made to the Middle West.

The expiration of the lease on the Bellevue property was still a year away, and the management of the Fibertex Plastic Corporation felt it had plenty of time to work out a satisfactory solution to the problem. Hence, it was reviewed in a casual way from time to time.

Case Discussion Questions

1. Assume you have been hired as a consultant to study the company's problem of plant location. Prepare a plan of how to organize and proceed with this study.

2. What are the possible advantages and disadvantages of Fibertex's remaining in its suburban location as compared to relocating in the metropolitan area?

3. Compare Seattle, Los Angeles, and Chicago as locations for Fibertex by selecting appropriate business statistics from census data and other sources.

4. Select your home city or town, or another city, and evaluate it as a potential location for Fibertex.

5. How do you evaluate the approach of Fibertex's management to its problem?

REFERENCES

ABERNATHY, W.J., and J.C. HERSHEY, "A Spatial-Allocation Model for Regional Health-Services Planning," *Operations Research*, Vol. 20 (May–June 1972), 629–42.

ATKINS, R.J., and R.H. SHRIVER, "New Approach to Facilities Location," *Harvard Business Review*, May–June 1968, pp. 70–79.

CORNUEJOLS, G., M. FISHER, and G.L. NEMHAUSER, "Location of Bank Accounts to Optimize Float: An Analytic Study of Exact and Approximate Algorithms," *Management Science*, Vol. 23 (April 1977), 789–810.

DUTTON, R., G. HINMAN, and C.B. MILLHAM, "The Optimal Location of Nuclear-Power Facilities in the Pacific Northwest," *Operations Research*, Vol. 22, No. 3 (May–June 1974), 478–87.

EFFROYMSON, M.A., and T.A. RAY, "A Branch-Bound Algorithm for Plant Location," *Operations Research*, Vol. 14 (May–June 1966), 361–68.

FITZSIMMONS, J.A., "A Methodology for Emergency Ambulance Deployment," *Management Science*, Vol. 19 (February 1973), 627–36.

FRANCIS, R., and J. WHITE, *Facility Layout and Location: An Analytical Approach.* Englewood Cliffs, N.J.: Prentice-Hall, 1974.

KEUHN, A.A., and M.J. HAMBURGER, "A Heuristic Program for Locating Warehouses," *Management Science*, Vol. 19 (July 1963), 643–66.

KHUMAWALA, B.M., "An Efficient Branch and Bound Algorithm for the Warehouse Location Problem," *Management Science*, Vol. 18 (August 1972), 718–31.

————, "An Efficient Heuristic Procedure for the Uncapacitated Warehouse Location Problem," *Naval Research Logistics Quarterly*, Vol. 20, No. 1 (March 1973), 109–21.

————, and D.C. WHYBARK, "A Comparison of Some Recent Warehouse Location Techniques," *The Logistics Review*, Vol. 7 (1971).

KOLESAR, P., and W.E. WALKER, "An Algorithm for the Dynamic Relocation of Fire Companies," *Operations Research*, Vol. 22 (March–April 1974), 249–74.

LEE, S.M., and L.J. MOORE, "Optimizing Transportation Problems with Multiple Objectives," *AIIE Transactions*, Vol. 5 (December 1973), 333–38.

MARKLAND, R.E., "Analyzing Geographically Discrete Warehousing Networks by Computer Simulation," *Decision Sciences*, Vol. 4 (April 1973), 216–36.

REVELLE, C., D. MARKS, and J. LIEBMAN, "An Analysis of Private and Public Sector Location Models," *Management Science*, Vol. 16, No. 11 (July 1970), 692–707.

SÃ, G., "Branch-and-Bound and Approximate Solutions to the Capacitated Plant-Location Problem," *Operations Research*, Vol. 17, No. 6 (November–December 1969), 1005–15.

SAVAS, E., "Simulation and Cost-Effectiveness Analysis of New York's Emergency Ambulance Service," *Management Science*, Vol. 15 (August 1969), B608–27.

SHANNON, R., and T. IGNIZIO, "A Heuristic Programming Algorithm for Warehouse Location," *AIIE Transactions*, Vol. II, No. 4 (December 1970), 334–39.

SWEENEY, D., and R. TATHAM, "An Improved Long-Run Model for Multiple Warehouse Location," *Management Science*, Vol. 22, No. 7 (March 1976), 748–58.

part FOUR

operation
of productive
systems

chapter 8

FORECASTING

Regardless of whether an organization's role in society is to provide medical care, police protection, safe streets, consumer goods, or consumer services, it needs accurate and timely forecasts. Hospitals need to predict the demand for resources such as X-ray facilities, surgical rooms, special nursing stations, and so on. Computer organizations must predict demand so that the appropriate hardware and software can be acquired. Farmers need weather forecasts for making planting and harvesting decisions. Automobile manufacturers need demand forecasts to develop the master schedules that are a necessary input to materials requirements planning and aggregate scheduling. In short, many planning decisions of the operations manager are based on various forecasts, and it is becoming increasingly important for the competitive firm to perform the forecasting function accurately and efficiently.

To emphasize this point, let us demonstrate the effect of a 10 percent error in the demand forecast for automobiles. Let us assume that demand for September is estimated at 100,000 automobiles. Based on this forecast, manpower planning, production schedules, inventory policies, and many other important planning decisions are made. Now assume that sales for September are 90,000 units rather than the 100,000 projected. If we oversimplify the consequences of the forecasting error by using the cost of holding additional inventory to measure the cost of that error, we can compute it in the following manner:

$$\text{Cost of forecast error} = (\text{Cost of auto})(\text{No. of excess autos produced})(\text{Cost of capital})$$

For illustrative purposes, let the per-unit cost of the automobile be \$5,000 and the cost of capital be 12 percent per year, or 1 percent per month. Then, the cost of the forecast error for September is:

$$(\$5,000)(10,000)(.01) = \$500,000$$

It ought to be obvious from this oversimplified example that accurate demand forecasts are not only important to the typical organization but are possibly the difference between surviving and not surviving in a competitive marketplace.

Regardless of whether the subject of the forecast is sales, cash flow, GNP, or the weather, forecasts can be categorized by their time horizon. As depicted in Figure 8-1, short-range forecasts (up to one year, but typically a quarter) help the operations manager make current operational decisions such as production scheduling and short-term financing. Medium-range forecasts (one to three years) aid in making planning decisions that have a longer lead time. For example, a computer installation may use

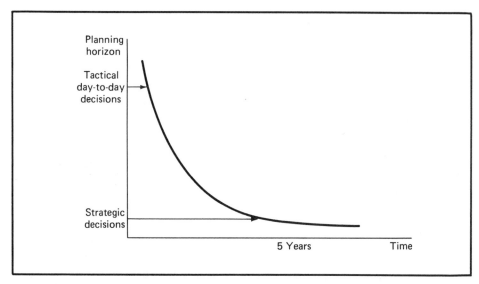

FIGURE 8-1   Forecasting Time Horizon

a three-year forecast of demand in order to make decisions concerning hardware acquisitions necessary to satisfy that demand. Long-range forecasts (three or more years) are used to make decisions that affect the organization further in the future. A utility company must make long-range forecasts concerning both its demand and the availability and cost of various fuels, in order to make decisions concerning new plant and equipment.

Forecasting techniques can be grouped into one of three categories: qualitative techniques, time series analysis, and causal methods. Qualitative techniques use qualitative data such as the aggregate opinion of the sales force to forecast the future. Time series analysis relies entirely on historical data, focusing on seasonal and cyclical variations and trend extrapolations. Causal methods attempt to define relationships between independent and dependent variables in a system of related equations. Each of these three general categories can be further subdivided into individual forecasting techniques. See Figure 8-2 for a breakdown of commonly used forecasting methods. Obviously, the decision of which technique to use is dependent on the parameters of the individual forecasting problem. In this chapter, however, we will attempt to indicate the comparative advantages, costs, and logical applications of the various techniques.

When selecting a forecasting technique, a decision maker must keep two types of costs in mind; cost of inaccuracy and cost of the forecast itself. The objective should be to minimize the total costs. In other words, it makes little sense to spend a large amount for a forecast of little significance to the organization. A "gut-feel" forecast from the sales manager might be adequate. Alternatively, an important decision that is very sensitive to future conditions may warrant the expenditure of thousands of dollars to improve the forecast by only a small amount.

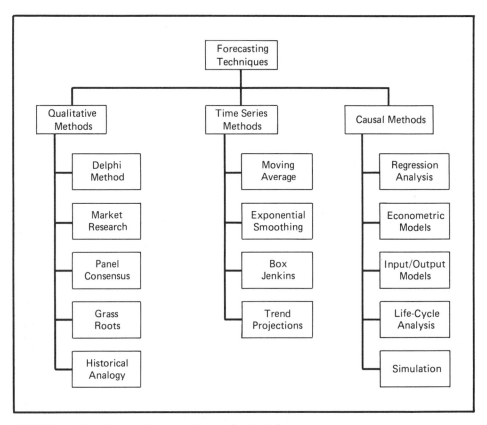

FIGURE 8-2   Breakdown of Common Forecasting Techniques

The selection of a forecasting technique depends on a multitude of factors. Many techniques require a substantial amount of historical data. If adequate and relevant historical data do not exist or are prohibitively expensive to accumulate, then many techniques can be automatically ruled out. Another factor to be considered is the planning horizon. Some techniques are more suited to short-term forecasts and some to long-term forecasts. The time available to make the forecast is an important consideration. If a manager needs a forecast for a current decision, he may not be able to wait six months to get it. Forecasting techniques vary as to cost and accuracy, and therefore it is important to identify the accuracy needed in the forecast and a reasonable cost for a given level of accuracy. Figure 8-3 gives some logical structure for deciding which forecasting technique is appropriate.

The first question to be asked concerns the availability of historical data. All quantitative forecasting techniques depend upon the existence of adequate and accurate historical data. Therefore, if adequate data do not exist, causal methods and time series analysis techniques are not feasible alternatives. However, even if adequate

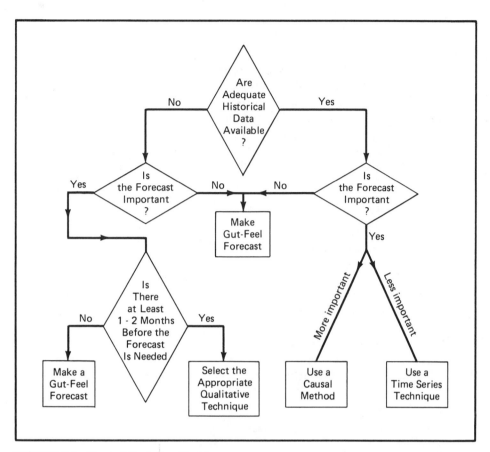

FIGURE 8-3   Forecast Technique Decision

data do not exist, if the forecast is important, there are qualitative techniques that can be employed that generally yield better results than a "gut-feel" or "seat-of-the-pants" forecast. The more sophisticated qualitative techniques, however, usually take several months to implement, and therefore, if the decision maker cannot wait several months, a "gut-feel" forecast is the forecaster's only alternative.

If adequate historical data do exist and the forecast is an important one, a wide variety of forecasting techniques are available. These methods range from quick-and-dirty time series techniques to very sophisticated econometric models containing hundreds of equations and hundreds of variables. The cruder and simpler methods require very little time and involve little cost. The more commonly used time series techniques are described later in this chapter. Some causal methods can require months and even years of development and thousands of dollars. The automobile demand forecast mentioned earlier in this chapter would be a likely candidate for a causal forecasting method such as multiple regression or econometric modeling.

Often, data necessary to generate a forecast using either time series analysis or some type of causal model are not available, and the manager is forced to use some kind of qualitative technique that substitutes human judgment for historical data. This situation frequently arises with the introduction of new products or services. The qualitative forecasting methods to be discussed in this chapter can be and often are formalized, technical procedures designed to incorporate human judgment in the forecasting process.

In this chapter, we describe five commonly used qualitative techniques:

1. The Delphi method
2. Market research
3. Panel consensus
4. Grass-roots forecasting
5. Historical analogy

The Delphi method establishes a panel of experts. This panel is interrogated, using a series of questionnaries in which the answers to each questionnarie are used as input to designing the next. In this way, information is shared among the experts without the disadvantage of having individual experts influencing each other; in other words, the bandwagon effect of majority opinion is eliminated. As indicated in Table 8-1, the Delphi method is effective regardless of the forecast's planning horizon. The cost, however, can be rather high.

Table 8-1   Qualitative Forecasting Methods

	DELPHI METHOD	MARKET RESEARCH	PANEL CON- SENSUS	GRASS ROOTS	HISTOR- ICAL ANALOGY
Accuracy					
Short-term	Fair to very good	Excellent	Poor to fair	Fair	Poor
Medium-term	Fair to very good	Good	Poor to fair	Poor to fair	Good to fair
Long-term	Fair to very good	Fair to good	Poor	Poor	Good to fair
Cost	$2,000 +	$5,000 +	$1,000 +	$1,000 +	$1,000 +
Time required	2 months +	3 months +	2 weeks +	2 months +	1 month +

SOURCE: Adapted from J.S. Chambers, S.K. Mullich, and D.D. Smith, "How to Choose the Right Forecasting Technique," *Harvard Business Review*, July–August 1971.

Market research is probably the most sophisticated of the qualitative techniques and also the most quantitative. "Market research" encompasses an entire family of techniques that are helpful in revealing predictions about the size, structure, and configuration of markets for various goods and services. Market researchers obtain information about markets of interest through the use of mail questionnaires, telephone surveys, panels, and personal interviews. The data obtained are then subjected to various statistical tests so that hypotheses about the market can be tested. Market research techniques are generally the most expensive form of qualitative forecasting, take the longest to implement, and if properly applied are often the most accurate.

Panel consensus is a technique based on the assumption that several heads are better than one. With this technique, a panel of experts is assembled for the purpose of jointly developing a forecast. Free communication is encouraged, and the job is finished when a consensus opinion is arrived at. Obviously, the relative merit of this approach depends heavily on the configuration of the panel of experts, but it is generally considered inferior to most other qualitative methods with respect to accuracy. It can, however, be accomplished in a relatively short amount of time at a modest cost.

Grass-roots forecasting refers to asking the people closest to the problem to make individual forecasts for their territory. These individual forecasts are then aggregated to form the overall forecast. Sales forecasts are frequently accomplished in this way. This type of approach depends on the quality of the individual forecasts coming from the field. If done conscientiously, grass-roots forecasting can be very effective. The major argument against it is the opportunity cost. It is often argued that the sales force should spend its time selling and minimize its administrative duties. In addition, if salespeople are working on a commission basis, it is very likely that they will put little thought into a sales forecast.

The final qualitative forecasting tool to be discussed is the *historical analogy* approach. Like other qualitative methods, this approach is used when specific data are scarce. For example, if a firm is introducing a new product that has strong similarities to an established product, it may use sales data relevant to the established product to predict the relative success or failure of the new product for which no data exist. This technique, while having a modest cost, is dependent on the availability of several years of data on the model product or service. Historical analogy forecasts seem to perform better for medium- and long-range planning horizons than for short-range.

TIME SERIES ANALYSIS

A time series is a set of raw data arranged chronologically; monthly sales is a good example. Time series analysis is used when several years of data exist and when trends are both clear and relatively stable. Because time series analysis is totally dependent upon historical data, its implicit assumption is that the past is a good guide to the future. Consequently, time series analysis performs better in the short-term than in the long-term forecast. In addition, time series analysis cannot predict turning points in trend. For example, typical seasonally adjusted sales for a textbook like this one over a four-year period might behave as shown in Figure 8-4. If our historical data were limited to 1975 and 1976 sales data, we might project sales to be 8,000 copies by 1980, when in fact sales dropped to 1,000. A turning point in sales was caused by the existence of the used-book market, and mere time series analysis does an extremely poor job of predicting turning points in trend. If the data exist, however,

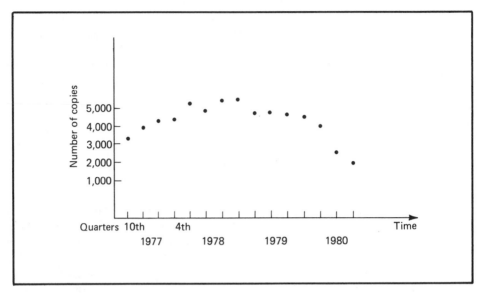

FIGURE 8-4   **Sales Time Sarles**

most time series analysis techniques are extremely inexpensive, and projections can be produced on a computer in a matter of seconds.

A time series is composed of four basic elements: a trend component, a seasonal component, a cyclical component, and an erratic or random component. Trend refers to long-term growth or decay. A seasonal fluctuation in the forecasted variable recurs regularly at periodic intervals. Many products experience seasonal fluctuations with respect to demand. Cyclical fluctuations about trend are explainable fluctuations but differ from seasonal fluctuations in that their length of time and amplitude are not constant. Finally, if a forecaster could precisely measure trend, seasonability, and the cyclical factor, there would still be an unexplained variation between the forecast and reality. This unexplained variation is usually referred to as the erratic or random component in a time series.

In this chapter, we describe three common types of time series forecasting techniques:

1. Moving average
2. Exponential smoothing
3. Trend projection

Simple Moving Average

The simple moving average forecasting method simply eliminates the effects of seasonal, cyclical, and erratic fluctuations by averaging the historical data points. Therefore, if seasonality, trend, and cyclical factors are not critical in the variable being forecast, the moving average method is of some value. The effect of the simple moving average technique can be seen in Figure 8-5.

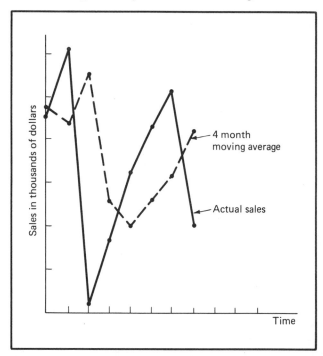

FIGURE 8-5 **Sales Forecast Using Simple Moving Average**

To compute a simple moving average, simply choose the number of points in the time series data to include in the average. Then, as each time period evolves, add the new time period data and subtract the oldest time period data, and calculate a new average.

Mathematically, then:

8.1
$$F_t = \frac{\sum_{i=1}^{N} S_{t-i}}{N}$$

where F_t = forecast for time period t

S_{t-i} = actual sales for period $t - i$

N = the number of time periods used in the averaging process

For example, let us calculate the moving average for the sales data contained in Table 8-2, using a four-month moving average. Since our data go back only to January 1978, our first possible sales forecast using a four-month moving average is for May 1978. The forecast for May 1978 can be computed as follows:

$$F_5 = \frac{S_1 + S_2 + S_3 + S_4}{4}$$

$$= \$238,250$$

Table 8-2   Sales Data for Time Series Analysis

YEAR	MONTH	SALES (DOLLARS)	SIMPLE 4-MONTH MOVING AVERAGE FORECAST
1978	January	250,000	
	February	210,000	
	March	223,000	
	April	270,000	
	May	245,000	238,250
	June	261,000	237,000
	July	212,000	249,750
	August	226,000	247,000
	September	241,000	236,000
	October	252,000	235,000
	November	261,000	232,750
	December	229,000	245,000
1979	January	247,000	245,750
	February	255,000	247,250
	March	271,000	248,000
	April	261,000	250,500
	May	258,000	258,500
	June	265,000	261,250
	July	250,000	263,750
	August	275,000	258,500
	September	245,000	262,000
	October	260,000	258,750
	November	255,000	257,500
	December	263,000	258,750

Once May sales data are available, the forecast for June can be computed:

$$F_6 = \frac{S_2 + S_3 + S_4 + S_5}{4}$$

$$= \$237,000$$

It is obvious from Figure 8-6 that the longer the period over which the averaging takes place, the smoother the forecast function.

Weighted Moving Average

Often, it is desirable to vary the weights given to historical data in order to forecast future demand or sales. Past history may show that a significantly better forecast is computed when the more recent data are given heavier weight. Mathematically, the weighted moving average is computed as follows:

8.2
$$F_t = \frac{\sum_{i=1}^{N} W_{t-i} S_{t-i}}{\sum_{i=1}^{N} W_{t-i}}$$

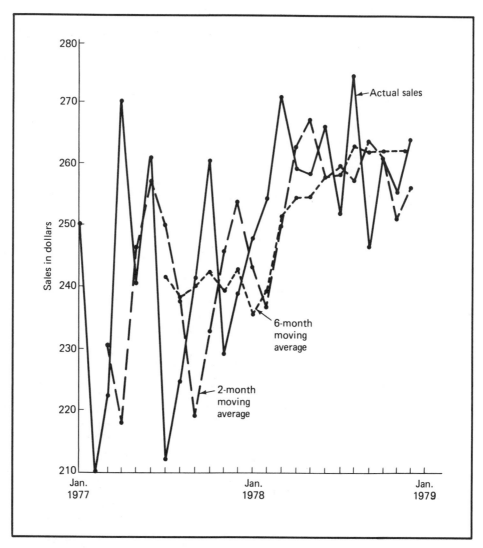

FIGURE 8-6   Sales Forecast Using Simple Moving Average

where F_t = forecast for time period t
S_{t-i} = actual sales for time period $t - i$
N = the number of time periods used in the averaging process
W_{t-i} = the weight given to the $t - i^{th}$ period in the averaging process

For example, assume that a weight of 50 is assigned to the most recent month, a weight of 25 to the next most recent month, and weights of 15 and 10 to the next two months respectively. Using the data in Table 8-2, the four-month weighted moving average for May 1977 is computed as follows:

$$F_5 = \frac{(50)(270,000) + (25)(223,000) + (15)(210,000) + (10)(250,000)}{100}$$

$$= \$247,250$$

The data shown in Table 8-3 are plotted in Figure 8-7.

Table 8-3   Four-Month Weighted Moving Average

YEAR	MONTH	ACTUAL SALES	4-MONTH WEIGHTED MOVING AVERAGE
1977	January	250,000	
	February	210,000	
	March	223,000	
	April	270,000	
	May	245,000	247,250
	June	261,000	244,450
	July	212,000	254,550
	August	226,000	235,000
	September	241,000	229,650
	October	252,000	234,900
	November	261,000	241,350
	December	229,000	252,250
1978	January	247,000	241,650
	February	255,000	245,100
	March	271,000	249,700
	April	261,000	259,200
	May	258,000	261,200
	June	265,000	260,400
	July	250,000	263,250
	August	275,000	256,050
	September	245,000	265,550
	October	260,000	255,250
	November	255,000	257,500
	December	263,000	256,750

The major advantage of the moving average technique is its simplicity, low cost, and little time necessary to implement. In general, however, the moving average technique does a poor job for long-range and medium-range forecasts. For "quick-and-dirty" short-term forecasts that don't require a great deal of accuracy, a moving average forecast may be a viable alternative to other forecasting methods.

Exponential Smoothing

Exponential smoothing refers to a family of forecasting models that are very similar to the weighted moving average. The simplest exponential smoothing model is of the following form:

8.3 $$F_t = F_{t-1} + \alpha(A_{t-1} - F_{t-1})$$

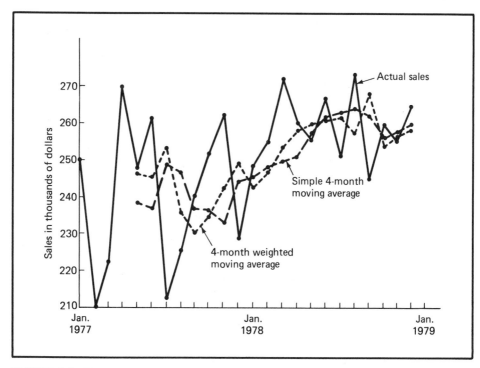

FIGURE 8-7   Simple Moving Average vs Weighted Moving Average

where F_t = forecast for time period t
  A_{t-1} = actual value of variable being forecast in period $t - 1$
  α = smoothing constant

The value of α, which can range from 0 to 1, determines the degree of smoothing that takes place and how responsive the model is to fluctuation in the forecast variable. The setting of α is not a scientific process and is usually done by trial and error. Let us assume an α of .15 and a January 1979 forecast of 250 units. The actual January demand turned out to be 260 units. The forecast for February could be computed as follows:

$$F_t = 250 + (.15)(260 - 250)$$
$$= 250 + 1.5$$
$$= 251.5 \text{ units}$$

Given the forecasts in Table 8-4, let us compare the effect of different smoothing constants by looking at Figure 8-8.

Other exponential smoothing models exist that compensate for the various components of a time series such as the seasonal or trend component. To illustrate more complex exponential smoothing models, let us consider a model that has an adjustment for trend built into it. If trend exists in either a positive or a negative form, there

Table 8-4   Effects of Various Smoothing Constants

	ACTUAL DEMAND	*FORECAST α = .05*	*FORECAST α = .25*	*FORECAST α = .4*
January	260	250,000	250,000	250,000
February	210	250,500	252,500	254,000
March	223	248,475	241,875	236,400
April	270	247,201	237,156	231,040
May	245	248,341	245,367	246,624
June	261	248,174	245,275	245,974
July	212	248,815	249,207	251,985
August	226	246,975	239,905	235,991
September	241	245,926	236,429	231,994
October	252	245,680	237,572	235,597
November	261	245,996	241,179	242,158
December	249	246,746	246,134	249,695

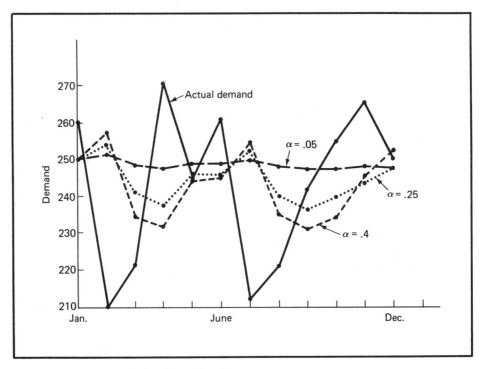

FIGURE 8-8   Effect of Various Smoothing Constants

will be a lag using the simple exponential smoothing model just described. See Figure 8-9. The basic idea behind the trend-adjusted model is to calculate a simple, exponentially smoothed forecast as described above and adjust the forecast for a trend lag.

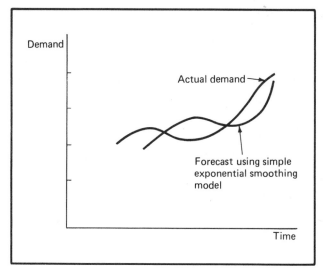

FIGURE 8-9   Trend Lag

Mathematically, the trend-adjusted model can be described as follows:

8.4
$$F_t' = F_t + \frac{1 - \beta}{\beta} T_t$$

where $F_t' =$ trend-adjusted forecast for time period t
$F_t =$ simple exponential smoothing forecast for time period t
$\beta =$ trend smoothing factor
$T_t =$ exponentially smoothed trend for time period t

T_t is computed using the following formula:

8.5
$$T_t = T_{t-1} + \beta(t_t - T_{t-1})$$

where

$$t_t = F_t - F_{t-1}$$

To compute a trend-adjusted forecast is a four-step process:

Step 1:   Compute a simple forecast for time period t (F_t).
Step 2:   Compute t_t by finding the difference between F_t and F_{t-1}.

$$t_t = F_t - F_{t-1}$$

Step 3:   Calculate the exponentially smoothed trend.

$$T_t = T_{t-1} + \beta(t_t - T_{t-1})$$

Step 4: Finally, calculate a trend-adjusted forecast by using the formula:

$$F_t' = F_t + \frac{1 - \beta}{\beta} T_t$$

Let us illustrate how to compute a trend-adjusted, exponentially smoothed forecast using the demand data in Table 8-5 and smoothing constants α and β, equal

Table 8-5   Time Series Data in Which Trend Is Present

PERIOD	DEMAND
1	12
2	17
3	19
4	16
5	22
6	24
7	30
8	29
9	33
10	34
11	37
12	38

to .3 and .25 respectively. Let the initial forecast be 11.5. The trend-adjusted forecast for period 2 is computed as follows:

The first step is to compute F_2:

$$F_2 = F_1 + \alpha(A_1 - F_1)$$
$$= 11.5 + .3(12 - 11.5)$$
$$= 11.65$$

The next step is to calculate t_2:

$$t_2 = F_2 - F_1$$
$$= 11.65 - 11.50$$
$$= .15$$

T_2 can now be calculated, assuming the initial trend adjustment is 0:

$$T_2 = T_1 + \beta(t_2 - T_1)$$
$$= 0 + .25(.15)$$
$$= .0375$$

Finally, the trend-adjusted forecast for time period 2 can be computed:

$$F_2 = F_2 + \frac{1 - .25}{.25} T_2$$

$$= 11.65 + 3(.0315)$$

$$= 11.7625$$

Doing the same calculations for the remaining time periods for the time series data shown in Table 8-5 results in the trend-adjusted forecasts reflected in Table 8-6. Figure 8-10 graphically contrasts the unadjusted and adjusted forecasts for the time series in Table 8-6.

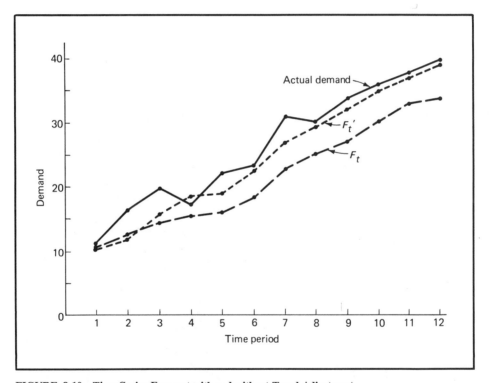

FIGURE 8-10   Time Series Forecast with and without Trend Adjustment

Generally, exponential smoothing is considered superior to the moving average methods previously discussed. Its cost is equivalent and its accuracy especially in the short term is usually better. Owing to their relatively small computational cost and computer storage requirement, exponential smoothing models are probably the most widely used of the time series techniques. For longer term forecasts, however, exponential smoothing is also considered a poor technique.

Table 8-6   Trend-Adjusted Forecasts

TIME PERIOD	ACTUAL DEMAND	F_t	t_t	T_t	F_t'
1	12	11.5000	0	0	11.5000
2	17	11.6500	.15000	.037500	11.7625
3	19	13.2550	1.60500	.429375	14.5431
4	16	14.9785	1.72350	.752906	17.2372
5	22	15.2849	3.06450	.641292	17.2088
6	24	17.2995	2.01451	.984598	20.2533
7	30	19.3096	2.01016	1.24099	23.0326
8	29	22.5167	3.20711	1.73252	27.7143
9	33	24.4617	1.94498	1.78563	29.8186
10	34	27.0232	2.56149	1.97960	32.9620
11	37	29.1162	2.09304	2.00796	35.1401
12	38	31.4814	2.36513	2.09725	37.7731

Trend Projection

Trend projection using a technique called least squares is a special case of a category of causal forecasting methods called regression analysis. The basic idea in trend projection using least squares is to fit a function to a set of time series data in which the independent variable is time and the dependent variable is the variable to be forecasted such as demand. This function can be linear or nonlinear and the basic idea and methodology are the same. In this chapter, however, we consider only linear trend projection.

Consider the scatter diagram in Figure 8-11. It is easy to imagine a straight line running through the data such that the sum of the differences between the data points and the trend line is minimized. If the equation of the trend line is a function of time then it is a simple matter to "plug" a future time period into the function and calculate a forecast.

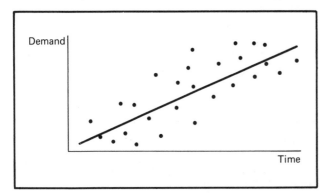

FIGURE 8-11   Scatter Diagram

Remember, the general equation for a straight line is

8.6 $$y = mx + b$$

where $\quad\quad\quad\quad\quad\quad\quad\quad y =$ the dependent variable
$b =$ the y intercept
$m =$ the slope of the line
$x =$ the independent variable

See Figure 8-12 for a graphical interpretation of a straight line.

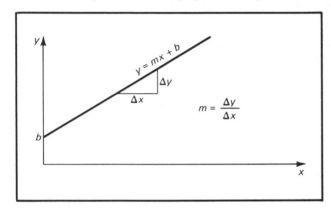

FIGURE 8-12 Graph of Linear Equation

Now, if we define x as time and y as demand, and b (the y intercept) and m (slope of the line) are known, then demand can be computed by merely letting x assume a value. For example, assume that the linear function is:

$$y = 150x + 5,000$$

If 1980 is the tenth time period in the time series, the demand forecast for 1980 can be forecast, substituting 10 into the equation:

$$y = 50(10) + 5,000$$
$$= 5,500 \text{ units}$$

Now let us turn to the method of deriving the "best fit" linear equation for a set of time series data. It is possible to find a line that provides a good fit of the data by merely "eyeballing" the scatter diagram and superimposing a line on it. Then, relying on the accuracy of the graph, a y intercept (b) can be read, and the slope of the line can be calculated as $\Delta y/\Delta x$. A more accurate way to find the linear equation that best fits the data is to solve the following equations simultaneously for b and m:

8.7 $$\sum_{i=1}^{n} y_i = nb + m \sum_{i=1}^{n} x_i$$

8.8 $$\sum_{i=1}^{n} x_i y_i = b \sum_{i=1}^{n} x_i + m \sum_{i=1}^{n} x_i^2$$

where y_i = dependent variable for the ith time period
                  n = number of historical time periods
                  x_i = independent variable for the ith time period

Equations 8.7 and 8.8 are called normal equations and are derived using the differential calculus. To illustrate how the simple linear regression equation is found, let
us use the data in Table 8-7.

Table 8-7   Historical Demand Data

TIME PERIOD	DEMAND
1	1200
2	1700
3	1900
4	1600
5	2200
6	2400
7	3000
8	2900
9	3300
10	3400
11	3700
12	3800

The dependent variable (y) is demand, whereas the time period is the independent
variable. Looking at normal equations 8.7 and 8.8, it is clear that several sums are
required. These values are computed in Table 8-8.

Table 8-8   Least Squares Calculations

x_i	y_i	$x_i y_i$	x_i^2
1	1,200	1,200	1
2	1,700	3,400	4
3	1,900	5,700	9
4	1,600	6,400	16
5	2,200	11,000	25
6	2,400	14,400	36
7	3,000	21,000	49
8	2,900	23,200	64
9	3,300	29,700	81
10	3,400	34,000	100
11	3,700	40,700	121
12	3,800	45,600	144
78	31,100	236,300	650

Substituting the appropriate sums into the two normal equations, we have the following two equations with two unknowns, b and m:

8.9
$$31{,}100 = 12b + 78m$$

8.10
$$236{,}300 = 78b + 650m$$

If we multiply both sides of equation 8.9 by 6.5 and subtract it from equation 8.10, the b terms will fall out:

$$
\begin{aligned}
236{,}300 &= 78b & + 650m \\
-\,202{,}150 &= -78b & -\,507m \\
\hline
34{,}150 &= 143m \\
m &= 238.811
\end{aligned}
$$

Solving for b by substituting m into equation 8.9, we find:

$$31{,}100 = 12b + 78(238.811)$$
$$b = 1{,}039.4$$

Therefore, the "best fit" linear forecasting equation is:

8.11
$$y = 238.811x + 1039.4$$

Once this equation has been derived, trend extrapolation is simply a mechanical procedure. If a prediction for the fourteenth time period is desired, simply set x equal to 14 and solve for y using equation 8.11. The forecast for time period 14 is therefore:

$$y_{14} = 238{,}811(14) + 1{,}039.4$$
$$= 4{,}382.754$$

If we compute a standard error of estimate to determine how well the regression line fits the data, it is possible that more information about a forecast can be obtained. See Figure 8-13. The standard error can be defined mathematically as

$$S_{yx} = \sqrt{\frac{\sum_{i=1}^{n}(y_i - Y_i)^2}{n-2}}$$

where
$y_i =$ the dependent variable for time period i (in our example demand)
$Y_i =$ value for the dependent variable obtained from the regression equation
$n =$ the number of historical time periods

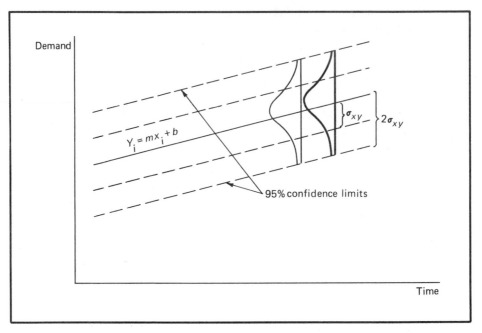

FIGURE 8-13   Least Squares Differences

To compute the standard error of estimate, we merely do the computation necessary to complete Table 8-9 using the data in Table 8-7 and the regression equation 8.11.

Table 8-9   Standard Error Computation

x_i	y_i	Y_i	$y_i - Y_i$	$(y_i - Y_i)^2$
1	1200	1278.21	−78.211	6116.96
2	1700	1517.02	182.978	33480.90
3	1900	1755.83	144.167	20784.10
4	1600	1994.64	−394.644	15574.40
5	2200	2233.45	−33.455	1119.24
6	2400	2472.27	−72.266	5222.37
7	3000	2711.08	288.923	83476.50
8	2900	2949.89	−49.888	2488.81
9	3300	3188.70	111.301	12387.90
10	3400	3427.51	−27.510	756.80
11	3700	3666.32	33.679	1134.28
12	3800	3905.13	−105.132	11052.70
				333,765.00

$$s_{yx} = \sqrt{\frac{333,765}{10}}$$

$$= 182.692$$

If we assume that demand is normally distributed around the regression line as depicted in Figure 8-13 and want 95.5 percent of the demand values to fall within our prediction interval, the prediction interval can be calculated as follows:

$$\text{Prediction interval for } Y_i = Y_i \pm 2s_{yx}$$

where

$$Y_i = \text{the regression equation value}$$
$$s_{yx} = \text{standard error of estimate}$$

In our example:

$$\text{Prediction interval for } Y_{14} = 4{,}382.754 \pm 2(182.692)$$
$$= 4{,}382.754 \pm 365.384$$

or

$$4{,}017.37 \leq Y_{14} \leq 4{,}748.14$$

Remember that we calculated Y_i and s_{yx} using historical data, and to say we are 95.5 percent confident that demand for time period 14 will fall between 4,017 and 4,748 units is to assume that the future is going to behave like the past. Also, a sample size of 12 is too small to assume normality, and a student's t distribution should be used when the sample size is small.

Simple linear regression using time period as the independent variable generally outperforms both moving average and exponential smoothing techniques with regard to forecast accuracy. Usually, very good short-term forecasts can be derived using trend projections, and often, good long-term forecasts can be based on least squares trend projections. If the historical data are available, the cost of the forecast is minimal and the time lapse required to derive the forecast is often less than one day.

In general, time series methods such as those discussed in this section provide fairly accurate and very inexpensive short-term forecasts. It is therefore very common for one or more of these techniques to be integrated into computerized multiproduct inventory systems such as IBM's IMPACT system. In automated multiproduct inventory systems in which forecasts are automatically generated using a time series technique such as exponential smoothing, it is necessary to consistently monitor the forecasting process to report to management when the forecast and actual demand for a time period differ significantly. This discrepancy may be due to keypunch errors, extraordinary market conditions, or the unsatisfactory performance of the forecasting technique. Whatever the reason, management must be alerted through some type of exception reporting that there is a need to investigate a product's forecast versus its demand and take the appropriate corrective action.

CAUSAL METHODS

When a particular forecast is of vital importance to an organization and adequate historical data exist, it is often advisable to develop a causal forecasting model in which the variable to be forecast is a function of several or many causal variables.

Sales may be a function of price, advertising budget, competitors' actions, quality control budget, disposable personal income, or other independent variables. If the relationship between these independent variables can be adequately defined mathematically, superior forecasts can result. Causal models are the most sophisticated type of forecasting model and generally require more data, more time, and substantially more money than the time series approaches discussed earlier.

There are two predominant causal forecasting methods:

1. Multiple regression models
2. Econometric models

Multiple Regression Models

Multiple regression analysis is a simple extension of simple linear regression. The difference is that instead of one independent variable in the regression equation, there are several or many independent variables. The general form of a multiple regression equation is:

$$Y = \sum_{i=1}^{n} a_i x_i + b$$

where
a_i = coefficient of independent variable x_i
b = constant
x_i = independent variable
Y = forecast variable
n = number of independent variables

The method for deriving a multiple regression equation is analogous to the simple linear case and will not be described in this text. Instead, let us look at the following example.

A typewriter manufacturing firm wishes to forecast demand for two years' maintenance contracts for its most popular typewriter. It is felt that demand is a function of the advertising budget, the premium for a one-year contract, the premium for a two-year contract, and trend. Historical data for the last ten years are available; they are shown in Table 8-10. These data were used to derive the following regression equation:

$$Y = .05085x_1 + 4.01746x_2 - 7.26361x_3 + 433.175784x_4 + 5,226.50$$

where
Y = demand for two-year maintenance contracts
x_1 = annual advertising budget
x_2 = premium for one-year contract
x_3 = premium for two-year contract
x_4 = time period, using 1968 as time period 1

Table 8-10 Maintenance Contracts Sales Data

YEAR	NUMBER OF 2-YEAR CONTRACTS SOLD	ANNUAL ADVERTISING BUDGET	PREMIUM FOR 1-YEAR CONTRACT	PREMIUM FOR 2-YEAR CONTRACT
1968	5,000	50,000	250	550
1969	6,000	50,000	250	500
1970	6,500	55,000	250	550
1971	7,000	55,000	300	600
1972	6,000	45,000	300	650
1973	7,500	60,000	350	650
1974	8,000	60,000	300	650
1975	9,000	70,000	300	600
1976	10,000	75,000	325	550
1977	10,500	75,000	325	550
1978	12,000	80,000	325	500

In order to calculate a forecast for 1979, values for x_1, x_2, x_3, and x_4 must be set. If the advertising budget for 1979 is set at \$90,000, the premium for a one-year contract at \$325, and the premium for a two-year contract at \$550, then forecast demand can be calculated as:

$$D = (.05085)(90{,}000) + (4.01746)(325) - (7.26361)(550) + (433.17578)(12)$$
$$+ 5{,}226.50$$
$$= 12{,}311.80 \text{ contracts}$$

Generally, multiple regression is less expensive but unfortunately frequently less accurate than econometric models. In other words, multiple regression is not as "quick-and-dirty" a method of forecasting as are the time series techniques discussed earlier, but it is quicker and dirtier than econometric models.

Econometric Models

An econometric model is a system of interdependent equations that describe some real phenomenon. For example, consider the following three-equation, eight-variable macroeconomic model:

$$C_t = x_1 I_t + x_3 Y_t + x_4 C_{t-1} + x_5 R_t + U_1$$
$$I_t = \beta_1 + \beta_2 Y_t + \beta_3 R_t + U_2$$
$$Y_t = C_t + I_t + G_t$$

where $\qquad C_t$ = aggregate consumption in time period t

I_t = gross investment in time period t

Y_t = gross national product in time period t

G_t = government spending in time period t

R_t = short-term interest rate

U_i = error terms

x_i = parameter estimates for first equation

β_i = parameter estimates for second equation

These equations are solved simultaneously to find the values for unknown variables C_t, I_t, and Y_t.

Econometric models are used extensively in economic forecasting, and some of the models are very complex, with hundreds of variables and hundreds of simultaneous equations. These models often provide superior forecasts but are very costly and time-consuming to build and to maintain. The Wharton School econometric model, for example, has over 200 equations and 80 exogenous variables and costs thousands of dollars to develop and more thousands to maintain.

SUMMARY

A good forecast is the primary input to the planning process. If an aggregate plan for use of labor, facilities, and inventory is to be of any value, the forecast or forecasts on which the aggregate plan is based must be accurate. The master schedule on which all automated production/inventory systems depend is based on the sales forecast for end items, and therefore the quality of any production/inventory system depends on the quality of end-item sales forecasts.

In this chapter we have attempted to describe the major forecasting methods and indicate areas of applicability. We have divided forecasting methods into three categories: qualitative methods, time series analysis techniques, and causal methods. In general, qualitative techniques are used when quantitative historical data are not available. Time series analysis techniques are used when the importance of the forecast is not great enough to justify the use of more expensive causal methods. Time series techniques have found wide usage in automated multiproduct inventory systems. Causal methods are used when their extra cost and time of implementation can be justified by the importance to the organization of the forecast accuracy.

SOLVED PROBLEMS

Problem Statement

For the demand data in Table 8-11, calculate the four-quarter moving average for the fourth quarter of 1979 and the first quarter of 1980.

Table 8-11   Calculator Demand

TIME PERIOD	TI-53 CALCULATOR DEMAND
1st Quarter 1976	1,000 units
2nd Quarter 1976	2,500 units
3rd Quarter 1976	3,000 units
4th Quarter 1976	4,000 units
1st Quarter 1977	10,000 units
2nd Quarter 1977	12,000 units
3rd Quarter 1977	15,000 units
4th Quarter 1977	14,000 units
1st Quarter 1978	20,000 units
2nd Quarter 1978	25,000 units
3rd Quarter 1978	40,000 units
4th Quarter 1978	50,000 units
1st Quarter 1979	65,000 units
2nd Quarter 1979	75,000 units
3rd Quarter 1979	80,000 units
4th Quarter 1979	100,000 units

Solution

$$\text{Forecast for the 4th quarter of 1979} = \frac{50,000 + 65,000 + 75,000 + 80,000}{4}$$

$$= 67,500 \text{ units}$$

$$\text{Forecast for the 1st quarter of 1980} = \frac{65,000 + 75,000 + 80,000 + 100,000}{4}$$

$$= 80,000 \text{ units}$$

Problem Statement

Using a weighted five-quarter moving average with the weights as described below, calculate the forecast for the first quarter of 1980 for Table 8-11 data.

	PERIOD	WEIGHT
Oldest data	1	.05
	2	.10
	3	.15
	4	.25
Most recent data	5	.45

Solution

The forecast for the first quarter of 1980 is computed as shown below:

$$F = \frac{(.05)(50{,}000) + (.1)(65{,}000) + (.15)(75{,}000) + (.25)(80{,}000) + (.45)(100{,}000)}{1.00}$$

$$= 85{,}250 \text{ units}$$

Problem Statement

Using a simple exponential smoothing model, calculate the forecast for the first quarter of 1980, given that the forecast for the last quarter of 1979 was 80,250 units. Use $\alpha = .15$.

Solution

The exponentially smoothed forecast for the first quarter of 1980 is computed as follows:

$$F_t = F_{t-1} + \alpha(A_{t-1} - F_{t-1})$$
$$= 80{,}250 + .15(100{,}000 - 80{,}250)$$
$$= 83{,}212.5 \text{ units}$$

Problem Statement

Using a trend-adjusted exponential smoothing model, calculate the forecast for the first quarter of 1980. Use a smoothing factor of .15 for the simple model forecast and a smoothing factor of .1 for the trend-smoothing factor.

Solution

The first step is to calculate the simple exponential smoothing forecast for the first quarter of 1980. This was accomplished in the preceding example:

$$F_t = 80{,}250 + .15(100{,}000 - 80{,}250)$$
$$= 83{,}212.5 \text{ units}$$

The next step is to calculate t_t:

$$t_t = F_t - F_{t-1}$$
$$t_t = 83{,}212.5 - 80{,}250$$
$$= 2{,}962.5$$

Now we must calculate T_t, assuming the initial trend adjustment is 0.

$$T_t = T_{t-1} + \beta(t_t - T_{t-1})$$
$$= 0 + .1(2,962.5)$$
$$= 296.25$$

Finally, the trend-adjusted forecast for the first quarter of 1980 can be computed as shown below:

$$F'_t = F_t + \frac{1 - \beta}{\beta} T_t$$

$$= 83,212.5 + \left(\frac{1 - .1}{.1}\right) 296.25$$

$$= 83,212.5 + 2,666.25$$

$$= 85,878.75 \text{ units}$$

Problem Statement

Using the least squares method, find the regression line for the data in Table 8-11 and calculate the forecast for the first quarter of 1980.

Solution

In order to derive the regression equation, it is necessary to solve the following two normal equations simultaneously:

$$\sum_{i=1}^{n} y_i = nb + m \sum_{i=1}^{n} x_i$$

$$\sum_{i=1}^{n} x_i y_i = b \sum_{i=1}^{n} x_i + m \sum_{i=1}^{n} x_i^2$$

In order to solve the two equations simultaneously, the four sums in the two equations must first be found. This is done in Table 8-12.

Substituting these sums into the two normal equations, we get:

$$516,500 = 16b + 136m$$
$$6,535,000 = 136b + 1,496m$$

To find what factor to multiply the first equation by to add it to the second to eliminate the b terms, we divide 136 by 16, getting 8.5. Therefore, if we multiply the first equa-

Table 8-12

x_i	y_i	$x_i y_i$	x_i^2
1	1,000	1,000	1
2	2,500	5,000	4
3	3,000	9,000	9
4	4,000	16,000	16
5	10,000	50,000	25
6	12,000	72,000	36
7	15,000	105,000	49
8	14,000	112,000	64
9	20,000	180,000	81
10	25,000	250,000	100
11	40,000	440,000	121
12	50,000	600,000	144
13	65,000	845,000	169
14	75,000	1,050,000	196
15	80,000	1,200,000	225
16	100,000	1,600,000	256
136	516,500	6,535,000	1,496

tion by -8.5 and add it to the second equation, we get:

$$
\begin{aligned}
6,535,000 &= 136b + 1,496m \\
-4,390,250 &= -136b - 1,156m \\
\hline
2,144,750 &= 340m
\end{aligned}
$$

Therefore:

$$m = \frac{2,144,750}{340}$$

$$= 6,308.0882$$

Once we have the value of one unknown, we can simply "plug" it into either normal equation to find the other unknown. Hence:

$$6,535,000 = 136b + (1,496)(6,308.0882)$$
$$6,535,000 = 136b + 9,436,900$$
$$136b = -2,901,900$$
$$b = -21,337.5$$

We can now write the regression equation:

$$Y = 6,308.0882x - 21,337.5$$

To calculate first quarter 1980 demand, we merely plug in the x value corresponding to the first quarter 1980, which is 17.

$$\text{Demand for 1st quarter } 1980 = Y = (6{,}308.0882)(17) - 2{,}133.75$$
$$= 85{,}900 \text{ units}$$

Problem Statement

Management of the calculator manufacturing firm feels that in addition to time period, the demand for calculators is also a function of price. After price data for the 16 time periods were fed into a multiple regression software package on the company computer, the following regression equation was produced:

$$Y = 8121x_1 - 1{,}045x_2 - 5{,}525$$

where
$$x_1 = \text{time period}$$
$$x_2 = \text{price}$$
$$Y = \text{demand}$$

What is the forecast for the first quarter of 1980 if the price of the TI-53 calculator is \$14.95?

Solution

Forecasting demand for first quarter 1980 is a mechanical procedure of plugging the multiple regression equation with values of the independent variables:

$$Y = 8{,}121(17) - 1{,}045(14.95) - 5{,}525$$
$$= 116{,}909.25 \text{ units}$$

REVIEW QUESTIONS

1. Define the three basic time horizons for forecasts.
2. List the three categories of forecasting techniques described in this chapter.
3. When are qualitative forecasting techniques most useful?
4. What is the major advantage of time series analysis?
5. How do causal methods differ from time series analysis?

6. What is the major disadvantage of time series analysis?

7. Which category of forecasting technique performs best for long-term forecasts?

8. List four factors to consider in selecting the proper forecasting techniques.

9. List five commonly used qualitative forecasting techniques.

10. Define the Delphi method.

11. Which of the qualitative forecasting techniques discussed in this chapter is the most sophisticated and the most expensive?

12. Which qualitative forecasting technique is generally considered to yield the most accurate forecasts?

13. How does panel consensus differ from a "grass-roots" approach?

14. Using a historical analogy approach depends on what?

15. What is a time series?

16. What are the four major components of a time series?

17. To what planning horizon is time series analysis best suited?

18. Distinguish between moving average, exponential smoothing, and trend projection.

19. What is the effect of changing the smoothing constant?

20. Why is simple exponential smoothing inadequate when trend exists in time series data?

21. Write the equation of a straight line and define each parameter and variable.

22. Why is it desirable to calculate the standard error of estimate?

23. Distinguish between simple linear regression and multiple regression.

PROBLEMS

1. Calculate the 4-year simple moving average for 1980, using the time series data in Table 8-13.

2. For the data in Table 8-13, calculate a 6-year weighted moving average for 1980, using the following weights: .1, .1, .1, .2, .2, and .3 from the oldest to the most recent year.

3. Using an α of .25, calculate the 1980 forecast using the simple exponential smoothing model. Use the data in Table 8-13 and assume a 1979 forecast of $500,000.

4. Using trial-and-error techniques, determine the best α, .10 or .25 for the data in Table 8-13. Assume a 1961 forecast of 250,000.

5. Again using Table 8-13 data, calculate the 1980 forecast using the trend-adjusted exponential smoothing model. Assume $\alpha = .15$, $\beta = .20$, and a 1979 forecast of $500,000.

Table 8-13   Time Series Data

YEAR	SALES
1961	$250,000
1962	262,000
1963	300,000
1964	351,000
1965	364,000
1966	365,000
1967	377,000
1968	402,000
1969	393,000
1970	400,000
1971	425,000
1972	415,000
1973	430,000
1974	440,000
1975	455,000
1976	457,000
1977	481,000
1978	492,000
1979	505,000

6. For problem 5, find an α and β that you think do a good job of forecasting sales by writing and running a computer search program.

7. Draw a scatter diagram for the time series data of Table 8-13.

8. Using the method of least squares, find the regression equation for the time series data in Table 8-13. Use the regression equation to forecast sales for 1981.

9. Find the interval estimate for the regression equation derived in problem 8 corresponding to a 95.5% confidence level. Assume normality.

10. Given the data in Table 8-14, compare a 6-month moving average forecast and a 3-month moving average forecast for the 12 months of 1979.

11. Choose weights for a 6-month moving average that do a better job of forecasting demand than the simple 6-month moving average calculated in problem 10.

12. Which is the better smoothing constant for the 1979 data in Table 8-14, $\alpha = .05$, or $\alpha = .25$? Justify your answer.

13. By a limited search procedure, define a good trend-adjusted exponential smoothing model for the 1979 time series data in Table 8-14.

14. Write a computer program that will accomplish the search required by problem 13.

15. Draw a scatter diagram of the time series data of Table 8-14 on graph paper and "eyeball" a regression line. Read the slope and intercept off the graph to construct the regression equation.

Table 8-14   Time Series Data for Part No. 215-22000

YEAR	MONTH	DEMAND
1978	January	25,450
	February	25,000
	March	25,150
	April	24,950
	May	24,500
	June	24,600
	July	24,250
	August	23,000
	September	23,100
	October	22,900
	November	22,000
	December	19,500
1979	January	19,750
	February	18,950
	March	19,150
	April	18,740
	May	18,500
	June	18,250
	July	17,475
	August	17,500
	September	17,650
	October	17,250
	November	17,100
	December	16,550

16. Find the simple linear regression equation for the Table 8-14 data using the least squares method.

17. How do the January 1980 demand forecasts differ using the "eyeballed" equation and the least squares equation derived in problem 16?

18. Given a confidence level of 90%, what is the prediction interval for demand for February 1980?

19. The number of pediatric admissions for one month can be forecasted using the following regression equation:

$$Y = 5.1 + 5.72x_1 + .002x_2 + 4.16x_3$$

where Y = number of pediatric admissions for one month
x_1 = number of pediatricians on the hospital staff
x_2 = city population of people under 20
x_3 = number of obstetricians on the hospital staff

If the hospital has seven pediatricians and nine obstetricians and the under-20 population is 14,000, what is the monthly forecast for pediatrics admissions?

Case: HARMON FOODS, INC.*

Introduction

John MacIntyre, general sales manager of the Breakfast Foods Division of Harmon Foods, Inc., was having difficulty in forecasting the sales of Treat. Treat was a ready-to-eat breakfast cereal with an important share of the market. It was also the major product in those company plants where it was manufactured. Mr. MacIntyre was responsible for sales forecasts from which production schedules were prepared.

In recent months, actual Treat sales had varied from 50% to 200% of his forecast. Most of his difficulty in preparing forecasts arose from the great variability in historical sales; that variability can easily be seen in Table 8-15. Since sales were debited on the day of shipment, Table 8-15 represents unit shipments as well as sales.

Table 8-15 Harmon Foods, Inc. Sales of Treat (Standard Cases)

| | YEAR | | | |
MONTH	1966	1967	1968	1969
January	425,075	629,404	655,748	455,136
February	315,305	263,467	270,483	247,570
March	432,101	468,612	429,480	732,005
April	357,191	313,221	260,458	357,107
May	347,874	444,404	528,210	453,156
June	435,529	386,986	379,856	320,103
July	299,403	414,314	472,058	451,779
August	296,505	253,493	254,516	249,482
September	426,701	484,365	551,354	744,583
October	329,722	305,989	335,826	421,186
November	281,783	315,407	320,408	397,367
December	166,391	182,784	276,901	269,096

*This case was prepared as a basis for class discussion rather than to illustrate either effective or ineffective handling of an administrative situation. Copyright © 1970 by the President and Fellows of Harvard College. Reproduced by permission. Distributed by the Intercollegiate Case Clearing House, Soldiers Field, Boston, Mass. 02163. All rights reserved to the contributors. Printed in the U.S.A.

Manufacturing Problems

Accuracy in production forecasts was essential for the health of the entire business. The individual plant managers received these forecast schedules and certified their ability to meet them. Acceptance of a schedule by a plant manager represented a "promise" to deliver; crews and machines were assigned, materials ordered, and storage space allocated to meet the schedule.

Schedule changes were expensive. On the one hand, the lead time on raw material orders was several weeks, so that ordering too little caused shortages which were expensive in lost production time and disappointed customers. After schedule reductions, on the other hand, the raw material could not be used as fast as it arrived. Storage space was short, and so some of the material had to be left on the truck, railroad car, or barge in which it had been shipped. The resultant tie-up of these vehicles was extremely expensive in demurrage charges.[1]

Even more important than the storage problem was the problem of efficient manpower utilization. Production schedules were kept tight to avoid unnecessary costs. Overtime was avoided because it was expensive and interfered with weekend maintenance. The labor force was highly skilled and difficult to increase in the short run. Layoffs, on the other hand, were avoided to preserve the skills of the crew. This job security resulted in a high level of employee morale and was an important part of the company's labor policy. Thus, the production manager had to try to make production schedules efficient for a constant-size work force and to use as little overtime as possible.

Advertising Expenditures

Inaccuracy of sales forecasts also led to a reduction in the effectiveness of Treat advertising expenditures. Most of the advertising dollars for Treat were spent on Saturday morning network shows for children, time for which was purchased up to a year or more in advance. This time was relatively expensive, costing $20,000 per one-minute commercial, but it was the opinion of all of the brand managers in the Breakfast Food Division that these network programs delivered the best value for each advertising dollar spent. This opinion was based upon cost per million messages delivered, viewer-recall scores, and measures of audience composition.

---

[1]Demurrage charges are assessments made by a carrier against a consignee for delays in unloading (or the initiation of unloading) of a transport vehicle. Typically, there is an allowance of one free hour in excess of normal unloading time for trucks. Rail cars and barges have typical allowances of three days and one day respectively, including unloading time. Typical charges for delays beyond these allowances range from as low as $5 per hour for a truck and $8 per day for a rail car to $1,000 per day for a large barge.

It was the policy at Harmon Foods, as at many companies, to budget advertising expenditures at a fixed amount per unit sold. Each year, monthly budgets for advertising were established, based on forecasted sales. Brand managers tended to contract for time on network programs to the limit of their budget allowance. When shipments ran high, however, brand managers tended to increase advertising expenditures to the level warranted by the actual sales. In such circumstances, they would seek contracts for time from other brand managers who were shipping below budget. Failing this, they would seek network time through the agencies, or if such time were unavailable, they would seek spot advertising as close to prime program time as possible. Thus, unplanned advertising expenditures could result in use of time which gave lower value per advertising dollar spent than did the best network time.

Budgets and Controls

The errors in forecasts were also the subject of complaints from the controller of the Breakfast Foods Division. Each brand prepared a budget based on forecasted shipments. This budget "promised" a contribution to division overhead and profits. Long-term dividend policy and corporate expansion plans were based in part on these forecasts. Regular quarterly increases in earnings over prior years had resulted in a high price-earnings ratio for the company. Since the market value of the common stock was a chief interest of the owners, profit planning was an important part of the management control system.

The discretionary "overspending" on advertising noted earlier tended to amplify the problems of profit planning. These expenditures did not have budgetary approval, and until a new "budget base" (sales forecast) for the fiscal year was approved at all levels, such overspending was merely borrowing ahead on the current fiscal year. The controller's office charged only the budgeted advertising to sales in each quarter and carried the excess over, since it was unauthorized. This procedure resulted in spurious accounting profits in those quarters with sales in excess of forecast, with counterbalancing reductions in profit in subsequent quarters.

The extent to which profits could be affected by deferred advertising expenditures had been demonstrated in the past fiscal year. Treat, along with several other brands, had overspent extensively in the early quarters, and as a result, divisional earnings for the fourth quarter were more than one million dollars below corporate expectations. The division manager, as well as his sales manager, brand managers, and controller, had felt very uncomfortable in the meetings and conferences which had been held as a result of this shortage of reported profits. The extra profits reported in earlier quarters had offset shortages of other divisions, but in the final quarter, there had been no division to offset the Breakfast Foods shortage.

The Brand Manager

Donald Carswell, the brand manager for Treat, prepared his brand's "budget base," or set of monthly, quarterly, and annual forecasts which governed monthly advertising and promotional expenditures. These forecasts, along with forecasts from the division's other brand managers, were submitted to Mr. MacIntyre for his approval. This approval was necessary because, in a given month, the sales force could support the promotions of only a limited number of brands. Once approved, the brand managers' forecasts served as the basis of the "official" forecasts made by Mr. MacIntyre.

The use of the brand managers' forecasts as the basis for the sales manager's official forecasts (and thus, the basis for production scheduling) required mutual confidence and understanding. From the sales manager came information on Harmon's, and also the competitors', activity and pricing at the store level. From the brand manager came knowledge of market trends for his brand and its competitors. The brand manager also kept records of all available market research reports on his and similar brands, and was aware of any package design and product formulations under development.

As brand manager, Mr. Carswell knew that the responsibility for improving the reliability of sales forecasts for Treat rested with him. After talking to analysts in the Market Research, Systems Analysis, and Operations Research departments, he concluded that better forecasts were possible, and Robert Haas of the Operations Research Department offered to work with him on the project. Carswell received enthusiastic support for his planned undertaking from both the sales manager and the controller. Although such projects were outside the normal scope of a brand manager's duties, Carswell recognized the opportunity to find a solution to his forecasting problem that would have companywide application.

Factors Affecting Sales

Carswell and Haas discussed at great length the factors that influenced sales. A twelve-month moving average of the data in Table 8-15 indicated a long-term rising trend in sales. This trend confirmed the A. C. Nielsen store audit, which reported a small but steady rise in market share for Treat, plus a steady rise for the commodity group to which Treat belonged.

In addition to trend, Carswell felt that seasonal factors might be important. In November and December, sales slowed down as inventory levels among stores and jobbers were drawn down for year-end inventories. Summer sales were often low because of plant shutdowns and sales vacations. There were fewer selling days in February. Salesmen often started new fiscal years with a burst of energy in order to get in a good quota position for the rest of the year.

Non-media promotions, which represented about 25% of the advertising budget for Treat, were known to have a very strong influence on sales. Such promotions were of two main types. Promotions targeted directly at the consumer were called "consumer packs," so named because the consumer was reimbursed in some way for each package of Treat which was purchased. Promotions which sought to increase sales by increasing the degree to which the brand was "pushed" by dealers were called "dealer allowances," so-called because allowances were made to dealers to compensate them for expenditures incurred in promoting Treat. Consumer packs and dealer allowances were each offered two or three times per year during different canvass periods. (A sales canvass period is the time required for a salesman to make a complete round of all customers in his assigned area. Harmon Foods scheduled 10 five-week canvass periods each year. The remaining two weeks, one at midsummer and one at year-end, were for holidays and vacations.)

Consumer Packs

Consumer packs usually took the form of a five-cent-per-package reduction in the price paid by the consumer. The offer could also take the form of a coupon, an enclosed premium, or a mail-in offer; but based on the results of consumer-panel tests of all such offers, Carswell was confident that each of these forms was roughly equivalent to the five-cent price reduction in its return to the brand. Consequently, he decided to group all forms of consumer packs together.

Consumer packs, along with supporting advertising material and special cartons, were produced ahead of the assigned canvass period for shipment throughout the five-week period. Any packs not shipped within this period would be allocated among salesmen for shipment in periods in which no consumer promotion was officially scheduled. From a study of historical data covering a number of consumer packs, Haas found that approximately 35% of a consumer-pack offering moved out during the first week, 25% during the second week, 15% the third week, and approximately 10% during each of the fourth and last weeks of the canvass period. Approximately 5% was shipped after the promotional period was over. Since they saw no reason for this historical pattern to change, Haas and Carswell were confident that they could predict with quite reasonable accuracy the monthly consumer-pack shipments that would result from a given promotion undertaken in the future.

The impact of consumer packs on total shipments was, of course, favorable in the month in which the consumer packs were actually shipped; but since the consumer ate Treat at a more or less constant rate over time, Carswell was convinced that part of this increase in total shipments was the result of inventory buildups on the part of jobbers, stores, and consumers. Thus it seemed reasonable to expect that consumer packs might have a negative impact on total ship-

Table 8-16   Harmon Foods, Inc. Consumer Packs (Standard Shipping Cases)*

			YEAR		
MONTH	1965	1966	1967	1968	1969
January	−15	75,253	548,704	544,807	299,781
February	−47	15,036	52,819	43,704	21,218
March	−7	134,440	2,793	5,740	157
April	−1	119,740	27,749	9,614	12,961
May	15,012	135,590	21,887	1,507	333,529
June	62,337	189,636	1,110	13,620	178,105
July	4,022	9,308	436	101,179	315,564
August	3,130	41,099	1,407	80,309	80,206
September	−422	9,391	376,650	335,768	5,940
October	−8	942	122,906	91,710	36,819
November	5	1,818	15,138	9,856	234,562
December	220	672	5,532	107,172	71,881

*Negative shipments are returns of consumer packs by customers.

ments, as these excess inventories were depleted in the first and possibly the second month after the packs were shipped.

Dealer Allowances

Sales seemed even more sensitive to allowances offered to dealers for cooperative promotional efforts. These allowances were provided to participating dealers via a $1 to $2 per-case discount on their purchases during the canvass period of the allowance.

The total expenditure for dealer allowances during a given promotional canvass period was budgeted in advance. As with consumer packs, any "unspent" allowances would be allocated to salesmen for disbursement after the promotional period was over. The actual weekly expenditures resulting from these allowances were found to follow approximately the same pattern as was found for the shipment of consumer packs, and consequently, Carswell felt that the monthly expenditures resulting from any given schedule of future dealer allowances could also be predicted with reasonable accuracy.

Promotional efforts by dealers took the form of "giant spectacular end-of-aisle displays," newspaper ads, coupons, or fliers, among others. The extent to which such efforts could affect sales is illustrated by the fact that an end-of-aisle display located near a cash register could give an average of five weeks' business in a single weekend. As with special packs, however, Carswell believed that much of the resulting sales increase was attributable to inventory buildups, and therefore he expected reactions to these buildups as late as two months after the initial sales increase.

Actual expenditures made for dealer allowances over the past four years are shown in Table 8-17.

Table 8-17   Harmon Foods, Inc., Dealer Allowances ($)

| | YEAR | | | | |
MONTH	1965	1966	1967	1968	1969
January	99,194	114,433	0	166,178	8,133
February	38,074	63,599	78,799	134,206	5,867
March	39,410	64,988	175,906	137,890	1,125,864
April	61,516	66,842	49,616	37,520	125,226
May	83,929	39,626	119,720	145,200	0
June	81,578	107,503	114,293	108,770	0
July	65,821	97,129	177,370	90,286	11,526
August	122,169	56,404	11,345	24,461	23,063
September	8,482	260,576	7,020	7,593	1,217,488
October	56,007	243,523	27,880	37,581	94,139
November	76,001	75,473	66,800	73,261	94,139
December	88,218	19,037	88,576	40,697	138,134

Conclusion

Carswell and Haas felt that they had identified, to the best of their ability, the most important factors affecting sales. They knew competitive advertising and price moves were important but unpredictable, and they wished to restrict their model to those variables which could be measured or predicted in advance.

Haas agreed to formulate the model, construct the data matrix, and write an explanation of how the solution of the model could be used to evaluate promotion strategies, as well as to forecast sales and shipments. Carswell and Haas would then join in planning a presentation to divisional managers.

Case Discussion Questions

1. Why was it of critical importance to do a better job of forecasting for Treat?
2. What factors did Carswell and Haas identify as being relevant to the Treat forecast?
3. Can any of the time series techniques discussed in this chapter be applied with success? Explain.
4. If available, use a multiple regression package on your computer to derive a multiple regression forecasting equation.
5. How would you convince management to use your regression analysis?

REFERENCES

ADAM, EVERETT E., and RONALD J. EBERT, *Production and Operations Management.* Englewood Cliffs, N.J.: Prentice-Hall, 1978.

BRIGHT, JAMES R., ed., *Technological Forecasting for Industry and Government Methods and Applications.* Englewood Cliffs, N.J.: Prentice-Hall, 1968.

BROWN, ROBERT G., *Smoothing, Forecasting, and Prediction of Descrete Time Series,* Englewood Cliffs, N.J.: Prentice-Hall, 1962.

I.S. CHAMBERS, S.K. MULLICH, and D.D. SMITH, "How to Choose the Right Forecasting Technique," *Harvard Business Review,* July–August 1971.

CHASE, RICHARD B., and NICHOLAS J. AQUILANO, *Production and Operations Management.* Homewood, Ill.: Richard D. Irwin, 1977.

CHOW, WEN M., "Adaptive Control of the Exponential Smoothing Constant," *Journal of Industrial Engineering,* Vol. 16, No. 5 (September–October 1965), 314–17.

CLARK, CHARLES T., and LAWRENCE, L. SCHKADE, *Statistical Methods for Business and Economics.* Cincinnati, O.: South-Western Publishing Company, 1977.

HOEL, PAUL G., and RAYMOND J. JESSEN, *Basic Statistics for Business and Economics.* New York: John Wiley, 1977.

PARKER, G.C., and EDELBERTO L. SEGURA, "How to Get a Better Forecast," *Harvard Business Review,* Vol. 49, No. 2 (March–April 1971), 99–109.

MONKS, JOSEPH G., *Operations Management: Theory and Problems.* New York: McGraw-Hill, 1977.

SHORE, BARRY, *Operations Management.* New York: McGraw-Hill, 1977.

chapter 9

AGGREGATE
PLANNING

Planning is one of the primary functions of a manager. It is through proper planning that an organization can hope to achieve its objectives. Along the dimension of time, planning breaks naturally into three phases: long-range, intermediate-range, and short-range.

Long-range or strategic planning typically involves the formulation of organizational objectives (and strategies for obtaining those objectives) for a planning horizon of several years. Long-range planning is the responsibility of top management and also includes growth policies, establishment of total budgets, and long-range capital investments such as building new facilities. In long-range planning, management has a great deal of flexibility in choosing courses of action. It may order new equipment, change products or services, select new management, or train a new labor force. The duration of the long-range planning horizon can vary from one to more than five years; it depends on the organization and how long it takes to respond to changes. For example, an electrical power company may need five years or more to plan and build a new plant to meet increasing demand, whereas a service company such as an engineering consulting firm can get into a new line of expertise in a year or two.

Intermediate-range planning usually involves from one month to a year or more. This type of planning is usually the function of middle management and involves tactical decisions such as quarterly plans, subdivisions of budgets, and arrangements to meet fluctuations in demand. Aggregate planning is the essence of intermediate-range planning, and that is what we shall study in this chapter. This type of planning has received significant attention, and several methods have been used for it. In intermediate-range planning, management must work within the limitations established in long-range planning, but still has some flexibility in selecting courses of action.

The short-range planning horizon is from a day up to possibly a month. The focus is on operational considerations such as schedules, short-run budgets, and daily or weekly plans. The objective is to meet planned production as economically as possible. Management participating directly in short-range planning is usually at the first level and involves supervisors and foremen. Their decisions must fit within the constraints imposed by the intermediate-planning decisions. In short-run planning, the details of scheduling particular jobs and implementing special projects must be carried out. The aggregate or general plans of intermediate planning must be disaggregated to specify the production or operation plan into time-phased weekly, daily, or hourly activities. Little flexibility exists to achieve these short-range objectives. In a later chapter, we shall turn to the specific methods of scheduling.

See Figure 9-1 for a graphical illustration of the time planning horizons of long-, intermediate-, and short-range planning.

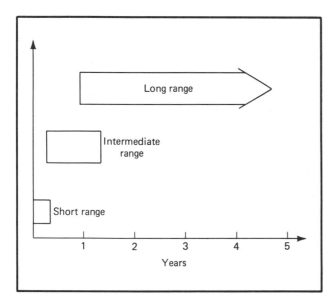

FIGURE 9-1 Planning Horizons of Types of Planning

DEFINITION AND REQUIREMENTS
OF AGGREGATE PLANNING

Aggregate planning is intermediate-range planning in which strategies are devised to economically absorb demand fluctuations. The output of aggregate planning should specify values for monthly manpower levels, output levels, inventory levels, overtime commitments, subcontracting needs, vacation plans, undertime levels, and hiring quantities. The objective is to minimize future operating costs over a particular planning horizon.

As the name implies, aggregate planning involves combining the relevant resources into general terms or an overall aggregate. Thus, an organization needs an overall measure of output in aggregate planning. These gross amounts include total demand, inventory, work force, or production capacity requirements—for example, barrels of oil in the oil industry, machine- or man-hours in a manufacturing plant, or beds in a hospital. Furthermore, aggregate planning requires some means of forecasting these aggregate levels for the planning horizon. Data pertaining to past sales, trends, and seasonal components are necessary, as well as an effective forecasting technique. See Chapter 8 for a thorough discussion of forecasting.

Successful aggregate planning requires a systems approach. Not only must the aggregate planner have forecasting input from the marketing function, but aggregate strategies must fall within the cash-flow constraints set by finance. Making intermediate operations plans without the input and cooperation of other functions of the organization can result in unworkable or, at least, suboptimal strategies. In order to be useful, aggregate plans must also be translatable into shorter-range assignments of personnel to specific work groups, operations, and products or services. In manufacturing organizations, these assignments make up the master schedule, which is the detailed report of the aggregate plan. The master schedule specifies job orders, machine utilization, and inventory purchases. It is through the master schedule that aggregate planning ties in with MRP, materials requirement planning for dependent demand (the topic of Chapter 11). Aggregate planning determines a tentative master schedule, and computerized MRP output checks the feasibility of future production plans. Through an information feedback process, the aggregate capacity plans can be refined and made realistic for final implementation. Figure 9-2 describes the development of the master schedule.

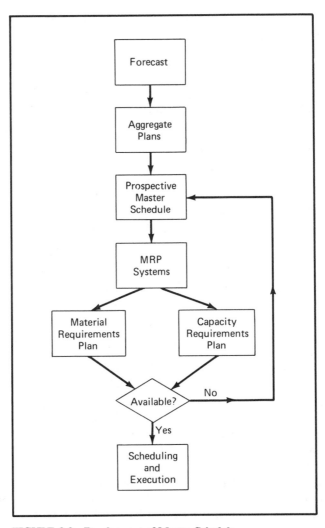

FIGURE 9-2   Development of Master Schedule

STRATEGIES FOR AGGREGATE PLANNING

In planning the future use of operations capacity, the organization can assume an active or a passive role. In the passive role, the planner tries to respond to demand fluctuations but not to affect the rate of demand itself. In the active role, the firm tries to influence or in some way change the demand pattern.

Active Strategies

The objective of active strategies is to smooth out the peaks and valleys of demand during the planning horizon. The goal is to obtain a smoother load on the productive facilities. During periods of low demand, increased sales of goods or services can be encouraged through price cuts. Thus, lawn and garden tools are sometimes cheaper during the off season, telephone calls are cheaper at night, and Miami Beach hotel rooms are most expensive during the winter months. Periods of low demand can also be tackled through expenditures on special advertising programs or promotional gimmicks.

During periods of high demand, management can choose simply to not meet all demand requirements. However this approach is not usually taken as it purposely ignores opportunities for increased revenue. A more reasonable alternative during high demand periods is to incur order backlogs. Backlogs, however, may be acceptable only for certain types of goods or services. The success of backlogging demand certainly depends upon the customer's willingness to wait. In some cases backlogs may result in customer ill will or losses of future sales; customers may be willing to wait for automobiles, but probably not airline tickets.

Another active approach to smoothing demand for productive resources is to select a product mix which consists of counterseasonal products. For example, a firm might manufacture air conditioners during the warm months and heat pumps or furnaces during the winter, another company might maintain a product mix of snow skiis and tennis rackets. Vergin found that the counterseasonal product line was by far the most widely used smoothing strategy among eight manufacturing firms with seasonal demand.

Passive Strategies

The objective of passive strategies is not to change demand but to somehow absorb the fluctuations in demand. The alternatives for passive responses include work-force size, work rate, inventory, subcontracting, and capacity utilization. Varying any one of these factors while holding all others constant is called a pure strategy. Thus, absorbing demand by increasing the size of the work force is a pure strategy. A mixed strategy involves the use of two or more pure strategies—for example, a buildup of inventory and subcontracting of work in order to meet peak demand levels.

The first passive strategy is to vary the size of the work force in accordance with fluctuations in demand. Thus, hiring would be used to absorb high demand, and laying off workers would be used to absorb low demand. From a behavioral and legal stand-point, this strategy has some obvious limitations in terms of morale and labor unions. It could be used to some extent, however, in labor-intensive industries. The strategy of varying the size of the work force requires cost data pertaining to hiring and laying off, but these costs are not always easy to determine. The hiring process would include time spent interviewing, testing, and training. Additionally, the learning-curve phenomenon would require that the typical worker be at his job a while to achieve full productivity. Layoff costs include severance pay, insurance, unemployment compensation, and unmeasurable ill will on the part of the worker and possibly the community.

A strategy that can be used to vary the output rate while keeping the work force constant in size is the use of overtime and undertime. Undertime implies that the workers are receiving full pay, whereas a shorter-workweek policy implies less than full-time pay. The costs of an overtime strategy can be directly measured in terms of increased wages; however, undertime involves opportunity costs, and shorter work-weeks involve intangibles such as worker dissatisfaction.

Inventory can be used to absorb demand even when the work force or work rate remains constant. The basic idea is to produce inventory during periods of low demand so that this inventory can be used to meet high demand in other periods. This strategy is usually limited to manufacturing firms, as most service-oriented organizations do not deal with inventoriable items. Maintaining an inventory, however, requires storage space and incurs costs involving capital opportunity cost, taxes, insurance, handling, and possibly obsolescence.

Subcontracting work is another pure strategy that can be used during periods of high demand. Usually, the per-unit production costs are higher when subcontracted rather than produced "in-house," so the benefits must be weighed against the costs. And in subcontracting, the firm also loses some control over the quality of the final product.

A final pure strategy, which is more common to service industries, is the utilization of capacity. Organizations that cannot store their product or service must plan for a capacity to meet peak demand. Examples include electric power companies, telephone companies, computer time-sharing companies, and even airlines. In this approach, all the available capacity is used only during periods of highest demand.

In summary, the pure strategies for absorbing fluctuating demand are:

1. Varying work-force size
2. Varying production rate
3. Increasing inventory
4. Subcontracting
5. Capacity utilization

Even though each of the pure strategies can effectively aid in absorbing demand, it is usually some combination or mixed strategy that works best. The problem of finding the best overall strategy has been approached by several methods, some of them quite simple and some quite sophisticated. In the next section, we first consider a simple graphical approach to aggregate planning and then look at some more effective mathematical and computerized approaches.

METHODS FOR AGGREGATE PLANNING

Graphical Method

Our first approach to aggregate planning is one of the most widely used and offers the advantage of enabling the decision maker to visualize the plans being considered. To illustrate the graphical method, we present an example.

Consider the Braden Company, which has developed monthly forecasts for its leading product. The expected monthly demand for the upcoming year is presented in Table 9-1. The Braden Company assumes that safety stock is 20 percent of monthly demand for planning purposes. (Safety stock is the amount of inventory that is stored in excess of expected demand.) In Table 9-1, we also see the calculated safety stock

Table 9-1   Demand and Safety Stock Forecasts

MONTH	EXPECTED DEMAND	DESIRED SAFETY STOCK	WORKING DAYS	IMPLIED PRODUC- TION RATE PER DAY
Jan.	9,000	1,800	22	409
Feb.	8,000	1,600	19	421
Mar.	7,000	1,400	21	333
Apr.	6,000	1,200	21	285
May	5,000	1,000	22	227
June	6,000	1,200	20	300
July	8,000	1,600	12	666
Aug.	10,000	2,000	22	454
Sept.	14,000	2,800	20	700
Oct.	15,000	3,000	23	652
Nov.	12,000	2,400	19	631
Dec.	10,000	2,000	21	476
	110,000	22,000	242	

and number of working days per month. The number of working days in July is low because of vacation time. The implied production rate per day in the last column of the table is calculated by dividing the expected demand by the working days in the month. Figure 9-3 graphically depicts the implied production rate per day for each month, and Table 9-2 presents the costs needed to assess any proposed aggregate plan.

If we assume a starting inventory of 1,000 units at the beginning of the year, we can now compare three proposed plans for absorbing demand fluctuations. In Plan 1, let's consider an approach that maintains a constant work force throughout the year. From Table 9-1 we can see that 110,000 units required and 242 working days yields

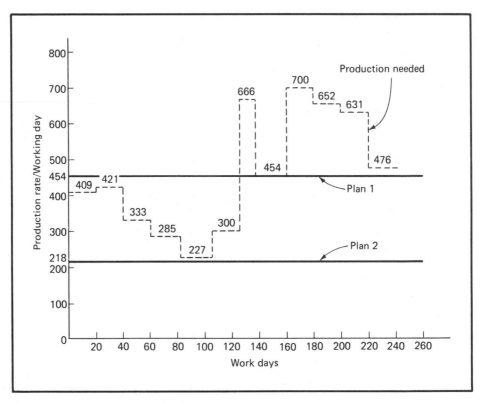

FIGURE 9-3   **Production rates for various plans**

Table 9-2   Cost Information

Manufacturing cost	=	$50 per unit
Inventory carrying cost	=	$2 per unit/month
Stockout cost	=	$6 per unit/month
Subcontracting cost	=	$65 per unit ($15 marginal increase)
Average pay rate	=	$5 per hour
Overtime pay rate	=	$7.50 per hour
Hiring costs	=	$220 per man
Layoff costs	=	$270 per man
Man-hours per unit	=	4

110,000/242 = 454.54 units per working day as an average. Considering that each man works eight hours and each unit requires four hours for production, we see that we need 454.54/2 = 227.27 full-time workers. In the first month, January, we have 1,000 units on hand, estimated demand of 9,000, and a desired safety stock of 1,800. This yields a needed production of 9,800 units. However, 227 full-time workers will produce 10,000 units in a 22-day work month, and the 200 excess units, along with 1,800 units of safety stock, push the inventory level to 2,000 in January.

In Plan 1, inventory costs are quite high, since units are stored early in the year to meet high demand later in the year. However, there are no hiring, firing, or stockout costs. Note that nominal subcontracting costs of $35,000 are incurred only if management insists on having the 2,000 extra units of inventory for safety stock in the last month. That is, $(110,000 + 2,000) - (110,000 + 1,000$ beginning inventory$) = 1,000$ units short. Figure 9-3 graphically illustrates the constant production rate of Plan 1.

In Plan 2, we investigate another pure strategy, in which a constant work force is maintained at a level necessary only for the lowest month, May; all demand above this level is met by subcontracting. During May, we have a forecasted demand of 5,000 units + 1,000 safety stock — April's safety stock of 1,200 = 4,800, and 22 workdays. Thus, we need 109 full-time workers. Under this plan, subcontracting is required in every month except May. No inventory costs (except for safety stocks) are incurred under Plan 2, as only subcontracting costs apply. The daily production rate of Plan 2 is shown in Figure 9-3.

In Plan 3, we consider a mixed strategy in which overtime and subcontracting are used to absorb demand. We assume that overtime is limited to 20 hours per week, or four hours per day for each employee. In Plan 3, we maintain a constant work force of 109 workers and subcontract work whenever demand exceeds regular plus overtime production capacity.

In Table 9-3, we see the costs broken down for each of the three plans. From the table you can see that Plan 1 offers the cheapest alternative for absorbing demand. In this problem, the labor cost was a dominant factor, but subcontracting proved more expensive. In some companies, management may be unable or unwilling to

Table 9-3 Cost Comparison of the Three Plans

COST	PLAN 1 (INVENTORY) WORK FORCE = 227	PLAN 2 (SUBCONTRACTING) WORK FORCE = 109	PLAN 3 (OVERTIME AND SUBCONTRACTING) WORK FORCE = 109
Regular labor (above 109 workers)	$1,142,240 (118 x $5/hr. x 242 days x 8 hr./day)	0	0
Overtime labor	0	0	$263,780 ($10 x 26,378 units made on overtime)
Inventory carrying cost (above safety stocks)	148,398 (74,199 units carried x $2)	0	0
Subcontracting cost	35,000 (1,000 units x $35)	2,038,540 ($35 x 58,244 units)	1,115,310 ($35 x 31,866 units)
Total incremental cost	$1,345,638	$2,038,540	$1,379,090

* The $35 subcontracting cost excludes the $30 manufacturing cost per unit.

resort to four hours of overtime each working day or to subcontract over 30 percent of the units demanded. Of course, other plans involving other pure or mixed strategies could be considered; we have examined only three possibilities.

Even though the charting method is widely used and useful, it is more helpful in evaluating strategies than in generating or constructing them. The graphical method does not guarantee an optimal or even a near-optimal solution. What is needed is a systematic method that will consider all costs and generate an effective solution. We now turn to some mathematical and computer models for aggregate planning problems.

Mathematical and Computer Techniques

Useful mathematical optimization models have been developed for various cases of aggregate planning problems. All these models, however, make certain assumptions about the cost structure or basic nature of the problem; for this reason, they are not always answers to the general aggregate planning problem. Each model we shall discuss is a useful planning tool for certain types of problems.

Transportation Model. The transportation model that was presented in the supplement to Chapter 2 is useful not only for distributing a product from plant to market, but also for planning production. The transportation model is applicable whenever the costs of production, inventory, and subcontracting are approximately linear in nature. Its most serious limitation for planning purposes is that it does not account for changeover costs, such as hiring and laying off workers from one period to the next. Thus, it would be most useful when management was exploring aggregate plans having a relatively stable work force over time.

The transportation model will determine an optimal aggregate plan assuming linear costs, and demand fluctuations that are to be absorbed only through overtime, undertime, inventory, subcontracting, and backorders. In the transportation model, the destinations or columns will represent product demand and the origins or rows will represent the means and their capacities to absorb demand. For example, Table 9-4 shows the general form of a transportation model for three planning periods. The R_i, O_i, and S_i represent regular time, overtime, and subcontracting capacities respectively in period i. The D_i represent product demand in period i, and I_b and I_f represent beginning and ending inventories. In the cells of the tableau, the costs in the upper left-hand corners are represented by c = inventory carrying cost, r = regular-time production cost, t = overtime production cost, s = subcontracting cost, b = backorder cost, and w = wage cost per idle employee on regular time. The squares or cells of the tableau represent a means of absorbing demand in a particular period by a particular resource. For example, cell 2,1 (second row, first column) represents the means of satisfying period 1 demand with regular production in period 1.

Let's apply the transportation model to the previous example of the Braden Company. To keep the model conveniently small, we will consider only the third quarter of the year. Assuming that the beginning inventory for July will be the safety

Table 9-4 General Form of Transportation Tableau for Three-Period Model

	PERIOD 1	PERIOD 2	PERIOD 3	FINAL INVENTORY	UNUSED CAPACITY	AVAILABLE CAPACITY
Beginning inventory	0	c	$2c$	$3c$	$4c$	I_b
Period 1 — Regular time	r	$r+c$	$r+2c$	$r+3c$	w	R_1
Overtime	t	$t+c$	$t+2c$	$t+3c$	0	O_1
Subcontracted	s	$s+c$	$s+2c$	$s+3c$	0	S_1
Period 2 — Regular time	$r+b$	r	$r+c$	$r+2c$	w	R_2
Overtime	$t+b$	t	$t+c$	$t+2c$	0	O_2
Subcontracted	$s+b$	s	$s+c$	$s+2c$	0	S_2
Period 3 — Regular time	$r+2b$	$r+b$	r	$r+c$	w	R_3
Overtime	$t+2b$	$t+b$	t	$t+c$	0	O_3
Subcontracted	$s+2b$	$s+b$	s	$s+c$	0	S_3
Demand requirement	D_1	D_2	D_3	I_f		

stock of June, we have the associated transportation tableau for the Braden Company in Table 9-5. The available capacity is figured on the basis of 109 workers, each of whom is able to produce two units each working day; overtime capacity is assumed to be 25 percent of regular capacity, and subcontracting is limited to 9,000 units per month. Demand requirements are calculated as forecasted demand plus the preceding month's safety stock minus the current month's safety stock. From Table 9-2 we obtain the following cost information:

Manufacturing cost = $50 per unit on regular time
Regular-time labor = $5 per hour × 4 hours per unit = $20
$w = 20$
$r = 30 + 20 = 50$
Overtime labor = $7.50 per hour × 4 hours per unit = $30
$t = 30 + 30 = 60$
Inventory carrying cost = $2 per unit per month
$c = 2$
Subcontracting cost = $65 per unit including outside materials, labor, etc.
$s = 65$
Backorder cost = $6 per unit per month
$b = 6$

The solution to the three-month planning problem is also shown in Table 9-5. The solution represents a mixed strategy; regular time, overtime, subcontracting, and

Table 9-5   Transportation Tableau and Solution for Braden Company

		JULY	AUG.	SEPT.	FINAL INVENTORY	UNUSED CAPACITY	AVAILABLE CAPACITY
	Beginning inventory	0 1,200	2	4	6	8	1,200
July	Regular tin.	50 2,616	52	54	56	20	2,616
	Overtime	60 654	62	64	66	0	654
	Subcontracted	65 3,930	67	69	71	0 5,070	9,000
Aug.	Regular time	56	50 4,796	52	54	20	4,796
	Overtime	66	60 1,199	62	64	0	1,199
	Subcontracted	71	65 4,405	67 350	69 3,000	0 1,245	9,000
Sept.	Regular time	62	56	50 4,360	52	20	4,360
	Overtime	72	66	60 1,090	62	0	1,090
	Subcontracted	77	71	65 9,000	67	0	9,000
	Demand requirement	8,400	10,400	14,800	3,000	6,315	

inventory are used to absorb demand. Inventory is stored in August to cover September demand and the desired 3,000 units of final inventory for the safety stock in October. Looking at September demand of 14,800, for example, we can see that 350 units are met by subcontracting and inventory from August, 4,360 units from regular time, 1,090 units from overtime, and 9,000 units from subcontracting in September.

We could have solved the aggregate planning problem for twelve months, but this would have required a larger, 37 × 14 transportation tableau. The transportation-model approach to aggregate planning has been around since 1956, when Bowman first suggested its use in aggregate planning.[2] It isn't widely used because it does not account for costs of production-level changes.

---

[2]E.H. Bowman, "Production Planning by the Transportation Method of Linear Programming," *Journal of the Operations Research Society*, February 1956.

Linear and Goal Programming. The transportation model is a special type of linear programming model. In general linear programming, the models developed do not have to fit a special form, as transportation models do. Thus, in linear programming models it is possible to account for the costs associated with hiring, firing, and other production change costs. (Refer to the supplement to Chapter 2 for more material on linear programming.) In 1960, Hanssmann and Hess proposed a linear programming approach to production and employment scheduling.[3]

Since general linear models vary from problem to problem, the user must develop his own model for his special application; this requires insight and a certain amount of time spent creating and then solving the model. Fortunately, linear programming models are efficiently solved by the simplex method on a computer. Many computer manufacturers offer standard LP software packages to their users. The potential drawback of linear programming for aggregate planning is the linearity assumptions. In linear programming, the objective function and all constraints must be linear. If production change costs, inventory costs, or problem relationships are not approximately linear, then linear programming would not be an appropriate tool.

Linear programming models also seek to optimize a simple objective such as cost minimization. Many decision problems, including aggregate planning, strive to meet several objectives. For instance, management may want to minimize costs but also maintain a relatively stable work force and keep inventory and overtime at acceptable levels. *Goal programming* is a recent mathematical programming method that attempts to handle multiple incompatible goals. Since it may be impossible to meet all goals, the goals are ranked and highest priority goals are met first. The final solution may result in "satisficing," or only getting as close as possible to some goals. Goal programming is an effective tool for multiple-criteria decision making, but most of the work on these models has been linear in nature. Thus, linearity assumptions can be a pitfall just as in linear programming. Some research is being done on nonlinear goal programming models, but these tend to be much more difficult to solve. Further research may enable goal programming to be a highly effective tool for aggregate planning.

Linear Decision Rule. Another aggregate planning method that attempts to optimize decisions for the intermediate planning horizon is the Linear Decision Rule (LDR). It was developed by Holt, Modigliani, and Simon in 1955.[4] It is possibly the best-known analytical method for aggregate planning, and a classical approach against which others have continued to compare their results.

Unlike the implication of the name, the LDR is actually based on a nonlinear cost function. However, the decision rules for production and work-force levels resulting from the LDR analysis are linear. The LDR minimizes the combined costs of regular payroll, hiring and layoff, overtime, and inventory.

---

[3]F. Hanssmann and S.W. Hess, "A Linear Programming Approach to Production and Employment Scheduling," *Management Technology*, Vol. 1 (January 1960), 46–52.

[4]C.C. Holt, F. Modigliani, and H.A. Simon, "A Linear Decision Rule for Production and Employment Scheduling," *Management Science*, Vol. 2, No. 2 (October 1955), 1–30.

A unique feature of the LDR is that it assumes that each of these four cost functions can be approximated by a quadratic cost curve. A quadratic function is a nonlinear function of the second degree containing products of variables or variables squared. Figure 9-4 illustrates the quadratic cost assumptions and their comparisons with the assumed actual costs.

In Figure 9-4(a), it is assumed that payroll costs rise proportionately with workforce size. The hiring and layoff costs vary with changes in the work force. Assuming linear increases for hiring and linear increases for firing, the V-shaped graph in Figure 9-4(b) is obtained. The hiring and layoff cost curve can be approximated by a second-degree parabola, as shown by the dashed line. In Figure 9-4(c), the overtime costs are assumed to rise at a nonlinear rate, since overtime productivity decreases but production bottlenecks tend to increase as the production rate increases. The inventory costs depicted in Figure 9-4(d) increase with high inventory or low inventory. High inventory levels increase carrying costs, whereas low inventory levels incur shortage costs and possibly more frequent setup costs.

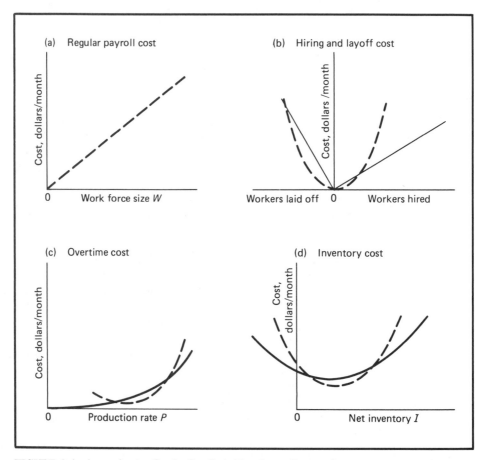

FIGURE 9-4 Approximate Quadratic Cost Functions Compared to Presumed Actual Costs

The exact nature of the approximating quadratic curves in Figure 9-6 must be determined by careful data collection and subsequent curve fit analysis to fit the data. The linear decision rules are then obtained by using calculus to differentiate the overall quadratic cost function and solving for the values that achieve the minimum cost.

Example: The authors of the LDR applied their model to data collected from a paint factory for the years 1949 to 1954. The quadratic cost function was determined from actual accounting data, along with subjective estimates of intangible costs. Their analysis yielded two equations or linear decision rules that specify work-force level and production rate for each month t. To interpret the decision rules, let us define the following decision variables:

W_t = number of employees required during month t

W_{t-1} = number of employees in work force at end of preceding month, $t - 1$

P_t = number of units that should be produced in month t

I_{t-1} = number of units in inventory less backorders at beginning of month t

F_t = forecast of number of units to be shipped in month t

F_{t+i} = forecast of number of units to be shipped in month $t + i$

The linear decision rules for the paint factory were calculated as:

$$P_t = \begin{cases} +.463F_t \\ +.234F_{t+1} \\ +.111F_{t+2} \\ +.046F_{t+3} \\ +.013F_{t+4} \\ -.002F_{t+5} \\ -.008F_{t+6} \\ -.010F_{t+7} \\ -.009F_{t+8} \\ -.008F_{t+9} \\ -.007F_{t+10} \\ -.005F_{t+11} \end{cases} + .993W_{t-1} + (153 - .464I_{t-1})$$

$$W_t = .743W_{t-1} + (2.09 - .010I_{t-1}) + \begin{cases} +.0101F_t \\ +.0088F_{t+1} \\ +.0071F_{t+2} \\ +.0054F_{t+3} \\ +.0042F_{t+4} \\ +.0031F_{t+5} \\ +.0023F_{t+6} \\ +.0016F_{t+7} \\ +.0012F_{t+8} \\ +.0009F_{t+9} \\ +.0006F_{t+10} \\ +.0005F_{t+11} \end{cases}$$

The first decision rule for number of units to be produced in time period t, P_t, incorporates a weighted average of forecasts extending 11 months into the future, the heaviest weights being on the most recent months. The value of P_t also depends on employment level in the preceding month and the preceding month's inventory. The second decision rule, for W_t, depends on the same variables.

The authors compared the performance of the LDR with that of the paint company's actual aggregate plans for the six-year period. Using a simple moving average forecast to calculate P_t and W_t, the LDR bettered the actual company performance by $173,000 per year.

Applying the LDR method to other companies would require new data collection and the derivation of new decision rules. However, to illustrate how simple it is to plug into the LDR equation, let's apply the LDR to the month of January in our previous Braden Company example. We assume that in the preceding month, 109 workers were employed.

$$P_1 = \begin{cases} +.463(9,000) \\ +.234(8,000) \\ +.111(7,000) \\ +.046(6,000) \\ +.013(5,000) \\ -.002(6,000) \\ -.008(8,000) \\ -.010(10,000) \\ -.009(14,000) \\ -.008(15,000) \\ -.007(12,000) \\ -.005(10,000) \end{cases} + .993(109) + 153 - .464(1,000)$$

$$W_1 = .743(109) + 2.09 - .010(1,000) + \begin{cases} +.0101(9,000) \\ +.0088(8,000) \\ +.0071(7,000) \\ +.0054(6,000) \\ +.0042(5,000) \\ +.0031(6,000) \\ +.0023(8,000) \\ +.0016(10,000) \\ +.0012(14,000) \\ +.0009(15,000) \\ +.0006(12,000) \\ +.0005(10,000) \end{cases}$$

Performing the calculations, we obtain:

$$P_1 = 6,398$$
$$W_1 = 432$$

Thus, the LDR recommends the production of 6,398 units in January for the Braden Company, with an increase in the work force from 109 to 432 workers. This unreasonably high addition to the work force can be explained by noting that the Braden Company is not the paint company for which these specific linear decision rules were developed. The example further illustrates the need to develop unique decision rules for each individual problem.

The LDR approach is limited, much like the linear programming approach, in that it assumes a specific type of cost function. If payroll, hiring and layoff, production, and inventory costs are not approximately quadratic in nature, then the LDR is not applicable. Second, the method requires significant data collection and curve fit analysis. Finally, the method imposes no constraints on the final values of the decision variables; this can possibly result in solutions that are negative in sign or otherwise unacceptable to management.

Heuristic Methods

The shortcomings of linear programming and the LDR are that they restrict the nature of the costs relevant to aggregate planning. These restrictions have caused aggregate planners to utilize heuristics in order to handle a wider variety of cost functions. Even though heuristics cannot guarantee an optimal solution, they allow us to drop the restrictive assumptions often required by optimization procedures. VAM, for example, is a heuristic that we used to obtain good solutions to transportation problems in the supplement to Chapter 2 and the transportation models in this chapter.

Search Decision Rule. One of the most successful and widely used heuristics is the Search Decision Rule (SDR) developed by Taubert.[5] It is a computerized approximation procedure that uses a direct-search method to find the decision variable values that minimize the total cost function. A high-speed computer is required to systematically search for points that yield a cost reduction. Thousands or even millions of points may be explored by this computerized trial-and-error process. Taubert used the Hooke-Jeeves method of direct search.[6] This type is called pattern search and requires a starting solution as a base point. From the base point, exploratory moves are made to see if improvements can be found. If a better point is found, then it becomes the new base point. From the new base point, a larger pattern move is made, followed by smaller exploratory searches. The procedure terminates when no improvements can be found within a given tolerance—say, .00001. See Figure 9-5 for an illustration of a two-dimensional pattern search.

Other types of direct-search methods can be used, but all have in common that they do not guarantee an optimal solution. They are optimal seeking procedures and often find the optimal solution, but since they employ heuristic search rules, they may

[5]W.H. Taubert, "Search Decision Rule for the Aggregate Scheduling Problem," *Management Science*, Vol. 14, No. 6 (February1968), 343–59.

[6]R. Hooke and T.A. Jeeves, "A 'Direct Search' Solution of Numerical Statistical Problems," *Journal of the Association for Computing Machinery*, April 1961.

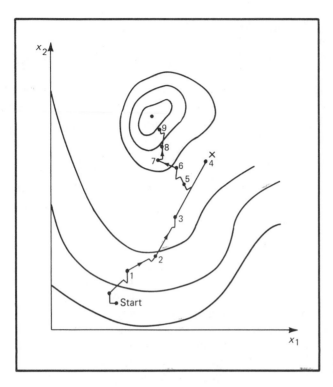

FIGURE 9-5 Exploratory Moves of Hooke-Jeeves Direct Search

not; the direct-search procedures terminate whenever no improvement can be found or a predetermined time limit is exceeded. The strength of the direct-search procedures is that they can be applied to virtually any cost function and will yield good results. This kind of flexibility is important in real-world decision making.

Other Heuristics. Heuristics usually have the property of being able to find a good solution to one class of problems but not necessarily others. The SDR is fairly robust, in that many cost functions can be used. However, other heuristics have also been found to perform well under various problem types and managerial assumptions. Three heuristics that have found some degree of acceptance are the following:

1. *Parametric production planning model.* This approach was developed by Jones,[7] and like the LDR it assumes a quadratic cost function for the same costs of work force, overtime, production rate, and inventory. Jones uses a heuristic search procedure to develop the coefficients for two decision rules for production rate and work size. Like the SDR, this approach can be applied to virtually any cost function.

2. *Management coefficients model.* This approach is unique in that it attempts to incorporate the manager's own performance and experience into a formal decision

[7]C.H. Jones, "Parametric Production Planning," *Management Science*, Vol. 13, No. 11 (July 1967), 843–66.

model. Developed by Bowman,[8] the procedure uses regression analysis of management's past behavior in similar decisions. The procedure incorporates management's bias (which is favored anyway) and attempts to minimize variance or deviations from this bias or average behavior. The regression coefficients form the basis of an equation from which future decisions can be made that will supposedly be acceptable to management.

3. *Simulation and search.* Vergin developed an approach that incorporates linear, quadratic, and step costs.[9] A heuristic is used to select various aggregate schedules, and simulation is used to evaluate the best alternative.

Comparison of Methods

We have considered several quantitative models for aggregate planning at this point, and each has its advantages and disadvantages. We would expect certain models to do well whenever their assumptions hold true. Thus, we would expect linear programming to perform well when all relationships are linear and the parameters of the model are deterministic. But how do these various methods perform under the true test of real-world experience? Some research has been done in this area. Eilon has considered five approaches to aggregate production planning; he thoroughly examines the limiting assumptions of each approach and the basic shortcomings of each method.[10]

In one interesting study, Lee and Khumawala compared the performance of four aggregate planning models on a firm in the capital-goods industry.[11] A computer simulation model was developed to simulate the aggregate operation of the firm. Past data pertaining to actual demand were used so that comparisons could be made between performance on demand forecasts (implied) and performance on known demand or perfect forecasts.

The four methods tested were the Linear Decision Rule, Search Decision Rule, management coefficients model, and the parametric production planning model. Compared with actual company decisions, all four methods resulted in increased profits. Figure 9-6 illustrates the profit increase for each method. Under perfect forecasts, all four methods performed well, with the Search Decision Rule being slightly better than the Linear Decision Rule. A more realistic comparison is obtained under imperfect forecasts, which is the usual operating state of a firm. In this case, a wider variation among the four methods occurs. The Search Decision Rule performed best, followed by parametric production planning, Linear Decision Rule, and the management coefficients model. The results of this study, together with the flexibility of the Search

---

[8]E.H. Bowman, "Consistence and Optimality in Managerial Decision Making," *Management Science*, Vol. 4 (January 1963), 100–103.

[9]R.C. Vergin, "Production Scheduling under Seasonal Demand," *Journal of Industrial Engineering*, Vol. 17, No. 5 (May 1966).

[10]Samuel Eilon, "Five Approaches to Aggregate Production Planning," *AIIE Transactions*, June 1975.

[11]W.B. Lee and B.M. Khumawala, "Simulation Testing of Aggregate Production Planning Models in an Implementation Methodology," *Management Science*, Vol. 20, No. 6 (February 1974), 903–11.

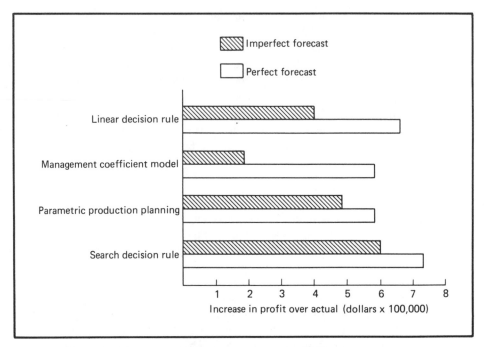

FIGURE 9-6   **Profit Comparison of Four Aggregate Planning Models**

SOURCE: W.B. Lee and B.M. Khumawala, "Simulation Testing of Aggregate Production Planning Models in an Implementation Methodology," *Management Science*, Vol. 20, No. 6 (February 1974), 903–11.

Decision Rule, suggest that it is currently the most effective quantitive approach to the aggregate planning problem.

LEARNING-CURVE EFFECTS ON PRODUCTION

Thus far we have assumed that productivity has remained constant. In many productive activities, however, the learning process results in improved efficiency as a function of output. You might expect this phenomenon more in labor-intensive industries, but wherever methods improve or work becomes more organized, you could expect productivity to increase with output. The *learning-curve phenomenon* has been recognized in machine shops and aircraft assembly plants. The Boeing Company, for example, has developed specified rates that decrease with increased output of various aircraft components. The Boeing formula states that each time the production quantity doubles, the number of unit worker-hours is reduced at a constant rate.

    A 90 percent learning curve is illustrated in Figure 9-7. Assuming that an activity required 20 hours for the first unit, the second would take 18, the fourth 16.2, and the eighth 14.58. Other learning-curve formulas exist that yield similar but slightly different curves.

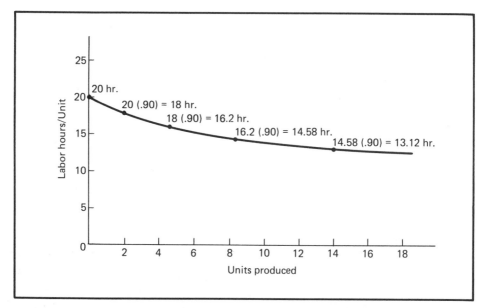

FIGURE 9-7 **Ninety Percent Learning Curve**

If the learning-curve phenomenon applies to a given product or service, then aggregate planners need to consider the learning-curve effect in production planning. Other functions of an organization, including marketing, purchasing, and scheduling, should also consider learning-curve effects; variable production costs will decrease over time, as well as per-piece average processing time. If the learning phenomenon exerts a significant effect, it should be incorporated into aggregate plans.

Traditional approaches to aggregate planning have assumed a constant work-force productivity factor. However, several factors can cause changes in work output capabilities over time. Ebert cites examples involving (1) changes in work methods, (2) product engineering modifications, (3) facilities relocation, (4) facilities layout, (5) equipment redesign, and (6) changes in employee skills or training.[12] Some of the resulting work output effects can be explained in terms of learning-curve phenomena.

Recently, Ebert has proposed a method for aggregate planning with learning-curve effects. His model uses the Holt et al. basic cost structure and various manufacturing progress function parameters.[13] A Hooke-Jeeves direct-search computer program is used to obtain approximate solutions that indicate work force and production rate for each time period. The method is capable of incorporating into the scheduling aspects of aggregate planning such established learning-curve applications as (1) cash-flow planning, (2) product pricing, and (3) manpower planning. Cash

---

[12]R.J. Ebert, "Aggregate Planning with Learning Curve Productivity," *Management Science*, Vol. 23, No. 2 (October 1976), 171–82.

[13]Holt, Modigliani, and Simon, "A Linear Decision Rule."

Table 9-6 Cost Estimates for Product Pricing

COST CATEGORY	LEARNING CURVE						CONSTANT PRODUCTIVITY
	70%	75%	80%	85%	90%	95%	100%
Scheduling Costs:							
overtime	$ 17,790.9	18,824.9	12,221.8	25,458.1	16,516.5	19,117.7	21,433.2
hiring	6,326.9	7,409.7	7,410.3	12,052.1	17,569.3	26,595.1	37,178.4
layoff	25,074.7	32,341.7	40,248.0	51,702.2	67,799.6	79,990.6	103,977.7
inventory carrying	3,532.5	4,960.0	6,570.0	8,787.5	12,087.5	14,030.0	17,085.0
inventory shortage	806.5	830.5	3,985.9	953.1	7,692.6	4,983.6	5,577.4
TOTAL	$ 53,531.5	64,366.2	72,436.0	98,952.0	121,565.5	144,717.6	185,251.7
Cost/unit	$ 2.723	3.274	3.684	5.033	6.183	7.361	9.422
Nonscheduling Costs:							
development	$ 250,000.	250,000.	250,000.	250,000.	250,000.	250,000.	250,000.
direct materials	1,572,880.	1,572,880.	1,572,880.	1,572,880.	1,572,880.	1,572,880.	1,572,880.
variable materials overhead	314,576.	314,576.	314,576.	314,576.	314,576.	314,576.	314,576.
administrative	430,000.	430,000.	430,000.	430,000.	430,000.	430,000.	430,000.
direct labor	369,322.	521,721.	741,890.	1,039,531.	1,458,758.	2,018,561.	2,765,225.
variable labor overhead	181,583.	256,512.	364,762.	511,102.	717,224.	992,462.	1,359,566.
TOTAL	$3,118,361.	3,345,689.	3,673,108.	4,118,089.	4,743,438.	5,578,479.	6,692,247.
TOTAL COST	$3,171,893.	3,410,055.	3,746,544.	4,217,041.	4,865,003.	5,723,197.	6,877,498.7
Selling Price (per unit)	$ 179.254	192.713	211.730	238.319	274.938	323.437	349.802

SOURCE: R.J. Ebert, "Aggregate Planning with Learning Curve Productivity," *Management Science*, Vol. 23, No. 2 (October 1976), 171–82.

flows associated with production scheduling can be combined with other cash flows to estimate total cash flow over the life of the product. Future manpower needs can be estimated with respect to various learning-curve rates by examining the output of the computer program. Pricing strategies are aided by a breakdown of the costs into scheduling and nonscheduling costs. For example, Ebert presents product pricing output for a hypothetical company, Dynapro Corp., in Table 9-6. From the total cost figures in the table, we can see that lower-percentage learning curves can really lower total costs by decreasing scheduling costs through greater production efficiency. It is also worthwhile to note that small-percentage changes in the learning-curve rate can have significant effect on total costs and selling price. This indicates the importance of estimating learning-curve parameters accurately.

Ebert's methodology is important in that it allows the aggregate planner to use a systematic procedure for incorporating learning-curve phenomena. Equally important is the inclusion of decision factors from the financial and marketing functions of the firm. This wider approach to the aggregate planning function represents a significant step toward a true systems approach to intermediate-range planning.

SUMMARY

Aggregate planning is concerned with the development of plans and strategies for utilizing capacity and absorbing demand fluctuations. It is intermediate-range planning, usually the longest-range plans that are dealt with by the operations manager; long-range or strategic plans are the concerns of top management.

The aggregate plans are key to a smooth production and operating system. They must be feasible in terms of men and machine capacities and they must include estimated work shifts, vacations, inventories, and subcontracts. The general information of the aggregate plans are input to a more detailed master production schedule. The master schedule breaks the aggregate plan into greater details and is the basis for *disaggregation*, scheduling, and computerized MRP (materials requirements planning) systems. The master schedule is updated by actual demand and production figures throughout the year and serves as a means for adjusting general aggregate plans. The successful implementation of aggregate plans requires an information feedback loop between the planning stages and the plant first-line scheduling and operational stages.

Aggregate planning for service and nonmanufacturing organizations can utilize many of the procedures presented in the chapter. The utilization of capacity and planning for personnel are the primary objectives. The main difference between service-oriented and manufacturing organizations is that service industries cannot use inventory as a strategy for demand absorption. The useful strategies include the variation of work force, hours worked, overtime, and capacity utilization.

In actual practice, the trial-and-error graphical methods and the counter-seasonal-products methods seem to be the most widely used in service and manufacturing organizations. In addition to the active and passive strategies mentioned in this chapter, some firms may engage in bargaining with suppliers and customers or coalition with other organizations. For example, electric power companies sometimes borrow power from each other during periods of peak demand.

Mathematical and computer techniques are used to a limited extent for aggregate planning. Not only do these methods have their limitations, but management is sometimes skeptical or uneducated in using them. In spite of their shortcomings, the quantitative methods can be useful planning tools; when used properly, they have outperformed "seat-of-the-pants" planning methods in real applications. The most promising approach appears to be the Search Decision Rule coupled with computer simulation to evaluate various aggregate plans.

Aggregate planning is an important part of operations management, and research continues to explore new and better ways of developing effective aggregate plans. Recently, the learning-curve phenomenon has been incorporated in an aggregate planning model. Future research should yield new methods for making more realistic aggregate plans. However, effective aggregate planning can be achieved now by making use of forecasting techniques and the tools that are currently available.

SOLVED PROBLEMS

Problem Statement

The Hafler Co. utilizes the counterseasonal-product strategy to smooth production resource requirements. It manufactures its spring product line during the first four months of the year and would like to employ a strategy that minimizes production costs while meeting demand during these four months. Hafler currently employs 30 men at an average wage of $1,000 per month. Each unit requires eight man-hours to produce, or one full day per worker. Hiring costs are estimated at $400, and layoff costs are $500 per person. Inventory carrying costs are $5/unit/month, and shortage costs are $100/unit/month. Given the forecasted demand figures below, determine the more effective of the proposed pure strategies:

Plan A: Vary work-force levels to meet demand.
Plan B: Maintain 30 employees and use inventory plus stockouts to absorb demand fluctuations.

MONTH	DEMAND	WORKING DAYS
Jan.	500	22
Feb.	600	19
Mar.	800	21
Apr.	400	21

Solution

Assuming that no inventory is available at the beginning of the year, and that safety stock (if used at all) is built into the monthly demand figures, we can compare the overall costs of both strategies.

Plan A

	JAN.	FEB.	MAR.	APR.	TOTAL
1. Men required	$\frac{500}{22} = 23$	$\frac{600}{19} = 32$	$\frac{300}{21} = 38$	$\frac{400}{21} = 19$	
2. Labor	$23,000	$32,000	$38,000	$19,000	$112,000
3. Hiring		9(400) = 3,600	6(400) = 2,400		6,000
4. Layoff	7(500) = 3,500			19(500) = 9,500	13,000
					$131,000

Plan B

	JAN.	FEB.	MAR.	APR.	TOTAL
1. Men used	30	30	30	30	
2. Labor	$30,000	$30,000	$30,000	$30,000	$120,000
3. Units produced	660	570	630	630	
4. Inventory	5(160)	5(130)		5(190)	2,400
5. Shortage			100(40)		4,000
					$126,400

Plan B, using inventory and shortages, appears to be the best plan economically, with a total cost of $126,400 versus $131,000 for Plan A. Additionally, Plan B would result in higher worker morale, smoother production, and a higher-quality product.

Problem Statement

Suppose that the Hafler Co. of the problem above has decided to maintain a steady work force of 30 men per month. However, the company wants to analyze the cost of a mixed strategy employing overtime and inventory as means to absorb demand. Inventory costs remain at $5/unit/month, and per-unit labor costs are $50 on regular time and $75 on overtime.

Solution

Given that work-force levels will remain constant, we can use the transportation model of linear programming to solve this problem. Setting up regular time and overtime options for each month and assuming backordering is not allowed, we obtain the following 8 × 5 transportation tableau:

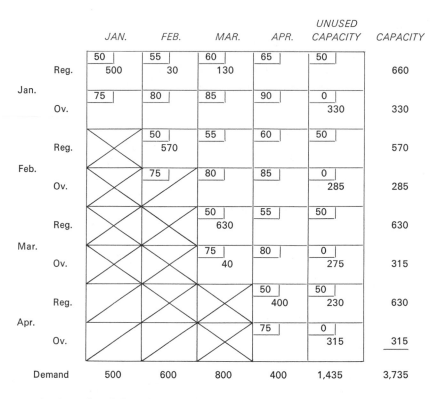

The costs in the cells of the tableau reflect only direct labor costs. This enables us to compare the transportation mixed strategy with the pure inventory strategy. A solution derived by inspection is presented in the tableau. Notice that certain cells are inadmissible, since backordering is not allowed. The final solution differs from Plan B only in that the firm satisfies the peak demand of March through overtime rather than choosing to only partially fulfill demand as in Plan B.

Problem Statement

Cornwell Design Corporation has recently received a contract to manufacture chair frames for a large furniture company. The production process is labor-intensive and a 95 percent learning curve applies. If it takes eight hours for a craftsman to make the first chair, how long will it take him to produce the 128th unit?

Solution

The 128th unit represents the seventh doubling of the original output of one unit. Thus, the total time for the 128th unit will be:

$$8 \text{ hours} \times (.95)^7 = 8 \times .6983 = 5.58 \text{ hours}$$

REVIEW QUESTIONS

1. What is the approximate length of the planning horizon for aggregate planning?
2. What is the objective of aggregate planning, and what are the active and passive strategies for implementing aggregate plans?
3. What are some constraints that the aggregate planner must consider?
4. Which methods are primarily used today by managers to absorb demand fluctuations?
5. Comment on the main shortcoming of the graphical method for aggregate planning.
6. Give some explanations of why mathematical or quantitative models aren't used more in actual aggregate planning.
7. Contrast aggregate planning alternatives for an aircraft manufacturing plant with those of a public accounting firm.
8. How can the following organizations employ active strategies—retail department store, savings and loan, electric power company?
9. What is the main difference between linear programming for aggregate planning and the Linear Decision Rule?
10. Why is the Search Decision Rule probably the best current approach to aggregate planning?
11. Explain how the estimated needs for aggregate capacity get refined through the production planning process.
12. Would you prefer to own a manufacturing company whose production rate was constant, or one that showed an 80% learning-curve rate? Why?
13. Explain the relationship between aggregate planning and master schduling.
14. What is management concerned with in the disaggregation problem?
15. In what sense does Ebert's learning-curve approach to aggregate planning represent a systems approach?

PROBLEMS

1. The forecasted demand for the last six months of the year is shown below. Develop a production requirement graph (like Figure 9-3) in which the implied production rate per day is plotted versus the working days each month.

MONTH	EXPECTED DEMAND	DESIRED SAFETY STOCK	WORKING DAYS
July	5,000	1,000	21
August	6,000	1,200	13
September	10,000	2,000	20
October	8,000	1,600	23
November	8,000	1,600	21
December	6,000	1,200	20

2. Using the 6-month data in problem 1, evaluate two pure strategies involving variation of work force and subcontracting. To hire and train a worker costs $220, and layoff costs are $240 per worker. Each worker can produce four units per working day, and subcontracting costs are $20 above manufacturing cost. Assume a beginning inventory of 800 units.

3. Can you improve upon the Plan 2 pure strategy of subcontracting for the data in Table 9-1? (Costs are given in Table 9-3.) You may use any strategy, pure or mixed.

4. Nickelson Tool and Die Co. has undertaken a new contract. Production of the first unit has required 40 hours. Assuming a 90% production learning curve, how long will it take to produce the second unit? the eighth unit?

5. American Products Corporation experiences a cyclical demand pattern, which they forecast as $y = 500 + 1,000x + (-1)^x 600$, where y = units of demand and x = quarter of the year.
   a. What is the forecasted demand for each of the four quarters of this year?
   b. What must be the level quarterly production rate to meet demand over the year?
   c. What types of demand absorption strategies would the level production plan entail?

6. Consider the following aggregate planning problem for one quarter:

	REGULAR TIME	OVERTIME	SUBCON-TRACTING
Production capacity/month	9,000 units	2,250 units	4,000 units
Production cost/unit	$8	$10	$13

   Assume no initial inventory and a forecasted demand of 12,000, 16,000, and 17,000 in the three months of the quarter. Carrying cost is $1.50/unit/mo., back-order cost is $2/unit/mo., and unused regular time costs $5 per unit. Set up the problem in a transportation tableau.

7. Solve problem 6 using Vogel's Approximation Method, which is a heuristic described in the supplement to Chapter 2.

8. Develop a general linear programming model for the aggregate planning problem in problem 6. Take into consideration work-force-level changes by letting the cost

of increasing output from one month to the next be $40 per unit, and the decrease cost be $50 per unit.

9. Suppose the following data apply to the paint company mentioned in the chapter. The beginning work force $w_{t-1} = 200$, beginning inventory is 500 gallons of paint, and the company has the following forecast for the year:

MONTH	GALLONS	MONTH	GALLONS
January	300	July	850
February	300	August	900
March	500	September	600
April	500	October	550
May	650	November	300
June	800	December	200

Calculate work and production levels for January and February, using the Holt et al. Linear Decision Rules.

10. Rockwood International has contracted with the federal government to build solar energy panels for orbital space stations. Work on the first panel took 120 worker hours, and estimates are that an 88% learning curve applies to this type of work. Assuming that Rockwood wants to build one panel per 8-hour workday, how many workers should they schedule for the 64th unit?

11. Refer to the Hafler Co. in the first Solved Problem, and evaluate the strategy of employing the minimum number of 19 men and absorbing demand with overtime (cost = $75 per unit) and inventory (cost = $5 per unit).

12. Refer to the Hafler Co. in the second Solved Problem. Consider the additional strategy of subcontracting for a unit cost of $70. Set up a transportation tableau for this problem and find the new solution.

13. A city administrator is trying to plan personnel requirements for city firemen in the upcoming year. Past years' demand and growth trends suggest the following needs:

January	27,000 man-hours	July	30,000 man-hours
February	22,000	August	32,000
March	23,000	September	28,000
April	24,000	October	21,000
May	25,000	November	19,000
June	29,000	December	26,000

Current work-force levels can provide 25,000 man-hours per month on a regular-time basis. Regular-time costs are $6.00 per hour, and overtime is $9.00 per hour; overtime can furnish only 10%, or 2,500 additional man-hours per month. Part-time firemen can be used, but they are usually not as well qualified and cost $7.00 per hour regular time and $10.50 on overtime. Training costs for firemen are

$500 per man, and laying-off costs are $300 per full-time employee. (No cost for laying off part-time firemen.)

 a. What should the monthly personnel levels be for the city firemen? What is the yearly cost?
 b. What pure or mixed strategies did you use?
 c. If you had access to a computer, what method might you prefer to use in solving this problem?

Case: YORK CONTAINER COMPANY*

The York Container Company was one of the large manufacturers in the container industry. The industry included large, medium, and small companies. Large companies had decentralized their production facilities throughout the country. They engaged in active competition with each other by emphasizing customer service. Smaller manufacturers competed by offering price reductions ranging from 2 to 6 percent, coupled with less service.

John Flint, production planning manager of the Midwest plant of York Container Company, faced a problem involving employment policy, inventory control, and production planning. Early in December, the home office in New York City had dictated a new policy directing all branch plants to stabilize employment of production-line workers to the extent that such a policy was possible without incurring unreasonable cost. During the past year, employment of production-line workers had fluctuated with seasonal requirements from a high of 150 to a low of 30.

The Midwest factory was one of the company's oldest plants and, although unionized, it enjoyed favorable relations with its employees. For years, this plant had followed a policy of hiring and laying off employees as required by market demands. It drew largely upon transient workers and college students to fill manpower needs during the busy summer and fall months. When college students left at the end of summer to go back to school, the factory had to hire

*From Cases in Manufacturing Management by Schrieber et al., © 1965 by McGraw Hill, Inc., used with permission of McGraw Hill Book Company.

 This adaptation will appear in *Case Book in Production and Operations Management* by Johnson et al. to be published by Prentice-Hall, Inc.

 Adopted from: Meyer, Johnson, Newell, and Schrieber, *Case Book in Production and Operations Management* (Prentice-Hall, 1980)

and train a new group of employees for one or two months' work. Joe Asplund, the personnel director, estimated that it cost $425 to hire and train a new employee, and $175 to terminate one. In contrast to the changes in employment levels of production-line workers, the supervisory, maintenance, lithographing and enameling, and tinplate department employees were hired on a permanent basis, and therefore, the number of people in these categories did not fluctuate with changes in seasonal demand.

The Midwest plant had twelve standard can lines and two frozen-food container lines. Cans manufactured were of several types and sizes. Most cans were classified as open-top cans; that is, the top was not sealed on the can until after the can had been filled. Some cans (such as beer cans) were manufactured differently from the typical fruit or vegetable can; they were sprayed with a protective coating on the inside. Frozen-food containers came in a variety of materials and shapes. For example, the carton for frozen strawberries was made of paper with metal ends. The can lines produced cans at rates varying from 100 to 450 per minute, depending upon the size and complexity of the can. As a general rule, the larger the can, the slower the rate of production. The two frozen-food container lines produced at an average rate of 180 per minute. Standard can lines could be used to produce only beer cans and open-top cans, and frozen-food container lines could be used to produce only frozen-food containers. A list of can sizes produced at this plant, together with production rates, appears in Table 9-7.

A line changeover typically withdrew the line from production for two days and resulted in a cost of $1,100. This cost included wages of two maintenance men who made the mechanical changeover, material scrap, and a charge for lost production capacity. Line operators and supervisors could be reassigned to other jobs during such changeovers. A line that had been idle, however, could be restarted again without any additional setup costs, provided it was used to produce the same-sized can. Machine lines scheduled to be in operating condition on January 1 included two beer lines, two frozen-food lines, and three open-top can lines producing for can numbers 4, 5, and 9.

In past years, the factory had operated two shifts during the peak season, running about ten can lines on the first shift and six on the second shift. In addition, two frozen-food container lines were operated on each shift. The average first-shift hourly pay rate for line operators and supervisors was $6.10 and $9.40, respectively. A 15 percent premium was paid to both line operators and supervisors for second-shift operations. A 50 percent overtime premium was paid for all overtime work not exceeding 20 hours per week per crew (maximum of four hours per day).

Storage space in the factory for finished cans amounted to 50,000 square

Table 9-7   Cans Manufactured at Midwest Plant of York Container

| | | PRODUCTION RATE | | |
CAN NUMBER[a]	APPROX. SIZE (DIAM. × HEIGHT IN INCHES)	CANS/ LINE-SHIFT[b]	CAR-LOADS/ LINE-MONTH[c]	MANUFAC-TURING COST, $/CARLOAD
1	2 3/4 × 4 3/4 (beer)	216,000	30	$5,200
2	3 1/4 × 4 1/4	168,000	30	4,800
3	4 × 4 3/4	156,000	45	4,300
4	3 × 4 3/4	168,000	25	4,500
5	3 1/2 × 2	168,000	15	7,000
6	3 × 4 1/2	168,000	25	4,800
7	6 1/4 × 7	48,000	50	3,500
8	4 × 5 1/2	139,000	50	4,100
9	Miscellaneous	144,000[d]	25	4,600
10	Frozen-food container	86,000	10	5,500

[a]Can number was a local plant code used for convenient identification. It was not related to the standard can-size number used in the industry. Can numbers 9 and 10 were used to designate groups of special-dimension cans or containers, most of which were infrequently produced and each of which required its own dimension identification.

[b]Line-shift is based on average output per line during eight hours of normal operation.

[c]Line-month is based on a single shift operating 21 days per month.

[d]Average production rate.

feet, and when stacked to a height of ten feet (the maximum), 500,000 cubic feet. The empty cans were stored in cardboard cartons that could be used to package the filled cans. A freight car contained approximately 3,200 cubic feet of shipping space.

There was no immediate alternative use for inside storage space; hence depreciation, building taxes, and the like were considered a fixed cost, and no specific charge was levied for the use of this space. A monthly charge, however, equal to 2 percent of the average monthly inventory value, was applied to cover variable costs for capital investment in the inventory, deterioration of inventory, other handling and maintenance costs, and so on, associated with the use of both inside and outside storage space.

Adequate warehouse space was available nearby at a monthly rate of 12 cents per square foot (ten feet high). The rent was determined by the maximum number of square feet used in any single month. To load, transport, and unload a freight car lot of cans from the factory to an outside warehouse cost $300 per car. Shipments were made directly to the customers from the outside warehouses.

Deliveries fluctuated from 30 to more than 300 cars per month. Table 9-8 shows the sales forecast that Flint intended to use in planning production for the next year. Flint expected to have 83 line operators and 7 supervisors on the payroll as of December 31. Finished-goods inventories as of the same date were estimated to consist of 72 carloads of can number 1, 20 carloads of can number 4, and 12 carloads of can number 5.

Table 9-8 Anticipated Inventory and Sales Forecast

| | | CAN NUMBER | | | | | | | | | | |
		1	2	3	4	5	6	7	8	9	10	TOTAL
INVENTORY ON HAND (DEC. 31)		72			20	12						104 CARLOADS
Sales:	Jan.	6			15	9						30 carloads
	Feb.	12			25	12			5			54
	Mar.	21			55	39				30		145
	Apr.	39			55	57				30	5	186
	May	36	24		50	42	40			25		217
	June	102	90				40		5	20	5	262
	July	150	81	18			20		20		28	317
	Aug.	111	81	81			20	10			43	346
	Sept.	90	42	81				40	25		21	299
	Oct.	81	21	81				10	25		33	251
	Nov.	15		54	15						17	101
	Dec.	27		36	15						41	119
	Total	690	339	351	230	159	120	60	75	110	193	2,327 carloads

Sales forecasts were typically optimistic, but not sufficiently so to justify either specific or general reductions by the production planning group. Production plans were made so that the amount forecast for any given month was planned for production in the same month. Sufficient flexibility existed in delivery dates and production capacity that more specific planning could be delayed until the month prior to actual production. Hence, if the sales forecast called for 15 carloads of can number 4, it was sufficient to plan for the production of 15 carloads of can number 4 anytime during the month of January.

Each type of can line required a specific number of workers. Beer cans, open-top cans, and frozen-food containers required thirteen, eleven, and twelve operators, respectively, plus a supervisor for each line. Detailed manpower requirements for each of these lines are shown in Table 9-9.

Table 9-9   Workers Required to Operate Lines

JOB TITLE	BEER CAN	OPEN-TOP CAN	FROZEN-FOOD CONTAINER
Slitter operator	1	1	1
Tin and body blank feeder	1	1	1
Spray operator and line tender	1	1	2
Bottom end feeder	1	1	1
Inspector	3	1	2
Packer and sealer	1	4	2
Folder and stitcher	2	0	1
Checker	1	1	1
Car loader	2	1	1
Total	13	11	12

Case Discussion Questions

1. What kinds of gains may accrue from stabilizing employment?
2. Outline the approach you would take in solving York's labor stabilization problem.
3. Develop a production plan for the operation of the plant during the coming year. (Assume that inventory levels predicted by Flint for December 31 were normal for the end of the year and that there are 21 working days per month.)
4. What are some of the advantages and disadvantages of your solution?

REFERENCES

BOWMAN, E.H., "Consistence and Optimality in Managerial Decision Making," *Management Science*, Vol. 4 (January 1963), 100–103.

———, "Production Planning by the Transportation Method of Linear Programming," *Journal of the Operations Research Society*, February 1956.

EBERT, R.J., "Aggregate Planning with Learning Curve Productivity," *Management Science*, Vol. 23, No. 2 (October 1976), 171–82.

EILON, SAMUEL, "Five Approaches to Aggregate Production Planning," *AIIE Transactions*, June 1975.

HANSSMANN, F., and S.W. HESS, "A Linear Programming Approach to Production and Employment Scheduling," *Management Technology*, Vol. 1 (January 1960), 46–52.

HOLT, C.C., F. MODIGLIANI, and H.A. SIMON, "A Linear Decision Rule for Production and Employment Scheduling," *Management Science*, Vol. 2, No. 2 (October 1955), 1–30.

HOOKE, R., and T.A. JEEVES, "A 'Direct Search' Solution of Numerical Statistical Problems," *Journal of the Association for Computing Machinery*, April 1961.

JONES, C.H., "Parametric Production Planning," *Management Science*, Vol. 13, No. 11 (July 1967), 843–66.

LEE, W.B., and B.M. KHUMAWALA, "Simulation Testing of Aggregate Production Planning Models in an Implementation Methodology," *Management Science*, Vol. 20, No. 6 (February 1974), 903–11.

ORLICKY, JOSEPH, *Materials Requirements Planning*. New York: McGraw-Hill, 1975.

TAUBERT, W.H., "Search Decision Rule for the Aggregate Scheduling Problem," *Management Science*, Vol. 14, No. 6 (February 1968), 343–59.

VERGIN, R.C., "Production Scheduling under Seasonal Demand," *Journal of Industrial Engineering*, Vol. 17, No. 5 (May 1966).

WIGHT, OLIVER W., *Production and Inventory Management in the Computer Age*. Boston: Cahners Books, 1974.

part FIVE

systems scheduling and control

INVENTORY
CONTROL
SYSTEMS

chapter 10

INTRODUCTION

An *inventory* is a stock of goods that is held for the purpose of future production or sales. Raw materials, work in progress, and finished goods can all be classified as inventory items, and the decisions about them as inventory are similar. Obviously, such decisions often have a critical effect on the health of an organization.

Organizations carry inventories for a number of the following reasons:

1. *Smooth production.* Often, the demand for an item fluctuates widely, owing to a number of factors, such as seasonality and production schedules. For example, 50 percent of all the toys manufactured in one year may be sold in the three weeks before Christmas. If toy manufacturers were to try to produce 50 percent of a year's output in three weeks, they would need a tremendous influx of labor as well as huge manufacturing facilities. Instead, firms find it more economical to produce goods over a longer, slower schedule and store them as inventory. Thus, they keep the labor force fairly stable, and expenditures for capital equipment are lower.

2. *Product availability.* Most retail goods and many industrial goods are carried in inventory to ensure prompt delivery to customers. Not only does a good inventory provide a competitive edge, it often means the difference between success and failure. If a firm gains a reputation for constantly being out of stock, it may lose a significant number of customers.

3. *Advantages of producing or buying in large quantities.* Most production runs involve machine setup time as well as production time. If setup time is significant, real savings can be achieved by producing in large lots. In addition, most firms offer quantity discounts for buying in large quantities.

4. *Hedge against long or uncertain lead times.* The time between ordering and receiving goods is known as *lead time.* Firms don't want to stop manufacturing or selling goods during lead time, so it is necessary to carry inventory.

If an organization does not effectively control its inventory, the cost of carrying inventory or the cost of being out of stock can have an extremely adverse effect on the financial health of the organization. The costs associated with inventory are traditionally classified into three basic categories: ordering costs, carrying costs, and shortage costs.

Ordering costs are the costs involved in ordering and receiving inventory. These costs typically consist largely of salaries in the purchasing and accounting departments and wages in the receiving area; they also include purchase and transportation charges. If a firm produces its own inventory instead of purchasing from an outside source, production setup costs are analogous to ordering costs. Ordering costs are usually expressed by a dollar amount per order.

Carrying costs, also referred to as *holding costs*, are the costs that holding inventory entails. Components of carrying costs are both direct and indirect, and they include:

1. Interest on the money invested in inventory
2. Storage or warehousing costs, including rent, electricity, wages, insurance, security, data processing, and so on
3. Obsolescence (If the good is held too long in inventory, its value may decrease substantially.)

Carrying costs are typically calculated as a percentage of inventory value or a dollar value per unit of inventory.

The third category of inventory costs is *shortage* or *stockout costs*. If demand for an off-the-shelf good exists and a firm does not have the good in inventory, there is an inevitable loss of customer goodwill as well as loss of the profit from the sale. The dollar value of this loss of goodwill is, at best, difficult to measure. If you had to assess it, relevant questions would include: Will the firm lose the sale? Will the firm lose the customer? What are the probabilities of these losses? What is the dollar value of that particular customer?

If the inventory is being carried for internal use (that is, production), a stockout can have very serious effects. It can shut down an assembly line, and to shut down a typical automobile assembly line, for example, can cost as much as $20,000 per minute.

Gene Woolsey, writing for *Interfaces*, emphasizes the importance of controlling inventories:

> The second stop on the required tour is the production line of machinists making part X. We proceed as follows. First look for a 5 by 5 by 3 foot bin of gears or parts that looks like it has been there awhile. Pick up a gear and ask, casually, "How much is this worth?" You then ask, "How many of these are in the bin?" followed by, "How long has this bin been here?" and, "What's your cost of money for this company?" I recall one case in a nameless South American country where the unit cost times the number of parts times the time it had been there times the interest rate resulted in a cost per day figure that would insure a comfortable retirement for the plant manager on the bank of the Rio de la Plata at one of the better resorts to be found there. The plant manager suddenly realized that what he was holding was not just a chunk of high-test steel, but was *real money*. He then pointed out that *he* now understood the value of the inventory but could I suggest a way to drive the point home to upper management? I suggested that he go to the accounting department and borrow enough money to be equal to the bin's value for as long as it had been sitting there, and pile it on the top of the bin. I further suggested that he do that for every bin on the production line. We rapidly figured out that by the time we had the money piled up on the bin, you would not even be able to *see* the bin. My opinion was that if the upper managers were given a tour of the line with the money piled up, they would *never forget it*.[1]

---

[1]Gene Woolsey, "On Doing Good Things and Dumb Things in Production and Inventory Control," *Interfaces*, Vol. 5, No. 5 (May 1975), 66–67.

There are two basic functions that must be performed in order to effectively control an organization's inventory. First, management must have a system for accounting or keeping track of inventory. This system can be either a periodic series of physical numerations or a continuous inventory system in which quantities in inventory are calculated each time units are added to or drawn from inventory. A continuous inventory accounting system can be either manual or computer-based. The second function that must be performed for effective inventory control is the decision-making function. Decisions must be made regarding how much to order and when to order. In order for him to make intelligent inventory decisions, accurate information about demand and the inventory status for each item must be available to the decision maker.

Demand for inventory items can be classified as dependent or independent. *Dependent demand* is demand for those items in inventory that is determined ultimately by the demand for an end item or final product for which the inventory items are components. An example would be the demand for engine pistons; if the demand for each type of automobile is forecasted, then the demand for engine pistons can be calculated directly based on the number of pistons required for each automobile. The demand for automobiles is an example of *independent demand*. Although dependent-demand items are very common to the manufacturing sector of the economy, the service sector is concerned almost exclusively with independent-demand items. Because the problems associated with each type of demand are essentially different, we treat the problems of independent demand in this chapter and those of dependent demand in the next chapter, on materials requirements planning.

Fortunately, a large number of optimization models have been developed for independent-demand inventories, to aid the decision maker in making good inventory decisions. Therefore, the organization that effectively and efficiently controls inventory has an effective inventory information system and makes use of appropriate mathematical models in making inventory decisions.

Obviously, using a computer-based inventory information system and sophisticated operations research techniques to control the paper-clip inventory might be absurd. For this reason, many organizations choose to classify inventory items into three basic categories, usually according to annual dollar volume. The logic of this classification scheme (ABC classification) is to spend money and time controlling only important inventory items, in the realization that the cost of closely controlling relatively unimportant inventory items cannot be justified. To give you a feel for how this classification is effected, let us assume that a firm has only twelve individual inventory items. These items and their annual dollar volume are shown in Table 10-1.

The ABC classification typically seeks to put approximately 15 percent of the items in category A, 35 percent in category B, and 50 percent in category C. There is nothing sacred about these percentages, but these are the ones often used. Since in our example we have twelve items, two would make up 16.6 percent and four would be 35.3 percent. Therefore, you might put items 22213 and 22157 in category A, and 22545, 22452, 22511, and 22457 in category B, with the remaining items in category C. Table 10-2 shows that if we closely controlled only two items, we would be controlling 75.5 percent of the annual inventory dollar volume.

Table 10-1   Annual Dollar-Volume Usage

ITEM NO.	ANNUAL DEMAND	PER-UNIT COST	TOTAL ANNUAL DOLLAR VALUE
22213	100	10,000	1,000,000
22157	2,000	500	1,000,000
22545	200	1,500	300,000
22432	400	500	200,000
22511	150	700	105,000
22457	240	100	24,000
22111	300	50	15,000
22331	10	100	1,000
22471	10	100	1,000
22512	25	25	625
25531	30	20	600
22122	50	10	500
			2,647,725

Table 10-2   ABC Analysis

CATEGORY	TOTAL ANNUAL DOLLAR VOLUME	PERCENT OF TOTAL
A	2,000,000	75.5
B	629,000	23.8
C	18,725	.7
	2,647,725	100.0

It is possible, of course, that an item that is placed in category C because of its low annual dollar volume may be of a critical nature and therefore deserves greater control. A simple solution is to arbitrarily place that item in category A.

INVENTORY ACCOUNTING SYSTEMS

Inventory accounting systems can be classified as physical or continuous. A *physical inventory system* is a system in which management periodically reviews inventory levels of the various items in order to make inventory decisions. A common example of this type of system might be in the small grocery store. Each day, various delivery men stop at the store to replenish inventory. For example, the milkman may come daily, take a physical inventory, and decide what he needs to leave in the dairy case. Each week it may be necessary to order canned goods and other relatively nonperishable items. In order to do this, the manager must look at each item and make a decision on whether to order the item and how much to order.

Continuous inventory systems are typically more sophisticated than periodic ordering systems. They keep track of the inventory level of each item on a continuous basis. In other words, as items are added to or drawn from inventory, these events are recorded and the new inventory level is computed.

Continuous inventory accounting systems can range from the extremely simple manual system to very sophisticated computer-based systems. An example of a manual but continuous inventory system might be the local blood bank. For each type of blood, there might be a card on which is recorded the number of units in inventory. As units are demanded or added to inventory, a clerk merely makes the appropriate notation on the card. Hence, there is a permanent record of the inventory status of each blood type at all times.

Computerized inventory accounting systems can be classified as batch-processing systems or real-time systems. A *batch-processing inventory system* is a system in which inventory transactions (additons to and withdrawals from inventory) are collected periodically, batched together, and processed to update the current inventory master file. In the simplified example, graphically represented in Figure 10-1, an inventory control clerk creates a transaction document each time an item is drawn from inventory and each time an order is received. Periodically, these documents are "batched" together and sent to data processing, where the information is transcribed into machine-readable form. These data are then processed against the current inven-

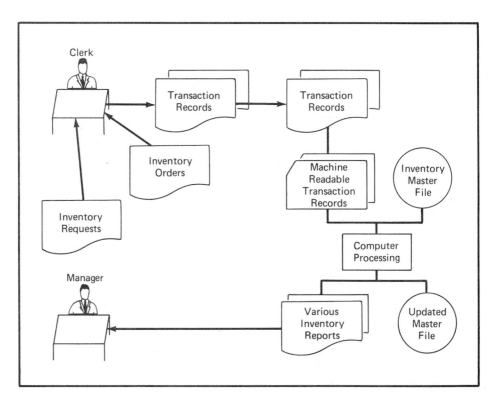

FIGURE 10-1   Simplified Example of Batch Inventory Accounting System

tory master file to create an updated master file. Output from this processing could include a list of items that need to be ordered, a list of the status of all inventory items, purchase orders, a value-of-inventory report, suggested order quantities, and so on. Therefore, in a batch-processing environment, the inventory master file is only as current as the data of the last update.

Real-time systems keep the inventory master file continuously up to date. When a unit is drawn out of or added to inventory, that event is recorded immediately and the master file reflects the change immediately. Figure 10-2 graphically depicts this process. Typically, real-time systems are significantly more costly than batch systems, but as the cost of computing continues to decrease, the number of real-time inventory systems will inevitably increase.

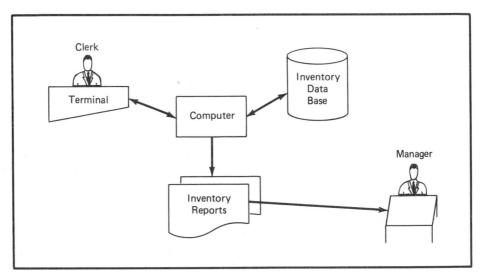

FIGURE 10-2 **Simplified Real-Time Inventory Accounting System**

Regardless of the mode of processing, a computer-based inventory system can vary according to the amount of inventory decision making that is delegated to the system. Some systems provide only information and all ordering decisions are made by people, whereas with some systems, the computer calculates reorder points and order quantities, and even writes the purchase order or shop order. These are two extremes, and many systems fall somewhere in between. Jack Bishop, Jr., reports a system he designed that calculated order quantities based on the information system and the appropriate inventory models.[2] He emphasizes, however, that the key to the success of the system was that order quantities were not dictated by the computer-based system but rather were just suggestions to operating personnel. His experience was that a system characterized by this kind of man–computer partnership has a far

---

[2]Jack L. Bishop, Jr., "Experience with a Successful System for Forecasting and Inventory Control," *Operations Research*, Vol. 22, No. 6, 1224–31.

better chance of success. Initially, people were overriding computer-generated order quantities 80 percent of the time. A year later, only 10 percent of the inventory decisions made by the computer were manually overridden.

MODELS FOR INVENTORY DECISION MAKING

As mentioned earlier in this chapter, there are two basic functions necessary to effectively control inventory. In this section, we deal with a scientific approach to performing one of those functions: namely, inventory decision making for independent-demand items.

The objective of any inventory model is to minimize total inventory cost. Minimizing just one of the three components of inventory cost is easy, and of little value. For example, to minimize carrying cost, a firm can simply stop carrying any inventory. This action, however, can be expected to create unreasonable stockout or order costs. The actual process for minimizing total inventory costs entails two basic decisions: how much and when to order. Understandably, these are the two decision variables that inventory models use in optimizing an inventory system.

In this section, we discuss the five essential steps in analyzing inventory problems: determining inventory properties, formulating and developing the appropriate inventory model, solving or manipulating the model, performing sensitivity analysis on the model, and incorporating the model in the inventory control system.

Determining System Properties

Inventory properties can be classified in four categories: demand properties, replenishment properties, cost properties, and constraints. In order to prevent the misapplication of an inventory model, it is extremely important to identify and consider each property of an inventory system properly.

Demand properties.   These characteristics include the size, and rate, of demand. The size of demand can be constant or variable, depending on the nature of the good. A constant demand merely means that for each time period, the quantity of goods demanded is constant. The size of demand for a good can be deterministic or stochastic. Given a production schedule, for example, it may be a simple calculation to determine demand for a particular period of time. However, the demand of many inventory items cannot be predicted with any degree of certainty; hence, the problem is a stochastic or probabilistic problem rather than a deterministic one.

The rate of demand is the size of demand over a particular unit of time. For example, Vulcan Valve Company has a total demand for the year of 600 valves, and its records verify that the monthly demand rate is 600/12, or 50 units per month. Clearly, demand rate can be variable or constant, deterministic or stochastic.

Replenishment properties.   When you analyze replenishment properties, it is necessary to define the *scheduling period*. The scheduling period is the length of time between decisions concerning replenishments. This time period can be prescribed or variable. For example, the local supermarket orders fresh lettuce twice a week (prescribed), whereas canned kidney beans are ordered when the inventory reaches a certain reorder point (variable). Variable scheduling periods require a continuous accounting for inventory. In most medium and large firms, an inventory accounting system is, or should be, totally computerized.

Lead time, you will recall, is the time between ordering a replenishment of inventory and actually receiving the goods into inventory. Lead time can be either a deterministic constant or variable, or a stochastic variable. If lead time is known with a high degree of certainty, its existence is easily treated in inventory modeling. On the other hand, if lead time is stochastic with a large variance, the difficulty in finding an appropriate inventory model is greatly increased.

Like demand, the *size of replenishment* can also be stochastic. In other words, the quantity ordered may not be the same as the quantity received, owing to undershipments, or quality rejections, Replenishment size is often called *lot size*.

The *replenishment period* is the time during which units of a particular order are added to inventory. In a purchasing situation, the replenishment period may be insignificant; but in a production environment, units are added to inventory over a period of time (that is, as they are produced).

Often, instead of specifying the lot size, an inventory policy specifies an *order level*. An order level is the quantity that will be in inventory after replenishment.

Cost properties.   Inventory costs are of three types: ordering cost, holding cost, and shortage cost. These parameters of an inventory model are rarely known with certainty. Consequently, the inventory manager usually should determine the sensitivity of the optimal solution to small and reasonable changes in these parameters.

Inventory constraints.   In addition to determining inventory properties, before you can decide on solution methodology you must analyze inventory constraints. For example, if the inventory storage area holds only 100 units, an optimal order quantity of 1,000 units is irrelevant. Similarly, if working capital is severely limited and the optimal inventory policy calls for carrying a high inventory, the optimal policy may not be feasible. Typical inventory constraints are these:

1. *Space*. The amount of storage space may put limits on the order quantity.
2. *Scheduling period*. If the scheduling period is prescribed, many inventory models cannot be used.
3. *Shortage*. Management may make a decision that stockouts cannot be allowed. On the other hand, shortages may be allowed and may or may not result in lost sales.
4. *Dependent demand*. In most inventory models, demand is considered independent of the demand of the preceding period. When independent demand is not characteristic of a particular inventory system, it is generally more difficult to optimize the system.

5. *Continuous nature of inventory units.* Most analytical models used for optimizing inventory systems depend on the calculus for their derivation. Consequently, if inventory units are not or cannot be considered continuous in nature, a majority of the analytical optimization models cannot be applied. Usually, when large quantities are involved, the assumption of continuousness is not damaging.

Determining inventory properties is crucial to analyzing inventory problems. If we expect to find or develop an appropriate model for the inventory item in question, we must analyze the item's properties and characteristics in depth.

Formulating the Model

The second step in analyzing inventory problems is to discover or derive the appropriate inventory model to solve the particular problem. Basically, there are two types of inventory models: deterministic models and stochastic models. The parameters of deterministic inventory models are assumed to be known with certainty. For example, demand is assumed to be perfectly predictable. Stochastic inventory models contain uncontrollable variables, such as demand or lead time, that are probabilistic in nature. Generally, stochastic inventory models are mathematically more difficult to derive and solve. As the number of stochastic variables increases, it becomes more difficult to derive an analytical optimization model. In addition, if a stochastic variable is not distributed according to a known probability density function, the likelihood of finding or deriving an analytical inventory model is drastically reduced. When an analytical model cannot be developed to model a particular inventory system adequately, simulation can usually be used to determine a good inventory policy. The decision of whether to simulate an inventory system hinges on the cost/benefit of the simulation. This is one area in which ABC analysis can be used.

Solving the Model

The third step in the analysis of inventory systems is to solve the analytical model or run the simulation model. This is typically the easiest part of the process if the first two steps have been performed properly. Because the solution of analytical inventory models is not an iterative process, a computer is not considered an absolute necessity. If a computer is used, very few computer resources (memory and time) are necessary to solve analytic inventory models.

An analytical model is preferable to a simulation model for two reasons. First, the cost in computer resources is considerably less. Second, an analytical model yields an optimal solution, whereas a simulation model can only search for a good solution. In short, analytical inventory models cost *much* less than simulation models to find the *best* answer. This is not to say, however, that a real system should be modeled using an analytical model whose assumptions do not adequately fit the real-system properties. This is a common error in practice, and it is for this reason that we state explicitly the assumptions of each model we present in this chapter.

Performing Sensitivity Analysis

Some models yield order quantities that are extremely sensitive. In other words, slight changes in the order quantity cause significant changes in the total cost of the inventory system. In addition, it is usually helpful to the decision maker to know the relative sensitivity of such inventory variables as demand, lead time, and replenishment quantity. Unlike LP, inventory models cannot easily determine the sensitivity of the system's various parameters and decision variables. Instead, the parameter or variable in question is perturbed, and the effect of the change is observed.

Integrating the Model into the Inventory Control System

Once a model has been found that makes good inventory decisions, it must be integrated into the inventory control system. For example, let us assume Model A calculates an order quantity for a particular item that minimizes cost. If that model is programmed into the software of the inventory system, then anytime that item reaches its reorder point, an order quantity can be calculated and suggested to management.

ANALYTICAL MODELS

In this chapter, we are going to consider several deterministic models and one stochastic model. These represent only a small sampling of the inventory models that have been developed and used since the first one was introduced in 1915.

Basic Economic Order Quantity Model (EOQ)

Before examining it, we must identify the assumptions of the basic EOQ model so that you will know under what conditions to apply it. If the following assumptions cannot be accepted, thereby indicating that the real-world inventory problem may not be adequately represented by the basic EOQ model, it is inappropriate to use it.

1. *Deterministic demand.* It must be possible to predict demand with a high degree of confidence.
2. *Constant rate of demand.* Not only must the total demand be known, but units must be drawn from inventory at a uniform rate. For example, if 365 units are used each year, these items must be drawn one per day during the year to strictly satisfy this assumption.
3. *No shortages.* Inventory replenishments are made whenever the inventory level reaches zero. Shortages are not allowed to occur. This assumption implies that, one of the three costs involved in an inventory system, stockout cost, does not exist in the basic EOQ model.
4. *Constant replenishment size.* The replenishment size, denoted by q, is the only decision variable in the basic EOQ model. The other decision variable—when to

reorder—is fixed, because demand is at a constant rate and replenishments occur when the inventory level reaches zero.

5. *Zero lead time.* It is assumed that no appreciable time elapses between placing an order and receiving that order. This assumption can be easily dealt with, as we shall explain later.

6. *Infinite replenishment rate.* Replenishment rate is defined as the rate at which units are added to inventory. An infinite replenishment rate implies that inventory replenishment occurs instantaneously. In other words, it takes zero time to receive an order. This assumption is reasonable for most purchased goods but is often unreasonable for manufactured goods. Typically, manufactured goods are put into inventory at some finite rate.

7. *Constant inventory costs.* Both costs in the basic EOQ model are constant. Ordering cost is expressed as dollars per order, and holding cost is expressed as dollars per unit per time period.

These assumptions for the basic EOQ model determine the graph in Figure 10-3.

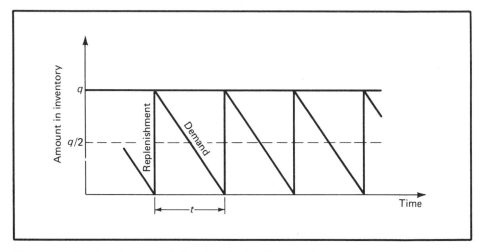

FIGURE 10-3   Graphic Representation of the Basic EOQ Model

It would be the rare inventory item for which all the assumptions above could be accepted without reservation. The key point is that you should be aware of these assumptions, and if your inventory problem violates one of them significantly, another inventory model may be more appropriate.

Inventory problems in which the decision variable is the order quantity have the objective function in equation 10.1:

10.1   Min $C(q) = A(q) + B(q) + D(q)$

where $C(q)$ = the total cost function
               $A(q)$ = a function of q that defines the holding cost

$$B(q) = \text{a function of } q \text{ that represents the shortage cost}$$
$$D(q) = \text{a function of } q \text{ that defines the ordering cost}$$

In order to determine the optimal value of q, it is necessary to develop the functions $A(q)$, $B(q)$, and $D(q)$ for the basic EOQ model. For holding cost we have

$$A(q) = C_1(q/2)$$

where $C_1 = \text{holding cost per unit of inventory}$

A look at Figure 10-3 will reveal to you that $q/2$ represents the average number of units in inventory. In other words, half the time there are more than $q/2$ units in inventory, and half the time the amount in inventory is less than $q/2$ units. Therefore, if we multiply a per-unit holding cost by the average number of units in inventory, that product is the holding cost. Since no shortages are allowed in the basic EOQ model, owing to the zero-lead-time and zero-reorder-point assumptions, $B(q)$ is not present in the total cost function. Ordering cost can be thought of as the cost of placing an order multiplied by the number of orders placed in a particular time period. More specifically:

$$D(q) = C_3(r/q)$$

where $C_3 = \text{the cost of processing one order}$
                $r = \text{total demand for a given period of time}$
        $r/q = \text{number of orders}$

Given the preceding defined functions, the total cost function can be written as shown in equation 10.2:

$$C(q) = A(q) + D(q)$$
10.2 $$C(q) = C_1(q/2) + C_3(r/q)$$

Remember, the question is to determine the value of q that minimizes the objective function $C(q)$. Figure 10-4 graphs the three functions $A(q)$, $C(q)$, and $D(q)$. From Figure 10-4, it is apparent that the minimum of $C(q)$ occurs at the same level of q where functions $A(q)$ and $D(q)$ intersect. It is possible, therefore, to set $A(q)$ equal to $D(q)$ and solve for q to find q^*, the optimal value of q. It must be noted that this relationship is not universally true.

$$A(q) = D(q)$$
$$C_1(q/2) = C_3(r/q)$$
10.3 $$C_1(q^2/2) = C_3 r$$
$$q^2/2 = C_3 r/C_1$$
$$q^2 = 2C_3 r/C_1$$
$$q^* = \sqrt{2C_3 r/C_1}$$

Now, let's look at an example of how to use the basic EOQ model. The Ace Aerospace Company uses 10,000 special bolts per year. Each bolt costs $1. The Materials Department estimates that it costs $25 to order a shipment of bolts, and the Accounting Department estimates the holding cost is 12.5 percent. All the assumptions of the basic EOQ model are valid.

$$C_1 = \$.125 \text{ per bolt per year}$$
$$C_3 = \$25 \text{ per order}$$
$$r = 10,000 \text{ bolts}$$
$$q^* = \sqrt{2C_3r/C_1}$$
$$= \sqrt{2(25)10,000/.125}$$
$$= \sqrt{4,000,000}$$
$$= 2,000 \text{ bolts}$$

If the Ace Aerospace Company buys 2,000 bolts every time inventory reaches zero, the total annual cost of this policy is:

$$C(q^*) = .125(2,000/2) + 25(10,000/2,000)$$
$$= 125 + 125$$
$$= \$250$$

Once q^* is calculated, it is a simple matter to calculate the optimal number of orders per year and the time between each two orders:

$$N^* = \text{optimal number of orders}$$
$$= r/q^*$$
$$= 10,000/2,000$$
$$= 5$$
$$t^* = \text{optimal time between orders (optimal reorder schedule)}$$
$$= \text{Planning period}/N^*$$
$$= 365/5 = 73 \text{ days}$$

Sensitivity of the Basic EOQ Model

As indicated in Figure 10-4, the shape of the total cost curve, $C(q)$, is relatively flat. Consequently, $C(q)$ is not very sensitive to small changes in q. To illustrate this fact, let us assume that the Ace Aerospace Company orders 1,000 bolts in each order instead of the optimal 2,000 bolts. The annual inventory cost for ordering 1,000 bolts each order is calculated below.

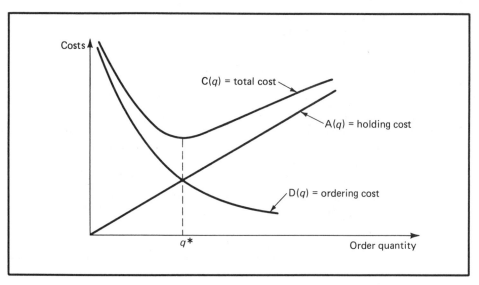

FIGURE 10-4   Inventory Cost Basic EOQ Model

$$C(1,000) = .125(1,000/2) + 25(10,000/1,000)$$
$$= 62.50 + 250$$
$$= \$312.50$$

Hence, a change of 50 percent in q resulted in only a 25 percent increase in the total inventory cost. (See Table 10-3 for a more complete sensitivity analysis.) This means that if total demand, r, is incorrectly estimated, thus causing a suboptimal q to be

Table 10-3   Sensitivity Analysis of Order Quantity

ORDER QUANTITY	ORDER COST ($)	CARRYING COST ($)	TOTAL COST ($)
100	2,500.00	6.25	2,506.25
500	500.00	31.25	531.25
750	333.33	46.88	380.21
1,000	250.00	62.50	312.50
1,250	200.00	78.13	278.13
1,500	166.65	93.75	260.40
1,750	142.85	109.38	252.23
2,000	125.00	125.00	250.00
2,250	111.11	140.63	251.73
2,500	100.00	156.25	256.25
3,000	83.33	187.50	270.83
4,000	62.50	250.00	312.50
10,000	25.00	625.00	650.00

calculated, the consequences are not as critical as they would be if the shape of the total cost curve were more peaked.

Basic EOQ System with Finite Replenishment Rate

Often, it is unrealistic to assume an infinite replenishment rate. If a firm is purchasing off-the-shelf items for its inventory, then typically, when an order is delivered, the entire replenishment quantity is delivered at one time; hence, an infinite replenishment rate. If, however, a company is producing for inventory, units are added to inventory over a finite period of time. Therefore, the inventory system has a finite replenishment rate. If it can be assumed that this replenishment rate is uniform and all other assumptions of the basic EOQ model hold, the appropriate model is the basic EOQ system with a finite replenishment rate. The graphic representation of the model is given in Figure 10-5.

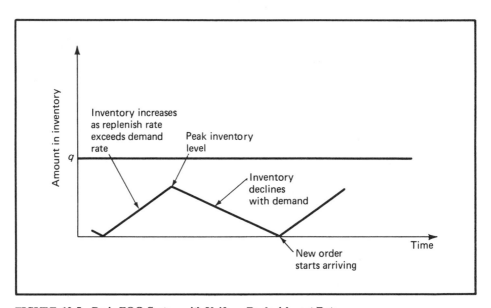

FIGURE 10-5   Basic EOQ System with Uniform Replenishment Rate

The total cost function of the inventory system depicted in Figure 10-5 is:

10.4
$$C(q) = \frac{C_1 q(1 - r/p)}{2} + \frac{C_3 r}{q}$$

The expression for the optimal order quantity is shown in equation 10.5:

10.5
$$q^* = \frac{\sqrt{2rC_3/C_1}}{\sqrt{1 - r/p}}$$

where r = the total demand for a given period of time
         C_3 = the setup cost per setup
         C_1 = the carrying cost per unit
         p = uniform replenishment rate expressed in units per time period

The minimum total inventory cost is given by the following function:

10.6 $$C^* = \sqrt{2rC_1C_3}\,\sqrt{1 - r/p}$$

where C^* = the minimum inventory cost

Let's alter our previous example just slightly so that the replenishment rate changes from infinite to a uniform 500 bolts per day. To restate, the Ace Aerospace Company uses 10,000 bolts per year. Each bolt costs \$1. The Production Engineering Department estimates setup costs at \$25, and the Accounting Department estimates that the holding cost is 12.5 percent of the value of inventory.

$$r = 10{,}000 \text{ bolts}$$

$$C_3 = \$25 \text{ per order}$$

$$C_1 = \$.125 \text{ per bolt per year}$$

$$p = 125{,}000 \text{ bolts per year}^3$$

$$q^* = \sqrt{\frac{2rC_3/C_1}{1 - (r/p)}}$$

$$= \sqrt{\frac{2(10{,}000)25/.125}{1 - (10{,}000/125{,}000)}}$$

$$= \sqrt{4{,}000{,}000/.92}$$

$$= \sqrt{4{,}350{,}000}$$

$$= 2{,}086$$

Therefore, the Ace Aerospace Company should order 2,086 bolts every time inventory for the bolts reaches zero. The total inventory cost of this ordering policy is calculated below:

$$C^* = \sqrt{2rC_1C_3}\,\sqrt{1 - (r/p)}$$

$$= \sqrt{2(10{,}000).125(25)}\,\sqrt{1 - (10{,}000/125{,}000)}$$

$$= \sqrt{62{,}500}\,\sqrt{.92}$$

$$\cong \$239.75$$

---

[3]It was necessary to convert the per-day production of bolts to per-year production of bolts because the time units must be compatible; that is, r was expressed in units per year. (250 workdays $\times$ 500 = 125,000 bolts per year.)

Therefore, if the Ace Aerospace Company orders 2,086 bolts approximately five times a year, inventory cost related to this particular bolt is minimized at about $240 per year.

Basic Order-Level System

The basic order-level system is very similar to the basic lot-size system previously described. In fact, all properties are the same except that shortages are allowed and backordered and the scheduling period is prescribed. This type of system is very common in the real world when an organization places orders for certain inventory items on a regularly scheduled basis, such as once a month. An advantage of a pre-scribed scheduling period is that it does *not* necessitate continuous monitoring of inventory levels.

The basic order-level system has the following properties:

1. Demand is deterministic.
2. The rate of demand is constant; that is, it is a linear demand function. ·
3. The scheduling period is prescribed.
4. The lead time is zero.
5. The replenishment rate is infinite.
6. Shortages are made up; that is, there are no lost sales.
7. The decision variable is the order level, S; that is, the decision variable is the amount of inventory after replenishment.
8. Holding cost is constant and is expressed as dollars per unit per time period.
9. Shortage cost is constant and expressed as dollars per unit per time period.

The basic order-level system is depicted in Figure 10-6.

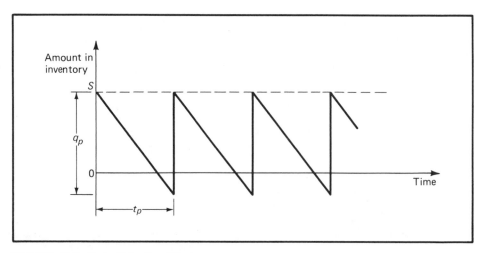

FIGURE 10-6 Basic Order-Level System

Since the scheduling period is prescribed, the only controllable inventory costs are the carrying and shortage costs. Since order level is the decision variable in this inventory model, the total cost function is a function of order level, S. It can be shown geometrically, using similar triangles, that the total cost function is:

10.7 $$C(S) = C_1 S^2/2q_p + C_2(q_p - S)^2/2q_p$$

where
$C_1 = $ carrying cost per unit per time period
$S = $ order level
$q_p = $ prescribed lot size (rate of demand multiplied by the prescribed time period)
$C_2 = $ shortage cost per unit per time period

minimizing this total cost function using classical optimization procedures of the differential calculus, the optimal order level is:

10.8 $$S^* = q_p C_2/(C_1 + C_2)$$

As an example, a local stereo store reviews its stock of Dynamo preamps every month, then orders for the next month. Last year, it sold 120 Dynamo preamps, and sales were spread evenly throughout the year. Predictions are that this year's sales will be approximately the same. Lead time is effectively zero, and shortages are made up. The holding cost is \$80 per preamp per year, and shortage cost has been determined to be \$10 per preamp per month (\$10 per preamp per month $\times$ 12 months equals \$120 per preamp per year). The optimal order level, therefore, is:

$$S^* = 10(120)/(80 + 120)$$
$$= 6 \text{ preamps}$$

To find the minimum cost of this solution, merely substitute S^* into the cost function:

$$C(6) = (80 \cdot 6^2)/(2 \cdot 10) + [120(10 - 6)^2]/20$$
$$= \$240$$

In summary, the inventory policy of the local stereo store is to order ten Dynamo preamps whenever backorders reach four.

This inventory policy costs \$240 per year in inventory cost; any other policy would cost the stereo store more. The graph of this inventory policy is shown in Figure 10-7.

A Stochastic Demand Model

Until now, we have assumed that all demand parameters of an inventory system are known with certainty. In addition, we have assumed that lead time is zero. If we loosen only this latter assumption, very little has to change except that we must order

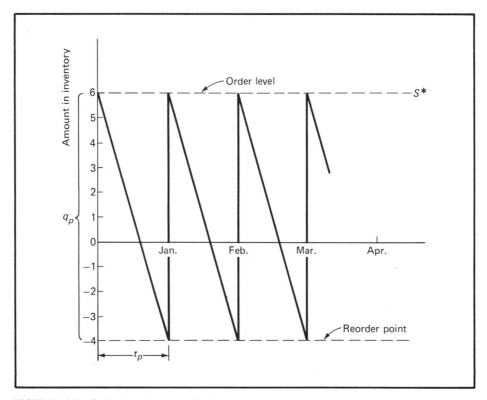

FIGURE 10-7   Order Level System with Stockouts

prior to running out of inventory to prevent stockouts. (Figure 10-8 illustrates the basic EOQ system with nonzero lead time.) In this situation, let's say, for example, that demand is ten units per day and lead time is known to be five days; then the reorder point, s, is equal to 50 units. Therefore, whenever inventory reaches 50 units, an order for q units should be processed.

If we loosen the assumption of known or certain demand, then the problem of when to order becomes more complicated. As you can see in Figure 10-9, there is now the danger of stockouts.

If an inventory system has all the properties of the basic EOQ system except that lead time is not zero and demand is not deterministic and constant, we can proceed in the following manner. The problem is still how much and when to order. If we assume that a reasonable estimate of the optimal order quantity can be calculated using the basic EOQ formula, then the problem reduces to merely determining the reorder point. In most real situations, using the EOQ formula when demand is not known with certainty has little effect on total inventory costs because of the relative insensitivity of total costs to moderate changes in the order quantity.

Since the order quantity is given, ordering costs should not be affected by

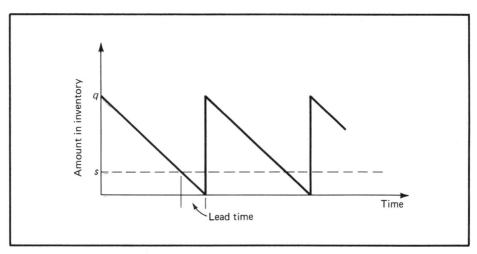

FIGURE 10-8 Basic EOQ with Nonzero Lead Time, Deterministic Demand

FIGURE 10-9 Stochastic Demand

changes in the reorder point. The inventory costs affected by changes in the reorder point are the carrying costs and the stockout costs. The problem, however, is that when stockout costs are lowered by increasing the safety stock, carrying costs are increased because the average value of inventory is increased.

To illustrate how to determine the reorder point, let us consider the following problem. A camera store wants to determine the proper reorder point for its Instamatic 2 camera. Annual demand is for 1,000 Instamatic 2 cameras, sold at a rate of approximately four per day. It takes five days between the day the order is placed and the receipt of the shipment from the manufacturer. The question is, At what point does the camera store order Instamatic 2 cameras? In order to answer the question, it is necessary to have some idea of the probability distribution of the number of cameras demanded in any five-day period. This information is summarized in Table 10-4. In

Table 10-4   Frequency Distribution of 5-Day Demand for Instamatic
2 Cameras

DEMAND FOR 5-DAY PERIODS	FREQUENCY OF SPECIFIED DEMAND	RELATIVE FREQUENCY	CUMULATIVE RELATIVE FREQUENCY
10	5	.10	.10
15	15	.30	.40
20	20	.40	.80
25	5	.10	.90
30	4	.08	.98
35	1	.02	1.00
	50	1.00	

order to determine a good reorder point, it is possible to look at six reorder points and calculate the expected cost of each, then simply choose the reorder level with the smallest total cost. Let us assume stockout cost is $10 per camera, and carrying cost is $5 per camera per year and ordering cost is $25 per order.

$$q^0 = \sqrt{[2(1,000)(25)/5]}$$
$$= \sqrt{10,000}$$
$$= 100$$

If the camera store reorders when inventory hits ten cameras, there is a high probability (90 percent) of having a shortage before the shipment is received. The shortage cost associated with this policy can be calculated in the following way:

10.9 $$C_2 = \left[\sum_{i=1}^{n} x_i P(x_i)c_2\right](r/q)$$

where
C_2 = shortage cost for year
x_i = number short during lead time
$P(x_i)$ = probability of being short x_i units
c_2 = per-unit shortage costs
r = total annual demand
q = order quantity
n = number of 5-day demand levels

Given that the reorder point is 10:

$$C_2 = [0(.1)10 + 5(.3)10 + 10(.4)10 + 15(.10)10 + 20(.08)10 + 25(.02)10]$$
$$\times (1,000/100)$$
$$= \$910$$

Stockout costs for other reorder points are shown in Table 10-5.

Table 10-5   Stockout Costs

REORDER POINT	STOCKOUT COSTS ($)
10	910
15	460
20	160
25	60
30	10
35	0

The incremental carrying costs for the various reorder points under consideration are represented by:

10.10
$$\Delta C_1 = \sum_{i=1}^{n} y_i P(y_i) c_1$$

where y_i = number of units in inventory at the time of replenishment
   ΔC_1 = incremental carrying cost
   $P(y_i)$ = probability of y_i units in inventory at the time of replenishment
   c_1 = per-unit carrying cost
   n = number of 5-day demand levels

Given a reorder point of 10:

$$\Delta C_1 = 0(.1)5 + 0(.2)5 + 0(.4)5 + 0(.2)5 + 0(.08)5 + 0(.02)5 = 0$$

For a reorder point of 25:

$$\Delta C_1 = 15(.1)5 + 10(.3)5 + 5(.4)5 + 0(.1)5 + 0(.08)5 + 0(.02)5 = \$32.50$$

Table 10-6 shows total incremental costs per year based on reorder point. Since
the total incremental cost of the various reorder-point policies is minimized when the
reorder point is 30, the optimal inventory policy for the camera store is to order 100
cameras ten times a year, whenever the inventory level reaches 30 cameras.

Table 10-6   Cost of Reorder-Point Policies

REORDER POINT	EXPECTED STOCKOUT COSTS ($)	EXPECTED INCREMENTAL CARRYING COSTS ($)	TOTAL INCREMENTAL COSTS ($) $C_2 + \Delta C_1$
10	910.00	0	910.00
15	460.00	2.50	462.50
20	160.00	12.50	162.50
25	60.00	32.50	92.50
30	10.00	55.00	65.00
35	0	79.50	79.50

SIMULATION APPROACH

Although there are many more inventory models than the few we have discussed in this chapter, it is very common for a real inventory problem not to have an analytical counterpart. In other words, a model may not exist or be derivable mathematically that adequately describes a real inventory problem. This is especially true when several properties are stochastic in nature. For example, many systems with stochastic demand, stochastic lead time, and nonconstant cost parameters have no mathematical model that can be solved analytically. As in the case of complex queuing systems, simulation can usually be applied when inventory systems become too complex to be optimized analytically. The trouble with simulation as a means for solving inventory system problems is that it is a descriptive technique, not an optimization technique. Simulation can answer questions regarding the desirability of various inventory policies; but it cannot, by itself, assign values to the various decision variables.

You can gain specific insight into how simulation is used to answer inventory questions by working through a simple inventory simulation. An industrial equipment company carries a particularly popular skill saw that sells for $120 and wishes to know how much and when to order. Because demand is not known with certainty (see Table 10-7) and lead time is not known with certainty (see Table 10-8), simulation appears to be a proper approach to the problem. The cost of the saws, which depends on the quantity ordered, is shown in Table 10-9. Ordering cost is estimated at $25 per order, and the carrying cost fraction is .2. Stockout cost is assumed to be $25 per unit.

In order to utilize simulation to solve this inventory problem, we must develop functions that can be used to generate the two stochastic variables in the problem—namely, demand and lead time. Let's assume that no known probability distribution can be fitted to the two sets of historical data and that we are forced to use these empirical distributions. Hence, the generating functions we need can be found merely by using the cumulative frequency distribution of the two stochastic variables. (See Tables 10-10 and 10-11 for these distributions.) You can refer back to Chapter 3, if necessary, for an explanation of how the two generating functions were derived.

Table 10-7   Historical Frequency of Demand

DEMAND PER DAY	NUMBER OF OBSERVATIONS	RELATIVE FREQUENCY
0	19	.095
1	27	.135
2	42	.210
3	49	.245
4	34	.170
5	17	.085
6	9	.045
7	2	.010
8	1	.005
	200	1.000

Table 10-8   Historical Frequency of Lead Time

LEAD TIME IN DAYS	NUMBER OF OBSERVATIONS	RELATIVE FREQUENCY
4	11	.22
5	7	.14
6	3	.06
7	21	.42
8	5	.10
9	2	.04
10	1	.02
	50	1.00

Table 10-9   Price Schedule

ORDER	PRICE PER SAW
Less than 25	$100
25 or more	95
50 or more	90
100 or more	80

Once we have the generating functions, the next step is to experiment with a particular inventory policy. For example, let's compare two inventory policies:

1. Order 25 saws when inventory reaches 10 saws.
2. Order 25 saws when inventory reaches 15 saws.

Table 10-10   Demand-Generating Function

RANDOM NUMBER RANGE	DEMAND PER DAY
0–.095	0
.095–.230	1
.230–.440	2
.440–.685	3
.685–.855	4
.855–.940	5
.940–.985	6
.985–.995	7
.995–1.00	8

Table 10-11   Lead-Time-Generating Function

RANDOM NUMBER RANGE	LEAD TIME IN DAYS
0–.22	4
.22–.36	5
.36–.42	6
.42–.84	7
.84–.94	8
.94–.98	9
.98–1.0	10

For illustrative purposes, we shall simulate one month manually. Then, using a computer, we'll simulate a number of different policies to determine a good inventory policy. Tables 10-12 and 10-13 reflect the results of the manual simulation for both inventory policies we established. Look at the carrying cost and the stockout costs for the two policies simulated in Tables 10-12 and 10-13. (Ordering costs and the cost of goods are constant for the two policies.) You can see that, by increasing the reorder level five units, the stockout cost is decreased by $150 with only a $1.50 increase in the month's carrying cost.

Obviously, other inventory policies need to be examined, and the number of days simulated must be significantly increased before we can have much faith in the results of the simulation experiments. To give you some idea of what it costs to "solve" the saw inventory problem using computer simulation, we wrote and ran a simulation program to determine the effects of various inventory policies. The program, Figure 10-10, was written in GPSS, a special-purpose simulation language. It took approximately two hours to write and debug. One experiment simulated four years and took .1214 minutes to run on a Xerox Sigma 6 computer. In all, 15 experiments were run, at a total computer cost of approximately $9. As you can see in Table 10-14, the best inventory policy of those simulated is to order 100 saws whenever inventory level reaches 25 saws.

Table 10-12 Simulation: Reorder point = 10, Order Quantity = 25

DAY	RANDOM NUMBER	DEMAND	AMOUNT ORDERED (PAIRS)	RANDOM NUMBER	LEAD TIME (DAYS)	AMOUNT RECEIVED (PAIRS)	ENDING INVENTORY	CARRYING COST ($)	STOCK-OUT COST ($)	COST OF GOODS ($)	ORDER COST ($)	TOTAL COST ($)
1	.134	1					14	1.06	0	0	0	1.06
2	.909	5	25	.344	5		9	.69	0	2,375	25	2,400.69
3	.204	1					8	.61	0	0	0	.61
4	.906	5					3	.23	0	0	0	.23
5	.387	2					1	.08	0	0	0	.08
6	.045	0					1	.08	0	0	0	.08
7	.894	5					0	0	100	0	0	100.00
8	.172	1				25	24	1.82	0	0	0	1.82
9	.380	2					22	1.67	0	0	0	1.67
10	.390	2					20	1.52	0	0	0	1.52
11	.513	3					17	1.29	0	0	0	1.29
12	.563	3					14	1.06	0	0	0	1.06
13	.670	3					11	.84	0	0	0	.84
14	.428	2	25	.633	7		9	.68	0	0	0	.68
15	.589	3					6	.46	0	0	0	.46
16	.040	0					6	.46	0	0	0	.46
17	.738	4					2	.15	0	0	0	.15
18	.460	3					0	0	25	0	0	25.00
19	.007	0					0	0	0	0	0	0.00
20	.775	4					0	0	100	0	0	100.00
21	.421	2				25	23	1.78	0	2,375	25	2,401.78
22	.072	0					23	1.78	0	0	0	1.78
							Totals	$16.26	$225	$4,750	$50	$5,041.26

Table 10-13 Simulation: Reorder Point = 15, Order Quantity = 25

DAY	RANDOM NUMBER	DEMAND	AMOUNT ORDERED (PAIRS)	RANDOM NUMBER	LEAD TIME (DAYS)	AMOUNT RECEIVED (PAIRS)	ENDING INVENTORY	CARRYING COST ($)	STOCK-OUT COST ($)	COST OF GOODS ($)	ORDER COST ($)	TOTAL COST ($)
1	.134	1	25	.344	5		14	1.06	0	2,375	25	2,401.06
2	.909	5					9	.69	0	0	0	.69
3	.204	1					8	.61	0	0	0	.61
4	.906	5					3	.23	0	0	0	.23
5	.387	2					1	.08	0	0	0	.08
6	.045	0					1	.08	0	0	0	.08
7	.894	5				25	20	1.52	0	0	0	1.52
8	.172	1					19	1.44	0	0	0	1.44
9	.380	2					17	1.29	0	0	0	1.29
10	.390	2	25	.633	7		15	1.14	0	2,375	25	2,401.14
11	.513	3					12	.91	0	0	0	.91
12	.563	3					9	.68	0	0	0	.68
13	.670	3					6	.46	0	0	0	.46
14	.428	2					4	.30	0	0	0	.30
15	.589	3					1	.08	0	0	0	.08
16	.040	0					1	.08	0	0	0	.08
17	.738	4					0	0	75	0	0	75.00
18	.460	3				25	22	1.67	0	0	0	1.67
19	.007	0					22	1.67	0	0	0	1.67
20	.775	4					18	1.37	0	0	0	1.37
21	.421	2					16	1.22	0	0	0	1.22
22	.072	0					16	1.22	0	0	0	1.22
							Totals	$17.80	$75	$4,750	$50	$4,892.80

```
            REALLOCATE DLO,50,XAC,50,FAC,1,STO,1,QUE,1
            REALLOCATE LOG,5,TAB,1,FUM,3,VAR,30,BVR,1,FSV,15
            REALLOCATE HOV,10,BUR,1,FMS,1,HMS,1,CHA,5,COM,5000
            SIMULATE
*  X1 = CARRYING COST
*  X2 = STOCKOUT COST
*  X3 = COST OF GOODS
*  X4 = ORDER COST
*  X5 = TOTAL COST
*  X6 = ENDING INVENTORY
*  X7 = REORDER POINT
*  X8 = ORDER QUANTITY
*  X9 = COST PER UNIT
            INITIAL    X6,30
            INITIAL    X9,8000
            INITIAL    X7,10
            INITIAL    X8,100
    1       VARIABLE   X9*X6*2/2500  CARRYING COST
    2       VARIABLE   X6*(-2500)  STOCKOUT COST
    3       VARIABLE   X9*X8  COST OF GOODS
    4       VARIABLE   X1+X2+X3+X4   TOTAL COST
    1       FUNCTION   RN2,D9  DEMAND FUNCTION
.095,0/.23,1/.44,2/.685,3/.855,4/.94,5/.985,6/.995,7/1,8
    2       FUNCTION   RN3,D7  LEAD TIME FUNCTION
.22,4/.36,5/.42,6/.84,7/.94,8/.98,9/1,10
            GENERATE   1,0,,1000  GENERATE 1 DAY
            SAVEVALUE  6-,FN1  ADJUST ENDING INVENTORY
            TEST GE    X6,0,NEG  CHECK FOR STOCKOUT
            TEST GE    X6,X7,ORDER  CHECK FOR REORDER LEVEL
            SAVEVALUE  1+V1  ACCUMULATE CARRYING COST
            TERMINATE  1
MEG         SAVEVALUE  2+,V2  ACCUMULATE STOCKOUT COST
            SAVEVALUE  6,0  ZERO ENDING INVENTORY
TEM         TERMINATE  1  END THE DAY
ORDER GATE LR   1,TEM  HAS ORDER BEEN MADE??
            LOGIC S    1  SET THE ORDER SWITCH
            SAVEVALUE  4+,2500  ACCUMULATE ORDERING COST
            SAVEVALUE  3+,V3  ACCUMULATE COST OF GOODS
            SAVEVALUE  1+,V1  ACCUMULATE CARRYING COST
            PRIORITY   10  SET PRIORITY OF AN INCOMING ORDER
            ADVANCE    FN2  LEAD TIME
            SAVEVALUE  6+,X8  INCREMENT ENDING INVENTORY
            LOGIC R    1  RESET ORDER SWITCH
            TERMINATE  1
            GENERATE   1001  GENERATE TIMER TRANSACTION
            SAVEVALUE  5,V4  ACCUMULATE TOTAL COST
            TERMINATE  1
            START      1001
```

FIGURE 10-10 GPSS Program

Table 10-14   Simulation Results, Total Adjusted Inventory Costs

ORDER QUANTITY	REORDER LEVEL				
	10	*15*	*20*	*25*	*30*
25	$283,258	$276,738	$271,863	$269,611	$269,055
50	$263,589	$259,330	$256,271	$255,367	$254,937
100	$232,559	$229,395	$228,529	$227,777	$227,828

SUMMARY

In order to implement truly effective inventory management, an organization must have an integrated management information system for the purpose of inventory control. In most organizations, inventory control is nothing more than an inventory accounting system. In other words, whether the system is computer-based or not, it merely keeps track of inventory items and alerts management when inventory levels get low. Typically, the system has little capacity for making decisions about when and how much to order. Some progressive organizations, however, are developing or using systems that actually integrate inventory models like the ones described in this chapter into their management information systems. These more progressive systems may be real-time or batch-oriented systems. What distinguishes the management information system from the inventory accounting system is the decision-making capabilities of MIS.

Management's primary challenge in relation to inventory problems is to use the systems approach for the successful application of existing theory and technology. More theory is potentially useful, but unless organizations can be persuaded to apply the inventory theory thus far developed, the marginal utility of new theory is questionable.

To apply existing inventory theory successfully, you must beware of two pitfalls. First, you must avoid the misapplication of various inventory models by carefully examining the properties of an existing inventory system and making sure system properties adequately match model assumptions. Too many firms are using the basic EOQ model when it is inappropriate. Second, to implement a decision-making management information system, many human factors must be dealt with carefully. People naturally resist change, especially when it threatens their security or self-image. Many times, it is more effective, for example, to have the management information system suggest an order quantity than to automatically print the purchase or production order. A major reason why models such as those presented in this chapter have not been accepted by many organizations is a failure to take into consideration the human factors connected with organizational change. Unless the people in an organization are in favor of a change, that change, regardless of its merits, will not succeed.

SOLVED PROBLEMS

Problem Statement

A local TV distributor has found from experience that demand for a certain model TV is fairly constant at a rate of 50 sets per month. Lead time is effectively zero and no shortages are to be allowed. If the sets cost $300, the carrying-cost fraction is 20 percent per year, and ordering cost is estimated to be $50, how many sets should be ordered, and how many orders must be processed per year?

Solution

Using the basic EOQ model, the optimal order quantity is:

$$q^* = \sqrt{\frac{2C_3 r}{C_1}}$$

where
$$C_3 = \$50 \text{ per order}$$
$$r = (12)(50) = 600 \text{ sets per year}$$
$$C_1 = (.2)(300) = \$60 \text{ per set per year}$$

$$q^* = \sqrt{\frac{(2)(50)(600)}{60}}$$
$$= 31.62 \text{ sets per order}$$

Owing to the relative insensitivity of q^*, we can round q^* up or down with little effect. Let $q^* = 32$ sets per order. This means that the number of orders processed per year is:

$$N = 600/32 = 18.75 \text{ orders}$$

Problem Statement

A basket factory has decided to try and apply an inventory model to its most popular item. Demand is fairly deterministic at a rate of 5,000 baskets per month. Lead time is zero and no shortages are allowed by management. The factory can produce the baskets at a rate of 15,000 per month. Carrying costs are $.20 per basket per year, and setup costs are $100. What is the optimal lot size?

Solution

Using the finite replenishment-rate model:

$$q^* = \frac{\sqrt{2rC_3/C_1}}{\sqrt{1 - r/p}}$$

where r = annual demand = (5,000 baskets per mo.)(12) = 60,000 baskets
          C_3 = setup cost = \$100
          C_1 = per-basket carrying cost per year = \$.20
          p = replenishment rate = 15,000 baskets/mo.

$$q^* = \frac{\sqrt{(2)(60,000)(100)/.2}}{\sqrt{1 - (5,000/15,000)}}$$

$$\cong 948.7 \text{ baskets}$$

The minimum cost of implementing an order quantity of 949 is:

$$C^* = \sqrt{2rC_1C_3} \sqrt{1 - r/p}$$

$$= \$1264.94$$

Problem Statement

A glass company has patented an extra-strength glass and currently sells it in 25-square-foot sheets. Because the product is patented, being out of stock does not result in a lost sale. A stockout, however, is bad for customer goodwill, and management has assigned a stockout cost of \$50 per sheet per month. The sheets cost \$1,000 to make, but because of the unusual process, orders can be filled in less than one day. Demand for the glass has averaged 150 sheets per month. Annual holding costs for the company are assumed to be 15 percent of the value of inventory. Lot sizes are 150 sheets (owing to production scheduling, the hi-test glass can be produced only once monthly). The pertinent question is, What is the optimal order level?

$$S^* = \frac{q_p C_2}{C_1 + C_2}$$

where q_p = 150 sheets
                      C_2 = (50)(12) = \$600
                      C_1 = (1,000)(.15) = \$150

$$S^* = \frac{(150)(600)}{150 + 600}$$

$$= 120$$

In other words, backorders would reach 30 sheets of glass before inventory was replenished.

The cost of the above inventory policy is:

$$C^* = \frac{C_1 S^2}{2q_p} + \frac{C_2(q_p - S)^2}{2q_p}$$

$$= \frac{(150)(120)^2}{2(150)} + \frac{600(150 - 120)^2}{2(150)}$$

$$= \$9{,}000$$

REVIEW QUESTIONS

1. List four reasons for carrying inventory.
2. Why is it critical to manage an organization's inventory effectively?
3. What are the two major functions that must be performed in order to effectively control an organization's inventory?
4. In your own words, explain the rationale behind ABC analysis.
5. Classify inventory accounting systems into two categories.
6. Distinguish between real-time inventory control systems and batch-processing systems.
7. Why is it likely that the number of real-time inventory systems will increase in the future?
8. What is the object of inventory models?
9. What are the two major decision variables in inventory models?
10. Describe the three components of inventory cost.
11. Briefly explain the five basic steps in analyzing an inventory system.
12. Why is the determination of system properties so important?
13. What is meant by demand patterns?
14. Define *lead time*.
15. Distinguish between stochastic demand and deterministic demand.
16. Define *replenishment period*.
17. Distinguish between order level and reorder level.
18. Why is it sometimes necessary to simulate an inventory system?
19. Why is sensitivity analysis an important step in analyzing inventory systems?
20. List the assumptions of the basic EOQ model.
21. Distinguish between finite and infinite replenishment rate.
22. What is the major difference between the basic EOQ model and the basic order-level model?
23. Why is simulation often used for inventory problems?

24. What are two major disadvantages of using a simulation approach to inventory problems?

25. What distinguishes a management information system from an inventory accounting system?

26. Why haven't inventory models been more widely applied?

PROBLEMS

1. Given the following information, perform an ABC analysis on the data. Discuss your results.

ITEM NO.	ANNUAL DEMAND	COST PER UNIT IN DOLLARS
157	100	25
222	50	30
315	1,000	50
719	250	15
244	300	20
367	400	25
219	2,000	20
234	345	20
577	500	25
619	750	10
621	1,000	35
322	900	5
357	432	10
192	150	15
334	225	30

2. You are asked by the manager of a blood bank to study its inventory problem and make recommendations for optimizing costs. The manager has been taking some night courses; he has been taught the following formula and wonders if it might be applied to the problem:

$$q^* = \sqrt{2C_3r/C_1}$$

Specifically, do the following:
   a. Indicate to the manager what an inventory model is meant to do.
   b. Discuss properties of this inventory problem.
   c. Recommend use of the aforementioned formula or state specific reasons why it shouldn't be used.

3. A drill-rig company has a contract with Saudi Arabia to produce 60 drill rigs during the next year. The plan is to produce these rigs at a rate of five per month. A valve used in the drill rig is purchased off the shelf from a nearby supplier; no lead time is required. Each drill rig requires four valves. The valves cost $100 each. Holding cost for the valves is $10 per year per valve. In addition, it costs $75 to order these valves and receive them from the vendor.
    a. What is the optimal order quantity?
    b. What is the optimal number of orders per year?
    c. How frequent should the orders be?
    d. What is the total inventory cost of ordering the optimal order quantity?
    e. Perform a limited amount of sensitivity analysis on the order quantity.

4. An automobile manufacturer plans to produce 30,000 cars in the next month. All cars planned for production use the same headlamps; therefore, demand for the headlights for the next month is known to be 60,000. The purchasing agent wants to know how many headlamps to buy at one time. Historically, headlamps have been received on the same day they were ordered. It costs $35 to order headlamps, and the carrying-cost fraction used by the auto company is 15% per year. The lamps cost $.87 each.
    a. What is the optimal order quantity?
    b. What is the optimal number of orders per year?
    c. What is the frequency of orders? Assume 22 working days.
    d. What is the total inventory cost of ordering the optimal order quantity?
    e. Show the inventory cost for q's of 10,000, 20,000, 25,000, 30,000, and 40,000 units.

5. a. Referring to problem 3, what should the drill-rig company do if lead time is one month rather than zero? In other words, what should the inventory policy be?
    b. Does the existence of lead time change the total inventory cost of the valves? If so, what is the total cost of the new inventory policy?

6. Management has decided to make the valves in problem 3 rather than buy them from an outside vendor. The demand is for 240 valves for the next year, or 20 valves per month. To make the valves costs the company $90 each, and setup time amounts to $100 per set up. Holding cost remains at $10 per valve. Since these valves are not being bought off the shelf, replenishment of inventory is not simultaneous. In fact, the production department says it can produce 200 valves per month given present human and capital resources.
    a. What is the optimal order quantity?
    b. What is the optimal number of setups per year?
    c. What is the optimal time between orders? Assume 250 working days.
    d. What is the total inventory cost of the optimal order policy?

7. The automobile manufacturer in problem 4 has decided to make the headlamps. It has been determined that 150,000 headlamps per month can be produced; but owing to various resource constraints, management has decided to buy half the necessary quantity of headlamps and make the other half. It costs the company $.75 to make each headlamp, and setup costs are $50 per setup. Refer to problem 4 for the parameters of the purchasing decision.

a. What is the optimal order quantity to be purchased from the outside supplier?
b. What is the EOQ for in-house production?
c. What is the total inventory cost for the headlamps?
d. What is the optimal number of purchase orders per month?
e. What is the optimal number of production runs per month?

8. A mail-order stereo firm reviews its stock of amplifiers each month and orders for the next month. Its most popular amp last year was the SEA-700. Last year, 600 amps were sold; these sales were spread evenly throughout the year. Predictions are that this year's sales will be approximately the same. Lead time from the manufacturer is effectively zero, and no sales are lost owing to shortages; instead, the amps are merely delivered one month later. A recent market survey revealed that 60 percent of the customers surveyed would not buy amps again from this firm if they were made to wait an extra month. Profit on an SEA-700 amp is $50. Management, therefore, has estimated stockout cost to be .6 (profit on two future sales), or $60, or $720 per amp per year. Holding cost per amp is $75 per year.
   a. What is the optimal order level?
   b. What is the minimum inventory cost for the SEA-700 amp?
   c. What is the order-level sensitivity?

9. A deluxe bicycle store sells a particular model men's bike for $200. The bike costs the store $150, including selling cost. The wholesale cost of the bike is $125. Demand for the bike is stochastic; past demand is reflected in the following table:

MONTHLY DEMAND	FREQUENCY
0	1
1	3
2	6
3	7
4	8
5	11
6	7
7	5
8	2
	50

Total demand for one year is forecast to be 52 units. Stockout cost is assumed to be the profit lost, or $50. Lead time is one month. Ordering costs are $50 per order. Carrying cost is 20% per year of the inventory value.
   a. What is the best inventory policy for the bicycle in this problem?
   b. What are the expected stockout and incremental carrying costs of the selected inventory policy?

10. Given the policy you recommended in problem 9, simulate manually one year's activity. Interpret your simulation results. Assume a beginning inventory of ten units.

11. A small charter airline company wants to know how much aviation fuel to buy. Demand for flight fuel has been somewhat constant at 50,000 gallons per month. Fuel costs are $.75 per gallon, and the company's annual carrying-cost fraction is .10. If it costs $100 to get a delivery with no lead time required:
     a. What is the optimal order quantity?
     b. What assumption did you make in answering *a* above?
     c. If storage capacity for the fuel were limited to 10,000 gallons, how would you analyze the problem?

12. Demand for pacemakers has been running at a rate of ten per month. The cost of a pacemaker to the hospital is $1,000. It costs $50 to place an order, and the hospital's carrying annual cost is 12% of inventory value.
     a. What information would you need to determine the optimal order quantity?
     b. Assuming the basic EOQ model, what are $q*$ and the minimum inventory cost?
     c. If lead time were seven days, what is the proper reorder point, assuming a constant rate of demand?

13. If lead time for the pacemakers in problem 12 is one day and daily demand is distributed according to the following table, what is the reorder point if stockouts are not allowed?

DAILY DEMAND	PROBABILITY
0	.30
1	.40
2	.15
3	.10
4	.05
	1.00

14. A sawmill has been operating at peak capacity for several years. To keep the mill running takes 2,000 trees per day. The supplier of raw material (trees) can deliver only 10,000 trees per day. Trees cost an average of $100. Ordering costs are extremely high at $5,000 per order. The annual carrying cost fraction is 12%. Assume a 365-day operation of the mill.
     a. What is the optimal order quantity?
     b. What is the total inventory cost?
     c. What assumption about system properties did you make in calculating the optimal order quantity?

Case: BLANCHARD IMPORTING
AND DISTRIBUTING CO., INC.*

Upon completing his first year at the Harvard Business School, Hank Hatch accepted summer employment with Blanchard Importing and Distributing Co., Inc., a Boston firm which dealt in the processing and wholesaling of alcoholic beverages. Early in June 1972, Hank had met with Toby Tyler, the general manager of the company, who was a recent graduate of the Harvard Business School. Toby had described the initial tasks which he wished Hank to perform, as follows:

> Hank, during your first few days at Blanchard, I'd like you to become familiar with the general scope of operations of the firm. As you investigate our various product lines, I think you will find that the most rapidly expanding demand for alchoholic beverages is in the wine market. At the present time we estimate that we can earn a before-tax return of 20% on any money we put into wine merchandising. However, to date, Carmen Petrillo, our Wine Division manager, and Dave Rubin, the Sales Department manager, have been unable to exploit this trend due to lack of funds needed to hire experienced wine salesmen and build up an adequate inventory of wines. Here is a recent balance sheet [see Table 10-15] which shows that we have just about reached the limit of our borrowing capability. It appears that a reduction in inventory level is the only substantial source of funds available to us. That's where you come in.
>
> After you've become acquainted with our operations, I'd like you to spend some time analyzing the inventory situation and recommend ways in which we can economize in that area. Initially, you can look into the method we use in scheduling production runs of those beverages which we bottle ourselves. The current scheduling system, which was initiated in October 1969, calls for bottling of an Economic Order Quantity (EOQ) of an item when the stock level of that item falls below a fixed Re-order Point (ROP). This Re-order Point trigger level is equal to 3 1/2 weeks' worth of the average weekly demand throughout the year ending October 31, 1969. I suspect that many of

Table 10-15 Blanchard Importing and Distributing Co., Inc. Balance Sheet as of January 31, 1972 (in thousands)

ASSETS		EQUITY	
Current Assets:		Current Liabilities:	
Cash	24	Payroll Withheld	1
A/R (net)	483	Unsecured Notes Payable	809
Inventory*	1,050	Accounts Payable	173
Prepaid Expenses	32	Federal Distilled Spirits	337
		Taxes Payable	
Total Current		Accrued Taxes	40
Assets	1,589	Accrued Expenses	11
Fixed Assets:		Total Current Liabilities	1,371
Plant and equipment,	287	Long-Term Debt	64
net of depreciation		Total Liabilities	1,435
Registered trademarks	8	Stockholders' Equity:	
Total Fixed Assets	295	Capital Stock	100
		Retained Earnings	349
Total Assets	1,884	Total Equity	1,884

*Inventory was subdivided into the following categories:

Finished case goods (uncontrolled stock)	311
Finished case goods (controlled stock)	362
Customs bond (raw bulk and uncontrolled finished case goods stock)	171
IRS bond (raw bulk)	175
Miscellaneous (bottles, cartons, labels, flavors, etc.)	31

the EOQ and ROP quantities calculated in 1969 should be recalculated based on changes in annual demand over the past 2 1/2 years. As a first assignment you can update the EOQ and ROP figures. While you're at it, keep thinking about ways in which we can reduce expenses and cut back on unnecessarily high stock levels—any cash which can be made available for wine merchandising will be greatly appreciated by Carmen and Dave.

BACKGROUND

Product Lines

During the first week of June, Hank learned that Blanchard was a full-line alcoholic beverage house which distributed both imported and domestic goods including wine, beer, distilled spirits, cordials, and pre-mixed cocktails. Blanchard purchased pre-bottled goods (called "uncontrolled stock") for resale to retail outlets at wholesale prices. Uncontrolled stock accounted for 45% of the firm's annual sales. The remaining 55% of Blanchard's revenue was attributed to sale of "controlled stock," those items which Blanchard bottled and sold under its own brands and private labels.

In June 1972, controlled stock consisted of 158 products which Blanchard processed in its own bottling facility. These 158 items were differentiated by bottle size, type and proof of beverage, and brand label. Blanchard produced 25 items in half-gallons, 63 in quarts, 42 in fifths, 12 in pints, and 16 in half-pints.

History of the Firm

The Blanchard name was originally established as a chain of retail liquor stores, the first of which was opened in 1938 by John D. Corey. In 1957, Mr. Corey became interested in the wholesaling of alcoholic beverages and began distributing case goods to retail outlets. In order to devote his full efforts to this new venture, he transferred ownership of the chain of Blanchard retail outlets to other members of the Corey family. In 1964, the present warehouse and office facility was completed, and in 1966, equipment was installed to permit the conversion of raw bulk spirits to bottled goods for sale under the firm's own brands and private labels. When Mr. Corey died in 1968, his son, John D. Corey, Jr., assumed responsibilities as president and treasurer of the company. As of June 1972, the firm's annual revenue was $4 million, of which $3 million represented sales to the seven Blanchard retail stores owned by other members of the Corey family.

Warehouse Layout

Figure 10-11 depicts the layout of the recently completed Blanchard warehouse. Most of the warehouse space was set aside for stocks of bottled case goods. These areas included a large margin for future growth, and actual finished-goods inventories had never occupied more than 50% of the reserved space.

In addition to the areas set aside for storage of finished case goods, space was occupied by two U.S. bonded warehouses and the rectification and bottling equipment used for processing controlled stock. The government required that all products imported to the United States by Blanchard, including both pre-bottled goods and raw bulk spirits, enter the Blanchard facility by way of the Customs Bonded Warehouse. In addition, all the raw bulk spirits which Blanchard purchased for processing in its bottling operation were required to pass through the IRS Bonded Warehouse prior to rectification. The flow of goods into and out of the two bonded warehouses was closely monitored by federal officials to ensure that the required tax and customs duty obligations were met by the company.

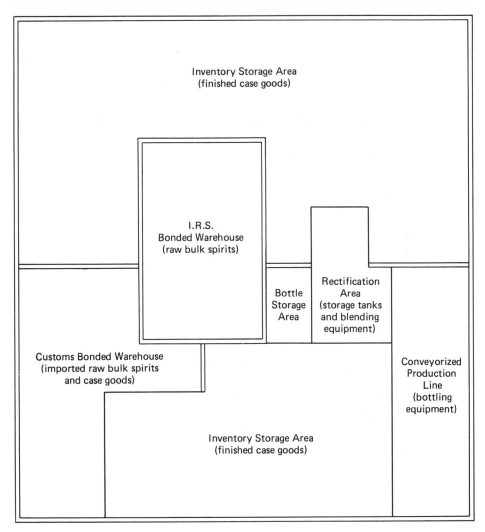

FIGURE 10-11   Blanchard Importing and Distributing Co., Inc.,
Warehouse Layout

CONVERSION OF RAW BULK SPIRITS
INTO BOTTLED CASE GOODS

In preparation for his first assignment, Hank made a thorough study of the
method used by Blanchard to process controlled stock. Hank learned that two
salaried employees, Bob Young and Eliot Wallace, were in charge of this operation. Bob Young, a skilled machinery operator, had worked for Blanchard since

1969, and Eliot Wallace, a chemistry expert with a degree in food technology, had worked for Blanchard for seven years. The combined annual wage of these two employees was $23,000. Bob and Eliot explained that the conversion process followed three steps: withdrawal of raw spirits from bulk storage, rectification of the spirits, and bottling of the finished product.

Withdrawal from Bulk Storage

Raw bulk was purchased by the barrel and stored either in the Customs Warehouse or the IRS Warehouse, depending on whether the spirits were imported or domestic. When a bottling run called for use of a particular type of raw bulk, Bob and Eliot withdrew the spirits from one of the two bonded warehouses and pumped it into mixing tanks for rectification; imports were withdrawn from the Customs Warehouse via the IRS Warehouse, incurring both a customs duty and federal distilled spirits tax liability, while domestic spirits incurred only the federal distilled spirits tax liability upon withdrawal from IRS Warehouse storage.

Rectification

Rectification of withdrawn bulk consisted of diluting the spirits with distilled water to attain the desired "proof," mixing several different types of spirits to form combinations such as blended whiskey, and adding nonalcoholic ingredients to yield cocktails such as screwdrivers and whiskey sours. Eliot Wallace was responsible for performing chemical tests on each rectified beverage to verify that the appropriate ratio of ingredients had been established before releasing the beverage to the bottling line.

Bottling

The bottling operation utilized a fully automated conveyorized line of equipment, including machines which filled each bottle, screwed on a cap, attached a brand label, and affixed the government seal which protected the consuming public against unauthorized opening of a container following bottling. Since 1966, the demand for controlled stock items had required operation of the bottling line less than one out of every three available working days. Thus, the capacity of the bottling line equipment was more than adequate to support the current level of sales. Bob Young was responsible for maintenance and repair of this equipment and verified the setup of each machine prior to initiating a bottling run.

Bob Young and Eliot Wallace worked together in completing all preparations for a bottling run, including the withdrawal and rectification of spirits and the setup of the bottling equipment for each size and label combination. When preparations were complete, Bob and Eliot were joined by five part-time workers drawn from the local area who were each paid $2.50 per hour. While Bob and Eliot supervised overall operation of the bottling line, these five laborers packed filled bottles into cartons, labeled and stamped each carton with appropriate information, and stacked the cartons on pallets for transfer to the controlled stock case goods storage area. The five temporary laborers were paid soon after completion of the bottling run.

Tax and Customs Duty Considerations

It was the practice at Blanchard to delay withdrawal of bulk spirits from storage in the two bonded warehouses until just before the start of a bottling run to avoid incurring tax and custom duty liabilities earlier than necessary. Consequently, the length of time between withdrawal of bulk spirits from storage and transfer of the bottled product to finished case goods storage never exceeded one week.

In addition to the federal distilled spirits tax and customs duty charge, two other taxes were levied against alcoholic beverages: a federal rectification tax was incurred during blending of certain items, depending on the mixing process, and a state tax was incurred upon sale of the finished product by Blanchard. Federal and state regulations required the company to pay the customs duty charge, federal rectification tax, and state tax within a few days after these liabilities were incurred; however, payment of the federal distilled spirits tax was not required until one month after sale.

FORMAL EOQ/ROP SCHEDULING SYSTEM

Before making corrections to the EOQ and ROP figures for each of the 158 items bottled by Blanchard, Hank located the documents showing how the formal scheduling system was developed in 1969. These records, which are reproduced in Table 10-16, indicate the general method used to determine EOQ and ROP quantities for each Blanchard product. During his review of the system, Hank made the following observations about the inputs to the EOQ calculations:

Setup Costs, *S*

Blending setup cost was based on the annual salaries of Bob Young and Eliot Wallace and the length of time required for these men to withdraw the appropriate spirits from bulk storage and complete rectification for a given item.

Table 10-16   Blanchard Importing and Distributing Co., Inc. EOQ and ROP Calculation Method

$$\text{EOQ} = \sqrt{\frac{2RS}{CK}} \qquad\qquad \text{ROP} = \frac{3.5}{52} \times R$$

where:

Annual Demand, R:
Demand for an item for year ending October 31, 1969, in cases of bottles.

Setup Cost, S:
Setup cost per bottle run of an item.

S = blending setup cost + size changeover cost + label change-over cost + order processing cost.

Blending setup cost = actual cost of labor for blending during rectification and is different for each item.

Size changeover cost = average cost of labor to reset all machines for a change in bottle size and is a constant $8.85 for all 158 items.

Label changeover cost = average cost of labor to reset labeling machine for a change in labels and is a constant $11.78 for all 158 items.

Order processing cost = average cost of administrative labor to process an order for a bottling run and is a constant $51.43 for all 158 items.

Unit Cost, C:
Cost per case of bottles of an item after bottling and packaging.

C = materials cost + bottling labor + fixed overhead allocation + variable overhead + customs duty + federal distilled spirits tax + federal rectification tax.

Materials cost = cost of raw bulk, bottles, caps, and labels.

Bottling labor = cost of part-time bottling line labor per case of bottles produced and is a constant $0.10 per case for all 158 items.

Fixed overhead allocation = total company fixed overhead for the year divided by the number of cases sold per year and is a constant $1.31 per case for all 158 items.

Variable overhead = total direct expense (other than material and direct labor costs) resulting from production of one case of an item and is a constant $.50 per case for all 158 items.

Customs duty = charge on imported spirits and varies with the alcoholic content of the beverage.

Federal distilled spirits tax = IRS tax on all spirits sold in the United States and varies with the alcoholic content of the beverage.

Federal rectification tax = IRS tax on certain mixed beverages and varies with the alcoholic content of the item.

Carrying Cost Percentage, K:
Percent of average inventory value which represents annual cost of carrying inventory of an item.

K = cost of capital + other carrying costs.

Cost of capital = 9% for all items.

Other carrying costs, including estimated costs of obsolescence, shrinkage, insurance, and year-end inventory tax = 2.5% for all items.

Size changeover cost equaled the cost of resetting all machinery for a change in bottle size divided by the average number of different items of a given size processed between size changeovers.[1] The cost of resetting all machines for a change in bottle size was based on the annual salaries of Bob and Eliot and the fact that it took these two men one full day to complete all the machinery adjustments required for a size changeover.

Label changeover cost was based on the average length of time that the bottling line was shut down to change from one label to another label of a given bottle size. This idle time was assumed to be 30 minutes, which included 20 minutes to reset the labeling machine and 10 minutes to restore the labeling machine to continuous error-free operation following the change in labels. Since the part-time bottling laborers remained idle during the label changeover, the cost of this 30 minutes of downtime was based on both the hourly wage rate of these five workers and the annual salaries of Bob and Eliot.

Order-processing cost equaled the yearly cost of two office workers, who earned a combined annual salary of $18,000, divided by the total number of separate item-bottling runs per year. These two clerks worked full time processing the customs duty forms, federal tax forms, state tax forms, and other paperwork required to support the bottling operation.

Unit Cost, *C*

Blanchard used a standard form titled "Cost and Price Data" to determine the wholesale price per case of each item. This price was based on a "full unit cost" figure, which included all direct expenses incurred in producing and selling an item plus an allocation of the total fixed expenses of the company. Since the state tax liability was not incurred until sale of the finished product, the "unit cost" used in the EOQ formula was determined by deducting the state tax from the "full unit cost" figure shown on the Cost and Price Data form.

Carrying Cost Percentage, *K*

The only substantial component of the inventory carrying cost was the cost of capital. Equity was not considered a source of funds, since all common stock was privately held by John D. Corey, Jr., who wished to maintain full control of the company. As a result, the cost of capital was assumed to be 9%, the prevailing interest rate for debt available to Blanchard. Components of the

---

[1] In a typical year, Blanchard operated the bottling line for 77 days during the year. The bottling equipment was adjusted approximately 35 times during the year for a change in bottle size; however, an average of 10 different items of a given bottle size were processed between size changeovers, resulting in about 350 separate item-bottling runs during the year.

carrying cost percentage other than cost of capital were small and amounted to only 2.5%.

ACTUAL SCHEDULING SYSTEM IN USE

Hank decided to make his first corrections to EOQ and ROP figures for the items to be produced during an upcoming bottling run. He learned that Bob and Eliot planned to bottle the following items during the last week in June:

NO. OF CASES TO BE BOTTLED	ITEM	NO. OF CASES ON HAND AS OF JUNE 20, 1972
1,000	Blanchard's 80 proof Vodka (quarts)	144
600	Blanchard's 80 proof Gin (quarts)	55
60	MacCoy & MacCoy 86 proof Scotch (quarts)	54
120	Triple 7 86 proof Blended Whiskey (quarts)	301
50	Blanchard's 80 proof Ron Cores Rum (quarts)	45

Hank then located the Cost and Price Data and the original EOQ and ROP Calculation Sheets for these five items and summarized the data in tabular form (see Tables 10-17 and 10-18). Hank compared the annual demand for the year ending October 31, 1969 (see Table 10-18) with the monthly sales summary report for the fiscal year ending January 31, 1972 (see Table 10-19) and noted significant shifts in demand between the years ending October 1969 and January 1972, especially for the MacCoy & MacCoy Scotch and Ron Cores Rum products.

On June 21, Hank finished recalculating the EOQ and ROP figures and decided to find out how the schedule for the upcoming bottling run had actually been determined. He found Bob and Eliot in the blending area, where they were withdrawing corn spirits from the IRS Warehouse prior to rectification of Triple 7 Blended Whiskey, and questioned them about the schedule:

HANK: How did you decide on these particular items for next week's run, Bob?

BOB: Well, every week the computerized inventory control system issues us a card for each item that has dropped below the 3 1/2-week ROP stock level. As of yesterday, we had several half-gallon and quart items which have dropped below their ROP levels, including the vodka and gin quart products scheduled for bottling next week.

Table 10-17   Blanchard Importing and Distributing Co., Inc. Summary of Cost and Price Data
                    (in $ per case)

	BLAN-CHARD'S 80 PROOF VODKA	BLAN-CHARD'S 80 PROOF GIN	MacCOY & MacCOY 86 PROOF SCOTCH	TRIPLE 7 86 PROOF BLENDED WHISKEY	BLAN-CHARD'S 80 PROOF RON CORES RUM
Wholesale price	$43.99	$43.99	$57.39	$49.87	$47.39
Materials—beverage	.93	1.08	4.46	2.52	2.74
Materials—packaging	1.27	1.27	1.27	1.27	1.27
Direct labor	.10	.10	.10	.10	.10
State tax	10.08	10.08	10.08	10.08	10.08
Federal distilled spirits tax	25.20	25.20	27.09	27.09	25.20
Federal rectification tax				.76	
Customs duty			1.55		
Variable overhead	.50	.50	.50	.50	.50
Fixed overhead allocation	1.31	1.31	1.31	1.31	1.31
Full unit cost	$39.39	$39.54	$46.36	$43.63	$41.20
Profit before income tax	$4.60	$4.45	$11.03	$6.24	$6.19

HANK: Why don't you bottle both the half-gallon and quart items next
           week?

BOB: It takes Eliot and me just about one full day to make all the
           adjustments to the bottling equipment required for a size change.
           Consequently, we limit each bottling run to a single size and
           process several combinations of beverages and labels in that size
           during the run. Since quarts are our most popular size, we plan to
           bottle only quarts next week. We'll try to make a run of half-
           gallons in three weeks. Hopefully, the 3 1/2-week advance notice
           will keep us from stocking out of any half-gallon items.

HANK: What about the rum, whiskey, and Scotch quart products: How
           did they get added to the schedule?

ELIOT: After we decided to bottle quarts based on the low gin and vodka
           inventories, we checked the stock level for each of the remaining
           61 quart items. We're going to try to make a run of quarts every
           four weeks for the next two months. So the June 20 stock level of
           any quart item which we *don't* schedule for bottling next week has
           to last at least six weeks until the following run is completed at the

Table 10-18 Blanchard Importing and Distributing Co., Inc. Summary of EOQ and ROP Calculation Sheet Data

	BLENDING SETUP COST	ALL OTHER SETUP COSTS	TOTAL SETUP COST (S)	ANNUAL DEMAND (R)	CARRYING COST % (K)	UNIT COST (C)*	EOQ $\sqrt{\dfrac{2RS}{CK}}$	ROP $\left[\dfrac{3.5}{52} \times R\right]$
Blanchard's 80 proof Vodka	$1.15	$72.06	$73.21	2,455	11.5%	$29.31	327	165
Blanchard's 80 proof Gin	1.08	72.06	73.14	1,421	11.5%	29.46	248	96
MacCoy & MacCoy 86 proof Scotch	3.24	72.06	75.30	800	11.5%	36.28	170	54
Triple 7 86 proof Blended Whiskey	2.62	72.06	74.68	3,096	11.5%	33.55	346	208
Blanchard's 80 proof Ron Cores Rum	2.33	72.06	74.39	449	11.5%	31.12	137	30

*Unit Cost (C) = Full Unit Cost (see Table 10-17) minus State Tax (see Table 10-7).

Table 10-19 Blanchard Importing and Distributing Co., Inc. Monthly Sales Summary Data (in Cases of Quart Bottles) (February 1971–May 1972)

		FEB.	MAR.	APR.	MAY	JUNE	JULY	AUG.	SEPT.	OCT.	NOV.	DEC.	JAN.	YEAR TOTAL
Blanchard's 80 proof Vodka	(1971)	128	136	233	219	284	343	368	230	162	246	252	114	2,715
	(1972)	210	303	275	463									
Blanchard's 80 proof Gin	(1971)	51	52	74	157	150	257	179	83	72	89	181	42	1,387
	(1972)	166	142	133	213									
MacCoy & MacCoy 86 proof Scotch	(1971)	79	82	151	66	127	96	85	61	67	103	131	39	1,087
	(1972)	82	68	66	38									
Briple 7 86 proof Blended Whiskey	(1971)	163	180	198	183	217	207	186	171	205	266	257	654	2,887
	(1972)	177	163	162	256									
Blanchard's 80 proof Ron Cores Rum	(1971)	10	34	44	26	33	35	51	16	15	26	43	22	355
	(1972)	11	28	61	55									

end of July. The stocks of MacCoy Scotch, Triple 7 Whiskey, and Ron Cores Rum were all below the six-week level when we checked yesterday, so we added them to the list.

HANK: How do you minimize the length of time that the line is idle when you shift from one item to another?

ELIOT: We process the lighter beverages first, so that we can switch from one item to the next with only a few bottles of distilled water in between to rinse the bottling machine. As a result, the bottling machine is ready after about only eight minutes of rinsing. We have sixteen tanks for storing rectified beverages prior to bottling which have a combined volume equivalent to 10,000 cases of half-gallons, quarts, pints, or half-pints. This is more than enough storage capacity for all items scheduled for a single bottling run. Since Bob and I finish rectification of all beverages during the week before a scheduled bottling run, each item is always ready when the schedule calls for bottling to begin. No adjustment for bottle shape is necessary, since we only run one size at a time and each size has a standard shape. That leaves label changeover as the controlling item; right, Bob?

BOB: Yes, every time we shift from one item to the next, I have to adjust the labeling machine and load in a stack of labels for the new item. This takes about 20 minutes, and during that time, the five part-time workers are idle. Once in a while the labels for two items in a row are the same shape, which permits me to make the change in about three minutes. At any rate, Eliot usually finishes purging the bottling machine and completes the shift to the new blending storage tank well before I have the labeling machine ready to resume bottling.

HANK: Once you have decided on the items you intend to bottle and the order in which you intend to bottle them, how did you determine the number of cases of each item to process? Did you use the EOQ figure that was calculated in 1969 when the scheduling system was originally developed?

BOB: Not exactly, Hank. Since we'll probably be bottling quarts every four weeks for a while, we tried to predict what the demand for each item will be between runs; then we took into account the inventory on hand and scheduled production of enough cases to last until the next scheduled bottling run for quarts.

HANK: How did you go about predicting what the demand for each item will be?

BOB:	We used the data from the monthly sales summary [see Table 10-19] to see what the demand was last month. Then we adjusted this May 1972 sales figure by adding a safety factor to offset any difference between sales in May and July.
HANK:	Then the planned production volume for each of the five items scheduled for bottling next week represents your predicted demand for July, with an adjustment made for the current inventory on hand?
BOB:	Yes, except for the gin and vodka. We're finding it difficult to accurately predict demand for these two items because sales are up substantially from last year. So we've decided to bottle enough gin and vodka to last us *two* months, through the end of August. If our predicted sales volumes for gin and vodka are correct, we can omit production of these products during the July bottling run of quarts and save the cost of blending and label changeover for these two items. However, if demand continues to spiral and exceeds our prediction, we can add these items to the July schedule and avoid a stockout.

CONCLUSION

The day after Hank's discussion with Bob Young and Eliot Wallace, Toby Tyler asked Hank to report what he had accomplisehd on his first assignment and to recommend appropriate action based on his findings. Hank realized that the scheduling system in use bore little resemblance to the formal EOQ/ROP system developed in 1969. In preparation for his meeting with Toby, Hank decided to evaluate the disadvantages of both the original scheduling system and the improvised system developed by Bob and Eliot. Based on this analysis, Hank felt that he could determine if improvements could be made which would warrant adoption of one of the two systems on a permanent basis.

Case Discussion Questions

1. What is wrong with applying the Basic EOQ Model to the inventory problem at Blanchard?
2. Why isn't the EOQ Model currently being used for making replenishment decisions?
3. What are the shortcomings of the present system for determining replenishment quantities and production scheduling?
4. How would you approach the problem?

REFERENCES

BERRY, W.L., "Lot Sizing Procedures for Requirements Planning Systems: A Framework for Analysis," *Production and Inventory Management*, 2nd Quarter 1972, pp. 19–34.

BIERMAN, HAROLD, JR., CHARLES P. BONINI, and WARREN H. HAUSMAN, *Quantitative Analysis for Business Decisions*, 4th ed. Homewood, Ill.: Richard D. Irwin, 1973.

BISHOP, JACK L., JR., "Experience with a Successful System for Forecasting and Inventory Control," *Operations Research*, Vol. 22, No. 6, 1224–31.

BUFFA, ELWOOD S., *Operations Management: The Management of Productive Systems*. New York: Wiley Hamilton, 1976.

———, *Production-Inventory Systems: Planning and Control*. Homewood, Ill.: Richard D. Irwin, 1968.

CHASE, RICHARD B., and NICHOLAS J. AQUILANO, *Production and Operations Management: A Life Cycle Approach*. Homewood, Ill.: Richard D. Irwin, 1977.

HADLEY, GEORGE, and T.M. WHITIN, *Analysis of Inventory Systems*. Englewood Cliffs, N.J.: Prentice-Hall, 1963.

LEE, W.B., and C.P. MCLAUGHLIN, "Corporate Simulation Models for Aggregate Materials Management," *Production and Inventory Management*, 1st Quarter 1974, pp. 55–67.

LEVIN, RICHARD I., and CHARLES A. KIRKPATRICK, *Quantitative Approaches to Management*, 4th ed. New York: McGraw-Hill, 1978.

NADDOR, ELIEZER, *Inventory Systems*. New York: John Wiley, 1966.

SCHMIDT, J.W., and R.E. TAYLOR, *Simulation and Analysis of Industrial Systems*. Homewood, Ill.: Richard D. Irwin, 1970.

SHORE, BARRY, *Operations Management*. New York: McGraw-Hill, 1973.

WAGNER, HARVEY M., *Principles of Operations Research*, 2nd ed. Englewood Cliffs, N.J.: Prentice-Hall, 1975.

WOOLSEY, GENE, "On Doing Good Things and Dumb Things in Production and Inventory Control," *Interfaces*, Vol. 5, No. 3 (May 1975), 66–67.

chapter 11

MATERIALS
REQUIREMENTS
PLANNING

In the preceding chapter, we examined classical statistical inventory methods. These methods are useful for managing distribution inventories or items subject to independent demand. Demand for a given inventory item is independent when it is unrelated to demand for other items. Thus, end products and items stocked to meet customer demand are subject to independent demand. Since independent demand is not known exactly, it must be forecasted, and statistical order-point or EOQ methods are appropriate.

In this chapter, we shall study the *materials requirements planning (MRP)* approach to dependent-demand items. An item has *dependent demand* whenever its demand depends on the demand for another item or product. For example, the demand for automobile engines or transmissions depends directly on the demand for the final product, automobiles. The MRP approach is particularly appropriate for manufacturing operations in which the demand for subassemblies, component parts, and raw materials is dependent upon an end product. These dependent-demand items have a demand pattern that is not smooth over time, but lumpy. Demand that is lumpy occurs in discrete batches at different points in time. This type of pattern is very unlike the steady-demand-rate assumption of the basic EOQ models. Thus, MRP was developed to better cope with the lumpy demand patterns of dependent-demand items.

THE DEVELOPMENT OF MRP

MRP has the distinction of being hailed by many as the new way of life in production and inventory management. It is a methodology that has been developed "on the firing line" in industry rather than by academicians or theoreticians. It has been in use by some companies for many years, and is now finding its way into academic courses. MRP has been successful largely because it addresses some of the basic time-phasing problems that confront the inventory manager. It is concerned with that all-important problem we mentioned in the first chapter: getting the right materials to the right place at the right time.

MRP has grown out of a certain disenchantment of practitioners with classical inventory methods for dependent-demand items. Some practitioners felt a need for better data processing and timing rather than better statistical or mathematical methods. MRP has experienced a very rapid growth and level of acceptance since 1970. Its adoption rate among practitioners is growing faster than that of any other inventory control method. This growth is partly attributed to the "MRP crusade" carried out by the APICS (American Production and Inventory Control Society). APICS is a 12,000-member professional society for the advancement of the practice of production and inventory management. The APICS effort to promote the utility of MRP was spearheaded by such professionals as Dr. Joseph Orlicky of IBM, Oliver Wight, George Plossl, and Walter Goddard. The list of firms using MRP has grown rapidly from 150 in 1971 to 700 by 1975, and over 1,000 in 1976; all indications are that the list will continue to grow.

THE NATURE OF MRP

MRP is a technique for determining when to order dependent-demand items and how to replan and reschedule orders to adjust for changes in demand estimates from the master production schedule. The MRP system consists of inventory records, bills of material, and usually computer programs that translate the master production schedule into time-phased net requirements and planned coverage of these requirements for each component item needed. Because of the large amounts of data that usually need to be manipulated, MRP systems are computerized; they are, in a sense, a data-processing approach to dependent-demand inventory control. Successful MRP systems are taking the systems approach to inventory; they coordinate not only inventory, but purchasing, manufacturing, scheduling, and planning.

MRP avoids the "averaging process" of statistical inventory methods in managing inventory and calculates a specific quantity of what parts to order and when. Thus, an essential feature of MRP is the *calculation* of exact inventory needs rather than a statistical estimation. The calculation is based on a planned production quantity of an end item and the bill of materials (BOM) for that item, which specifies a list of all subassemblies and parts required to produce the end item. The MRP system interacts with production scheduling to correctly time the release orders for all required items.

The purpose of an MRP system is more than to maintain inventory levels by ordering the right quantities of items at the right time. A properly functioning MRP system aids in priority and capacity planning. It helps to establish valid order due dates and order priorities; it also maintains order priority by revising due dates that have been invalidated. An MRP system is an integral part of the priority planning system. It provides valuable information for both purchasing and production operations. However, it cannot cause due dates for purchasing or operations to be met. Thus, MRP must be supplemented by a priority control system in the factory. The control system provides the means to enforce adherence to plans.

A primary tool of priority control is the dispatching list or departmental schedule, which indicates the relative priorities of jobs. The list is based on operations priorities, which are closely tied to the order priorities. Thus, the priority control systems for both dispatching and purchasing cannot function effectively without an information base that maintains timely and valid due dates. MRP can provide this information and the key to a systems approach to manufacturing operations.

MRP, in conjunction with capacity planning, has already been mentioned in Chapter 9 on aggregate planning. By utilizing future tentative production quantities as specified by the master schedule, MRP systems can generate load reports for production work centers by period of time. Unrealistic load reports signal that a revision is required in the master production schedule. The MRP load report can be used repetitively to ensure manageable production quantities and the capability to plan accurately for the future. Figure 11-1 illustrates the MRP system in relation to priority and capacity planning.

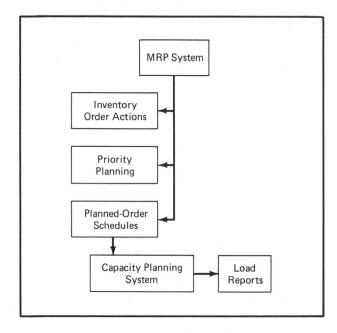

FIGURE 11-1 Priority and Capacity Planning in MRP

Prerequisites and Assumptions of MRP

MRP is primarily intended for manufacturing operations and has been used in such general applications as assembly operations, general machine shops, and fabrication assembly operations. It can be applied to any operation provided that certain assumptions or prerequisites are satisfied. The following conditions are the primary prerequisites for using MRP:

1. The existence of a realistic master production schedule that can be stated in bill-of-material terms.
2. An accurate bill of material for each product that not only lists all components of the product, but also reflects how the product is actually made in steps.
3. Having each inventory item identified with a unique code or part number.
4. Data-file integrity pertaining to inventory status data and bill-of-material data. The system will not function properly without accurate input data.
5. Known lead times on all inventory items.

Benefits and Costs of MRP

The benefits and costs of using an MRP system will vary with individual companies, and efficiency increases will depend on how well the company was doing with its previous inventory system. However, successful adopters of MRP have noted the following potential benefits:

1. Lower inventories. The ability to plan ahead and the flexibility to reschedule rather than maintain large safety stocks allows significant reduction in inventory levels; reductions of up to 50% are not unusual.
2. Improved customer service. The percentage of late orders and stockouts is reduced, sometimes up to 75%.
3. Reduced overtime and idle time—the result of smoother and better planned production.
4. Reduced sales price and improved response to market demands.
5. Ability to modify the master schedule and respond to unanticipated changes in demand.
6. Ability to aid in capacity and priority planning. MRP not only aids the expediting of "hot orders," but also helps in de-expediting orders that must be delayed.
7. Reduced subcontracting the purchasing costs.

The largest cost or disadvantage of any MRP system is the cost of purchasing or leasing a computer system to support the function. However, with increasing inventory and production costs, along with decreasing computation costs, an MRP system is getting easier to justify. An MRP system will also require personnel with MRP expertise and computer programmers to interact with the system, although the actual MRP system software is usually purchased from major computer manufacturers. Additional costs include system maintenance costs and the trials and tribulations of a system changeover.

But once functioning smoothly, the MRP system offers really significant advantages to weigh against the costs. The actual benefits depend upon how bad the performance of the current system really is. For example, one company that had some serious inventory problems installed an MRP system and achieved a 12 percent reduction in finished inventories, a work-in-process inventory reduction of 30 percent, and a 35 percent increase in the number of on-time deliveries.[1]

Illustration of Lumpy Demand

Having briefly discussed the nature of MRP and its potential benefits, let's look at an example of dependent or lumpy demand (requirements) to demonstrate the superiority of MRP in handling this type of inventory problem. Let us assume we are to

---

[1]Jeffrey G. Miller and Linda G. Sprague, "Behind the Growth in Materials Requirements Planning," *Harvard Business Review*, September–October 1975, pp. 83–91.

produce a final product A whose demand is uniform at the rate of four units per week. From Figure 11-2, which illustrates the product structure tree for product A, we can see that it takes one unit of component B and two units of component C to make one unit of A. Also, each B requires three Ds, and each C requires one. Even though demand for product A is uniform, the production of A occurs in lot sizes of 20 units every five weeks. This is shown in Figure 11-3.

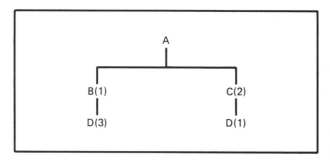

FIGURE 11-2   Product Structure for A

	Week 1	Week 2	Week 3	Week 4	Week 5	Week 6
Demand for Product A	4	4	4	4	4	4
Production	20					20

FIGURE 11-3   Master Production Schedule for Product A

Given that 20 units of A take one week to produce and that parts B, C, and D have lead times (for internal production or external ordering) of two, four, and one week respectively, when should we release orders so that 20 units of A can be ready for distribution at the end of week 6? We are faced with the basic problem of time phasing and getting the right parts to the right place at the right time.

In order to have 20 units of product A ready at the end of week 6 (we are concentrating only on these 20 units in week 6), we can see from the product structure in Figure 11-2 that we will need 20 units of B and 2 × 20 = 40 units of C at the beginning of week 6. Given the lead times of B and C, we should place orders for 20 units of B at the beginning of week 4 and 40 units of C at the beginning of week 2. This in turn would require 60 units of D to be ordered (for the assembly of B) at the beginning of week 2 and 40 units of D to be ordered at the beginning of week 1. These order release dates are summarized in Figure 11-4. Looking at the gross requirements for part D in that figure, we see that the requirements follow a "lumpy pattern" of 0 40 0 20 0 0. In spite of the fact that the demand for the end product A is uniform at four per week, the resulting dependent demand for part D is quite lumpy.

Figure 11-5 illustrates the large amount of error that can result in trying to

Item B Leadtime 2 weeks	Week					
	1	2	3	4	5	6
Gross requirements						20
Planned order releases				20		

Item C Leadtime 4 weeks	1	2	3	4	5	6
Gross requirements						40
Planned order releases		40				

Item D Leadtime 1 week	1	2	3	4	5	6
Gross requirements		40		40		
Planned order releases	40		20			

FIGURE 11-4   Illustration of Lumpy Demand

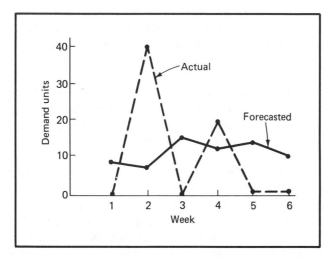

FIGURE 11-5 MRP Calculated Demand versus Statistically Forecasted Demand

statistically forecast demand when in fact you can calculate it after end-item production quantities have been established. The forecast in Figure 11-5 is based on exponential smoothing, where Forecast = Previous period forecast + α(Previous demand − Previous forecast), and α = the smoothing constant. For example, using an α of

.2, and assuming a previous period forecast of 10 units and demand of 0 units, we obtain:

$$\text{Forecast in period } 1 = 10 + .2(0 - 10) = 8$$
$$\text{Forecast in period } 2 = 8 + .2(0 - 8) = 6.4$$
$$\text{Forecast in period } 3 = 6.4 + .2(40 - 6.4) = 14.12$$
$$\text{Forecast in period } 4 = 14.12 + .2(0 - 14.12) = 11.3$$
$$\text{Forecast in period } 5 = 11.3 + .2(20 - 11.3) = 13.0$$
$$\text{Forecast in period } 6 = 13.0 + .2(0 - 13.0) = 10.4$$

It is clear from the figure that dependent-demand quantities should be calculated once firmed production quantities have been determined from the master production schedule.

PRINCIPLES OF MRP

The example above dealing with lumpy demand illustrates the basic process in MRP—working backward from the scheduled completion dates of end products to determine the dates when the various component parts and materials are to be ordered, and the quantities to be ordered. Of course, the example was a simple one, but the basic process is the same for large-scale real-world manufacturing operations.

The calculations of dependent-demand quantities and order dates are performed by the MRP computer program. The computer program is but one aspect of the overall MRP system, whose structure Figure 11-6 depicts. Chronologically, the MRP system begins with the aggregate production plans, which are refined into a master production schedule. Forecasts of independent-demand items such as end products serve as input to aggregate plans and the master schedule. The master schedule is broken into firm and tentative plans. Firm production schedules are needed for short-range time frames covering up to a month or two; tentative production plans may range from a month up to a year. Tentative plans are sometimes revised according to market reactions, new forecasts, and capacity output reports of the MRP computer program.

The MRP computer program has three major sources of input—the master production schedule, the inventory records file, and the product structure or bill-of-materials file. Using these three inputs, the MRP computer program schedules order releases and production dates for the entire manufacturing operation. The MRP computer program must schedule not only orders for regular customer demand, but also random orders or orders external to the planned master schedule. These external orders can include service and repair parts, interplant orders, and items specially selected for experimentation or testing.

Given dependent demand, the MRP computer program schedules orders by combining information from the master schedule, the bill-of-materials file, and the inventory record file. The master schedule specifies production quantities and due dates, the inventory record file states the number of units on hand and an order for each item, and the bill-of-materials file lists all the items needed to produce a given end product. The logic processor within the MRP computer program then "explodes" the net requirements for the production of the end product and schedules order releases, taking into account any lead times of items.

As can be seen in Figure 11-6, there are three important output reports from the MRP computer program. Order release reports are the principal output, and they represent planned orders in the current period. They form the basis for new shop orders, new purchase requisitions, and due dates for production scheduling. The order reschedule reports call for changes in due dates for open orders. These reports are major input for priority planning and rescheduling, and they also provide expediting information. The planned order reports tentatively schedule orders for release in future periods. These provide information in forecasting inventory and future work-center loads. This visibility into the future is very helpful in capacity planning and the development of realistic master schedules. Other, secondary reports not shown in Figure 11-6 can include performance reports for forecasted usages and costs, and

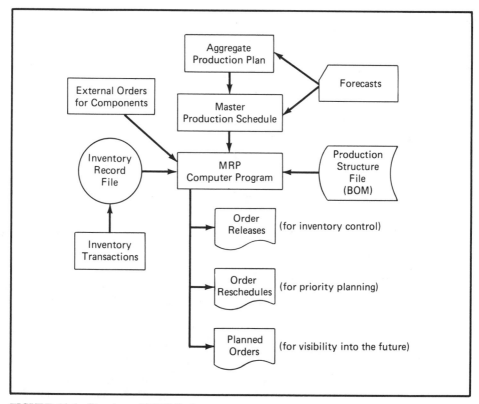

FIGURE 11-6 Structure of MRP System

exception reports, which signal errors such as late orders, nonexistent parts numbers, or a due date of an open order outside the planning horizon.

Master Production Schedule

The *master production schedule* is the hub of the MRP system, since it essentially "drives" the system. It is a refinement of the rougher aggregate plan and it specifies what manufacturing actually plans to produce, not just sales forecasts. The master schedule specifies a time-phased schedule of production quantities of end items. The initial production quantities for end items serve as the first stage of capacity planning. The MRP computer program can "run" on the tentative master schedule production quantities to generate order releases and estimated demands upon plant capacity and various work centers. Revisions may be necessary to reach an authorized master schedule. Figure 11-7 shows the development of an authorized master production schedule.

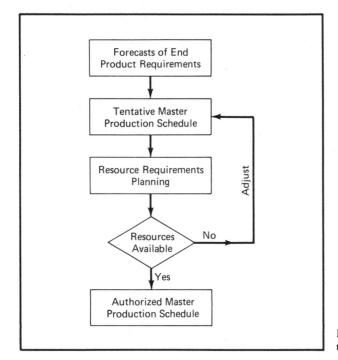

FIGURE 11-7   Development of a Master Production Schedule

The authorized master schedule is a flexible plan that must be able to incorporate changes as they occur. It also serves as the basis for making decisions whenever due dates, capacity, or lead time cannot be satisfied. It is essential that the master schedule be realistic, and hence its development should include input and shared responsibility from not only manufacturing, but also marketing and finance. Marketing is usually responsible for forecasts of demand, product mix, and storage and distribution.

Finance must be able to cover the cash flows required in manufacturing operations and finished-goods inventory.

The master production schedule serves two major functions. It is the basis for materials planning, priority planning, and capacity planning over the cumulative production lead time; it is also the basis for estimating long-term resource requirements beyond the cumulative production lead time. The master schedule is usually broken down into a firm and a tentative portion of the planning horizon. Even though last-minute changes can cause the firm schedule to differ slightly from the final assembly schedule, it is usually representative of the scheduled production. Figure 11-8 depicts the master production schedule for three end products, A, B, and C.

| | | ←—Firm—→ | | | ←——————————Tentative——————————→ | | | | | | | |
Product	Month J	F	M	A	M	J	J	A	S	O	N	D
A	40		30		70		35	25		50		
B		45		67			88				100	
C	50	60	40	70	70	65	75	90	80	75	95	100

FIGURE 11-8   Master Production Schedule for A, B, and C

Inventory Record File

The inventory record file serves as a main source of inventory information for the MRP computer program. The inventory record file consists of the following three data segments:

1. Item Master Data Segment
2. Inventory Status Segment
3. Subsidiary Data Segment

These three data segments are called the logical record, since they are related to each other. Each of them may exist for thousands of items, and each segment can contain a significant amount of information. The resulting need to access and move large amounts of data rapidly necessitates a high-speed computer and an efficient information system.

The Item Master Data Segment includes information on item identity, characteristics, and planning factors such as lot size, lead times, safety stock, and scrap allowances. The Inventory Status Segment contains current information on gross requirements, scheduled receipts, on-hand quantities, and planned order releases.

The Subsidiary Data Segment includes four types of data: (1) order details, such as open orders and released portions of blanket orders; (2) records of pending action, such as purchase requisitions outstanding and order changes; (3) counters and accumulators that indicate usage to date, demand-history details, and forecast errors; and (4) keeping-track records, which indicate firm planned orders and unused scrap allowance.

These three inventory data segments must be kept up to date in order to be useful. Status data are kept up to date by noting inventory transactions as they occur; these transactions may include stock receipt, disbursements, and scrap losses. The status data are updated frequently—say, daily—whereas planning factors are changed at the user's discretion. The inventory transactions are initially stored on the inventory transactions file (see Figure 11-6) and can subsequently be used to update the Status Data Segment.

Bill-of-Materials File

The bill-of-materials file (BOM), or product structure file, represents the way a product is manufactured. It is in a sense a directory for visiting item record files of a "parent's" components. Consider, for example, the product tree structure for product X shown in Figure 11-9.

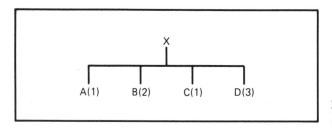

FIGURE 11-9 Product Structure for Product X

There are two standard methods for structuring a BOM, the indented file and the single-level file. The single-level file is much more convenient for computer representation, so let's consider it. The single-level bill of material specifies the immediate component items for a given parent item, as well as specific usage quantities of each component. The single-level bill also provides a "pointer" to facilitate retrieval of the bills of material for the components. Figure 11-10 illustrates the single-level BOM for product X.

With the aid of the pointers, the computer can move from one storage location to another to find the appropriate BOM for particular components. This is particularly helpful, since a component can exist in its own right or as a subassembly or part of another parent item. Through the use of pointers, the computer can move from one single-level BOM to another in order to determine net requirements for order releases.

When the individual single-level bills of material are grouped together graphically, they form a hierarchial, pyramidlike structure. This defines the hierarchy in

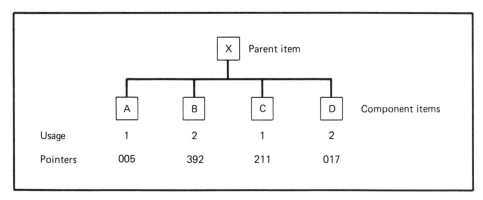

FIGURE 11-10   Single-Level Bill of Material for X

the BOM of the end product. Figure 11-11 shows the hierarchy and resulting levels in the BOM for product X.

By convention, we keep all identical components at the same level relative to the same parent end item. For example, look at component M in Figure 11-11. It appears at level 4 under components L and D respectively. Component M could have been placed at level 2 under component D, but then it would not have been at the same level as its counterpart under component L. The purpose in keeping all identical components at the same level is to facilitate the computer's calculation of net requirements for parts. If all identical items are on the same level, the computer can scan across a single level of the BOM to summarize all requirements for the components at that level.

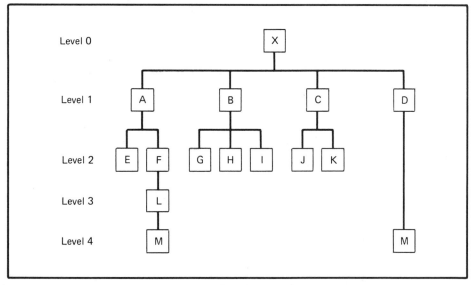

FIGURE 11-11   BOM Levels and Hierarchy for Product X

We have examined the basic structure of the MRP system and seen how the master schedule, inventory records file, and BOM file are the main input to the MRP computer program. We are now ready to study the logic behind the MRP computer program as it explodes item requirements from the BOM file and time-phases planned order releases. The basic logic is the same as that presented in the previous example of lumpy demand, but we formalize and extend the concepts involved.

Netting Requirements

The materials requirements planning process takes the end-item production quantities as specified by the master schedule and uses the BOM file as well as inventory status data to determine component material needs and their planned order releases. This explosion process is logically simple but can involve hundreds or thousands of calculations for complex products or for determining simultaneously the requirements of many end items.

Two primary concepts needed to accurately calculate the number of subassemblies and parts needed are those of gross and net requirements. The *gross requirement* for an inventory item equals the quantity of the item that will have to be disbursed to support a parent order; it is not necessarily the number of units that will be used by the end product, since there may be hidden inventories of the item in higher-level items in the product structure tree.

Consider, for example, the data in Figure 11-12 pertaining to the manufacture of heavy-duty electrical motors. What are the gross requirements for item D in order to produce 100 units of motor X? The figure is not 100. There are already 20 units of D in any finished subassembly A. Therefore, only 80 units of D need to be disbursed

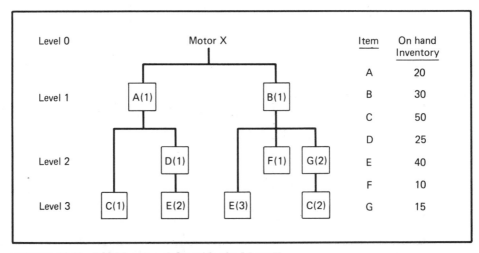

FIGURE 11-12   BOM Levels and Quantities for Motor X

to produce 100 motors, and the gross requirement is 80. The gross requirement is equivalent to demand at item level rather than at product or master production schedule level.

The *net requirements* of an item represent how many additional units must be procured to support the parent item. A formula for net requirements is:

$$\text{Net requirements} = \begin{cases} \text{Gross requirements} - \text{Scheduled receipts} - \text{Inventory on hand} \\ 0 \text{ if quantity above is negative} \end{cases}$$

In our example of the motor X, we have no scheduled receipts, so the net requirement for item D is gross requirements minus inventory on hand, or $80 - 25 = 55$ units. Table 11-1 summarizes the gross and net requirements for all items.

Table 11-1   Gross and Net Requirements to Produce 100 Motors

LEVEL			INVEN-TORY	GROSS REQUIREMENT	NET REQUIREMENT
1	2	3			
A(1)			20	100	$100 - 20 = 80$
	D(1)		25	$100 - 20 = 80$	$80 - 25 = 55$
		C(1)	50	$100 - 20 = 80$	$80 - 50 = 30$
		E(2)	40	$(100 - 45) \times 2 = 110$	$110 - 40 = 70$
B(1)			30	100	$100 - 30 = 70$
	F(1)		10	$100 - 30 = 70$	$70 - 10 = 60$
	G(2)		15	$(100 - 30) \times 2 = 140$	$140 - 15 = 125$
		E(3)	—	$(100 - 30) \times 3 = 210$	$210 - 0 = 210$
		C(2)	—	$(140 - 15) \times 2 = 250$	$250 - 0 = 250$

Time-Phasing

In calculating the net requirements of items, we have basically answered the question of how much. The *time-phasing* aspect of MRP is a key feature distinguishing it from classical inventory methods; it enables us to answer the all-important question of *when*.

There are two basic approaches for relating time to inventory status data, the date/quantity approach and the time-bucket approach. The time-bucket approach is more popular and more widely used; it is the approach we shall study here. A time bucket is a discrete segment of time, usually representing more than one day. It is a coarse division of time that can span five workdays, a week, or a month. Normally, a time bucket corresponds to one week.

To illustrate the logic of time phasing, let's consider component F (a coil), which is used in the manufacture of motor X. Suppose the production schedule of the end item, motor X, calls for gross requirements in the amounts indicated in Figure 11-13. The figure shows the time buckets in which component F is needed and receipts

		Week								Total
		1	2	3	4	5	6	7	8	
Gross requirements			16		22		30	12		80
Schedule receipts				30						30
On hand	20									

FIGURE 11-13 **Time-Phased Status of Component F before Net Requirements Computation**

are expected. From this information, we can calculate time-phased net requirements. Using abbreviations, the formula for net requirements becomes:

$$NR = \begin{cases} GR - SR - OH \\ 0 \text{ if } (GR - SR - OH) < 0 \end{cases}$$

Incorporating the time-phased net requirements in the time-phased display, we have Figure 11-14. Notice that it is not until the sixth and seventh weeks that additional

		Week								Total
		1	2	3	4	5	6	7	8	
Gross requirements			16		22		30	12		80
Schedule receipts				30						30
On hand	20									
Net requirements							18	12		30

FIGURE 11-14 **Time-Phased Status after Net Requirements Computation**

units of component F are needed. The next logical concept involves the timing of planned order releases to ensure that 18 and 12 units are available in the sixth and seventh weeks respectively.

Planned order releases are new orders scheduled in the future to cover net requirements. If no lead time exists, then planned orders can be released in the same period that net requirements occur; however, some lead time usually exists. The timing of planned order releases can be expressed as:

$$\text{Release date} = \text{Due date} - \text{Planned lead time}$$

If we assume a two-week lead time for component F, then the schedule of planned order releases is as shown in Figure 11-15.

			Week							Total
		1	2	3	4	5	6	7	8	
Gross requirements			16		22		30	12		80
Schedule Receipts				30						30
On hand	20									
Net requirements							(18)	(12)		30
Planned order releases					(18)	(12)				

FIGURE 11-15   Time-Phasing Planned Order Releases with Lead Time of 2 Weeks

Lot Sizing

Lot sizing is usually associated with classical inventory control, but it can also be used in MRP to economize on the setup and inventory carrying charges associated with an inventory item. There are several lot-sizing methods to choose from, including the EOQ method that was covered in the previous chapter.

Suppose that a lot size of 50 units has been calculated for component F using the standard EOQ formula. Figure 11-16 shows the effect on planned order releases. In this case, the lot size exceeds the net requirements for the eight-week planning horizon. This may not pose a problem in this case, but it can where the item is located at a high level near the end item in the product structure tree. An error in the order quantity filters down, becoming more and more exaggerated at the lower levels. Thus, lot sizing can be economical but is generally used for lower-level items in the product structure tree.

Time-Phased Order Point (TPOP)

We have examined the basic system structure and processing logic for MRP systems applied to dependent demand. The time-phased order point (TPOP) allows the MRP methodology to be applied to distribution or independent-demand items. Of course,

		Week								Total
		1	2	3	4	5	6	7	8	
Gross requirements			16		22		30	12		80
Scheduled receipts				30						30
On hand	20									
Net requirements							(18)	(12)		30
Planned order releases					(50)					50

FIGURE 11-16　Time-Phasing with a Lot Size of 50

the demand for such items must be forecasted rather than calculated, but the same MRP logic can be applied by simply including provisions for safety stock in the scheduling of planned order releases.

Let's consider an example of an end item whose demand is independent. Suppose the following inventory factors apply to the item:

$$\text{Lead time} = 2 \text{ weeks}$$
$$\text{Safety stock} = 100 \text{ units}$$
$$\text{Lot size} = 40$$
$$\text{Forecasted demand} = 19 \text{ per week}$$

Using a statistical order-point approach, the order point would be calculated as:

$$\text{Safety stock} + \text{Period demand} \times \text{Lead time} = 100 + 19 \times 2 = 138$$

The TPOP approach is shown in Figure 11-17. The results of the TPOP approach are similar to those of the order-point approach, but planned order releases are triggered not by an order point but rather by the on-hand quantity dropping down to the safety-stock level (100 in this case).

The MRP system requires no modifications to handle the independent-demand case and has the advantages of offering the same approach for both independent- and dependent-demand cases. Additional advantages include the ability to:

1. Plan gross requirements for subparts of the item
2. Develop full schedule of planned orders
3. Keep open order due dates valid
4. Provide an input to capacity planning
5. Plan the priority of dependent and independent items jointly

		Week							
		1	2	3	4	5	6	7	8
Gross requirements		19	19	19	19	19	19	19	19
Scheduled receipts									
On hand	150	131	112	93	74	55	36	17	−2
Planned order releases		40		40		40			

Safety stock reached in week 3

FIGURE 11-17   Time-Phased Order Point

Regenerative and Net-Change Systems

All MRP systems are executed as either regenerative or net-change systems. The conventional and most commonly used approach is the schedule regeneration implementation, in which the system is run every week or two. This method affords high data-processing efficiency but is not always up to date. The regenerative approach breaks down the new master schedule every week or two into detailed time-phased requirements for each item. This periodic batch-processing approach entails massive data-handling tasks in retrieving BOMs, exploding requirements, and computing the inventory status of all items. The process is executed level by level, starting with end items and proceeding down the levels of the BOM tree structure. Typically, volumes of output are generated pertaining to inventory and requirements data.

Net-change systems allow the user to monitor or replan the MRP system more frequently. In this approach, partial explosions of items that undergo status change are performed. Thus, only part of the master schedule is exploded at any one time and the volume of output is reduced. The approach is analogous to the periodic review system. Few MRP adopters are using the net-change approach even though it offers the capability to keep closer tabs on the system. Some may feel that the more timely information is not worth the additional frequency of computer runs.

TOWARD SUCCESSFUL IMPLEMENTATION

MRP is not a panacea for all inventory problems; people still make errors, and unexpected changes in the master schedule can occur. A properly functioning MRP system can, however, aid in time-phasing decisions and planning for the future. It is safe to say that MRP is currently revolutionizing the management of production and inventory control in the United States.

Since all real-world MRP systems entail the use of a computer and massive amounts of data manipulation, they need to function in a highly controlled environment. As in any computer system, the slogan "GIGO" (garbage in, garbage out) applies. An MRP system will fail if the input data is full of errors. It is not possible to prevent input errors entirely, but it is extremely important to minimize them. It is possible to incorporate a variety of internal checks in the MRP system to prevent and correct errors. Three types of preventive measures are (1) barriers to prevent errors from entering the system, (2) detectors to find errors in the input data, and (3) eradicators to eliminate undetected errors.

Barriers can consist of input audits, diagnostic computer routines, and rigid control on external factors such as stockrooms or warehouses. Internal detection routines can be programmed to check against the file being updated; tests of reasonableness can also be employed. Errors that escape barriers and detectors can be tolerated if they are low in percentage and do not accumulate. Error accumulation can be minimized by periodically reconciling differences in planned versus actual requirements and by file purging.

The accuracy of input data, BOM files, and master schedules is necessary, but just as important are the human factors in an MRP system. The people primarily concerned with the system, such as inventory managers, foremen, buyers, and clerks, must be educated as to the basic functioning of MRP systems. Top management must be committed to implementing the system, and sometimes a new attitude toward computers is needed by all concerned, especially during the installation of a new system.

MRP systems can be developed internally, but many commercial MRP software packages are available. Major computer manufacturers such as IBM and Honeywell offer packages, as do companies such as Software International. The time required to get an MRP system on line varies with different companies. For example, one $5 million fabrication/assembly company implemented a simple MRP system in six months, whereas a similar $20 million company began to reap benefits only after five years of stop-and-start evolutionary effort on MRP, a larger computer, and a great deal of data-processing support.[2]

Some efforts have been made to implement MRP systems within a broader-reaching control system that performs additional functions. One such system is the Production and Information Control System (PICS) developed by IBM. PICS was developed to aid in the management of dependent demand for fabrication and assembly types of manufacturing. It includes such functions as forecasting, purchasing, scheduling, and shop loading, as well as materials requirements planning.

An even broader-range system that IBM is still developing is called the Communication Oriented Production Information and Control System (COPICS). This computerized system will integrate functions ranging from forecasting, inventory management, and processing control to plant maintenance. COPICS will be a dynamic on-line system linked to computer terminals and will provide capabilities for management to test alternate decision strategies. The completion of the COPICS system will

---

[2]Miller and Sprague, "Behind the Growth."

bring manufacturing management another step closer to the embodiment of a true systems approach.

SUMMARY

MRP is a systems approach to the management of items subject to dependent demand. It has evolved through the practice of the art in industry and is gaining acceptance rapidly, although a few firms used similar approaches many years ago.

The basic idea in MRP is to calculate component requirements and then time-phase order releases in order to have needed materials available on time. The MRP computer program takes input from the master production schedule, the inventory records file, and the BOM file. The logic processor then explodes the net requirements for the production of end items and the scheduling of order releases.

MRP systems also provide visibility into the future and the ability to do priority and capacity planning. Other benefits include reduced inventories, fewer late orders, and the ability to adapt to changes in a systematic manner. The only disadvantages pertain to the costs associated with implementing a computerized inventory system. These costs range from around $200,000 to $500,000 for the average company. However, the resulting savings can often recover the initial cost in one to three years.

MRP is most useful for assembly-type manufacturing operations, but it is applicable to any operation involving dependent inventoriable items. MRP has been applied very little (if any) to service-oriented operations. However, just as the time-phased order point (TPOP) extended MRP methodology to independent-demand items, it does seem conceivable that MRP could be applied to allocating and time-phasing service resources. Only time will tell if this systems approach will be utilized in nonmanufacturing.

Meanwhile, the revolution continues among manufacturing firms. MRP is not yet the most widely used inventory technique—ABC analysis and the EOQ model are used more[3]—but its rate of growth is the greatest, and if it continues, MRP will be the dominant dependent-demand inventory method in the near future.

SOLVED PROBLEMS

Problem Statement

An end item X is assembled from three main subassemblies: A, B, and C. Subassembly A requires two units of part D and three of part E. Subassembly C requires one unit each of components F and G. Furthermore, component G requires four of part H.

---

[3]Edward W. Davis, "A Look at the Use of Production-Inventory Techniques: Past and Present," *Production and Inventory Management*, Vol. 16, No. 4 (December 1975), 1–19.

Given that there are 30, 70, and 90 units on hand of D, G and H, what are the net requirements of A, B, C, D, E, F, G, and H in order to produce 400 units of end item X?

Solution

In determing net requirements, it is helpful to look at the product structure tree.

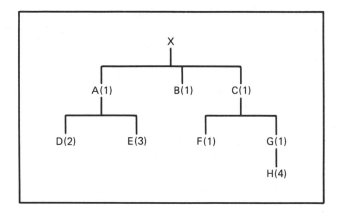

Using the formula $NR = GR - OH$ (in this case, there are no scheduled receipts), we can calculate net requirements as follows:

ITEM	INVENTORY	GROSS REQUIREMENT	NET REQUIREMENT
A	0	400	400 − 0 = 400
B	0	400	400 − 0 = 400
C	0	400	400 − 0 = 400
D	30	2 × 400 = 800	800 − 30 = 770
E	0	3 × 400 = 1,200	1,200 − 0 = 1,200
F	0	400	400 − 0 = 400
G	70	400	400 − 70 = 330
H	90	4 × (400 − 70) = 1,320	1,320 − 90 = 1,230

Problem Statement

The table below shows the scheduled receipts, current inventory, and gross requirements of component E. Given a lead time of one week and a lot size of 100, determine the timing of planned order releases.

		Week							
		1	2	3	4	5	6	7	8
Gross requirements		100		300	75		200		
Scheduled receipts		100				100			
On hand	90								

Solution

First we must calculate net requirements and then adjust for lot sizes and lead time.

		Week							
		1	2	3	4	5	6	7	8
Gross requirements		100		300	75		200		
Scheduled receipts		100				100			
On hand	90								
Net requirements (cumulative)				210	285		385		

Assuming that all production runs for component E must be in lot-size multiples of 100 or more, we obtain the following planned order releases:

		Week							
		1	2	3	4	5	6	7	8
Gross requirements		100		300	75		200		
Scheduled receipts		100				100			
On hand	90								
Net requirements				210	285		385		
Planned order releases			300			100			

The planned order release of 300 in week 2 will cover gross requirements through week 4. Only 85 more units of component E are required for week 6, but the minimum lot size of 100 requires an order release of size 100 in week 5.

Problem Statement

The scheduling of operations and the execution of jobs is closely tied to the MRP system. Order and dispatch schedules can be created from the due dates established by an MRP system. However, one of the most widely used methods for establishing sequencing priorities for operations is the *critical ratio*. The critical-ratio priority rule is calculated as:

$$\text{Critical ratio} = \frac{\text{Due date} - \text{Today's date}}{\text{Lead time for balance of work}}$$

Given the following three jobs and their associated operation times and due-date information, calculate critical ratios and establish processing priorities. Assume that today is day number 200.

JOB	DUE DATE	REMAINING OPERATIONS TIME IN DAYS
A	202	3.0
B	204	2.0
C	202	1.5

Solution

JOB	CRITICAL RATIO
A	$(202 - 200)/3 = .67$
B	$(204 - 200)/2 = 2.0$
C	$(202 - 200)/1.5 = 1.33$

Job A has a critical ratio of less than 1, which is an expedite ratio and is the highest priority. Jobs C and B have lower priorities, and these correspond to de-expedite ratios. A ratio of 1.0 represents a job that is exactly on schedule.

REVIEW QUESTIONS

1. What is the difference between dependent and independent demand?
2. Explain how errors can arise in applying statistical order-point procedures to lumpy demand.

3. Where did MRP originate?
4. Explain what additional capabilities an MRP system offers besides the time-phasing of order releases.
5. What are the three main inputs to any MRP computer program?
6. How often are most MRP systems run?
7. What kind of information is held in the BOM file? the inventory records file?
8. Explain the TPOP, or how MRP is applied to independent-demand situations.
9. How can the ability to de-expedite be almost as helpful as the ability to expedite?
10. For what types of items should the use of lot sizing be considered when generating planned order releases?
11. Characterize regenerative and net-change systems.
12. What steps can be taken to prevent input errors from entering the MRP input data?
13. What is the COPICS system?
14. Describe the process by which a tentative master schedule becomes an authorized master schedule.
15. Discuss the relative difficulties in managing manufacturing priorities in businesses that manufacture:
    a. A one-piece product made to order
    b. A one-piece product made to stock
    c. An assembled product made to order
    d. An assembled product made to stock

PROBLEMS

1. Compute the net requirements for items A, B, and C if we want to produce 40 units of X.

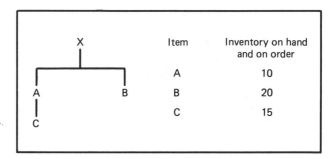

2. Statistical order-level systems sometimes try to store enough safety stock so there is no stockout over a specified percentage of the time. Suppose that enough safety is maintained so that subassemblies A, B, C, and D below will not stock out over 90% of the time. What is the actual probability that you will be able to produce end item X?

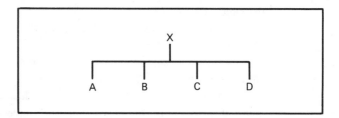

3. Given the following product structure tree, design the associated BOM, showing the hierarchy and components at the correct levels.

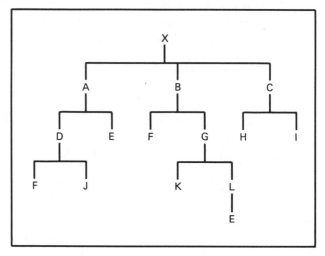

4. Calculate the gross and net requirements for the following BOM and quantities. Assume that you want to produce 50 end items.

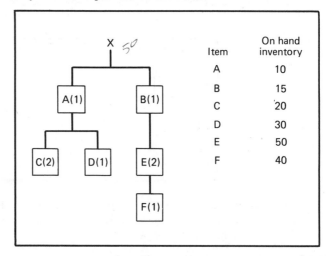

5. Time-phase the net requirements for component C below by placing the appropriate net requirements in the correct time buckets.

		Week					
		1	2	3	4	5	6
Gross requirements			40		55		70
Scheduled receipts		30		10		30	
On hand	25						
Net requirements							

6. Suppose that a lead time of two weeks applies to the orders in problem 5. Time-phase the planned order releases in order to satisfy net requirements.

7. Recalculate the net requirements for the example in Figure 11-14, given that the on-hand inventory is 35 rather than 20.

8. Determine the timing of planned order releases for the example in Figure 11-15, given an on-hand inventory of 35 and a lead time of three weeks.

9. Suppose that component C of problems 5 and 6 is a lower-level item, and a lot size of 40 units is to be used as the order quantity. Specify the planned order releases for problem 6 assuming a lot size of 40.

10. An end item Y consists of two main subassemblies, A and B. In order to produce A, components C, D, and two units of E are required. In order to make one B, component F and two units of G are required. Finally, component F requires three units of part H.
    a. Construct the product structure tree for Y.
    b. Determine the quantities of A, B, C, D, E, F, G, and H required to produce 1,000 end items.

11. Advanced Audio Systems is a company specializing in state-of-the-art electronic equipment. It has recently pioneered a new class D amplifier (D for digital), and demand of 52,000 units is expected for the upcoming year. The amplifier is simple in design, consisting externally of only a metal case plus an L.E.D. peak-overload indicator. Internally, the amp contains a separate power supply for each of the two channels. Each channel contains a digital processor, which in turn consists of an IC bias regulator, a positive and a negative Darlington driver, and a DC servo control.
    a. Develop your own master production schedule for a planning horizon of eight weeks.
    b. Specify the product structure tree.
    c. Given a lead time of two weeks on power supplies and three weeks on all other components, develop an MRP plan for production, including gross

and net requirements and planned order releases (assume no on-hand inventories).

12. Establish the scheduling priorities of the following four jobs. Assume that today is day number 50.

JOB	DUE DATE	REMAINING WORK TIME IN DAYS
W	51	1.0
X	49	.5
Y	52	1.0
Z	50	3.0

13. Prepare a dispatch list for the following five jobs. That is, list the jobs according to their scheduling priorities. Assume that today is March 1 (8:00 A.M.) and each workday is eight hours.

JOB NO.	DUE DATE	OPERATION TIME REMAINING IN HOURS
1253	3-2	7
1729	3-1	8
5623	3-3	28
2011	2-28	2
4192	3-3	15

Case: THE CROFT RECEIVER COMPANY*

You are the new general manager who has just moved into this position at the Croft Receiver Company, having been brought in from a smaller plant in the South. The problems at the Croft Receiver Company are many. Inventories are very high; customer service is so poor that your phone is ringing a good deal of the time with calls from irate customers. The business plan spells out a shipping budget, but the best Croft has been able to do in the last three months is to ship about 75 percent of the budget.

---

*Oliver W. Wight, *Production and Inventory Management in the Computer Age* (Boston, Mass., 1974). Reprinted by permission of CBI Publishing Co.

Croft makes portable receivers for citizens' band radios and similar equipment. A small percentage of it is made to stock, but most of it is made to order. It is really custom-assembled, since most of the modules are fairly standard. The difference between one receiver and another might be just a small number of frequency-sensitive components. Croft's sales run around $20 million a year. They've been a good profit generator over the past years, but since April of this year, disaster has followed upon disaster.

It all started about two years ago, when the corporate auditors were highly critical of the low rate of inventory turnover (1.7 turns at cost). They recommended the installation of a new inventory management system. A number of consulting firms were called in to bid on the job. The consultant that wound up designing the system had a slight edge right from the beginning, since one of his firm's principals sits on the board of directors of Croft's parent corporation.

The old production and inventory management system consisted of manual inventory records that were posted by a battery of clerks. As an order came in, they would "reserve" the components required for it and order any needed components. This system did have plenty of flaws. There was no time phasing and it was essentially an order-point system where the reservation simply served to generate orders sooner. These were deducted from the inventory, which meant that the order point would be reached sooner.

The system the consultant installed was very much the same type of system, only transferred to a computer and embellished with techniques like exponential smoothing and the mean absolute deviation used for calculation of the order point. Some of the production and inventory management people had read about MRP and were anxious to install it, but the engineering department said that the bills of material were not in any shape to put on a computer and that it would take several years before they could be corrected. The consultant had pointed out that because of the great product variety, customer orders could not really be forecast, and that order points on components would probably work as well or better.

The young man who was sent in by the consulting firm didn't seem particularly experienced in any area except systems. He could draw flow charts at a furious pace and seemed to know all the latest buzz words. He never went down to talk with the foremen in the shop and, in fact, made it very clear that this system was intended to get control *away* from *them* and that they would have to follow instructions to the letter when the computer reports started to come out. He made recommendations that resulted in transferring three of the oldest inventory clerks and giving retirement to two expediters.

It was this consultant who also insisted that the system be installed across the board. He said that this offered the advantage that people would have to sink or swim.

The system went on the air April 1 across the board, and by April 15 shipments had virtually stopped. One of the interesting features of the system as designed was that each assembly order that went into the computer reserved its components but *could not be released* until all components were available. It wasn't very long before there were many assembly orders in the system and none of them could be released. Since the earliest one had reserved the available components, the next one found fewer components available, and so on. There was no provision in the system to remove these orders without completely rebuilding the files. And with things in such a hectic state, this was hardly a desirable project to get started on.

The plant superintendent was the man of the hour when everything collapsed. He stepped forward, brought his foremen in to work early in the morning, and kept them late at night. They pulled material out of the stockroom against customer orders, found out what the real shortages were, expedited material, and finally got shipments out the door. They were not going out at the budgeted rate, but at least *something* was happening.

One of the people you talked to when you came on board was the materials manager. You asked him how he could have let this happen. While he was extremely upset by what had happened, his point was that he felt there was no way a large reputable consulting firm could have failed so badly. He had virtually delegated the responsibility to them for developing a system and, quite frankly, their representative had taken the initiative.

Recently, the consulting firm recommended that the materials manager be fired. They felt that he had not backed the system 100 percent and had been quick to let the foremen come in and go back to their manual methods for working around the system. They felt that the system simply had not been given a fair trial.

As the new general manager, you have a number of problems that you are facing. The division is paying $28,000 a month for the computer and the activities that support it. This system is certainly no better than the manual system and, in many cases, seems to be worse. What do you think the chances are of reconstructing the old informal system? It is obvious that this is what really worked, since the manual system couldn't do a very effective job of putting proper priorities on components. On the other hand, should the present computer system be discarded in favor of a sound one? In short, the problem is to go backward or go forward—standing still is not a sound choice.

Case Discussion Questions

1. Should you keep the materials manager, or fire him? What should you do about the consulting firm?
2. Sketch out the kind of system you think Croft Receiver requires. Justify why it would work better than the manual approach the company has been using

or the computer approach it has installed. Also give management some recommendations for working with a consultant in case they ever have to do that again.

REFERENCES

AMERICAN PRODUCTION and INVENTORY CONTROL SOCIETY, *APICS Special Report: Materials Requirement Planning by Computer*. Washington, D.C., American Production and Inventory Control Society, 1971.

CHASE, R.B., and NICHOLAS T. AQUILANO, *Production and Operations Management*. Homewood, Ill.: Richard D. Irwin, 1977.

DAVIS, EDWARD W., "A Look at the Use of Production-Inventory Techniques: Past and Present," *Production and Inventory Management*, Vol. 16, No. 4 (December 1975), 1–19.

EVERDELL, ROMEYN, "Master Production Scheduling," *APICS Training Aid*. Washington D.C.: APICS, 1974.

INTERNATIONAL BUSINESS MACHINES CORPORATION, *Communications Oriented Production Information and Control System*, Publications G320–1974 through G320–1981.

MILLER, JEFFREY G., and LINDA G. SPRAGUE, "Behind the Growth in Materials Requirements Planning," *Harvard Business Review*, Vol. 53, No. 5 (September–October 1975), 83–91.

ORLICKY, JOSEPH, *Materials Requirements Planning*. New York: McGraw-Hill, 1975.

PLOSSL, G.W., and O.W. WIGHT, "Materials Requirement Planning by Computer," APICS, Washington, D.C., 1971.

————, *Production and Inventory Control*. Englewood Cliffs, N.J.: Prentice-Hall, 1967.

THURSTON, PHILLIP H., "Requirements Planning for Inventory Control," *Harvard Business Review*, May–June 1972, pp. 67–71.

WIGHT, OLIVER W., *Production and Inventory Management in the Computer Age*. Boston: Cahners Books, 1974.

chapter

12

SCHEDULING

INTRODUCTION

Regardless of what kind of activity an organization is involved in, scheduling plays an important role. A hospital must schedule operations, admissions, and personnel. Local, state, and federal governments must schedule court cases, transportation systems, a wide variety of projects, mail systems, and a host of other activities. Manufacturing organizations must schedule production, the engineering effort, and materials acquisition. Educational institutions have to schedule classes, buses, and classrooms. The list could go on indefinitely.

Most scheduling problems can be classified into one of three different categories: (1) project scheduling, (2) production scheduling, and (3) scheduling of services. We could further categorize scheduling problems by the type of system being scheduled. In Chapter 1 we said there were basically three types of transformation systems: one-shot systems, intermittent-flow systems, and continuous-flow systems. This relationship between system type and scheduling problems is depicted in Figure 12-1.

Project scheduling refers to the scheduling of unique, one-shot projects. Projects are major tasks that require a significant amount of time to accomplish. The construction of a building, the design of a computer-based information system, and the development of a weapons system are all examples. It is obvious that these large projects require a great deal of detailed scheduling in order to complete them in a reason-

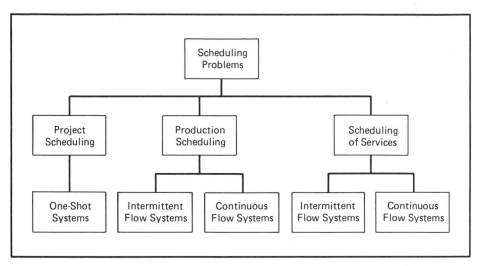

FIGURE 12-1 Classification of Scheduling Problems

able length of time. Fortunately, several quantitative techniques have been developed that significantly aid in the project-scheduling process. These techniques are described later in this chapter.

Production scheduling refers to the scheduling of any productive process, but for our purposes, we shall limit it to exclude project scheduling. The scheduling of jobs in a computer center, the scheduling of an automotive plant, and the scheduling of a refinery are all examples of production scheduling.

The methods and techniques used to schedule production depend primarily on the production process itself. Scheduling a job-shop or intermittent system is a totally different task from scheduling a continuous system or an assembly-line type of production. Therefore, we shall break production scheduling into two categories, the scheduling of intermittent systems and the scheduling of continuous systems.

The final type of scheduling to be discussed in this chapter is the *scheduling of services*. Provision of services accounts for more than 25 percent of our gross national product, and hence the proper scheduling of these services is of no little consequence. Again, scheduling methodology depends on system type. Obvious examples of services that must be scheduled are medical services, legal services, banking services, transportation services, and police protection.

PROJECT SCHEDULING

Project managers must know how long a specific project will take to finish, what the critical tasks are, and, very often, what the probability is of completing the project within a given time span. In addition, it is often important to know the effect on the total project of delays at individual stages. For these and other reasons, several techniques have been created upon which project managers rely. This section examines how the manager can integrate the use of a *work-breakdown structure* (WBS), *Gantt charts*, *project evaluation and review technique* (PERT), and the *critical path method* (CPM) to solve the problems of scheduling and controlling projects.

The scheduling techniques we discuss in this chapter can be applied to a wide variety of projects. Government contractors are almost always required to use scheduling techniques such as PERT for projects of even moderate size. Construction companies often use these techniques for scheduling moderate to large-scale projects. One construction company, for example, applies PERT to all projects with a cost greater than $150,000. Designers of computerized information systems are using analytical scheduling techniques more and more. In short, almost any project is a likely candidate, because the cost of using these techniques is usually outweighed by the benefit.

Work-Breakdown Structure

When confronted with the task of scheduling and controlling a project of significant size and scope, you must identify each of the tasks involved. In addition, time estimates for each task must be developed, and the necessary resources, both human and nonhuman, must be identified. In order to accomplish this primary task, it is often desirable to use a WBS. WBS is actually a graphical representation of the tasks involved in a particular project; it is a way of classifying individual tasks by a natural breakdown of the project in a manner analogous to an organization chart. (See Figure 12-2.) Indeed, WBS is the organizational structure of the project. It starts with a word description of the project and then breaks down the project into major tasks. These major tasks are reduced to tasks, then to minor tasks, and so on. Finally, the smallest element in the WBS, the *work package*, is defined in detail. Each work package identifies the resources and time it requires, all important precedent relationships, and the person who is responsible for it. When all work packages are completed, the project is complete.

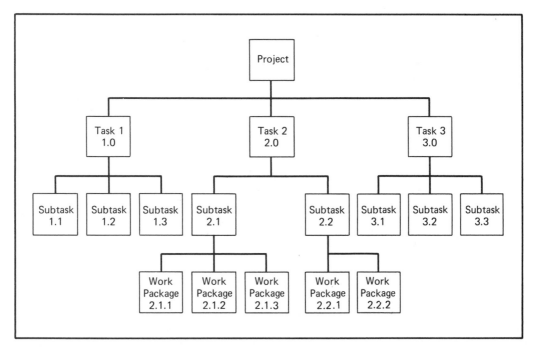

FIGURE 12-2   General Form of Work-Breakdown Structure (WBS)

Let us use the construction of an apartment building to illustrate the use of WBS. As you can see in Figure 12-3, the entire project can be broken down into six major tasks. These major tasks can then be broken into subtasks, as shown in Figure 12-4. Finally, the subtasks can be broken into work packages, as in Figure 12-5. It should be emphasized that WBS is not a solution to the project-scheduling problem but rather a preliminary, structured approach to collecting the data necessary for use with one of the more sophisticated techniques, such as PERT or CPM. Once the project has been broken down using WBS, the next step is to choose a way to schedule and control the project.

FIGURE 12-3   Second Level, WBS

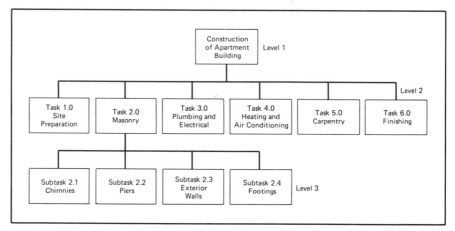

FIGURE 12-4   Third Level, WBS

Gantt Charts

For relatively small projects, a simple Gantt milestone chart, or a series of them, may be the best scheduling tool. A Gantt chart is simply a bar chart that plots tasks against time. Once the project manager has created the WBS for a project, the *Begin* and *Finish* dates for the various tasks, subtasks, and work packages can be scheduled. A single Gantt chart for major tasks and subtasks might be designed for management review, but any real scheduling must be done at the lowest level in the WBS. Each work package must have beginning and ending dates.

A relatively small project, such as building a house, might be effectively scheduled and controlled by means of a Gantt chart. Ordinarily, however, Gantt charts are primarily record-keeping tools used for monitoring projects. They are limited, in that they cannot generate information about the interrelationships among various tasks or about the minimum possible completion times for various tasks. Figure 12-6 shows a typical Gantt chart for an apartment construction project at the major-task level.

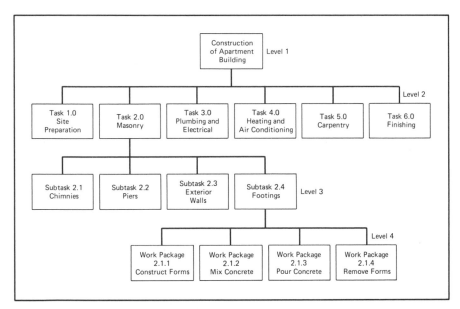

FIGURE 12-5   Fourth Level, WBS

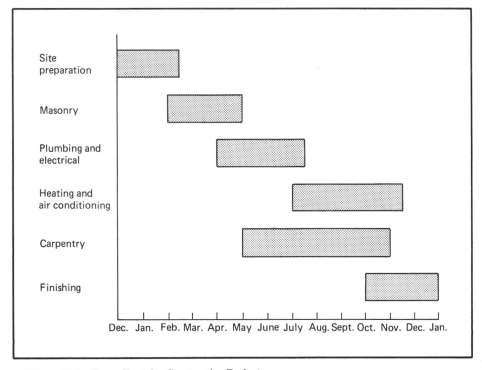

FIGURE 12-6   Gantt Chart for Construction Project

Deterministic PERT

PERT (project evaluation and review technique) evolved from Gantt charts in the late 1950s and was first applied to the U.S. Navy's Polaris submarine project. This project was so large that it actually necessitated the creation of a planning and control technique such as PERT. The project had more than 3,000 contractors, many of whom were performing multiple functions. Because of PERT's success in this and subsequent programs, major federal contracting agencies, such as the Department of Defense and NASA, require contractors to utilize PERT in scheduling and controlling their projects.

What, specifically, can PERT do for the project manager? PERT can be used as a planning tool as well as a controlling tool. In its planning function, PERT can be used to compute the total expected time needed to complete a project, and it can identify "bottleneck" activities that have a critical effect on the project-completion date. Stochastic PERT, to be discussed later in this chapter, allows the project manager to estimate the probability of meeting project deadlines. One of PERT's greatest benefits is that it forces the project manager to plan the project in explicit detail.

Once a project has been scheduled using PERT, you might think that the technique is of no further use. This is not the case; PERT is typically used throughout the project as a control technique. Used periodically, PERT monitors progress and calls attention to any delays that threaten the success of the project as a whole. In addition, PERT and similar techniques, such as the critical path method (CPM), can be used to evaluate and make decisions concerning time and cost tradeoffs of specific project activities.

Before we examine PERT as a methodology for scheduling and controlling a project, it is important for you to know certain terminology that we shall relate to a specific example.

An *activity* is a task the project requires. Because of the nature of PERT, an activity corresponds to the smallest task in the WBS—namely, the work package. Each activity must have associated with it a *time estimate*, and any *precedence relationships* must be defined. Table 12-1 depicts this pertinent information for a small project.

Table 12-1   Project Table

ACTIVITY	IMMEDIATE PREDECESSOR	TIME ESTIMATE (IN DAYS)
A	—	3
B	A	4
C	A	5
D	B, C, F	7
E	—	3
F	E	6

As these data show, work on activities A and E can begin immediately. Activities B and C cannot be started until activity A has been completed. Activities B, C, and F must be completed before activity D can be started.

One of the problems that PERT addresses is the determination of the minimum time required to complete the project. In order to analyze our project more completely, a *network diagram*, or *PERT chart*, is introduced. The PERT chart (Figure 12-7) is a graphical representation of the entire project. An arrow represents an activity and a circle represents an *event*, which is defined as the completion of an activity.

FIGURE 12-7   PERT Chart Showing Critical Path E-F-D

The network depicts the precedence relationships involved in the project. As the project table states, the PERT chart shows graphically that it is necessary to finish activity A before beginning activities B and C. The *dummy activity* depicted in Figure 12-7 is a way to indicate diagrammatically that both B and C must be finished before D can be started. A *path* through a PERT network is a sequence of connected activities. In our example, there are three paths, A-B-D, A-C-D, and E-F-D. The length of each path can be computed by adding the times for each activity on the path. Thus, the length of path A-B-D is $3 + 4 + 7 = 14$ days, and the lengths of paths A-C-D and E-F-D are 15 and 16 days, respectively.

The longest path through the network is called the *critical path*. The length of the critical path corresponds to the minimum time required to complete the project; thus, the critical nature of the longest path. The activities on the critical path are *critical activities*, because a delay in any of them results in a delay of the entire project. In other words, there is no slack time in the activities on the critical path. *Slack time* is defined as the latest time an activity can be completed without delaying the project minus the earliest time the activity can be completed. In other words, slack time is the amount of time an activity can be delayed without delaying the entire project.

Returning to our example, it is a simple process to identify the critical path by comparing the lengths of each path. Path E-F-D can be completed in 16 days from the start of the project; delay of activities E, F, or D will delay the entire project.

Path A-B-D has a total of two days of slack time, and path A-C-D has one day of slack time.

As the number of activities increases, drawing a chart and finding the critical path by inspection or complete enumeration becomes more and more impractical. Therefore, we need an algorithm (a systematic approach) to find the critical path. To explain the algorithm, four variables must be defined. Let:

ES_i = the earliest start time for activity i, assuming all predecessor activities started at their earliest start time

EF_i = the earliest finish time for activity i
$\quad = ES_i + t_i$, where t_i is the time estimated for activity i

LF_i = the latest finish time for activity i without delaying the project

LS_i = the latest start time for activity i without delaying the project
$\quad = LF_i - t_i$

Let us return to our example to illustrate how these four variables are calculated and how the critical path is identified. The algorithm to find the critical path is basically a three-step process. The first step is to calculate the earliest starting time (ES_i) and the earliest finish time (EF_i) for each activity. The second step is to calculate the latest start time (LS_i) and the latest finish time (LF_i). Finally, the slack time is calculated for each activity, and the critical path is the sequence of activities that has zero slack time.

To calculate the earliest start time, let all activities that have no predecessors start at time zero. To calculate the earliest finish time for these initial activities, merely add the time it takes to complete the activities. Hence, the earliest start time for activities A and E of our example is zero, and the earliest finish time for both activities is $LS_i + t_i$, or $0 + 3$. The earliest start time for the other activities is the largest earliest finish time of all immediate predecessor activities for that activity. In our example, activity A has to be finished before B and C are started. Therefore, the earliest start time for activities B and C is 3 (which is the earliest finish time for predecessor A). The earliest finish time for B is $ES_B + t_B$, or $3 + 4 = 7$. Similarly, the earliest finish time for C is 8, and the earliest finish time for F is 9. Consequently, because activity D cannot be started until B, C, and F are finished, the earliest start time for D is 9 (the largest earliest finish time of all immediate predecessors).

Calculating the latest finish times and latest start times is a similar procedure, but to do it, we must start at the other end of the PERT network. For all ending activities, set the latest finish time equal to the largest earliest finish time. In our example, there is only one ending activity; hence, the latest finish time is equal to the earliest finish time for activity D. Subtracting the end activity's time from its latest finish time yields the latest start time. The latest finish time for the other activities is equal to the smallest latest start time for all immediate successor activities. Therefore, the latest finish time for activities B, C, and F is 9. The latest start time for activity B is $9 - 4 = 5$.

The latest start time for activity C is $9 - 5 = 4$. Activity A has two successor activities, B and C. Remember, activity A's latest finish time is the minimum latest start time for its successor activities. Hence, the latest time activity A can finish is 4. If activity A finishes after the fourth day, the project will be delayed.

Once the four times have been calculated for each activity, it is a simple procedure to identify the critical path. Slack time is calculated by subtracting the earliest finish time from the latest finish time. Activities with zero slack time are on the critical path. In other words, a delay in any activity on the critical path results in a delay of the entire project. Table 12-2 indicates that the critical path is made up of activities E-F-D. (See Figure 12-8 for the graphical representation of this situation.) Any activity

Table 12-2 Data for PERT Algorithm

ACTIVITY	IMMEDIATE PREDECESSOR	TIME	ES	EF	LS	LF	SLACK
A	—	3	0	3	1	4	1
B	A	4	3	7	5	9	2
C	A	5	3	8	4	9	1
D	B, C, F	7	9	16	9	16	0
E	—	3	0	3	0	3	0
F	E	6	3	9	3	9	0

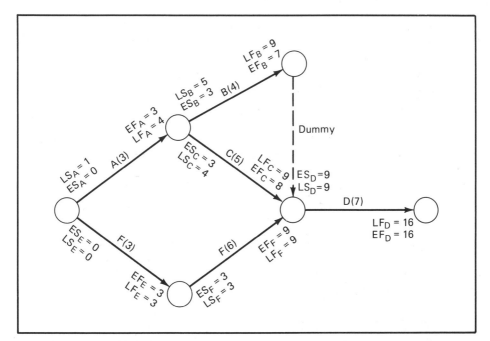

FIGURE 12-8 Evaluated PERT Chart

that has a nonzero slack time is not critical and can be delayed as much as the slack time without delaying the project.

Stochastic PERT

Until now, we have treated PERT as a deterministic technique in which all activity times are known with certainty. It is obvious that for most projects, these activity times are random variables. If these random times take on values significantly different from those point estimates used in the PERT analysis, the output from PERT (that is, the critical path, project completion time, and so on) is rendered invalid. To compensate for the lack of certainty in many of the time estimates, the project manager is often asked to give three subjective time estimates for each activity. These time estimates are:

a_i = the most optimistic time required for activity i

m_i = the most likely time required for activity i

b_i = the most pessimistic time required for activity i

These three time estimates are used to define a probability distribution of time for each activity. The distribution used almost exclusively is the *beta distribution*. There is no rigorous mathematical proof that the beta distribution is most appropriate, but three properties make it a logical choice. First, it is a continuous probability distribution; second, it is not necessarily symmetrical; and finally, it has a bounded range of values. In addition, empirical investigations support the use of the beta distribution for PERT times.

The mean of the distribution, the expected time for an activity, is calculated using the following function:

$$\bar{t}_i = (a_i + 4m_i + b_i)/6$$

where

$$\bar{t}_i = \text{the expected time for activity } i$$

The standard deviation of the beta distribution can be approximated using:

$$\sigma_i = (b_i - a_i)/6$$

Suppose, for example, the three time estimates for activity 5 are $a_5 = 2$ days, $m_5 = 6$ days, and $b_5 = 10$ days. Then the expected time for activity 5 is $\bar{t}_5 = (2 + 24 + 10)/6 = 6$ days. The standard deviation of time required for activity 5 is $\sigma_5 = (10 - 2)/6 = 8/6 = 1.33$.

The reason for calculating the standard deviation is to provide a means of computing the probability of completing the project on or before the scheduled completion date. To explain how this probability is computed, let's look at a stochastic version of our original problem. The first step is to calculate the expected time and standard deviation for each activity using the formulas specified by the beta distribution. This is done in Table 12-3. The next step is to find the *expected critical path*. (Since the calculated critical path may not, in fact, be the actual critical path, we can only refer to it as an expected critical path.) The expected critical path is found by using the algorithm previously developed for deterministic PERT. The only difference is that in this situation, you use the expected activity time instead of the single time estimate. As you can see in Table 12-4, the expected critical path is E-F-D.

Table 12-3   Stochastic PERT Table

ACTIVITY	IMMEDIATE PREDECESSOR	a_i	m_i	b_i	t_i	σ_i	σ_i^2
A	—	1	3	5	3.00	.67	.45
B	A	1	4	5	3.67	.67	.45
C	A	3	5	7	5.00	.67	.45
D	B, C, F	3	7	12	7.16	1.50	2.25
E	—	2	3	4	3.00	.33	.11
F	E	2	6	9	5.83	1.17	1.37

Table 12-4   Data for Stochastic PERT Algorithm

ACTIVITY	IMMEDIATE PREDECESSOR	EXPECTED TIME	ES	EF	LS	LF	SLACK
A	—	3.00	0.00	3.00	.83	3.83	.83
B	A	3.67	3.00	6.67	5.16	8.83	2.16
C	A	5.00	3.00	8.00	3.83	8.83	.83
D	B, C, F	7.16	8.83	15.99	8.83	15.99	0.00
E	—	3.00	0.00	3.00	0.00	3.00	0.00
F	E	5.83	3.00	8.83	3.00	8.00	0.00

Once the expected critical path has been identified, it is often useful to know the probability of completing it within a given length of time. For example, what is the probability that the tasks on the expected critical path will all be complete by the end of the project's seventeenth day? In order to compute a probability of this type, it is necessary to calculate the variance (σ_i^2) for each activity's time. This is done by simply squaring the standard deviation. If we assume that the activities on a given path are independent (that is, that the duration of one task has no effect on the length of time necessary to complete another task), then the variance related to an entire path's length is the sum of the variances of the individual activities on that path. Therefore, assuming independence, the variance for path E-F-D is .11 + 1.37 + 2.25 = 3.73. In addition, if there are many activities on a given path (that is, more than 30), the distribution of the total time of the path is often assumed to be normally distributed.

Given the mean and variance of a normally distributed random variable (path length), it is possible to determine the probability of completing that path within a certain length of time. For example, what is the probability of completing path E-F-D within 17 days? The standard deviation of the total time that it takes to complete path E-F-D is $\sqrt{3.73}$, or 1.93, and the mean is 15.99. Given these facts, the distribution of times necessary to complete path E-F-D is shown in Figure 12-9. The probability of completing path E-F-D within 17 days is represented by the shaded portion of the normal curve in Figure 12-10.

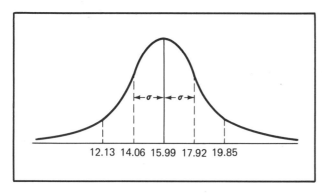

FIGURE 12-9 Normal Distribution of Days Necessary to Complete Path E-F-D

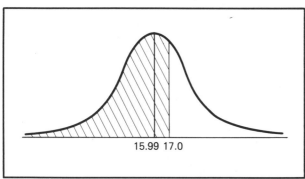

FIGURE 12-10 Normal Distribution Showing Probability of Completing E-F-D within 17 Days

To compute this probability, it is necessary to transform our normal distribution into the standard normal with a mean of 0 and a standard deviation of 1. This is done by using the following Z transformation:

$$Z = \frac{x - \mu}{\sigma}$$

where μ = the mean of the nonstandard normal
σ = the standard deviation of the nonstandard normal
x = the nonstandardized normal variate

Therefore, the probability of completing path E-F-D is calculated by first calculating Z. Thus, $Z = (17 - 15.99)/1.93 = .5233$. Once Z has been computed, the probability of $Z \leq .5233$ is found by using a standard normal table such as the one in Appendix A at the back of this book. The probability that path E-F-D will be finished within 17 days is approximately .699. (To find this, look up $Z \leq .5233$ in the table. Be sure to verify it for yourself.) In other words, $P(x \leq 17) = P(Z \leq .5233) = .699$. It is important to remember that the normality assumption postulates the existence of a large number of random variables (that is, activities on a path). For rough approximations, 30 random variables is usually acceptable; for more rigorous applications, however, an n closer to 100 is preferable.

Having computed the probability of completing the expected critical path within 17 days, can you then conclude that this is the probability of completing the project in 17 days or less? The answer is no. Since activity times are random variables, it is possible that a path different from the expected critical path might cause the project to last longer than 17 days. To illustrate this idea, let's consider path A-C-D. The expected time for path A-C-D $(t_{\text{A-C-D}})$ is $3 + 5 + 7.16 = 15.16$, and the standard deviation for path A-C-D is $\sqrt{.45 + .45 + 2.25} = 1.775$. Thus, $Z = (17 - 15.16)/1.775 = 1.037$. Therefore, $P(t_{\text{A-C-D}} \leq 17) = P(Z \leq 1.037) \cong .849$. Similarly, the probability of completing path A-B-D within 17 days is approximately .963. Now, if we assume that the lengths of the paths are independent random variables, we can compute the probability of completing the project within 17 days as the joint probability of completing each path within 17 days. In other words, $P(\text{Project time} \leq 17 \text{ days}) = P(\text{Path A-B-C} \leq 17 \text{ and Path A-C-D} \leq 17 \text{ and Path E-F-D} \leq 17)$. If independence is assumed, $P(\text{Project time} \leq 17) = (.963)(.849)(.699) = .5715$.

If the various assumptions necessary to compute the probability of project completion cannot be made (that is, if the individual paths are not independent or do not have a large number of activities), *computer simulation* is often used to estimate the probability of project completion within a specific time period. For each activity, the computer merely samples from a beta distribution for which the parameters have been established as previously described. On each iteration, a project completion time is computed and is added to a frequency distribution of project lengths. Given enough iterations, it is reasonable to use this frequency distribution to describe the probabilities of various project durations.

Evaluating Time–Cost Tradeoffs

So far, we have discussed two variations of PERT that emphasize time factors in project evaluation. *Deterministic PERT* is useful when a project's time parameters are known with a good degree of certainty. *Stochastic PERT*, on the other hand, allows uncertain times to be estimated so that probabilities concerning such activities' duration and completion can be computed. In a third technique, the critical path method (CPM), cost was introduced as a companion factor to time for project evaluation.

In their early use, PERT and CPM actually differed in two ways. First, PERT allowed for stochastic times, using the three-point estimate discussed in the preceding section. CPM, however, assumed that times are known with certainty. This distinction is still valid to some extent. When a project is rather uncertain in nature (as, for example, a research project or an out-of-the-ordinary undertaking), PERT is the logical technique to use for planning and control. For more common projects, such as certain construction projects in which the times necessary to complete individual tasks can be closely estimated, deterministic PERT or CPM may be more desirable.

As we have mentioned, the second distinction between PERT and CPM lay in the area of project costs. CPM made use of a dual perspective—namely, time and cost. You should realize, however, that this difference between PERT and CPM has faded as both techniques have evolved. In fact, most PERT software packages now include provisions for evaluating time–cost tradeoffs. Four that reason, the discussion of time and cost factors that follows refers to using "versions of PERT and CPM," because, in fact, both methods have been used to make valid analyses of the kind to be discussed.

Until now, we have talked about these project-evaluating techniques primarily as descriptive and predictive tools. Versions of PERT and CPM, however, are used to make decisions concerning how best to shorten a project's completion time. A project manager often has the prerogative of increasing resource allocation to specific tasks so that the project can be finished at an earlier date. In other words, a project manager may have such options as hiring additional workers or working personnel overtime to expedite the completion of a task. To give you an idea of how these time–cost tradeoff decisions are made, let's consider our previous deterministic example. Table 12-5 reflects the costs of feasible reductions in each activity's completion time.

Table 12-5   Time–Cost Tradeoff Data

ACTIVITY	NORMAL TIME ESTIMATE	CRASH TIME ESTIMATE	INCREMENTAL COST OF CRASH TIME ($)
A	3	2	150
B	4	$3\frac{1}{2}$	100
C	5	4	200
D	7	5	300
E	3	3	—
F	6	5	75

The crash time estimate in Table 12-5 represents the amount of time it would take to complete an activity if management wished to allocate additional resources to that activity. The incremental cost of crashing an activity is also reflected in the table. Remember that there were three paths in the PERT network of our original problem. These paths are summarized in Table 12-6.

In terms of shortening the total project, it is clear that to shorten paths A-B-D or A-C-D without shortening path E-F-D does no good. Remember, the minimum length of the project is the length of the longest individual path. Therefore, we must look at path E-F-D to determine how to expedite the completion of the total project. Table 12-7 indicates that we have two alternatives for shortening path E-F-D. Because of the lower per-day cost, it seems logical to add resources to activity F (that is, activ-

Table 12-6   PERT Paths

PATH	LENGTH
A–B–D	14 days
A–C–D	15 days
E–F–D	16 days

Table 12-7   Alternatives for Shortening E–F–D

ACTIVITY	EFFECT OF CRASH	COST OF CRASH	COST PER DAY OF CRASH
E	—		—
F	1 day		$75 per day
D	2 days		$150 per day

ity F is crashed) so that the length of the project is reduced from 16 days to 15 days at a cost of $75.

In order to shorten the project further, both paths A-C-D and E-F-D must be shortened. Since D is the only activity that can still be shortened on path E-F-D, there is no alternative. Fortunately, D is common to all three paths, and a reduction in D results in shortening all three. For $300, D can be reduced from seven days to five days, and each path can be reduced two days. Therefore, paths E-F-D and A-C-D would take 13 days, and path A-B-D would take 12 days. Further reduction in paths A-B-D or A-C-D would not be fruitful, because the length of path E-F-D cannot be reduced. To summarize, we can reduce the project schedule from 16 days to 13 days at a cost of $375.

A major advantage of WBS, Gantt charts, PERT, and CPM is that each of these techniques forces the project manager to explicitly plan and schedule his project in great detail. WBS is a necessary first step in planning a project, in that the output from the WBS analysis is the input for any utilization of PERT or CPM. PERT or CPM can then be used to identify critical tasks and to estimate project-completion times with various degrees of confidence. If the normality and independence assumptions of stochastic PERT cannot be accepted, the project manager can always use computer simulation to find the probabilities associated with various completion deadlines. Keep in mind also that more sophisticated versions of PERT exist that can answer such questions as how to shorten the project schedule with the least additional cost, and what to do about various resource constraints.

PRODUCTION SCHEDULING

The way in which production scheduling is approached by an organization depends on many factors. In a firm that produces highly standardized products, such as automobiles, boxes of detergent, children's toys, or the like, the scheduling function is more a function of process design than day-to-day scheduling. In other words, if an assembly line or continous system has been designed and balanced, then the rate of production has been set, and the only scheduling decision that can be made in the short term is how long the assembly line should operate (that is, whether the workday should be shortened or lengthened). In the longer term, however, the assembly line could feasibly be redesigned or rebalanced to alter the output schedule. How to design and balance a continuous-flow system was discussed in Chapter 5 on process design. If the assembly line is to move smoothly, then raw materials and subassemblies must be available on a timely basis or the assembly line will be interrupted. The avoidance of this type of costly interruption is the function of the inventory control system or the materials requirements planning system.

Scheduling intermittent-flow productive systems that are not assembly-line-type systems is difficult and has received a great deal of attention in the operations management literature. Before describing how firms actually accomplish the production scheduling of intermittent systems, it is helpful to list the objectives of a good production-scheduling system. First, firms seek to maximize labor utilization. Idle workers obviously have a negative effect on profitability. Machine utilization is also important and should be used as a criterion to determine the utility of the production-scheduling system. A third objective is to minimize the number of tardy jobs and their degree of tardiness. Minimizing in-process inventory costs and average waiting time for jobs is also an important objective of any production-scheduling system.

With these major objectives in mind, we will examine the ways in which organizations schedule their productive systems. A productive system can be categorized as a flow shop or a job shop. A *flow shop* is a production facility in which each job flows through the same sequence of processing (that is, from one work center to the next). Figure 12-11 depicts the pure flow shop. A *job shop* is one in which each job has to be

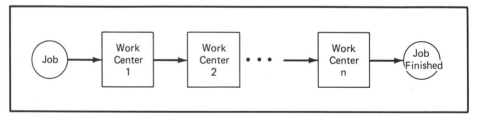

FIGURE 12-11   Flow-Shop Schematic

processed by a different sequence of work centers. If there were three work centers in a job shop, a random job could take one of the many paths indicated in Figure 12-12.

The ways organizations use to schedule flow-shop and job-shop production can be grouped into two major categories, *work-center loading* and *detailed scheduling*. Loading schemes typically take the form of a queue discipline that is used at the various work centers to determine which job is processed next. Detailed scheduling systems compute an operational schedule that defines for each job when processing is to begin and end at each work center.

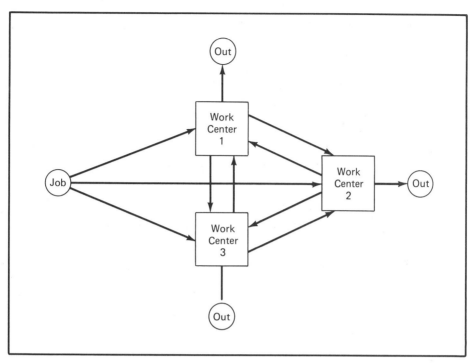

FIGURE 12-12   Job-Shop Schematic

Work-Center Loading

Work-center or machine-loading schemes have received a large amount of attention by researchers in the area of operations management. The job-shop scheduling research was initiated in the late 1950s when it was recognized that a job shop is merely a complex queuing system. Since that time, much has been done to evaluate various scheduling rules under various conditions. (Many of the references at the end of this chapter contain such evaluation. For a concise description of the job-shop scheduling research, see Buffa and Taubert.)[1] More than 100 rules have been tested by researchers operating in different environments, using queuing theory and computer simulation. Some of the queue disciplines or scheduling rules tend to minimize job lateness, some seek to minimize in-process inventory costs, and others seek to maximize the number of jobs that flow through the shop. Some scheduling rules perform better in machine-limited systems (where ample labor is always available), and some perform better in labor-limited systems (where machines are always in ample supply). You should be aware that much has been accomplished in job-shop scheduling research, and that

[1]E.S. Buffa and William H. Taubert, *Production-Inventory Systems: Planning and Control*, rev. ed. (Homewood, Ill.: Richard D. Irwin, 1972.

most job shops could benefit from using this research to improve their scheduling function.

To illustrate the use of simple dispatching or machine-loading schemes, let us look at three commonly used scheduling rules in a two-work-center job shop. The dispatching rules to be examined are:

1. First come, first served.
2. Least slack time. (This rule gives priority to jobs whose due date minus processing time is least.)
3. Shortest processing time. (This rule gives priority to jobs with the least remaining processing time.)

Table 12-8 reflects job-processing characteristics for five jobs to be used in illustrating the three dispatching rules. If we assume that jobs A through E are released

Table 12-8 Dispatching-Rules Illustration

JOB	DUE DATE IN MANUFACTURING DAY	TIME REQUIRED IN MACHINE CENTER 1 (IN HOURS)	TIME REQUIRED IN MACHINE CENTER 2 (IN HOURS)
A	213	8	6
B	212	15	5
C	225	41	40
D	214	5	10
E	214	4	9

to the shop by manufacturing day 210, that there are eight hours available each day, and that work proceeds on all jobs from machine center 1 to machine center 2, Tables 12-9, 12-10, and 12-11 summarize the results of using the three dispatching rules.

To illustrate how the machine on and off times are calculated, let's look at job A. Job A arrives on M-day 210 ahead of jobs B, C, D, and E. Therefore, according to the FCFS rule, job A is put on machine center 1 at the beginning of the first hour of M-day 210. Since processing time is eight hours, job A is finished after the eighth hour of M-day 210. Therefore, the next job in line, job B, can begin at the beginning of M-day 211. Since job A is finished at the end of M day 210 on machine center 1, it can begin processing on machine center 2 the following day.

The priority for the least-slack-time heuristic is calculated in the following manner:

Priority = (M-day due date)(8) − Time required for processing

Using the expression above for job A, the priority is:

$$(213)(8) - 14 = 1,690$$

Table 12-9   First Come, First Served

JOB	PRIORITY	DATE ON MACHINE CENTER 1	HOUR ON MACHINE CENTER 1	DATE OFF MACHINE CENTER 1	HOUR OFF MACHINE CENTER 1
A	1	210	1	210	8
B	2	211	1	212	7
C	3	212	8	217	7
D	4	217	8	218	4
E	5	218	5	218	8

JOB	DATE ON MACHINE CENTER 2	HOUR ON MACHINE CENTER 2	DATE OFF MACHINE CENTER 2	HOUR OFF MACHINE CENTER 2	HOURS LATE
A	211	1	211	6	0
B	212	8	213	4	4
C	217	8	222	7	0
D	222	8	224	1	73
E	224	2	225	2	82

For job B, the priority is:

$$(212)(8) - 20 = 1{,}676$$

Therefore, job B has the highest priority and is loaded on machine center 1 at the beginning of M-day 210, and job A is loaded on machine center 1 as soon as job A is finished.

The shortest-processing-time priorities are calculated by simply adding the processing times for each job, with the highest priority (lowest number) being the smallest combined processing time. The combined processing times for jobs A through E are 14, 20, 80, 15, and 13 hours respectively. Therefore, the priorities are 2, 4, 5, 3, and 1 respectively.

A review of Tables 12-9, 12-10, and 12-11 reveals that the FCFS dispatching rule performed poorly with respect to job tardiness. Machine utilization under FCFS was also worse than under the other two rules. As expected, the least-slack-time heuristic did the best job of minimizing job tardiness. Research has shown that the shortest-processing-time rule typically yields the lowest average flow time, which results in a low in-process inventory cost.

Once an organization has decided on a proper scheduling rule or queue discipline, a decision must be made concerning who is going to actually administer the rule. Should the chore of dictating which job is to be processed next at a particular work center or machine be delegated to the person operating the machine or manning the work center? Or should a foreman determine the sequencing? Or should machine loading be more centralized by letting a computer handle it?

Obviously, the answer to the question of who is going to determine job

Table 12-10   Least Slack Time

JOB	PRIORITY	DATE ON MACHINE CENTER 1	TIME ON MACHINE CENTER 1	DATE OFF MACHINE CENTER 1	HOUR OFF MACHINE CENTER 1
A	1,690	211	8	212	7
B	1,676	210	1	211	7
C	1,720	214	1	218	8
D	1,697	212	8	213	4
E	1,699	213	5	213	8

JOB	DATE ON MACHINE CENTER 2	TIME ON MACHINE CENTER 2	DATE OFF MACHINE CENTER 2	HOUR OFF MACHINE CENTER 2	HOURS LATE
A	212	8	213	5	0
B	211	8	212	4	0
C	219	1	223	8	0
D	213	6	214	7	0
E	214	8	215	8	8

Table 12-11   Shortest Processing Time

JOB	PRIORITY	DATE ON MACHINE CENTER 1	TIME ON MACHINE CENTER 1	DATE OFF MACHINE CENTER 1	TIME OFF MACHINE CENTER 1
A	2	210	5	211	4
B	4	212	2	213	8
C	5	214	1	219	1
D	3	211	5	212	1
E	1	210	1	210	4

JOB	DATE ON MACHINE CENTER 2	TIME ON MACHINE CENTER 2	DATE OFF MACHINE CENTER 2	TIME OFF MACHINE CENTER 2	HOURS LATE
A	211	6	212	3	0
B	213	6	214	2	10
C	219	2	224	1	0
D	212	4	213	5	0
E	210	5	211	5	0

sequencing depends on many things. First, the size of the organization has much to do with the decision. Second, the nature of the work force would have an influence; if your work force is reliable and mature, there would be more of a tendency to let the individual worker make sequencing decisions. Third, management philosophy concerning job design and job enrichment might dictate that job sequencing be totally decentralized.

Detailed Scheduling

Detailed scheduling of job shops is not widespread in today's manufacturing firm. Only a small percentage of firms produce detailed schedules for each job released to the shop. However, the technical feasibility exists, and the economic feasibility of scheduling each job in the shop will be a reality for most firms in the very near future.

Earlier attempts at detailed job scheduling failed because the technology necessary to do the job just didn't exist. Gantt charts attempted to model a dynamic problem with a basically static model. In other words, as each job is released to manufacturing, production planning dictates the operations to be performed and the sequence of those operations. Variables connected with each job, such as machine time and transportation time, are typically stochastic in nature, whereas Gantt charts assume deterministic times. Therefore, Gantt charts were always out of date, costly to maintain, and generally a total failure at performing the detailed-scheduling function. However, with the advent of computers, the major disadvantage of Gantt charts as a production scheduling tool, lack of timeliness, was deleted, and detailed scheduling is at least technically feasible.

The first attempts at computer-based systems to compute operational shop schedules prescribing starting and finishing times for each job and each operation were batch-oriented systems. Today, most firms using computer-based detailed shop scheduling use real-time systems, which can better cope with the dynamic nature of the job shop. The major advantage of computer-based detailed shop scheduling systems is that the criteria and decision rules used to determine the detailed schedule for a job can be much more complex than simple queue discipline and can use an integrative approach that considers the entire productive system or job shop rather than just a local work center.

Figure 12-13 is a schematic representation or system flow chart of a simplified detailed-scheduling system. As the diagram shows, there are two basic inputs to the detailed-scheduling system. First, work orders are released to the shop from production planning or another automated system such as an MRP system. This work-order file includes all pertinent information regarding processing requirements, such as sequence of operations, setup and processing time required at each operational step, resources required, due dates, and so on. Second, the work-center description file contains pertinent information concerning capacities and capabilities of each functional area in the shop. These data would include hours available each day, maintenance schedules, and other pertinent parameters. These two files, the work-order file and work-center file, provide the raw data that the computer system uses to produce various scheduling reports. The computer system itself can vary through a wide range of complexity. The computer can be programmed to produce schedules based on simple dispatching heuristics like those previously mentioned, or it can be programmed

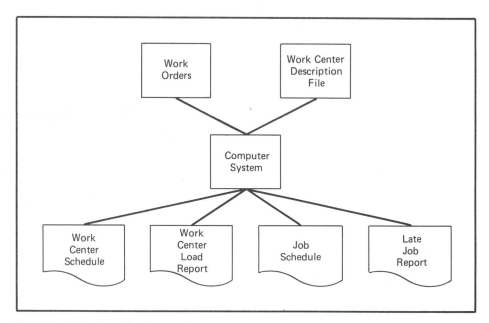

FIGURE 12-13   Simplified Detailed-Scheduling System Flow Chart

to use more sophisticated techniques, such as linear programming, dynamic programming, and the assignment method, to derive detailed schedules. These more sophisticated techniques, which typically yield better results, are precluded from a manual system for two reasons. First, the more sophisticated techniques require more timely, accurate, and complete information, and second, the computation can be accomplished only by using a computer.

Figure 12-13 shows four outputs from the computer system. Obviously, these four reports are only representative of those reports being produced by ongoing detailed-scheduling systems. The work-center schedule is a report dictating or suggesting the production schedule to each work center. The work-center load report tells each work center by M day how many hours that work center is scheduled to work. The job schedule reflects the detailed schedule for each job or work order (that is, when the job is to be loaded on a work center and when it is to be finished). The late job report is an example of the exception reporting that is possible with a computerized system. It merely lists jobs that are scheduled to be finished after the due date on the work order.

The issue of whether the system depicted in Figure 12-13 is a real-time or batch system must be decided by the individual firm. It is generally conceded that because of the rapidly changing nature of the work-order file, this system is a strong candidate for real-time processing. If a firm does not have real-time capability or isn't able to pay the extra cost of a real-time system, detailed-scheduling systems can be batch-oriented if the system is updated frequently to incorporate changes such as changes in processing times, new work orders, and changes in shop capacities.

Although the services sector is a significant sector in the American economy, the majority of work done in rationalizing the scheduling function pertains to project scheduling and production scheduling. Today, most organizations that provide services schedule them without the aid of any quantitative technique. More often than not, doctors schedule patients, universities schedule classes, and cities schedule buses without any sophisticated techniques to aid in the process.

There is a trend, however, toward improving the scheduling function in the service sector by using queuing models and computer simulation. Examples of this type of research appear often in the literature. The following examples are representative of the kinds of research on the scheduling of services that are currently being reported. (See the references at the end of this chapter for other successful approaches to scheduling services.)

Practically every community in the United States has problems of scheduling school buses. In majority of school districts, this scheduling is done manually, without the aid of any quantitative techniques. A school district in Tennessee, however, saved approximately a quarter of a million dollars per year by scheduling the school buses using quantitative techniques. The number of buses was reduced from 13 to 9, and the total distance traveled by the buses was nearly cut in half.[2] A similar application involved the scheduling of commercial garbage trucks. By changing the schedule of pickups, a firm was able to reduce the distance traveled by the trucks by approximately 25 percent, and the payback period for the cost of the study was less than two weeks.[3]

Simulation was used by Kwak, Kuzdrall, and Schmitz to investigate scheduling policies for surgical patients in a St. Louis hospital. It was found that just by changing the scheduling strategy, significant manpower reductions could be made, or alternatively, more surgeries could be undertaken using existing facilities and human resources.[4] In a somewhat related study, Smith and Wiggins developed a computer-based system for scheduling nursing personnel in a large St. Louis hospital.[5]

SUMMARY

In this chapter, we have tried to emphasize the importance of the scheduling function in all organizations. We have seen that the scheduling task can be classified into one of three different categories—project scheduling, production scheduling, and the

[2]P. Krolak, "Empirical and Theoretical Bounds on Generalized Vehicle Scheduling," paper presented at the ORSA/TIMS meeting, Las Vegas, Nevada, November 1975.

[3]Thomas M. Cook and Robert A. Russell, "A Simulation and Statistical Analysis of Stochastic Vehicle Routing with Timing Constraints" *Decision Sciences* Vol. 9, No. 4 (October 1978), 673–87.

[4]N.K. Kwak, P.J. Kuzdrall, and Homer H. Schmitz, "The GPSS Simulation of Scheduling Policies for Surgical Patients," *Management Science*, Vol. 22, No. 9 (May 1976), 982–89.

[5]L.D. Smith and A. Wiggins, "A Computer Based Nurse Scheduling System," *Computers and Operations Research* (forthcoming).

scheduling of services. To help the project manager schedule and control a project of considerable size, several widely used techniques such as PERT and CPM are available. By now, you should understand the basic steps involved in applying PERT/CPM to scheduling a large project.

As with project scheduling, much work has been done in the area of scheduling the productive process. This work can be categorized as either working-center loading or computer-based detailed scheduling. It should be noted that as the cost of computing continues to decrease, the economic feasibility of timely detailed scheduling will increase, and more and more firms will turn to the computer to schedule their productive systems.

The scheduling of services has received the least amount of attention from researchers and practitioners; the most room for improvement is in this area. It is highly likely that scheduling in the service sector will enjoy increased attention as that sector of the economy continues to grow in absolute and relative terms.

SOLVED PROBLEMS

Problem Statement

Consider the project information in the table below.

TASK	IMMEDIATE PREDECESSOR	TIME ESTIMATE (DAYS)
A	—	5
B	—	4
C	A	6
D	A	3
E	B	3
F	B	6
G	E	2
H	F	5
I	C, D	8
J	G, H	5

1. Draw the PERT network for the project.
2. Use the PERT algorithm to find the critical path.
3. What is the minimum project-completion time?

Solution

1. The PERT chart is:

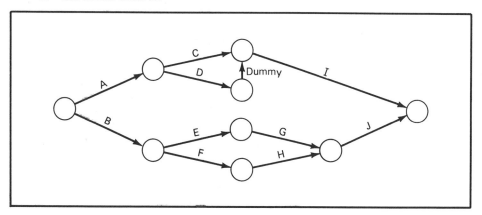

2. To find the critical path, it is necessary to compute the slack time for each task. This is done below using the PERT algorithm.

TASK	TIME	ES	EF	LS	LF	SLACK TIME
A	5	0	5	1	6	1
B	4	0	4	0	4	0
C	6	5	11	6	12	1
D	3	5	8	9	12	4
E	3	4	7	10	13	6
F	6	4	10	4	10	0
G	2	7	9	13	15	6
H	5	10	15	10	15	0
I	8	11	19	12	20	1
J	5	15	20	15	20	0

The critical path consists of those activities that have zero slack time. Therefore, the critical path is B-F-H-J.

3. The minimum project-completion time is the length of the critical path. The length of the critical path is the latest finish time for activity J, which is 20 days.

Problem Statement

Consider the project information in the table below.

1. Draw the PERT network for this project.
2. Compute the mean and variance in time for each activity.

3. Find the expected critical path.

4. What is the expected length of the critical path?

5. Assuming normality and path independence, what is the probability of completing the project in less than 22 days?

TASK	IMMEDIATE PREDECESSOR	TIME ESTIMATES a_i	m_i	b_i
A	—	4	5	7
B	A	2	3	5
C	A	5	7	11
D	B	2	2	2
E	B	3	4	6
F	D	3	5	6
G	C	3	3	3
H	C	2	2	2
I	G, H	3	4	6
J	E, F	4	6	7

Solution

1. The PERT network is:

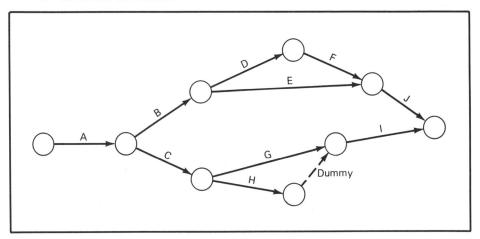

2. The mean time for task A is computed as follows:

$$\bar{t}_A = \frac{4 + 4(5) + 7}{6}$$

$$= \frac{31}{6} = 5.167$$

The standard deviation for task A is computed:

$$\sigma_A = \frac{7-4}{6} = \frac{3}{6} = \frac{1}{2}$$

Therefore, the variance for task A is:

$$\sigma_A^2 = \left(\frac{1}{2}\right)^2 = \frac{1}{4} = .25$$

The mean time and variances for the remaining tasks are shown below.

TASK	MEAN TIME	VARIANCE
A	5.167	.25
B	3.167	.25
C	7.333	1.00
D	2.000	0.00
E	4.167	.25
F	4.833	.25
G	3.000	0.00
H	2.000	0.00
I	4.167	.25
J	5.833	.25

3. The expected critical path is composed of all those activities whose slack time is zero. Slack times are computed below.

TASK	EXPECTED TIME	ES	EF	LS	LF	SLACK TIME
A	5.167	0.000	5.167	0.000	5.167	0.000
B	3.167	5.167	8.333	5.167	8.333	0.000
C	7.333	5.167	12.500	6.500	13.833	1.333
D	2.000	8.333	10.333	8.333	10.333	0.000
E	4.167	8.333	12.500	11.000	15.167	2.667
F	4.833	10.333	15.167	10.333	15.167	0.000
G	3.000	12.500	15.500	13.833	16.833	1.333
H	2.000	12.500	14.500	14.833	16.833	2.333
I	4.167	15.500	19.667	16.833	21.000	1.333
J	5.833	15.167	21.000	15.167	21.000	0.000

Therefore, the expected critical path is A-B-D-F-J.

4. The expected length of the critical path is the latest finish time of the ending activity (activity J), which is 21 days.

5. The probability of completing the project in 22 days is the probability completing all paths within 22 days. If we make the necessary assumptions, the probability of

completing path A-B-D-F-J in 22 days is found as follows:

$$Z = \frac{X - \mu}{\sigma}$$

$$= \frac{22 - 21}{\sqrt{.25 + .25 + 0 + .25 + .25}}$$

$$= \frac{1}{1} = 1$$

$$P(\text{Path A-B-D-F-J} \leq 22) = P(Z \leq 1) = .8413$$

Similarly, $P(\text{Path A-B-E-J})$ is computed:

$$Z = \frac{22 - 18.334}{\sqrt{.25 + .25 + .25 + .25}} = 3.667$$

$$P(\text{Path A-B-E-J} \leq 22) \cong 1.0$$

$P(\text{A-C-G-I} \leq 22)$ is:

$$Z = \frac{22 - 19.667}{\sqrt{.25 + 1.0 + 0 + .25}}$$

$$= 1.905$$

$$P(\text{A-C-G-I} \leq 22) = P(Z \leq 1.905)$$

$$= .9713$$

$P(\text{A-C-H-I} \leq 22)$ is:

$$Z = \frac{22 - 18.667}{\sqrt{.25 + 1.0 + 0 + .25}}$$

$$= 2.72$$

$$P(\text{A-C-H-I} \leq 22) = P(Z \leq 2.72)$$

$$= .9967$$

The probability of all paths being complete in 22 days, assuming independence of paths and normality, is the product of the individual probabilities, or:

$$P(\text{Project time} \leq 22) = (.8413)(1)(.9713)(.9967)$$

$$= .814$$

REVIEW QUESTIONS

1. Classify scheduling problems into three categories.
2. Distinguish between project scheduling and production scheduling.
3. Distinguish between Gantt charts and PERT.

4. What are the basic elements in a work package?

5. What is the basic purpose of using WBS?

6. On what type of projects would you use deterministic PERT rather than stochastic PERT?

7. What can PERT do for the project manager?

8. Define *critical path*.

9. How is slack time computed?

10. Why is the beta distribution used for PERT times?

11. Why compute σ_i?

12. What are the assumptions made in order to make probabilistic statements about project-completion schedules?

13. Distinguish between PERT and CPM.

14. How is the scheduling function accomplished in an assembly-line type of production system?

15. List four objectives of production scheduling.

16. Distinguish between a flow shop and a job shop.

17. Distinguish between the two major methodologies used by job shops to schedule production.

18. Why is detailed job scheduling not widespread in today's job shop?

19. Why did Gantt charts fail as a job-shop scheduling tool?

20. Why is detailed job scheduling likely to become more common in the future?

PROBLEMS

1. Prepare the WBS for a project with which you are familiar. In addition to identifying each task and subtask, prepare the necessary work packages.

2. Draw Gantt charts for the various task levels of the WBS prepared for problem 1.

3. Consider the information in the table below.

TASK	IMMEDIATE PREDECESSOR	ESTIMATED TIME (DAYS)
A	—	4
B	—	3
C	A	7
D	B	5
E	B, C	6
F	E	4

a. Draw the PERT network diagram for this project.

b. Use the PERT algorithm for finding the critical path.

    c. What is the minimum project-completion time?

    d. Would the critical path change if F were to take 5 days rather than 4? Explain.

 Consider the project information in the table below.

TASK	IMMEDIATE PREDECESSOR	ESTIMATED TIME (DAYS)
A	—	5
B	—	6
C	A	3
D	A	5
E	B	4
F	C, D	2
G	E	1
H	G	4
I	F, G	3
J	H	1
K	I, J	7

    a. Draw the PERT network diagram for the project.

    b. Use the PERT algorithm for finding the critical path.

    c. What is the minimum project-completion time?

5. Consider the project information in the table below.

TASK	IMMEDIATE PREDECESSOR	TIME ESTIMATE IN DAYS		
		a_i	m_i	b_i
A	—	2	4	7
B	A	3	5	8
C	B	1	3	6
D	B	2	3	7
E	C	2	5	9
F	D	1	2	4
G	E	2	2	4

    a. Draw the PERT network diagram for this project.

    b. Compute the mean and variance in time for each activity.

    c. Find the critical path by inspection.

    d. What is the expected length of the expected critical path?

    e. Assuming the time required to complete a path is normally distributed, what is the probability of completing the critical path in 15 days or less?

    f. Again assuming normality and path independence, what is the probability of completing the entire project in 15 days or less?

    g. If you wanted to be at least 95% sure of completing the project on time, what schedule would you quote?

6. Consider the information in the table below.

TASK	IMMEDIATE PREDECESSOR	TIME ESTIMATES a_i	m_i	b_i
A	—	3	4	7
B	—	4	9	12
C	A	5	11	15
D	A	3	5	8
E	B	5	7	12
F	D, C	3	4	7
G	D, C	2	3	4
H	E	7	11	18
I	E	7	10	14
J	F	4	6	9
K	G	5	7	9
L	H, I	2	3	5
M	J, K	7	8	9
N	L	1	3	4
O	M, N	14	17	23

a. Draw the PERT network diagram for this project.

b. Compute the mean and variance in time for each activity.

c. Find the critical path using the PERT algorithm.

d. What is the expected length of the expected critical path?

e. Assuming the time required to complete a path is normally distributed, what is the probability of completing the critical path in 50 days or less?

f. Again assuming normality and path independence, what is the probability of completing the entire project in 50 days or less?

g. If you wanted to be at least 95% sure of completing the project on time, what schedule would you quote?

7. State University is planning a holiday basketball tournament and has decided to use PERT to schedule the project. The following tasks and time estimates have been identified:

TASK	DESCRIPTION	IMMEDIATE PREDECESSORS	TIME ESTIMATES a_i	m_i	b_i
A	Team selection	—	1	3	5
B	Mail out invitations & receive acceptances	A	4	5	10
C	Arrange accommodations	—	8	10	15
D	Plan promotional strategy	B	2	3	5
E	Print tickets	B	4	5	8
F	Sell tickets	E	15	15	15
G	Complete arrangements	B, C	7	8	10
H	Develop practice schedules	C	2	3	4
I	Practice sessions	H	2	2	2
J	Conduct tournament	F, I	3	3	3

      a. Draw the PERT diagram and identify the expected critical path.

      b. If the tournament is to be held starting December 27, when should team selection begin if we want to be 98% confident that the tournament will be held as scheduled?

8. Consider the project in problem 3. Assume crash times and crash costs as set forth in the table below.

ACTIVITY	NORMAL TIME ESTIMATE	CRASH TIME ESTIMATE	IMCREMENTAL COST OF CRASH TIME
A	4	3.0	100
B	3	2.5	100
C	7	5.0	150
D	5	3.0	400
E	6	6.0	—
F	4	4.0	—

      a. What is the shortest time in which the project can be completed?

      b. What is the total incremental cost of part *a* above?

      c. What is the minimum incremental cost of completing the project in 19 days?

9. Consider the project in problem 4, assuming the crash times set forth in the table below.

ACTIVITY	NORMAL TIME ESTIMATE	CRASH TIME ESTIMATE	INCREMENTAL COST OF CRASH TIME
A	5	4.0	100
B	6	4.0	400
C	3	2.5	100
D	5	5.0	—
E	4	3.0	100
F	2	1.5	150
G	1	1.0	—
H	4	3.0	175
I	3	2.0	125
J	1	1.0	—
K	7	4.0	500

      a. What is the shortest time in which the project can be completed?

      b. What is the total incremental cost of part *a* above?

      c. What is the incremental cost of completing the project in 18 days?

10. Apply PERT to the project described in your WBS for problem 1.

11. Describe what you think would be reasonable criteria in evaluating dispatching rules or the effectiveness of a detailed-scheduling system.

12. Develop two dispatching rules and evaluate them using the following productive system and work orders:

JOB	DUE DATE M DAY	TIME REQUIRED ON MACHINE CENTER 1	TIME REQUIRED ON MACHINE CENTER 2
A	173	15	7
B	180	20	10
C	175	10	5
D	177	8	9
E	171	12	6
F	182	4	4

Assume all jobs arrive on M day 165 and the factory works 8-hour days. In answering this problem, first list any additional assumptions you are making and then define your dispatching rule explicitly. Finally, specifically define the measures of effectiveness you think are appropriate when comparing the two rules. *Note:* If you are unable to think of alternative dispatching rules yourself, consult the references for Buffa and Taubert, or Conway and Maxwell, for ideas.

13. Compare your results in problem 12 with results you would get in using FCFS, least-slack-time, and shortest-processing-time rules illustrated in this chapter.

Case: **REYNOLDS CONSTRUCTION COMPANY***

In 1973, Reynolds Construction Company had received a contract to construct a water purification system for the city of Oakmont. By the fall of 1974, work was nearly complete on the main system; however, it was apparent that work on a special remote-control building would have to be finished earlier than originally planned if the main system was to be completed on time.

Mr. James Alison, field construction supervisor for Reynolds, had arranged a meeting with Mr. Henry Phillips, project engineer, to restudy the arrow diagram of their critical path schedule for the construction of the remote-

---

control building in an effort to determine the shortest possible time in which the job could be done without spending more money than necessary.

Reynolds used the critical path method as a tool to assist in project planning and control. Two documents are used in this control system, an activity network and a cost table. A list of the activities for the remote-control site is in Table 12-12. The activity network, Figure 12-14, shows all the activities and

Table 12-12   Reynolds Construction Company

JOB LABEL	JOB DESCRIPTION	IMMEDIATELY PRECEDING JOBS	NORMAL TIME
A	Procure materials	Start	3
B	Prepare site	Start	6
C	Prepare request for Oakmont Engineering Dept. approval	Start	2
D	Prefabricate building and deliver to site	A	5
E	Obtain Oakmont Engineering Dept. approval	C	2
F	Install connecting lines to main system	A	7
G	Erect building and equipment on site	B, D, E	4

the sequence in which they can be performed. No activity can begin until all the previous ones on its path have been completed. The Cost Table, Table 12-13, lists the activities and their duration, along with the cost needed to complete them in this "normal time." The Cost Table also lists the minimum amount of time for each activity, called the "crash" time, and the costs needed to achieve this minimum time. In addition, a final listing in the Cost Table showed how much it would cost to shorten each activity one week. The sequence of consecutive activities requiring the longest time to complete before the end of the project is known as the "critical path" for that project. The path is considered "critical" because any delay in the particular sequence will delay the completion of the entire project.

Mr. Alison had the original arrow diagram for the remote control building project (Figure 12-14) in his office. It was, of course, considerably simpler than the similar diagrams for the control of the entire construction job.

It was apparent to Mr. Alison that the critical path for this project followed the sequence of activities A-D-G and would require 12 weeks. The original project cost was estimated at $61,000. Mr. Alison could also see that the sequence of activities along one path, C-E-G, could lag as much as four weeks behind schedule without affecting the planned time for the completion of the project.

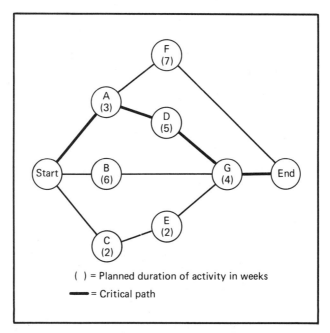

FIGURE 12-14 Reynolds Construction Company, Critical-Path Diagram for Remote-Control Building Project

Table 12-13   Reynolds Construction Company Cost Table for Remote-Control Building Project

	NORMAL		*CRASH**		*COST SLOPE,*
ACTIVITY	*WEEKS*	*DOLLARS*	*WEEKS*	*DOLLARS*	*DOLLARS/WEEK*
A	3	$ 5,000	2	$ 10,000	$5,000**
B	6	14,000	4	26,000	6,000
C	2	2,500	1	5,000	2,500
D	5	10,000	3	18,000	4,000
E	2	8,000	2	8,000	—
F	7	11,500	5	17,500	3,000
G	4	10,000	2	24,000	7,000
Total		$61,000		$108,500	

*Crash weeks shown represent the minimum possible time for the given activity.

**This is the cost of gaining one week over the normal time by use of "crash" methods.

Although a computer was necessary for the rapid solution of critical path problems in larger projects, Mr. Phillips had manually worked out a schedule for this project which indicated that the job could be completed in nine weeks at a total cost of $77,000. The additional cost of $16,000 was largely attributable to the cost of extra shift operations necessitated by a "crash" program. It will be noticed that in his revised schedule (Figure 12-15), three paths had become critical to the completion of the project as rescheduled.

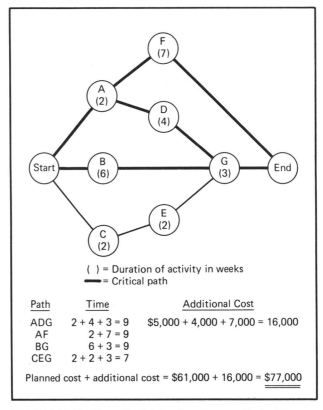

Path	Time	Additional Cost
ADG	2 + 4 + 3 = 9	$5,000 + 4,000 + 7,000 = 16,000
AF	2 + 7 = 9	
BG	6 + 3 = 9	
CEG	2 + 2 + 3 = 7	

Planned cost + additional cost = $61,000 + 16,000 = $77,000

FIGURE 12-15   Reynolds Construction Company Revised Program Schedule for Remote-Control Building Project

Case Discussion Questions

1. Reduce total project duration as much as possible without unnecessary additional costs. Indicate the new critical path or paths. Show how much slack time remains in the noncritical paths.

2. Assume that the situation proves to be less urgent than it seems to Messrs. Alison and Phillips. Revise the schedule in order to complete the job within ten weeks. Indicate the new cost and critical path or paths.

3. Suppose Reynolds were proceeding on the 10-week schedule and it became

obvious that it would take not two but five weeks to prepare the necessary data for the request for Oakmont approval, and that this step alone would now cost $7,000. What steps would you take to keep on schedule? What would be your new critical path or paths? What would happen to project costs?

4. Assume this project is planned to be completed in six weeks. If there is a penalty cost of $10,000 per week for every week the project is late, what action would you take?

REFERENCES

ABERNATHY, W.J., N. BALOFF, J.C. HERSHEY, and S. WANDEL, "A Three-Stage Manpower Planning and Scheduling Model—A Service Sector Example," *Operations Research*, Vol. 22, No. 3 (May–June 1973), 693–711.

ALLEN, M., "The Efficient Utilization of Labor under Conditions of Fluctuating Demand," Chap. 16 in *Industrial Scheduling*, eds. J.F. Muth and G.L. Thompson. Englewood Cliffs, N.J.: Prentice-Hall, 1963.

BAKER, C.T., and P.B. DZIELINSKI, "Simulation of a Simplified Job Shop," *Management Science*, Vol. 6, No. 3 (April 1960), 311–23.

BAKER, K.L., "Scheduling Full-Time and Part-Time Staff to Meet Cyclical Requirements," *Operational Research Quarterly*, Vol. 25 (March 1974).

BIERMAN, HAROLD, JR., CHARLES P. BONINI, and WARREN H. HAUSMAN, *Quantitative Analysis for Business Decisions*, 4th ed. Homewood, Ill.: Richard D. Irwin, 1973.

BOWMAN, E.H., "The Schedule Sequence Problem," *Operations Research*, Vol. 7 (September 1959), 621–24.

BUFFA, ELWOOD S., *Operations Management: The Management of Productive* Systems. New York: John Wiley, 1976.

————, and WILLIAM H. TAUBERT, *Production-Inventory Systems: Planning and Control*, rev. ed. Homewood, Ill.: Richard D. Irwin, 1972.

CARROLL, D.C., "Heuristic Sequencing of Single and Multiple Component Jobs," unpublished Ph.D. dissertation, Sloan School of Management, M.I.T., 1965.

CHASE, RICHARD B., and NICHOLAS J. AQUILANO, *Production and Operations Management*. Homewood, Ill.: Richard D. Irwin, 1973.

CONWAY, R.W., and W.L. MAXWELL, "Network Scheduling by the Shortest Operation Discipline," *Operations Research*, Vol. 10, No. 1 (1962), 51–73. Reprinted as Chap. 17 in *Industrial Scheduling*, eds. J.F. Muth and G.L. Thompson. Englewood Cliffs, N.J.: Prentice-Hall, 1963.

COOK, THOMAS M., "Schedule-Constrained Job Scheduling in a Multiprogrammed Computer," *Proceedings of the 1974 Winter Simulation Conference*, Vol. 2, 675–87.

COOK, THOMAS M., and ROBERT A. RUSSELL, "A Simulation and Statistical Analysis of Stochastic Vehicle Routing with Timing Constraints," *Decision Sciences*, Vol. 9, No. 4, October 1978, 673–687.

COOK, THOMAS M., and ROBERT H. JENNINGS, "Estimating a Project's Completion Time Distribution Using Intelligent Simulation Methods," Paper presented at the 1977 Fall Joint ORSA Items Meeting.

ELMAGHRABY, S.E., and R.T. COLE, "On the Control of Production in Small Job Shops," *Journal of Industrial Engineering*, Vol. 14, No. 4 (July–August 1963), 186–96.

EMERY, J., "An Approach to Job Shop Scheduling Using a Large-Scale Computer," *Industrial Management Review*, Vol. 3 (Fall 1961), 78–96.

EVARTS, HARRY F., *Introduction to PERT*. Boston: Allyn & Bacon, 1964.

GERE, W.S., JR., "Heuristics in Job Shop Scheduling." *Management Science*, Vol. 13, No. 3 (November 1966), 167–90.

HARRIS, R.D., "An Empirical Investigation of a Job Shop as a Network of Queueing Systems," unpublished Ph.D. dissertation, UCLA, 1965.

HEALY, W.C., "Shift Scheduling Made Easy," *Factory*, Vol. 117, No. 10 (October 1969).

HELLER, N.B., J.T. MCEWEN, and W.W. STENZEL, *Police Manpower Scheduling*. St. Louis: Board of Police Commissioners, St. Louis Police Department, 1972.

HOLSTEIN, W.K., and W.L. BERRY, "Work Flow Structure: An Analysis for Planning and Control," *Management Science*, Vol. 16, No. 6 (February 1970), 324–36.

JACKSON, J.R., "Job Shop-Like Queueing Systems," *Management Science*, Vol. 10, No. 1 (October 1963), 131–42.

———, "Networks of Waiting Lines," *Operations Research*, Vol. 5 (August 1957), 518–21.

LEGRANDE, E., "The Development of a Factory Simulation System Using Actual Operating Data," *Management Technology*, Vol. 3, No. 1 (May 1963). Reprinted as Chap. 9 in *Readings in Production and Operations Management*, ed. E.S. Buffa. New York: John Wiley, 1966.

LEVIN, RICHARD I., and CHARLES A. KIRKPATRICK, *Planning and Control with PERT/ CPM*. New York: McGraw-Hill, 1966.

MANN, A.S., "On the Job Shop Scheduling Problem," *Operations Research*, Vol. 8 (October 1960), 219–23.

MONROE, G., "Scheduling Manpower for Service Operations," *Industrial Engineering*, Vol. 2, No. 28 (August 1970), 10–17.

MURDICK, ROBERT G., and JOEL E. ROSS, *Information Systems for Modern Management*. Englewood Cliffs, N.J.: Prentice-Hall, 1975.

NANOT, Y.R., "An Experimental Investigation and Comparative Evaluation of Priority Disciplines in Job Shop-Like Queueing Networks," unpublished Ph.D. dissertation, UCLA, 1963. Also Management Sciences Research Project, Research Report No. 87, UCLA, 1963.

NELSON, R.T., "Labor and Machine Limited Production Systems," *Management Science*, Vol. 13, No. 9 (May 1967), 648–71.

————, "A Simulation Study of Labor Efficiency and Centralized Labor Assignment Control in a Production System Model," *Management Science*, Vol. 17, No. 2 (October 1970), 97–106.

REITER, S., "A System for Managing Job-Shop Production," *Journal of Business*, Vol. 39, No. 3 (July 1966), 371–93.

ROTHSTEIN, M., "Hospital Manpower Staff Scheduling by Mathematical Programming," *Health Services Research*, Vol. 8 (Spring 1973), 60–66.

WARNER, D.M., and J. PRAWDA, "A Mathematical Programming Model for Scheduling Nursing Personnel in a Hospital," *Management Science*, Vol. 19, No. 4 (1972), 411–22.

WIEST, J., and F.K. LEVY, *Management Guide to PERT/CPM*. Englewood Cliffs, N.J.: Prentice-Hall, 1969.

chapter 13

QUALITY ASSURANCE

INTRODUCTION

The final control function of the operations manager is control of the quality of the organization's product or service.

Webster defines the term *quality* as "the degree of excellence a thing possesses." The problem with this definition is that it defines a vague word, *quality*, in terms of another vague word, *excellence*. Everyone has some notion about what the term *quality* means. In stereo equipment, in education, in medical care, quality means different things to different people. Regardless of your subjective definition, you should recognize that decisions concerning product or service quality must be made by the management of an organization and that these decisions are crucial to the success enjoyed by that organization.

Determinants of Product/Service Quality

There are four major determinants of the quality of a product or service:

1. Policy decisions
2. Engineering/Design
3. Manufacturing/Operational Process
4. Field support

Policy decisions concerning product quality must be made by management. In making these decisions, management must consider several factors. The primary factor to be considered is the market, or target market, for which the product is aimed. Obviously, Volkswagen and Mercedes auto makers are aiming at totally different markets, and hence, quality policy decisions affecting the final products are different. The target market and the price customers are willing to pay determine to some extent the money that can be spent to enhance the product's quality. There is generally a strong relationship between quality level and product price. Typically, as the level of quality increases, so must the price increase. As shown in Figure 13-1, the level of product quality typically reaches a point where additional cost buys little or no additional increase in quality.

In addition to considering the target market and the price customers are willing to pay, management must be conscious of the organization's image. It might not be in the best interests of the firm to produce a product of a quality inconsistent with the firm's image, even though a market exists. Another factor affecting quality policy decisions is management's duty to act in a socially responsible manner. The administration of a ghetto hospital, for example, cannot afford to run a hospital with quality

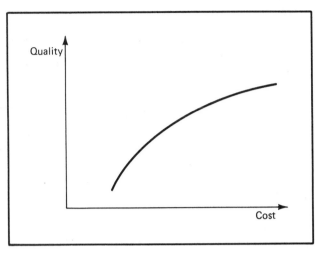

FIGURE 13-1   Quality Cost Relationship

control to match its target customers' ability to pay. A minimum level of quality is dictated by society.

Once policy decisions concerning quality have been made, it is the designer's job to translate those decisions into the design of the product or service—for instance, what materials should be used in making the product, and what tolerances are acceptable. These decisions have an important impact on the variable cost of the product as well as the overall level of its quality. In a nonmanufacturing environment, these same kinds of decisions must be made. For example, after a patient is admitted to the hospital, a doctor must decide on the type of care, the length of stay, and often what tests are to be run on the patient. Again, these decisions affect both quality of health care and cost of health care.

A third determinant of quality level is the input made during the operational process. In a manufacturing firm, a product's quality is largely a function of the manufacturing process. Engineering can design a truly high-quality product, but unless manufacturing builds it as it was designed, the resultant product can be of poor quality. The same dependent relationship exists in service organizations. The owners of a fine restaurant may have decided to serve the best food in town regardless of cost, and they may have hired the best chef in the city to carry out their policy decision, but if the people actually preparing and serving the food don't perform up to these high standards, the product's quality will suffer.

Sometimes a product's quality will be determined by the support it receives from the supplier after it has been sold. It is well known in the computer industry that IBM doesn't have the best computer hardware for the money. However, IBM has captured more than 60 percent of the computer hardware market, and one reason for this success is the quality level of the firm's customer support function. Therefore, although its finished product is not of higher quality than others, many organizations select IBM because its overall quality, including field service, is perceived to be superior.

THE QUALITY ASSURANCE SYSTEM

As depicted in Figure 13-2, the quality system in any organization combines people with information for the purpose of ensuring that the quality of the organization's product conforms to the quality desired by those making policy decisions about it.

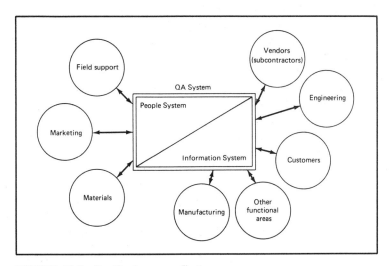

FIGURE 13-2   Quality Assurance System

The people working for the quality assurance department of an organization are responsible for ensuring that product quality conforms to the quality decisions of management. These people must interact with virtually all functional departments, as well as organizations outside the firm, such as vendors and customers. In addition to the human subsystem, there exists an information subsystem that provides the communication link between the quality assurance department and other organizations. As with any information system, the quality assurance system has a formal and an informal component.

In describing a quality assurance system, we are going to define a typical organizational structure of a large manufacturing firm and discuss the informational needs of any quality control system.

Because a product's quality should be the concern of virtually every employee in an organization, it makes good sense that the quality function be placed high in the organizational hierarchy. Therefore, many large firms place it on the same level as marketing, finance, engineering, and manufacturing. Many manufacturing firms, however, have quality control reporting to the manufacturing vice-president. This can be injurious to overall quality, if manufacturing personnel are allowed to dictate to quality inspectors. Many small firms don't even have a formal quality control department. In most of these firms, quality control is the responsibility of the worker or foreman. Obviously, where the quality function fits in an organization depends on the nature and size of the firm.

The nature and size of the firm also determine the scope of the information system that is part of any quality control system. As the size of a firm increases, the need for a very formal and comprehensive computer-based information system increases. Also, the scope of the information system is highly correlated with the importance of quality control to the success of the firm. Therefore, a quality control information system can fall anywhere in a continuum between a very informal, word-of-mouth system and a real-time computer-based system.

In order to give you more insight into what a quality control system is in today's large manufacturing firm, let us describe the system of a large hypothetical aerospace firm. Remember that the quality control system is composed of basically two parts—people and information. Therefore, this description will consist of a description of the organizational structure of the people in the system and the structure of the information system contained in the total quality control system.

The organizational structure of Aerospace Inc. is shown in Figure 13-3. Notice that the vice-president of quality assurance reports directly to the president of Aerospace Inc., and consequently manufacturing or engineering is not asked to police its own operation. This does not mean, however, that the functional areas such as manufacturing have no responsibility for quality. It merely means that the job of ensuring quality conformity falls on the quality assurance department. The job of producing quality products still rests with each of the functional areas.

FIGURE 13-3   Organizational Structure of a Hypothetical Aerospace Company

There are five major divisions of responsibility within the quality assurance department at Aerospace Inc., as depicted in Figure 13-3. First, a group is charged with ensuring quality and reliability in design. Typically, the Department of Defense invites proposals on aerospace contracts. These invitations define in considerable detail the specifications to which the product must conform. Specifications concerning mean time between failure (MTBF), weight, strength of components, and so on, are all included. The aerospace firm responds to a request for proposal (RFP) with a design proposal and a cost proposal. The design proposal defines how the firm is going to meet the specifications spelled out in the RFP. It is the job of engineering reliability to ensure that the product that is designed conforms to the specifications of the design proposal. In other words, if the technical proposal says that the MTBF of the forward-looking radar would be greater than 50 flight hours, it is the job of engineering reliability to ensure that the forward-looking radar has an MTBF in excess of 50 flight hours.

Manufacturing quality control must perform several functions. First, it must plan the "in-shop" quality control system. This includes participating in decisions concerning the choice of machines and processes, the design of tools, the choice of inspection criteria, and the planning of process quality control. Second, manufacturing quality control must be responsible for inspection and testing of parts in the manufacturing process and the investigation of why parts are being rejected and what the appropriate corrective action is. The design and acquisition of test equipment is also a function of manufacturing quality control.

Vendor quality assurance is an important functional area in any aerospace firm. Typically, outside vendors furnish at least half the components of an end item such as an airplane. Consequently, Aerospace Inc. cannot possibly build a high-quality, reliable product if subcontractors are supplying low-quality components. The vendor quality department is charged with the responsibility of ensuring the quality of vendor parts and components. It does this in several ways. Quality control engineers from the vendor quality department visit major subcontractors to see that proper quality assurance systems are being used. Parts and components are inspected and tested upon receipt from a vendor, and if they are rejected for poor quality, it is the responsibility of the vendor quality department to ensure that the vendor takes appropriate corrective action.

The field support unit has responsibility for ensuring quality performance after the product has been sold or delivered to the customer. At Aerospace Inc., the field support unit includes a field engineering staff to investigate problems occurring after delivery. Data collection concerning performance and field failures is performed by the customer, the Department of Defense. In many industries, this type of data collection is the responsibility of a field support unit within the quality assurance department.

The final organizational unit in the quality assurance department is administration. This unit is responsible for several staff functions. Preparing and controlling the departmental budget is one. Another is the responsibility for planning and evaluating the entire quality program at Aerospace Inc. Two technical functions are also performed: statistical services such as sampling plans and the establishment of control charts and operating characteristic curves (statistical quality control is described later in this chapter), and the design and maintenance of the formal computer-based quality assurance information system.

This system of data collection and information dissemination is crucial to the success of the quality assurance program, so we shall describe in some detail the computer-based information system at Aerospace Inc. The quality assurance information system is composed of five essential modules (see Figure 13-4) that produce more

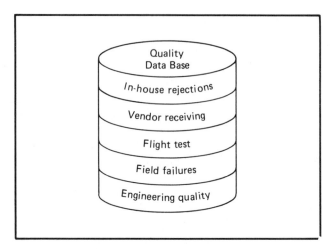

FIGURE 13-4   Quality Assurance Data Base

than 100 different reports using more than 70 computer programs. Reports produced by this system vary in level of detail, depending on their use. Some reports are distributed to the vice-presidential level and some to individual machine operators.

The in-house rejection module consists of rejection reports written up by inspectors in the manufacturing area for each part or component that is rejected. A copy of each report, which reflects the corrective action that was taken, is forwarded to data processing, where it is keypunched and the data entered into the quality data base. Monthly, more than 30 reports are produced from this module and distributed to various interested departments in Aerospace Inc.

In the receiving area, as shipments are received, they are inspected using various sampling plans. A source document is created at that time that is used as input to the vendor receiving module. Reports are produced monthly that reflect vendor component quality as well as rating the suppliers of various components.

Each time an airplane rolls off the assembly line, it is towed to flight operations for a series of flight tests. After each flight test, the test pilot fills out a source document, called a pilot's crab sheet, reflecting areas of dissatisfaction with the airplane. The data contained on these crab sheets are input to the flight test module, and reports are generated periodically for distribution within Aerospace Inc.

Every time a part or component of an airplane fails in the field after it has been delivered to either the U.S. Navy or the U.S. Air Force, a record is created describing the failure. These records, made worldwide, are mailed monthly to a central processing center and loaded on magnetic tape. These tapes are sent to major DOD contractors. Once received by Aerospace Inc., the field failure tapes are used to update the field failure module of the quality assurance data base, and from it, more than 30 reports are generated to be used internally to improve the reliability of the airplanes produced by the company.

Finally, engineering has its own data-base module that aids in the control of engineering design quality. Designs are reviewed by quality control engineers, design errors are input to the data base, and necessary corrective action is taken.

The quality assurance system that has been described is not meant to be a model to be followed by every firm. It is only one company's approach to the job of ensuring quality conformity. The organizational structure of people and information in a quality assurance system is a function of the type and size of the organization.

STATISTICAL QUALITY CONTROL

There are very few environments in which a firm can afford to inspect the entire population of goods and services. With certain products, in which quality is a matter of life and death, the high cost of total inspection can be rationalized. Most firms, however, rely for inspection purposes on statistical sampling procedures, in which inferences are made about the population based on sample statistics.

As seen in Figure 13-5, statistical quality control can be divided into two broad categories, *process control* and *acceptance sampling*. The objective of process control is to determine when the productive process needs to be investigated to determine if corrective action must be taken. For example, a machine that produces valve housings may produce them satisfactorily for a number of weeks and then start violating engineering specifications. This change from satisfactory performance to unsatisfactory performance may be caused by any of a number of factors, such as a change in machine operators or variation in machine adjustments. It is important for management to know as soon as possible that the process, or a portion of the process, is out of control, so that necessary corrective action can be taken. Therefore, process control

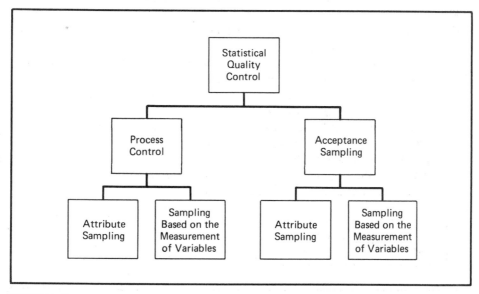

FIGURE 13-5   Classification Scheme for Statistical Quality

necessitates a continuous monitoring of each process in the system through sampling. Samples are taken, and attributes and measurements are compared to an acceptable range of variation. If the sample indicates that the process is out of control, the process is usually interrupted so that the problem causing the excessive variance can be found and corrected.

The other broad category of quality control, acceptance sampling, occurs after a "lot" of goods has been produced or received. A sample of the lot is taken to determine the overall quality of the total population. If the sample has more unacceptable components than specified in the sampling plan, either the shipment is rejected or a more complete inspection is necessitated.

Both process control and acceptance sampling can be broken into two subcategories, depending on what determines the quality of the product. The quality of a product is determined either by some qualitative attribute that dictates an accept or reject decision, or by the measurement of some variable. An example of attribute sampling might be the case of an electrical switch, where the attribute being examined is whether or not the switch works. Another example might be whether the color of the product is acceptable or not. Examples of sampling based on the measurement of some variable include measuring the diameter of a piston head or the harmonic distortion curve of a stereo amplifier.

Process Control

The purpose of process control is to determine as soon as possible when the process is out of control. The variations in a given characteristic of a manufacturing product can be attributed to one of two classes of causes, assignable and random. *Assignable variations* are those that can be attributed to specific causes. If the quality of a product decreases significantly, the cause may be a degradation in human expertise or motivation, or a deterioration in the machine side of the man–machine system— perhaps the machine is out of adjustment or needs maintenance. Another possible assignable cause may lie in the raw material going into the production process. Whatever the cause, it must be identified and the necessary corrective action taken. The object is to keep the transformation process, as described in Figure 13-6, under control. Given a steady-state man–machine system and uniform raw-material quality, *random variations* in the finished product will still occur. The magnitude of these variations depends on the design of the man–machine system and the specifications placed on the raw material. If the random fluctuations in the end product are too

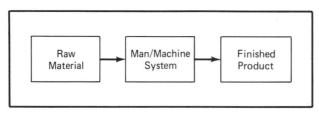

FIGURE 13-6 Transformation Process

large, then changes must be made in the transformation process or raw material to tighten the range of those fluctuations.

For example, let us look at a hypothetical transformation process. The raw material of this process is square steel stock. The man–machine system consists of a lathe and an operator that transform the square raw stock into a cam shaft, as pictured in Figure 13-7. The cam shaft has four critical dimensions, as shown in the figure. If random fluctuations in dimension A, B, or C are too large, it may be necessary to buy a more expensive lathe or hire a better operator. If, however, the random fluctuation in dimension D is too large, the source of raw material might have to be changed.

FIGURE 13-7   Example of Transformation Process

Once the random fluctuations are within a tolerable range, it is the function of the quality assurance department to ensure that the transformation process stays under control and to identify problems as soon as they arise. In order to ensure timely notice when the process goes out of control, continuous sampling or surveillance is necessary. With each sample, a test of significance must be made to decide whether or not to accept the hypothesis that variations in the population are due to random causes (that is, that the process is still in control). For the continuous monitoring of a process and to perform the numerous tests of hypotheses, control charts are frequently used. Two types of control charts are described in this chapter, one for attribute testing and the other for variable testing.

Control Chart for $\bar{x}$.   Let us return to the transformation process described in Figure 13-7. Let us assume that the variable to be measured is the diameter of the cam shaft. Every two hours, a sample of four cam shafts is taken so that quality personnel can see whether the process is still under control. Table 13-1 reflects two days of sampling. During this two-day period, special precautions were taken to ensure that all variations in shaft diameter were due to random causes and not assignable causes. The first step in developing a control chart for the mean cam-shaft diameter is to estimate the parameters of the population probability distribution.

Table 13-1   Measurement of Cam-Shaft Diameters

SAMPLE NO.	SAMPLE POINTS 1	2	3	4	$\bar{x}$	s^2
1	2.15	3.46	3.40	2.32	2.83	.36
2	3.20	2.47	3.53	3.27	3.12	.15
3	2.72	2.80	3.18	2.68	2.84	.04
4	2.30	2.87	3.73	2.52	2.86	.29
5	3.16	2.73	3.18	1.89	2.74	.27
6	3.07	2.50	4.11	3.96	3.41	.44
7	2.42	2.41	3.22	3.50	2.89	.23
8	2.20	2.76	3.28	2.36	2.65	.17
9	3.47	3.47	3.16	3.01	3.28	.04
10	2.41	2.53	2.81	3.99	2.94	.39
11	3.27	2.55	2.30	2.44	2.64	.14
12	2.90	3.22	3.28	3.61	3.25	.06
13	3.26	3.32	3.50	2.32	3.10	.21
14	3.39	3.72	3.28	2.50	3.22	.20
15	2.91	3.40	3.07	4.17	3.39	.23
16	3.56	2.92	2.39	3.43	3.07	.21
17	2.67	2.94	2.86	2.99	2.86	.02
18	3.14	3.22	2.69	3.16	3.05	.04
19	2.50	2.59	2.19	3.32	2.65	.17
20	2.84	3.01	2.76	3.47	3.02	.08
21	3.35	3.50	2.39	2.17	2.85	.33
22	3.35	2.68	2.18	3.12	2.83	.20
23	3.20	2.80	2.81	3.07	2.97	.03
24	3.38	3.14	2.54	3.39	3.11	.12
					71.57	4.42

The mean of the universe can be estimated directly by using the mean of the aggregate sample, $\bar{x}$.

$$\bar{x} = \frac{\sum_{i=1}^{24} \bar{x}_i}{24}$$

$$= \frac{71.57}{24}$$

$$= 2.98$$

In our example, the standard deviation of the population can be estimated using the following function:

$$\hat{\sigma} = \sqrt{\frac{\sum_{i=1}^{n} s_i^2}{N} \frac{n}{n-1}}$$

where $\hat{\sigma}$ = unbiased estimator of the standard deviation
       n = sample size for each sample
       N = number of samples

$$s_i^2 = \text{variance for sample } i = \frac{\sum\limits_{j=1}^{n}(x_j - \bar{x})^2}{n}$$

In our example, we obtain the following result:

$$\hat{\sigma} = \sqrt{\frac{4.42}{24}\frac{4}{4-1}}$$

$$= \sqrt{.24}$$

$$= .49$$

The next step is to compute the standard error of the mean, using the following function:

$$\hat{\sigma}_{\hat{x}} = \frac{\hat{\sigma}}{\sqrt{n}}$$

In our example, we obtain the following result:

$$\hat{\sigma}_{\hat{x}} = \frac{.49}{\sqrt{4}} = .245$$

Once the standard error of the mean has been computed, it is a fairly simple procedure to define the confidence interval, which is the essence of the control chart. It is common if not almost universal to use a confidence interval of three standard errors; using a range of $\pm 3\sigma_{\hat{x}}$ almost ensures that the process is out of control if a sample mean falls outside the confidence interval. In other words, the probability of rejecting the hypothesis that the process is in control incorrectly is equal to .0027. This type of error, you might remember, is a Type I error. The reason for using a confidence interval that yields such a low probability of a Type I error is that management typically wants to avoid unnecessary interruption of the production process if in fact the process is not out of control. In other words, the wider the confidence interval, the lower the probability of false alarms. Obviously, a small probability of a Type I error means that the probability of a Type II error is large. That is, although the probability of a "false alarm" is small, there is a high probability of accepting the false hypothesis that the process is in control. If it is more important to identify an out-of-control condition early than to avoid unnecessary disruption, a narrower confidence interval could be chosen. This condition might exist when the cost of the part or component being measured is high in relation to the cost of stopping the operation for investigation into the cause of the variation.

The control chart for the cam-shaft diameter is shown in Figure 13-8. The upper

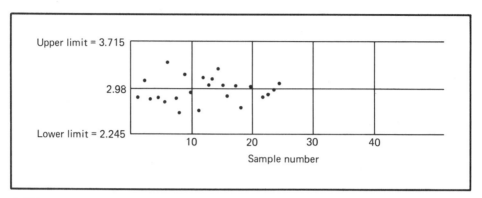

FIGURE 13-8 Control Chart for $\bar{x}$ of Cam-Shaft Diemeter

limit is calculated as follows:

$$UL = \bar{x} + 3\sigma_{\bar{x}} = 2.98 + (3)(.245) = 3.715$$

The lower limit is:

$$LL = \bar{x} - 3\sigma_{\bar{x}} = 2.98 - (3)(.245) = 2.245$$

Control Chart for Fraction Defective. As mentioned earlier in this chapter, controlling the transformation process statistically may mean measuring a critical variable or testing an attribute in order to make an accept or reject decision. If an item is rejected or accepted on the basis of some test, then a control chart for fraction defective can be used in the same manner as a control chart for $\bar{x}$. Because the statistic being measured is p (fraction defective), this type of control chart is often called a p chart. Because of the nature of the statistic, small sample sizes, which are common with control charts for $\bar{x}$, are not acceptable for p charts. Sample sizes of 100 or larger are common. A p chart can be used to test the hypothesis as to whether the process remains in control. The basic steps in the construction of a p chart are the same as those in the construction of any control chart. The difference is the sampling distribution and how the standard error is calculated.

To illustrate the use of a p chart, let us consider the following example. Metal tennis rackets are welded in several places. Daily, a sample of 100 rackets is taken off the assembly line for the purpose of X-raying the welds. The data contained in Table 13-2 were collected for the purpose of defining a p chart for the tennis-racket welds.

The first step in constructing the p chart is to estimate the population fraction defective. This can be done using the sample fraction defective. Therefore:

$$\hat{p} = \frac{\sum_{i=1}^{n} x_i}{N}$$

Table 13-2   Fraction Defective for Tennis-Racket Welds

SAMPLE NO.	SAMPLE SIZE	NUMBER DEFECTIVE	FRACTION DEFECTIVE
1	100	5	.05
2	100	4	.04
3	100	3	.03
4	100	4	.04
5	100	5	.05
6	100	6	.06
7	100	5	.05
8	100	4	.04
9	100	3	.03
10	100	7	.07
11	100	6	.06
12	100	5	.05
13	100	6	.06
14	100	4	.04
15	100	3	.03
16	100	4	.04
17	100	5	.05
18	100	3	.03
19	100	6	.06
20	100	3	.03
21	100	7	.07
22	100	12	.12
		$\overline{110}$	

where $\hat{p}$ = estimate of population fraction defective
$\quad x_i$ = number of defective parts in sample i
$\quad n$ = number of samples
$\quad N$ = total sample size

$$\hat{p} = \frac{110}{2,200}$$
$$= .05$$

In order to find the confidence interval for the sample fraction defective, we can use the following function to calculate the standard error:

$$\hat{\sigma}_p = \sqrt{\frac{pq}{n}}$$

where $\hat{\sigma}_p$ = standard error of p
$\quad p$ = population fraction defective
$\quad q = 1 - p$
$\quad n$ = sample size

For our example:

$$\hat{\sigma}_p = \sqrt{\frac{(.05)(.95)}{100}}$$

$$= .02179$$

Therefore, the range of the confidence interval at the 3σ level is $.05 \pm 3(.02179)$, or $0 < p < .11537$. According to this confidence interval, the last sample shown in Table 13-2 indicates that the welding process is out of control. In other words, that hypothesis that the fraction defective in the population is .05 must be rejected for the 22nd sample. The line must be stopped, the cause of the defective welds found, and the appropriate corrective action taken. Since sample 22 is not representative of the "in-control" process, the p chart should be constructed using only samples 1 through 21 to estimate p. Therefore:

$$\hat{p} = \frac{98}{2,100}$$

$$= .04667$$

and

$$\hat{\sigma}_p = \sqrt{\frac{(.04667)(.95333)}{100}}$$

$$= .02109$$

The range of the new confidence interval at the 3σ level is $.04667 \pm 3(.02109)$, or $0 < p < .10995$. Figure 13-9 shows the original and revised limits for the p chart for the welding process.

Acceptance Sampling

Acceptance sampling is done to determine whether to accept or reject a "lot" of goods that has been produced. The most common use of acceptance sampling is in the receiving department of a firm. As orders are received from various suppliers, a decision must be made of whether or not to accept each shipment. This decision can be made by inspecting each item received or by inspecting a sample. Typically, when a shipment is received, a sample is taken, the appropriate inspection or testing procedure is performed, and a decision based on the sample is made. This decision, as depicted in Figure 13-10, can be to accept the shipment, reject the shipment, or take another sample because the first did not yield enough information to make an accept/reject decision. If the sample results dictate rejection, a firm can elect to return the entire shipment to the supplier or to inspect or test each component and send back only defective units. The latter course of action is common when the shipment is critically needed by the receiving firm.

Acceptance sampling schemes can be classified as single, multiple, or sequential.

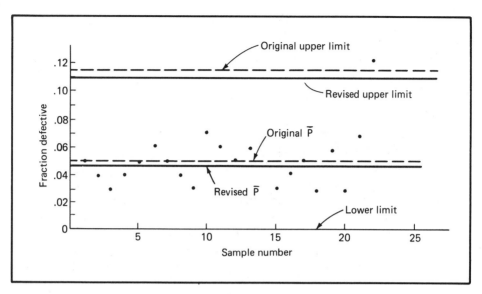

FIGURE 13-9 *P* **Chart for Tennis-Racket Welds**

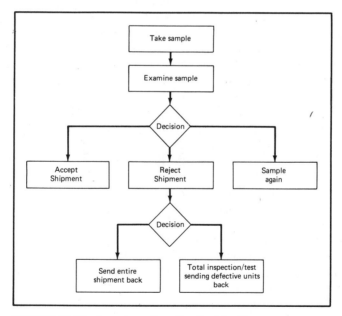

FIGURE 13-10   **Acceptance Sampling Decision Process**

With single sampling plans, a decision to accept or reject the shipment is made on the basis of one sample. With multiple plans, additional samples are taken if an accept/ reject decision cannot be made based on a single sample. In other words, if a sample gives a clear indication of either good quality or bad, it is not necessary to go to the expense of testing another sample. For example, if a supplier and its customer have agreed to 2 percent defective items as acceptable, and a sample of 100 items from a shipment is tested and none is defective, additional sampling may not be necessary. If ten out of 100 were found defective, a decision to reject could be made without additional sample information.

Sequential sampling plans call for testing or inspecting smaller samples and and accumulating the results until a decision can be made. As soon as a decision can be made, the sampling is terminated. Sequential sampling plans are generally more powerful, in that the accept/reject decision can be made based on a smaller total sample size.

Single-Sample Acceptance Plan. To give you an idea of some of the issues and techniques in acceptance sampling, let us consider a single-sample acceptance plan for a large data-processing firm. Universal Computing Inc. (UCI) subcontracts a considerable amount of keypunching to smaller service-bureau companies. It has been generally agreed upon that 1 percent error in keypunched data is acceptable. Universal Computing Inc. wants to devise a single-sample acceptance plan that will fairly discriminate between "good" and "bad" batches of keypunched data. As with all tests of hypotheses, there is danger of making two different kinds of errors based on sample results. First, UCI could reject a batch of data that in fact is of acceptable (errors $< 1\%$) quality. This type of error is known as a Type I error. The probability of a Type I error is usually denoted by the letter α. In a sense, α defines the producer's risk. The second type, a Type II error, occurs when a bad hypothesis is accepted or not rejected. In UCI's case, this would mean that a batch of data containing in excess of 1 percent errors was accepted as a good shipment. The probability of a Type II error is referred to as the consumer's risk and denoted by the Greek letter β.

Ideally, it would be nice if α and β (the probability of a Type I error and a Type II error) could both equal zero. This ideal situation is not possible if UCI does not want to verify each data card upon receipt. Let's look at a proposed sampling plan for UCI. Upon receipt of a batch of data cards, let a random sample of 100 cards be drawn and checked for errors. If more than two errors are found, reject the entire batch (in other words, the acceptance number is 2). Because each card verification could be considered a Bernoulli trial, the appropriate distribution for describing the probability of x errors in n trials, given a percent defective, is the binomial distribution, which for large n can be approximated using the Poisson distribution. Table 13-3 relates the actual percentage of error to the probability of accepting the shipment, using a sample size of 100 and an acceptance number of 2. The information in Table 13-3 is graphed in Figure 13-11. The curve in the figure is known as an operating characteristic curve, or simply an OC curve.

Looking at Table 13-3 or Figure 13-11, it is apparent that the probability of making a Type I error is $1 - .920$, or .08. If the actual percentage of errors is 2 percent, the probability of accepting the batch is 67.7 percent, which may be much too high. Consequently, it is necessary to balance the probability of making Type I and Type II errors. In other words, the consumer's risk must be balanced against the producer's

Table 13-3   Probability of Accepting Shipments
with Various Percentages of Errors

N = 100		ACCEPTANCE NUMBER = 2
p (TRUE PROPORTION OF ERRORS)	$\lambda = np$	PROB (ACCEPTING THE SHIPMENT GIVEN p)
.01	1	.920
.02	2	.677 —
.03	3	.423
.04	4	.238
.05	5	.125
.06	6	.062
.07	7	.030
.08	8	.014
.09	9	.006
.10	10	.003

* λ = the parameter of the Poisson distribution.

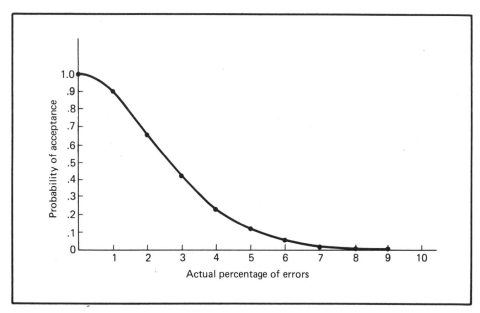

**FIGURE 13-11   OC Curve for a Sample of 100 and
an Acceptance Number of 2**

risk, and if an imbalance exists in an acceptance sampling plan, either the acceptance number or the sample size, or both, can be changed.

Figure 13-12 shows an OC curve for UCI if all cards in the batch of 10,000 were verified. Notice that α and β are both equal to 0. Figure 13-13 shows the effect

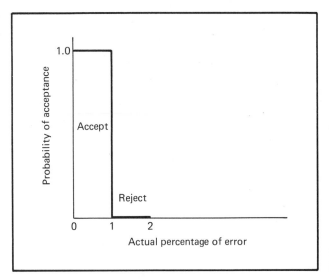

FIGURE 13-12 OC Curve with Exhaustive Verification

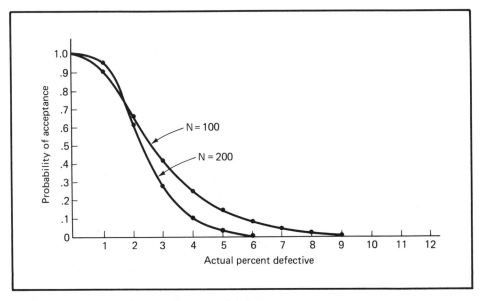

FIGURE 13-13   Effect of Sample Size on an OC Curve

on the OC curve if the sample size were doubled. Comparing Table 13-4 to Table 13-3, you can see that the probability of rejecting an acceptable shipment is .08 (1 — .92) for $n = 100$, and .053 for $n = 200$. In addition, the β error or consumer's risk decreased with an increase in sample size. If the actual percentage error was 2 percent, the probability of accepting the shipment was decreased from .677 to .629 with a doubling of sample size. Figure 13-14 shows the changes in the OC curve if the acceptance number were changed.

Table 13-4 Probability of Accepting Shipments with Various Percentage Errors and a Sample Size of 200 and Acceptance Number of 4

p	$\lambda = np$	PROBABILITY OF ACCEPTING SHIPMENT GIVEN p
.01	2	.947
.02	4	.629
.03	6	.285
.04	8	.100
.05	10	.029
.06	12	.008
.07	14	.002
.08	16	.0004

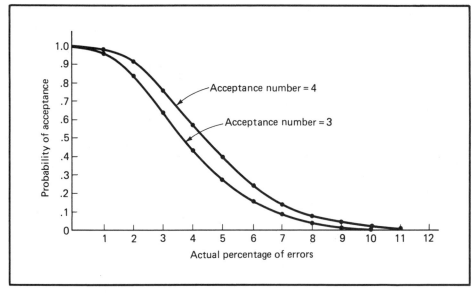

FIGURE 13-14 The Effect of the Acceptance Number on an OC Curve

As reflected in Tables 13-5 and 13-6, increasing the acceptance number reduces the probability of rejecting a good shipment (producer's risk) but at the same time increases the probability of accepting a bad shipment (consumer's risk). Consequently, it should be clear that the only way of reducing both producer's risk and consumer's risk simultaneously is to increase the sample size. As with all inspection and test procedures, an increase in sample size usually results in an increase in the cost of quality control. A decision about the cost/benefit of increasing the sample size is a subjective decision, but one that must be made.

Table 13-5   Probability of Accepting Shipments with Various
Percentages of Errors

SAMPLE SIZE = 100	ACCEPTANCE NUMBER = 3	
p	$\lambda = np$	PROBABILITY OF ACCEPTING THE SHIPMENT GIVEN *p*
.01	1	.981
.02	2	.857
.03	3	.647
.04	4	.433
.05	5	.265
.06	6	.151
.07	7	.082
.08	8	.042
.09	9	.021
.10	10	.010
.11	11	.005
.12	12	.002

Table 13-6   Probability of Accepting Shipments with Various
Percentages of Errors

SAMPLE SIZE = 100	ACCEPTANCE NUMBER = 4	
p	$\lambda = np$	PROBABILITY OF ACCEPTING THE SHIPMENT GIVEN *p*
.01	1	.996
.02	2	.947
.03	3	.815
.04	4	.629
.05	5	.440
.06	6	.285
.07	7	.173
.08	8	.100
.09	9	.055
.10	10	.029
.11	11	.015
.12	12	.008

QUALITY CONTROL IN SERVICE INDUSTRIES

Up until this point, you may have thought that quality control is a subject relevant primarily to manufacturing firms. This is simply not the case. Quality assurance is equally important in the service sector of our economy. The difference between quality assurance programs in manufacturing and nonmanufacturing organizations is not one of necessity but typically one of structure. Quality assurance in a hospital is no less important than in a large manufacturing company, and it is for this reason that considerable human and informational resources are committed to the assurance of quality health care. In order to gain an appreciation for quality control in nonmanufacturing environments, let us describe a quality assurance system of a typical hospital.

In the early 1970s, two key court cases, *Darling* v. *Charlston* and *Gonzales* v. *Mercy General Hospital*, resulted in something of a quality assurance revolution in hospitals. Essentially, the decisions in these two cases held that a hospital's board of trustees is legally responsible for ensuring quality health care to patients. Today's hospital is required to have an established and formal mechanism or system to ensure quality health care. In order to give you an understanding of quality assurance programs in hospitals, let us describe in general terms the quality system in a 600-bed midwestern hospital. Figure 13-15 shows a representative organizational structure for the quality assurance system in today's hospital. As seen in Figure 13-15, responsibility for quality health care ultimately rests with the hospital's board of trustees. The board relies on the medical staff through an extensive committee structure to ensure quality health care. Our representative hospital has a standing quality care committee staffed by doctors reporting to the medical executive committee, which in turn reports to the hospital's medical director, who is responsible to the board of trustees. The many quality care standing subcommittees composed of doctors range from a committee that investigates each surgical mortality to one that seeks to ensure that proper medical records are kept on each patient. In addition to these standing committees, each medical section—such as pediatrics, internal medicine, and general surgery—has a special committee dedicated to ensuring quality care in its specialty. These section committees establish criteria for quality care for various types of ailments. For example, if a patient is admitted to the coronary care unit with a suspected heart attack, certain tests should be given and procedures followed. The necessary tests and procedures are determined by the appropriate section QA committee. Periodically, in order to ensure that a coronary patient receives proper care, the medical charts of a sample number of coronary patients are pulled and compared to the criteria for quality care established by the section committee. Those cases that do not meet the criteria are reviewed on an individual basis by the section quality care committee. If adequate explanations exist for individual variances from established criteria, it is the responsibility of the committee to ascertain those explanations. If the variance is due to either physician negligence or other assignable causes, the necessary corrective action is taken by the committee.

SUMMARY

In this chapter, we have identified the major determinants of product or service quality, which are policy decisions, design, operational processes, and often, field support. The quality assurance system of an organization is composed of people and information. Various human organizational considerations have been discussed, such as where organizationally the quality assurance department should fit and what the major functions of such a department are. Complementing the human organiza-

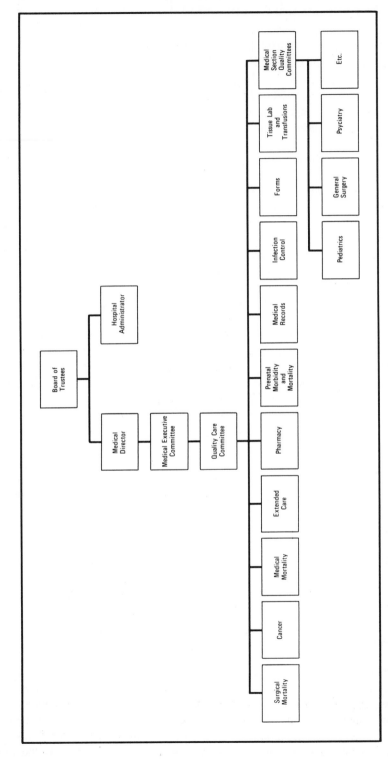

FIGURE 13-15 Organizational Structure for Quality Assurance in Today's Hospital

484

tional structure must be a quality assurance information system, which can vary from a very informal, word-of-mouth system to a highly formalized computer-based system.

Statistical quality control includes sampling procedures and various statistical techniques to effect process control and acceptance sampling. Control charts for $\bar{x}$ and p have been discussed as typical ways of controlling the production process. Types of acceptance sampling include single-sample, multiple-sample, and sequential sampling plans. The use and construction of OC curves in relation to single-sample acceptance plans was explained.

SOLVED PROBLEMS

Problem Statement

Construct a control chart for the thickness of sheets of plywood for ± 3 standard errors based on the data below. All samples contain five sheets of plywood.

SAMPLE NO.	THICKNESS IN CENTIMETERS				
1	2.111	2.101	2.115	2.015	2.213
2	2.011	2.059	2.143	2.114	2.221
3	2.125	2.215	2.114	2.141	2.321
4	2.055	2.043	2.100	2.097	2.189
5	2.210	2.120	2.012	2.099	2.177
6	2.178	2.213	2.014	2.019	2.191
7	2.189	2.187	2.217	2.143	2.154
8	2.212	2.125	2.200	2.099	2.117
9	2.194	2.087	2.094	2.049	2.196
10	2.287	2.097	2.189	2.205	2.111

Solution

The first step is to calculate an estimate of the mean. This can be done by calculating each sample's mean and then finding the mean of these sample means.

SAMPLE NO.	$\bar{x}_i$	SAMPLE NO.	$\bar{x}_i$
1	2.111	6	2.123
2	2.109	7	2.178
3	2.183	8	2.151
4	2.097	9	2.124
5	2.124	10	2.178

$$\bar{x} = \frac{\sum_{i=1}^{10} \bar{x}_i}{10} = 2.138$$

The next step is to estimate the standard error, using the following formula:

$$\hat{\sigma}_{\bar{x}} = \frac{\hat{\sigma}}{\sqrt{n}}$$

In order to solve for $\hat{\sigma}_{\bar{x}}$, it is necessary to calculate an estimate of the population standard deviation ($\hat{\sigma}$). This is done using:

$$\hat{\sigma} = \sqrt{\frac{\sum_{i=1}^{N} s^2}{N} \frac{n}{n-1}}$$

where $s^2 = \dfrac{\sum_{i=1}^{N} (x_i - \bar{x})^2}{n}$

N = number of samples
n = sample size

SAMPLE NO.	s^2	SAMPLE NO.	s^2
1	.0039	6	.0077
2	.0052	7	.0007
3	.0060	8	.0021
4	.0026	9	.0036
5	.0047	10	.0048

$$\hat{\sigma} = \sqrt{\frac{.0413}{10} \frac{5}{4}}$$

$$= .07185$$

$$\hat{\sigma}_{\bar{x}} = \frac{.07185}{\sqrt{5}}$$

$$= .03213$$

$$\text{UL} = 2.138 + 3(.03213)$$

$$= 2.234 \text{ centimeters}$$

$$\text{LL} = 2.042 \text{ centimeters}$$

Control Chart for $\bar{x}$

Problem Statement

Switches manufactured by a small manufacturing company are tested in batches of 50. Historically, 3 percent of the switches have failed to pass the test. Construct a control chart for testing the switches.

Solution

Since p historically has been .03, it is possible to use p as the estimate of the true population proportion defective. Therefore, the standard error of estimate is:

$$\sigma_p = \sqrt{\frac{pq}{n}}$$
$$= \sqrt{\frac{(.03)(.97)}{50}}$$
$$= .024$$

If we use a range of three standard errors, then the upper limit of the p chart is:

$$\text{UL} = .03 + (3)(.024)$$
$$= .03 + .072 = .102$$

The lower limit would normally be calculated as follows:

$$\text{LL} = .03 - (3)(.024)$$
$$= -.042$$

Since negative values have no meaning, the lower limit would default to zero.

REVIEW QUESTIONS

1. List four major determinants of product quality.
2. How does the law of diminishing returns relate to quality assurance?
3. What are the two major components of a quality assurance system?
4. Discuss where the quality department should be placed organizationally.
5. What are the two major determinants of the type of quality information system needed in an organization?
6. Why is there a need for statistical inference in quality control?
7. What are the two broad categories of statistical quality control?
8. What is the object of process control?

9. Distinguish between attribute sampling and sampling based on measurement of variables.

10. Define what is meant by acceptance sampling.

11. What are the two classes of causes of product variation?

12. Give three examples of assignable causes for product variation.

13. Briefly explain the purpose of a control chart.

14. Distinguish between a Type I error and a Type II error.

15. Why is a $\pm 3\sigma$ range standard for control charts?

16. What is the difference between a p chart and an $\bar{x}$ control chart?

17. What is the basic purpose of acceptance sampling?

18. What quality options does a company have when receiving a shipment from a vendor?

19. Distinguish between sequential sampling and a single-sample acceptance plan.

20. What is the purpose of an OC curve?

21. Distinguish between consumer's risk and producer's risk.

22. Define *acceptance number*.

23. How can α and β be reduced simultaneously?

24. Why is the Poisson distribution used in constructing OC curves?

PROBLEMS

1. Visit one of the types of organizations listed below and investigate its quality assurance system. Specifically, define the organization structure of the human resources committed to quality control and also define the information system used by people in the quality assurance system.

   Police department
   Street-maintenance department
   Fire department
   Hospital
   Manufacturing firm
   Airport
   Zoo
   Supermarket
   Restaurant
   Utility company
   Computer firm
   Other

2. Construct a control chart for a machine that produces bearings that have a mean diameter of 1.5 centimeters and a standard deviation of .005 centimeters. Construct a control chart for this machine. The table below shows the diameters of samples taken every four hours. Determine when the machine is out of adjustment at the 3σ level.

Bearing Table

SAMPLE NO.	BEARING 1	BEARING 2	BEARING 3	BEARING 4
1	1.501	1.505	1.502	1.501
2	1.493	1.495	1.501	1.502
3	1.505	1.502	1.503	1.501
4	1.493	1.497	1.503	1.502
5	1.505	1.499	1.505	1.500
6	1.515	1.511	1.514	1.520

3. As tennis balls roll off the assembly line, samples of three are taken to test inside air pressure. Construct a control chart for the mean pounds per square inch (psi) for tennis balls, using the following data:

SAMPLE NO.	PSI OF TENNIS BALL 1	PSI OF TENNIS BALL 2	PSI OF TENNIS BALL 3
1	26.1	27.2	24.4
2	25.4	27.1	26.1
3	25.5	25.5	27.0
4	26.1	26.7	25.8
5	25.9	25.6	26.1
6	25.1	24.9	25.0
7	26.0	25.5	25.3
8	25.4	24.8	25.1
9	27.5	28.5	29.0
10	26.0	25.5	24.3

4. In an attempt to control the process of a medical laboratory, the following sampling plan has been instituted for a particular urine test in which human life is not involved. The results of tests are classified as either positive or negative, and it is known that the national average of positive results is 10%. Five samples of 100 tests each have yielded the following results:

SAMPLE NO.	SAMPLE SIZE	NUMBER DEFECTIVE
1	100	.11
2	100	.09
3	100	.12
4	100	.13
5	100	.07

Construct a p chart and determine if the urine test process is under control or not.

5. Emergency calls coming to a central ambulance dispatcher result in some unnecessary ambulance responses; in other words, sometimes ambulances are dispatched when not needed. It is the dispatcher's responsibility to ascertain the presence of

a real need for the emergency care. Each day, 50 emergency dispatches are used to determine whether or not the dispatcher is doing an adequate job in screening emergency calls. Use the following data to construct a *p* chart for the process described above:

SAMPLE NO.	SAMPLE SIZE	NUMBER OF FALSE ALARMS
1	50	5
2	50	6
3	50	7
4	50	4
5	50	7
6	50	6
7	50	5
8	50	3
9	50	2
10	50	3

6. At the beginning of each soccer season, a local sports store orders 5,000 soccer balls. For the balls to be tested, they must be inflated, tested, and then deflated.
   a. Construct an OC curve for a sample size of 50 and an acceptance number of 1.
   b. Using $\alpha \leq .10$ as a guide, examine several different sample sizes and acceptance numbers in an effort to reduce the probability of accepting a shipment with 5% defective. Define a good shipment as 2% defective. Discuss your results.

7. A professor has been teaching for a long time, and over the years, he would like to know when his grading standards deteriorate. Using the last ten semesters as a control group, he calculates the following means and variances based on samples of 15 students:

SEMESTER NO.	$\bar{x}_i$	s_i^2
1	77.1	11.1
2	75.2	9.5
3	73.1	11.9
4	75.7	10.7
5	74.2	12.0
6	79.1	14.0
7	77.1	21.6
8	74.3	10.8
9	78.1	17.2
10	72.9	15.3

Construct a control chart at ± 2 standard errors for the professor.

8. The professor in problem 7 prides himself on the proportion of students he sends on to graduate school. For the last ten years, the proportion has been 60%. Construct a p chart that will alert the professor when his process is deviating from the historical 60%. Assume a sample size of 50 students.

Case: THE AKRON RUBBER COMPANY*

The Akron Rubber Company, located at Akron, Ohio, is a ranking manufacturer of tires. For a good many years its products have been widely accepted by individual consumers and commercial users. The company has reached a point of considerable maturity and has adopted conservative policies to govern most of its activities. One of its principal "informal" objectives is to "keep everyone happy." "Everyone," as interpreted by the company's president, includes customers, employees, stockholders, et al.

At the October meeting of the board of directors, Sam Chestnut, a minority representative on the board, raised a question about the company's method of computing payment for crude rubber. The crude rubber is invoiced to the company on the basis of a weight determined by an independent weighmaster acting as an agent for the seller. Upon receipt at the warehouse, the lot is weighed by the company. The company policy is to accept the seller's invoiced weight and make payment on it if there is no more than $\frac{1}{2}$ of 1 percent difference between the two weights.

Quoting a paragraph from the rules and regulations governing transactions between buyers and sellers of crude rubber, published by the Rubber Manufacturers Association, Mr. Chestnut demanded to know why a tolerance of $\frac{1}{2}$ percent is used in the payment rule rather than $\frac{1}{8}$ percent as stated in the Association code. The quoted paragraph states: "If final weights fall within $\frac{1}{8}$ percent more or less than invoiced weights, payments shall be made on basis of invoiced weights. If final weights vary from invoiced weights by more than $\frac{1}{8}$ percent, payments shall be made on basis of actual final weights. . . ." William Northcut, vice-president of purchasing, volunteered to discuss the matter further with Mr. Chestnut at a later time. This offer was accepted by Mr. Chestnut, and the discussion ended.

A discussion of Mr. Chestnut's question was included on the agenda of the following meeting of the purchasing staff. It was introduced by Mr.

*This case was prepared by Professor Raymond V. Ziegler, President James Stamp Co., Lakeland, Florida, and was reprinted with his permission.

Northcut: "A nosey board member has questioned why we accept a tolerance of $\frac{1}{2}$ percent in crude rubber weights rather than $\frac{1}{8}$ percent as set by the Association."

Various answers were suggested: "It is traditional." "It is satisfactory and acceptable." "No real loss is present under the system. Sure, sometimes we pay too much by not insisting on a closer tolerance, but we also find the balance in our favor. All in all, it balances out." It was suggested that Mr. Chestnut be ignored: "He is a minority member and is just looking for some place to make trouble."

In view of management's position regarding management–director relations, the group finally decided that an objective answer to Mr. Chestnut's question would be the best course of action. Bill Trent, a recent addition to the staff, was given the assignment.

Present Procedure

Mr. Trent's investigation of the procedure showed that invoiced weights are determined by an independent weighmaster acting as agent for the seller. Ten percent of each lot is weighed as it is taken from the shipment. Only one bale is weighed at a time. The bale is stripped, and any wraps or ties are removed, to give a true net weight. This 10 percent sample determines the weight of the lot. A beam scale is used and its accuracy is tested daily.

When the rubber is received at the factory, it is loaded on pallets, eight bales to the pallet. It is then transported to the scales, where the eight-bale load is weighed. The pallets have been weighed before loading, and the total pallet weight will be deducted when the total gross weight is tallied. The tare weight is determined by stripping off the wrap and ties from one or two bales, weighing them, and using this average for all bales. This total tare is deducted from the total gross, as was the pallet weight, to simplify computations and reduce the chance of clerical error that would be present if the tare weight were deducted from each bale.

The scales are checked weekly for accuracy by the Instrument Department and recalibrated if necessary. The Receiving Department places certified test weights on the scales daily. In case of any variation between the dial reading and the known weights, the net weight of the lot is adjusted by this amount on the tally sheet. No attempt is made at this time to recalibrate the scale. The adjustment, if any, does not usually run over one pound on a 1,500-pound test weight.

The company's scales are not of the recording type. Any error in reading the dial or writing the weight on the tally slip would be impossible to detect without reweighing the entire lot, unless, of course, the error was of obvious magnitude. Clerical checks have been set up to make it virtually impossible for clerical errors to occur in totaling the individual scale readings and subtracting the tare weights.

In cases where the weights differ by more than the prescribed percentage, the vendor has the option of sending in a crew to the buyer's warehouse to reweigh the entire lot, with the party in error liable for the costs of this operation.

Data Assembled

To make a statistical comparison of the seller's weight and the buyer's weight, Trent assembled the following data. Buyer's lot No. 825, a shipment of 500 bales of rubber, is received and loaded onto 63 pallets, which have been previously weighed at 6,300 pounds. The tare is found to be 4 pounds per bale. In the daily scale test, the 1,600-pound test weight had produced a reading of 1,601 pounds. The gross weight of the lot, as it crossed company scales, was 119,773 pounds.

Certified bale weights on which the invoiced weights were based are contained in Table 13-7.

Table 13-7   Seller's Weights Recapitulation of Bale Weights Reported by Certified Weighmaster

NUM-BER	WEIGHT	x	x^2	NUM-BER	WEIGHT	x	x^2
1	223.50	−0.16	0.026	26	223.00	−0.66	0.436
2	222.00	−1.66	2.756	27	224.25	+0.59	0.348
3	223.00	−0.66	0.436	28	223.25	−0.41	0.168
4	223.50	−0.16	0.026	29	223.50	−0.16	0.026
5	224.00	+0.34	0.116	30	223.25	−0.41	0.168
6	224.00	+0.34	0.116	31	222.50	−1.16	1.346
7	226.00	+2.34	5.476	32	224.00	+0.34	0.116
8	223.75	+0.09	0.008	33	223.25	−0.41	0.168
9	224.00	+0.34	0.116	34	224.00	+0.34	0.116
10	223.50	−0.16	0.026	35	226.00	+2.34	5.476
11	223.50	−0.16	0.026	36	222.50	−1.16	1.346
12	224.00	+0.34	0.116	37	223.25	−0.41	0.168
13	224.00	+0.34	0.116	38	225.00	+1.34	1.796
14	223.50	−0.16	0.026	39	223.00	−0.66	0.436
15	223.25	−0.41	0.168	40	223.25	−0.41	0.168
16	224.00	+0.34	0.116	41	224.50	+0.84	0.706
17	223.25	−0.41	0.168	42	222.25	−1.41	1.988
18	224.00	+0.34	0.116	43	223.50	−0.16	0.026
19	223.25	−0.41	0.168	44	225.00	+1.34	1.796
20	223.50	−0.16	0.026	45	224.50	+0.84	0.706
21	223.50	−0.16	0.026	46	223.25	−0.41	0.168
22	224.00	+0.34	0.116	47	223.00	−0.66	0.436
23	223.50	−0.16	0.026	48	224.00	+0.34	0.116
24	224.25	+0.59	0.348	49	223.50	−0.16	0.026
25	223.25	−0.41	0.168	50	223.50	−0.16	0.026
				Total	11,183.00	0	29.108

$\bar{X} = 223.66$

Case Discussion Questions

1. What is Mr. Trent's investigation to determine?
2. If you were Mr. Trent, what changes in the company's acceptance procedure for crude rubber would you advocate? Be specific in explaining the reasons for your proposed changes.

REFERENCES

BESTERFIELD, DALE H., *Quality Control*, Englewood Cliffs, New Jersey: Prentice-Hall, 1979.

CHASE, RICHARD B., and NICHOLAS J. AQUILANO, *Production and Operations Management: A Life Cycle Approach.* Homewood, Ill.: Richard D. Irwin, 1973.

COWDEN, D.J., *Statistical Methods in Quality Control.* Englewood Cliffs, N.J.: Prentice-Hall, 1957.

DUNCAN, ACHESON J., *Quality Control and Industrial Statistics*, 3rd ed. Homewood, Ill.: Richard D. Irwin, 1965.

FETTER, Robert B., *The Quality Control System.* Homewood, Ill.: Richard D. Irwin, 1967.

HAGEN, J.T., *A Management Role for Quality Control.* New York: American Management Association, 1968.

JURAN, JOSEPH M., *Quality Control Handbook*, 2nd ed. New York: McGraw-Hill, 1967.

————, and F.M. GRYNA, JR., *Quality Planning and Analysis.* New York: McGraw-Hill, 1962.

KIRKPATRICK, ELWOOD G., *Quality Control for Managers and Engineers.* New York: John Wiley, 1970.

SMITH, C.S., *Quality and Reliability: An Integrated Approach.* New York: Pitman, 1969.

STOCKTON, JOHN R., and CHARLES T. CLARK, *Introduction to Business & Economic Statistics*, 4th ed. Cincinnati, O.: South-Western Publishing Co., 1971.

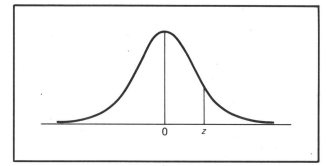

The entries in Table 1 are the probabilities that a random variable having the standard normal distribution assumes a value between 0 and z; they are given by the area of the white region under the curve in the figure shown above.

Table 1   Normal Curve Areas

z	.00	.01	.02	.03	.04	.05	.06	.07	.08	.09
0.0	.0000	.0040	.0080	.0120	.0160	.0199	.0239	.0279	.0319	.0359
0.1	.0398	.0438	.0478	.0517	.0557	.0596	.0636	.0675	.0714	.0753
0.2	.0793	.0832	.0871	.0910	.0948	.0987	.1026	.1064	.1103	.1141
0.3	.1179	.1217	.1255	.1293	.1331	.1368	.1406	.1443	.1480	.1517
0.4	.1554	.1591	.1628	.1664	.1700	.1736	.1772	.1808	.1844	.1879
0.5	.1915	.1950	.1985	.2019	.2054	.2088	.2123	.2157	.2190	.2224
0.6	.2257	.2291	.2324	.2357	.2389	.2422	.2454	.2486	.2517	.2549
0.7	.2580	.2611	.2642	.2673	.2704	.2734	.2764	.2794	.2823	.2852
0.8	.2881	.2910	.2939	.2967	.2995	.3023	.3051	.3078	.3106	.3133
0.9	.3159	.3186	.3212	.3238	.3264	.3289	.3315	.3340	.3365	.3389
1.0	.3413	.3438	.3461	.3485	.3508	.3531	.3554	.3577	.3599	.3621
1.1	.3643	.3665	.3686	.3708	.3729	.3749	.3770	.3790	.3810	.3830
1.2	.3849	.3869	.3888	.3907	.3925	.3944	.3962	.3980	.3997	.4015
1.3	.4032	.4049	.4066	.4082	.4099	.4115	.4131	.4147	.4162	.4177
1.4	.4192	.4207	.4222	.4236	.4251	.4265	.4279	.4292	.4306	.4319
1.5	.4332	.4345	.4357	.4370	.4382	.4394	.4406	.4418	.4429	.4441
1.6	.4452	.4463	.4474	.4484	.4495	.4505	.4515	.4525	.4535	.4545
1.7	.4554	.4564	.4573	.4582	.4591	.4599	.4608	.4616	.4625	.4633
1.8	.4641	.4649	.4656	.4664	.4671	.4678	.4686	.4693	.4699	.4706
1.9	.4713	.4719	.4726	.4732	.4738	.4744	.4750	.4756	.4761	.4767
2.0	.4772	.4778	.4783	.4788	.4793	.4798	.4803	.4808	.4812	.4817
2.1	.4821	.4826	.4830	.4834	.4838	.4842	.4846	.4850	.4854	.4857
2.2	.4861	.4864	.4868	.4871	.4875	.4878	.4881	.4884	.4887	.4890
2.3	.4893	.4896	.4898	.4901	.4904	.4906	.4909	.4911	.4913	.4916
2.4	.4918	.4920	.4922	.4925	.4927	.4929	.4931	.4932	.4934	.4936
2.5	.4938	.4940	.4941	.4943	.4945	.4946	.4948	.4949	.4951	.4952
2.6	.4953	.4955	.4956	.4957	.4959	.4960	.4961	.4962	.4963	.4964
2.7	.4965	.4966	.4967	.4968	.4969	.4970	.4971	.4972	.4973	.4974
2.8	.4974	.4975	.4976	.4977	.4977	.4978	.4979	.4979	.4980	.4981
2.9	.4981	.4982	.4982	.4983	.4984	.4984	.4985	.4985	.4986	.4986
3.0	.4987	.4987	.4987	.4988	.4988	.4989	.4989	.4989	.4990	.4990

Appendix B   Poisson Cumulative Distribution Function

$$F(k) = \sum_{x=0}^{k} \frac{\lambda^x e^{-\lambda}}{x!}$$

k	.5	1.0	1.5	2.0	2.5	3.0	3.5	4.0	4.5	5.0	5.5	6.0	6.5	7.0	7.5	8.0
0	.607	.368	.223	.135	.082	.050	.030	.018	.011	.007	.004	.002	.002	.001	.001	.000
1	.910	.736	.558	.406	.287	.199	.136	.092	.061	.040	.027	.017	.011	.007	.005	.003
2	.986	.920	.809	.677	.544	.423	.321	.238	.174	.125	.088	.062	.043	.030	.020	.014
3	.998	.981	.934	.857	.758	.647	.537	.433	.342	.265	.202	.151	.112	.082	.059	.042
4	1.000	.996	.981	.947	.891	.815	.725	.629	.532	.440	.358	.285	.224	.173	.132	.100
5	1.000	.999	.996	.983	.958	.916	.858	.785	.703	.616	.529	.446	.369	.301	.241	.191
6	1.000	1.000	.999	.995	.986	.966	.935	.889	.831	.762	.686	.606	.527	.450	.378	.313
7	1.000	1.000	1.000	.999	.996	.988	.973	.949	.913	.867	.809	.744	.673	.599	.525	.453
8	1.000	1.000	1.000	1.000	.999	.996	.990	.979	.960	.932	.894	.847	.792	.729	.662	.593
9	1.000	1.000	1.000	1.000	1.000	.999	.997	.992	.983	.968	.946	.916	.877	.830	.776	.717
10	1.000	1.000	1.000	1.000	1.000	1.000	.999	.997	.993	.986	.975	.957	.933	.901	.862	.816
11	1.000	1.000	1.000	1.000	1.000	1.000	1.000	.999	.998	.995	.989	.980	.966	.947	.921	.888
12	1.000	1.000	1.000	1.000	1.000	1.000	1.000	1.000	.999	.998	.996	.991	.984	.973	.957	.936
13	1.000	1.000	1.000	1.000	1.000	1.000	1.000	1.000	1.000	.999	.998	.996	.993	.987	.978	.966
14	1.000	1.000	1.000	1.000	1.000	1.000	1.000	1.000	1.000	1.000	.999	.999	.997	.994	.990	.983
15	1.000	1.000	1.000	1.000	1.000	1.000	1.000	1.000	1.000	1.000	1.000	.999	.999	.998	.995	.992
16	1.000	1.000	1.000	1.000	1.000	1.000	1.000	1.000	1.000	1.000	1.000	1.000	1.000	.999	.998	.996
17	1.000	1.000	1.000	1.000	1.000	1.000	1.000	1.000	1.000	1.000	1.000	1.000	1.000	1.000	.999	.998
18	1.000	1.000	1.000	1.000	1.000	1.000	1.000	1.000	1.000	1.000	1.000	1.000	1.000	1.000	1.000	.999
19	1.000	1.000	1.000	1.000	1.000	1.000	1.000	1.000	1.000	1.000	1.000	1.000	1.000	1.000	1.000	1.000
20	1.000	1.000	1.000	1.000	1.000	1.000	1.000	1.000	1.000	1.000	1.000	1.000	1.000	1.000	1.000	1.000
21	1.000	1.000	1.000	1.000	1.000	1.000	1.000	1.000	1.000	1.000	1.000	1.000	1.000	1.000	1.000	1.000
22	1.000	1.000	1.000	1.000	1.000	1.000	1.000	1.000	1.000	1.000	1.000	1.000	1.000	1.000	1.000	1.000
23	1.000	1.000	1.000	1.000	1.000	1.000	1.000	1.000	1.000	1.000	1.000	1.000	1.000	1.000	1.000	1.000
24	1.000	1.000	1.000	1.000	1.000	1.000	1.000	1.000	1.000	1.000	1.000	1.000	1.000	1.000	1.000	1.000
25	1.000	1.000	1.000	1.000	1.000	1.000	1.000	1.000	1.000	1.000	1.000	1.000	1.000	1.000	1.000	1.000
26	1.000	1.000	1.000	1.000	1.000	1.000	1.000	1.000	1.000	1.000	1.000	1.000	1.000	1.000	1.000	1.000
27	1.000	1.000	1.000	1.000	1.000	1.000	1.000	1.000	1.000	1.000	1.000	1.000	1.000	1.000	1.000	1.000
28	1.000	1.000	1.000	1.000	1.000	1.000	1.000	1.000	1.000	1.000	1.000	1.000	1.000	1.000	1.000	1.000
29	1.000	1.000	1.000	1.000	1.000	1.000	1.000	1.000	1.000	1.000	1.000	1.000	1.000	1.000	1.000	1.000
30	1.000	1.000	1.000	1.000	1.000	1.000	1.000	1.000	1.000	1.000	1.000	1.000	1.000	1.000	1.000	1.000
31	1.000	1.000	1.000	1.000	1.000	1.000	1.000	1.000	1.000	1.000	1.000	1.000	1.000	1.000	1.000	1.000

Appendix B   *(Continued)*

k	8.5	9.0	9.5	10.0	10.5	11.0	11.5	12.0	12.5	13.0	13.5	14.0	14.5	15.0	15.5	16.0
0	.000	.000	.000	.000	.000	.000	.000	.000	.000	.000	.000	.000	.000	.000	.000	.000
1	.002	.001	.001	.000	.000	.000	.000	.000	.000	.000	.000	.000	.000	.000	.000	.000
2	.009	.006	.004	.003	.002	.001	.001	.001	.000	.000	.000	.000	.000	.000	.000	.000
3	.030	.021	.015	.010	.007	.005	.003	.002	.002	.001	.001	.000	.001	.001	.001	.000
4	.074	.055	.040	.029	.021	.015	.011	.008	.005	.004	.003	.002	.004	.003	.002	.000
5	.150	.116	.089	.067	.050	.038	.028	.020	.015	.011	.008	.006	.010	.008	.006	.001
6	.256	.207	.165	.130	.102	.079	.060	.046	.035	.026	.019	.014	.024	.018	.013	.004
7	.386	.324	.269	.220	.179	.143	.114	.090	.070	.054	.041	.032	.048	.037	.029	.010
8	.523	.456	.392	.333	.279	.232	.191	.155	.125	.100	.079	.062	.088	.070	.055	.022
9	.653	.587	.522	.458	.397	.341	.289	.242	.201	.166	.135	.109	.145	.118	.096	.043
10	.763	.706	.645	.583	.521	.460	.402	.347	.297	.252	.211	.176	.220	.185	.154	.077
11	.849	.803	.752	.697	.639	.579	.520	.462	.406	.353	.304	.260	.311	.268	.228	.127
12	.909	.876	.836	.792	.742	.689	.633	.576	.519	.463	.409	.358	.413	.363	.317	.193
13	.949	.926	.898	.864	.825	.781	.733	.682	.628	.573	.518	.464	.518	.466	.415	.275
14	.973	.959	.940	.917	.888	.854	.815	.772	.725	.675	.623	.570	.619	.568	.517	.368
15	.986	.978	.967	.951	.932	.907	.878	.844	.806	.764	.718	.669	.711	.664	.615	.467
16	.993	.989	.982	.973	.960	.944	.924	.899	.869	.836	.798	.756	.790	.749	.705	.566
17	.997	.995	.991	.986	.978	.968	.954	.937	.916	.890	.861	.827	.853	.819	.782	.659
18	.999	.998	.996	.993	.988	.982	.974	.963	.948	.930	.908	.883	.901	.875	.846	.742
19	.999	.999	.998	.997	.994	.991	.986	.979	.969	.957	.942	.923	.936	.917	.894	.812
20	1.000	1.000	.999	.998	.997	.995	.993	.988	.983	.975	.965	.952	.960	.947	.930	.868
21	1.000	1.000	1.000	.999	.999	.998	.996	.994	.991	.986	.980	.971	.976	.967	.956	.911
22	1.000	1.000	1.000	1.000	.999	.999	.998	.997	.995	.992	.989	.983	.986	.981	.973	.942
23	1.000	1.000	1.000	1.000	1.000	1.000	.999	.999	.998	.996	.994	.991	.992	.989	.984	.963
24	1.000	1.000	1.000	1.000	1.000	1.000	1.000	.999	.999	.998	.997	.995	.996	.994	.991	.978
25	1.000	1.000	1.000	1.000	1.000	1.000	1.000	1.000	.999	.999	.998	.997	.998	.997	.995	.987
26	1.000	1.000	1.000	1.000	1.000	1.000	1.000	1.000	1.000	1.000	.999	.999	.999	.998	.997	.993
27	1.000	1.000	1.000	1.000	1.000	1.000	1.000	1.000	1.000	1.000	1.000	.999	.999	.999	.999	.996
28	1.000	1.000	1.000	1.000	1.000	1.000	1.000	1.000	1.000	1.000	1.000	1.000	1.000	.999	.999	.998
29	1.000	1.000	1.000	1.000	1.000	1.000	1.000	1.000	1.000	1.000	1.000	1.000	1.000	1.000	1.000	.999
30	1.000	1.000	1.000	1.000	1.000	1.000	1.000	1.000	1.000	1.000	1.000	1.000	1.000	1.000	1.000	.999
31	1.000	1.000	1.000	1.000	1.000	1.000	1.000	1.000	1.000	1.000	1.000	1.000	1.000	1.000	1.000	1.000

Appendix C   Exponential Functions

x	e^{-x}	x	e^{-x}	x	e^{-x}
.0	1.000	2.4	.091	4.9	.007
.1	.905	2.5	.082	5.0	.007
.2	.819	2.6	.074	5.1	.006
.3	.741	2.7	.067	5.2	.006
.4	.670	2.8	.061	5.3	.005
.5	.607	2.9	.055	5.4	.005
.6	.549	3.0	.050	5.5	.004
.7	.497	3.1	.045	5.6	.004
.8	.449	3.2	.041	5.7	.003
.9	.407	3.3	.037	5.8	.003
1.0	.368	3.4	.033	5.9	.003
1.1	.333	3.5	.030	6.0	.002
1.2	.301	3.6	.027	6.1	.002
1.3	.273	3.7	.025	6.2	.002
1.4	.247	3.8	.022	6.3	.002
1.5	.223	3.9	.020	6.4	.002
1.6	.202	4.0	.018	6.5	.002
1.7	.183	4.1	.017	6.6	.001
1.8	.165	4.2	.015	6.7	.001
1.9	.150	4.3	.014	6.8	.001
2.0	.135	4.4	.012	6.9	.001
2.1	.122	4.5	.011	7.0	.001
2.2	.111	4.6	.010		
2.3	.100	4.7	.009		
		4.8	.008		

glossary

Acceptance sampling—Sampling from a "lot" of goods to determine whether to accept or reject the lot.

Activity—A task to be accomplished in the completion of a project.

Aggregate planning—Intermediate-range planning in which strategies are devised to economically absorb demand fluctuations for the organization's product or service.

Assembly chart—A chart that shows the component parts of a product, the sequence of assembly, and the flow-of-materials pattern.

Assembly-line balancing—The process of smoothing the assembly process and minimizing worker or machine idle time.

Assignable variations—Variations in a given characteristic of a product or service that can be attributed to a specific cause.

Batch-processing system—A data-processing system in which transactions are accumulated and master files are updated periodically.

Beta distribution—A continuous probability distribution often used in stochastic PERT analysis.

Bill of materials (BOM)—A list that specifies all component items that a product comprises.

Calling population (also called *input source*)—Consists of all customers or calling units that can arrive to a queuing system. When the calling population is finite, it is referred to as a finite calling population or limited-source calling population. An infinite calling population refers to a calling population containing an infinite number of calling units.

Carrying cost (also called *holding cost*)—One of three components of inventory costs. Carrying costs are those costs incurred for holding inventory.

Chi-square test—A nonparametric goodness-of-fit test used to test the hypothesis that a random variable is distributed in a specified manner.

Computer simulation—A numerical technique that involves modeling a stochastic system on a digital computer with the intention of predicting the system's behavior.

Constraints—Mathematical expressions that state resource limitations or other physical restrictions in a particular decision model.

Continuous inventory system—A system of accounting for inventory that updates inventory levels whenever there is an inventory replenishment or decrement.

Critical activities—Activities in a PERT network that are on the critical path and consequently have zero slack time.

Critical path—The longest path through a PERT network. The critical path is composed of activities with zero slack time.

Critical-path method—A project scheduling and control method similar to PERT.

Critical ratio—A ratio used for establishing sequencing priorities in a job shop. The critical ratio for a job equals (Due date — Today's date)/Lead time for balance of work.

Cycle time—The length of time between completed products' coming off an assembly line.

Delphi method—A qualitative forecasting technique that utilizes a panel of experts and a series of questionnaires to develop a forecast.

Dependent demand—Demand whose magnitude depends on the demand for another item or product.

Detailed scheduling—A centralized method of scheduling a job shop that outputs a detailed schedule for each job released to the shop.

Deterministic PERT—A project-scheduling technique in which the activity times are assumed to be known with certainty.

Disaggregation—The process by which aggregate plans are broken down into greater details for various work centers and operations.

Event—In PERT analysis, the completion of an activity or task.

Expected critical path—The path in a stochastic PERT network that would be the critical path if length of each activity were the expected time.

Flow shop—A production facility in which each job flows through the same sequence of processing.

Gantt chart—A simple bar chart depicting the starting time and completion time for various project tasks.

Goal programming—A mathematical programming technique that solves optimization problems having multiple and sometimes incompatible goals.

Grass-roots forecasting—A qualitative forecasting technique in which individual forecasts are generated at the end of the distribution channel and are aggregated to generate the total forecast.

Gross requirements—The quantity of an item that will have to be disbursed to support the production of a parent item.

Heuristic—A method or rule of thumb that determines good but not necessarily optimal solutions to a problem.

Historical analogy—A qualitative forecasting technique that forecasts demand based upon past experience with a similar product or service.

Holding costs (see *Carrying costs*)

Independent demand—Demand that is not dependent on the demand for an end item.

Input source (see *Calling population*)

Inventory—A stock of goods that is held for the purpose of future production or sales.

Job shop—A productive system typified by each job's having to be processed by a different sequence of work centers.

Kolmogorov-Smirnov Test—A nonparametric goodness-of-fit test.

Lead time—The time between the release of an order and the time the goods start being added to inventory.

Learning-curve phenomenon—A phenomenon by which human productivity and efficiency increase as a function of experience or volume of output.

Least-squares method—A method for deriving a function that best fits a set of data.

Linear programming—A mathematical technique that can be used to maximize (minimize) a linear objective function subject to certain linear constraints.

Management information system—A system designed to collect, store, and process data so that they are useful for decision making.

Management science—The discipline devoted to studying and developing scientific procedures to help in the process of managerial decision making (see *Operations research*).

Market research—A family of qualitative forecasting techniques that is helpful in revealing predictions about the size, structure, and configuration of markets for various goods and services.

Master production schedule—A refinement of the aggregate plans; it specifies what is to be produced (and in what quantities) for a specified period of time (six months to one year).

Materials requirements planning (MRP)—A system of logically related records, procedures, and decision rules that translate the master schedule into time-phased net requirements and planned coverage of these requirements for all component items needed.

Model—A representation or an abstraction of an object or a particular real-world phenomenon.

Monte Carlo simulation—A simulation using a sampling technique that consists of the generation of random variates from a specified probability distribution.

Net requirements—The quantity of additional component items to procure in order to support the production of a parent item. Net requirements = Gross requirements — Scheduled receipts — Inventory on hand.

Network—A graphical representation of a problem or situation consisting of a collection of nodes connected by links (lines).

Network diagram (see *PERT chart*)

Objective function—A mathematical expression used to represent the goal or objective of a particular decision problem.

Operations management—The discipline devoted to the effective management of productive systems.

Operations research—The discipline devoted to studying and developing scientific procedures to help in the process of making decisions (see *Management science*).

Order costs—The costs incurred when processing an order for inventory.

Order level—The inventory level after replenishment.

Panel consensus—A qualitative forecasting technique that involves assembling a panel of experts for the purpose of jointly developing a forecast.

Path—A sequential series of activities in a PERT network.

PERT (see *Project evaluation and review technique*)

PERT chart—A network diagram of a project.

Physical inventory system—An inventory accounting system in which management periodically reviews levels of the various items in inventory in order to make inventory decisions.

Poisson probability density function—A discrete probability function that yields the probability of *n* events occurring in a given time interval.

Poisson process—Usually refers to a random arrival process where the number of arrivals in a time period is distributed according to a Poisson probability distribution.

Process contol—A category of statistical quality control whose object is to determine when the productive process needs to be investigated to determine if corrective action must be taken.

Process generator—A function that transforms a uniformly distributed random number into a nonuniform random variate.

Production scheduling—The scheduling of the production process.

Productive system—A system that transforms inputs into outputs for the purpose of creating goods and services.

Project evaluation and review technique (*PERT*)—A technique for scheduling and controlling large projects.

Project scheduling—The scheduling of major tasks that require a significant amount of time to accomplish.

Queue discipline (also called *service discipline*)—The decision rule that determines which calling unit in the queuing system receives service.

Queuing system—Any system that has a waiting line as an element of the system.

Queuing theory—A branch of operations research that through mathematical models describes the behavior of queuing systems.

Random variations—One of four components of a time series. Random variations are fluctuations in the dependent variable of a time series that cannot be assigned to trend, seasonality, or some cylical component.

Real-time system—A computer-based system that is on-line to the computer. This enables instantaneous response to inquiries and often instantaneous update of a data base.

Regression analysis—A forecasting technique yielding a forecasting equation that gives the dependent variable as a function of one or more independent variables.

Reorder level—The inventory level at the time of placing the order.

Replenishment period—The time it takes to replenish inventory once replenishment has begun.

Sensitivity analysis—The analysis of how an optimal solution and the value of its objective function are affected by changes in the various inputs or components of the decision model.

Service discipline (see *Queue discipline*)

Service facility—The server in a queuing system.

Shadow price—The marginal value of a resource associated with a linear programming constraint at optimality.

Shortage costs (also called *stockout costs*)—Inventory costs associated with being out of stock.

Simplex method—A mathematical procedure for solving linear programming problems.

Slack time—In PERT analysis, the amount of time an activity can be delayed without delaying the entire project.

Steady state—A queuing system is in a steady-state condition when its behavior is not a function of time.

Stochastic PERT—A project-scheduling technique in which the activity times are of a probabilistic nature.

Stockout costs (see *Shortage costs*)

System—A whole comprising interrelated parts intended to accomplish a specific objective.

Systems approach—A modern integrated approach to decision making in which all relevant factors (including intra-organizational and environmental or external factors) are considered in the decision process. The objective is to achieve the goals of the organization as a whole.

Time phasing—The process of timing inventory needs to arrive at the point in time when they are needed.

Work-breakdown structure—The top-down organizational structure of a project.

Work-center loading—One of two major categories of ways to schedule a job shop. Loading schemes typically take the form of a queue discipline, which is employed at each work center.

Work package—The smallest element in the work-breakdown structure.

index